ANTE-NICENE CHRISTIAN LIBRARY

TRANSLATIONS OF

THE WRITINGS OF THE FATHERS

DOWN TO A.D. 325

EDITED BY THE

REV. ALEXANDER ROBERTS

AND

JAMES DONALDSON

VOL. 2

Elibron Classics
www.elibron.com

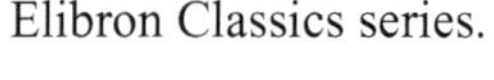

ISBN 0-543-97221-6 (paperback)
ISBN 0-543-97220-8 (hardcover)

This Elibron Classics Replica Edition is an unabridged facsimile of the edition published in 1867 by T. & T. Clark, Edinburgh.

ANTE-NICENE

CHRISTIAN LIBRARY:

TRANSLATIONS OF

THE WRITINGS OF THE FATHERS

DOWN TO A.D. 325.

EDITED BY THE

REV. ALEXANDER ROBERTS, D.D.,

AND

JAMES DONALDSON, LL.D.

VOL. II.

JUSTIN MARTYR AND ATHENAGORAS.

EDINBURGH:

T. AND T. CLARK, 38, GEORGE STREET.

MDCCCLXVII.

MURRAY AND GIBB, PRINTERS, EDINBURGH.

THE WRITINGS

OF

JUSTIN MARTYR AND ATHENAGORAS.

TRANSLATED BY

REV. MARCUS DODS, A.M., REV. GEORGE REITH. A.M.,

AND

REV. B. P. PRATTEN.

EDINBURGH:

T. & T. CLARK, 38, GEORGE STREET.

LONDON: HAMILTON & CO. DUBLIN: JOHN ROBERTSON & CO.

MDCCCLXVII.

NOTE BY THE EDITORS TO VOL. II.

The whole of the certainly and probably genuine works of Justin Martyr, and the two extant treatises of Athenagoras, are comprised in this volume of the Ante-Nicene Christian Library. Of these, the two *Apologies* of Justin, the *Address to the Greeks*, the *Exhortation*, and the *Martyrium*, have been translated by the Rev. M. Dods, M.A.; the *Dialogue with Trypho*, and the treatise *On the Sole Government of God*, by the Rev. G. Reith, M.A.; and the writings of Athenagoras by the Rev. B. P. Pratten, Bristol. The fragment of Justin *On the Resurrection* has been translated by Mr Dods, and the other fragments of the same writer by Dr Roberts.

CONTENTS OF VOL. II.

WRITINGS OF JUSTIN MARTYR.

INTRODUCTORY NOTICE.

USTIN MARTYR was born in Flavia Neapolis, a city of Samaria, the modern Nablous. The date of his birth is uncertain, but may be fixed about A.D. 114. His father and grandfather were probably of Roman origin. Before his conversion to Christianity he studied in the schools of the philosophers, searching after some knowledge which should satisfy the cravings of his soul. At last he became acquainted with Christianity, being at once impressed with the extraordinary fearlessness which the Christians displayed in the presence of death, and with the grandeur, stability, and truth of the teachings of the Old Testament. From this time he acted as an evangelist, taking every opportunity to proclaim the gospel as the only safe and certain philosophy, the only way to salvation. It is probable that he travelled much. We know that he was some time in Ephesus, and he must have lived for a considerable period in Rome. Probably he settled in Rome as a Christian teacher. While he was there, the philosophers, especially the Cynics, plotted against him, and he sealed his testimony to the truth by martyrdom.

The principal facts of Justin's life are gathered from his own writings. There is little clue to dates. It is agreed on all hands that he lived in the reign of Antoninus Pius, and the testimony of Eusebius and most credible historians renders it nearly certain that he suffered martyrdom in the reign of Marcus Aurelius. The *Chronicon Paschale* gives as the date 165 A.D.

The writings of Justin Martyr are among the most important that have come down to us from the second century. He was not the first that wrote an Apology in behalf of the

Christians, but his Apologies are the earliest extant. They are characterized by intense Christian fervour, and they give us an insight into the relations existing between heathens and Christians in those days. His other principal writing, the Dialogue with Trypho, is the first elaborate exposition of the reasons for regarding Christ as the Messiah of the Old Testament, and the first systematic attempt to exhibit the false position of the Jews in regard to Christianity.

Many of Justin's writings have perished. Those works which have come to us bearing his name have been divided into three classes.

The first class embraces those which are unquestionably genuine, viz. the two Apologies, and the Dialogue with Trypho. Some critics have urged objections against Justin's authorship of the Dialogue; but the objections are regarded now as possessing no weight.

The second class consists of those works which are regarded by some critics as Justin's, and by others as not his. They are: 1. An Address to the Greeks; 2. A Hortatory Address to the Greeks; 3. On the Sole Government of God; 4. An Epistle to Diognetus; 5. Fragments from a work on the Resurrection; 6. And other Fragments. Whatever difficulty there may be in settling the authorship of these treatises, there is but one opinion as to their earliness. The latest of them, in all probability, was not written later than the third century.

The third class consists of those that are unquestionably not the works of Justin. These are: 1. An Exposition of the True Faith; 2. Replies to the Orthodox; 3. Christian Questions to Gentiles; 4. Gentile Questions to Christians; 5. Epistle to Zenas and Serenus; and 6. A Refutation of certain Doctrines of Aristotle. There is no clue to the date of the two last. There can be no doubt that the others were written after the Council of Nicæa, though, immediately after the Reformation, Calvin and others appealed to the first as a genuine writing of Justin's.

There is a curious question connected with the Apologies of Justin which have come down to us. Eusebius mentions two Apologies,—one written in the reign of Antoninus Pius, the other in the reign of Marcus Aurelius. Critics have disputed much whether we have these two Apologies in those now extant. Some have maintained, that what is now called the Second Apology was the preface of the first, and that the second is lost. Others have tried to show, that the so-called Second Apology is the continuation of the first, and that the second is lost. Others have supposed that the two Apologies which we have are Justin's two Apologies, but that Eusebius was wrong in affirming that the second was addressed to Marcus Aurelius; and others maintain, that we have in our two Apologies the two Apologies mentioned by Eusebius, and that our first is his first, and our second his second.

THE FIRST APOLOGY OF JUSTIN.

CHAP. I.—*Address.*

TO the Emperor Titus Ælius Adrianus Antoninus Pius Augustus Cæsar, and to his son Verissimus the philosopher, and to Lucius the philosopher, the natural son of Cæsar, and the adopted son of Pius, a lover of learning, and to the sacred senate, with the whole people of the Romans, I, Justin, the son of Priscus and grandson of Bacchius, natives of Flavia Neapolis in Palestine, present this address and petition in behalf of those of all nations who are unjustly hated and wantonly abused, myself being one of them.

CHAP. II.—*Justice demanded.*

Reason directs those who are truly pious and philosophical to honour and love only what is true, declining to follow traditional opinions,[1] if these be worthless. For not only does sound reason direct us to refuse the guidance of those who did or taught anything wrong, but it is incumbent on the lover of truth, by all means, and if death be threatened, even before his own life, to choose to do and say what is right. Do you, then, since ye are called pious and philosophers, guardians of justice and lovers of learning, give good heed, and hearken to my address; and if ye are indeed such, it will be manifested. For we have come, not to flatter you by this writing, nor please you by our address, but to beg that you pass judgment, after an accurate and searching investigation, not flattered by prejudice or by a desire of pleasing superstitious men, nor induced by irrational impulse or evil

[1] Literally, "the opinions of the ancients."

rumours which have long been prevalent, to give a decision which will prove to be against yourselves. For as for us, we reckon that no evil can be done us, unless we be convicted as evil-doers, or be proved to be wicked men; and you, you can kill, but not hurt us.

CHAP. III.—*Claim of judicial investigation.*

But lest any one think that this is an unreasonable and reckless utterance, we demand that the charges against the Christians be investigated, and that, if these be substantiated, they be punished as they deserve; [or rather, indeed, we ourselves will punish them.][1] But if no one can convict us of anything, true reason forbids you, for the sake of a wicked rumour, to wrong blameless men, and indeed rather yourselves, who think fit to direct affairs, not by judgment, but by passion. And every sober-minded person will declare this to be the only fair and equitable adjustment, namely, that the subjects render an unexceptionable account of their own life and doctrine; and that, on the other hand, the rulers should give their decision in obedience, not to violence and tyranny, but to piety and philosophy. For thus would both rulers and ruled reap benefit. For even one of the ancients somewhere said, "Unless both rulers and ruled philosophize, it is impossible to make states blessed."[2] It is our task, therefore, to afford to all an opportunity of inspecting our life and teachings, lest, on account of those who are accustomed to be ignorant of our affairs, we should incur the penalty due to them for mental blindness;[3] and it is your business, when you hear us, to be found, as reason demands, good judges. For if, when ye have learnt the truth, you do not what is just, you will be before God without excuse.

[1] Thirlby regarded the clause in brackets as an interpolation. There is considerable variety of opinion as to the exact meaning of the words amongst those who regard them as genuine.

[2] Plat. *Rep.* v. 18.

[3] That is to say, if the Christians refused or neglected to make their real opinions and practices known, they would share the guilt of those whom they thus kept in darkness.

CHAP. IV.—*Christians unjustly condemned for their mere name.*

By the mere application of a name, nothing is decided, either good or evil, apart from the actions implied in the name; and indeed, so far at least as one may judge from the name we are accused of, we are most excellent people.[1] But as we do not think it just to beg to be acquitted on account of the name, if we be convicted as evil-doers, so, on the other hand, if we be found to have committed no offence, either in the matter of thus naming ourselves, or of our conduct as citizens, it is your part very earnestly to guard against incurring just punishment, by unjustly punishing those who are not convicted. For from a name neither praise nor punishment could reasonably spring, unless something excellent or base in action be proved. And those among yourselves who are accused you do not punish before they are convicted; but in our case you receive the name as proof against us, and this although, so far as the name goes, you ought rather to punish our accusers. For we are accused of being Christians, and to hate what is *excellent* (Chrestian) is unjust. Again, if any of the accused deny the name, and say that he is not a Christian, you acquit him, as having no evidence against him as a wrong-doer; but if any one acknowledge that he is a Christian, you punish him on account of this acknowledgment. Justice requires that you inquire into the life both of him who confesses and of him who denies, that by his deeds it may be apparent what kind of man each is. For as some who have been taught by the Master, Christ, not to deny Him, give encouragement to others when they are put to the question, so in all probability do those who lead wicked lives give occasion to those who, without consideration, take upon them to accuse all the Christians of impiety and wickedness. And this also is not right. For of philosophy, too, some

[1] Justin avails himself here of the similarity in sound of the words Χριστὸς (Christ) and χρηστὸς (good, worthy, excellent). The play upon these words is kept up throughout this paragraph, and cannot be always represented to the English reader.

assume the name and the garb who do nothing worthy of their profession; and you are well aware, that those of the ancients whose opinions and teachings were quite diverse, are yet all called by the one name of philosophers. And of these some taught atheism; and the poets who have flourished among you raise a laugh out of the uncleanness of Jupiter with his own children. And those who now adopt such instruction are not restrained by you; but, on the contrary, you bestow prizes and honours upon those who euphoniously insult the gods.

CHAP. V.—*Christians charged with atheism.*

Why, then, should this be? In our case, who pledge ourselves to do no wickedness, nor to hold these atheistic opinions, you do not examine the charges made against us; but, yielding to unreasoning passion, and to the instigation of evil demons, you punish us without consideration or judgment. For the truth shall be spoken; since of old these evil demons, effecting apparitions of themselves, both defiled women and corrupted boys, and showed such fearful sights to men, that those who did not use their reason in judging of the actions that were done, were struck with terror; and being carried away by fear, and not knowing that these were demons, they called them gods, and gave to each the name which each of the demons chose for himself. And when Socrates endeavoured, by true reason and examination, to bring these things to light, and deliver men from the demons, then the demons themselves, by means of men who rejoiced in iniquity, compassed his death, as an atheist and a profane person, on the charge that "he was introducing new divinities;" and in our case they display a similar activity. For not only among the Greeks did reason (Logos) prevail to condemn these things through Socrates, but also among the Barbarians were they condemned by Reason (or the Word, the Logos) Himself, who took shape, and became man, and was called Jesus Christ; and in obedience to Him, we not only deny that they who did such things as these are gods,[1] but assert that they are wicked and impious demons,[1] whose actions will not bear comparison with those even of men desirous of virtue.

CHAP. VI.—*Charge of atheism refuted.*

Hence are we called atheists. And we confess that we are atheists, so far as gods of this sort are concerned, but not with respect to the most true God, the Father of righteousness and temperance and the other virtues, who is free from all impurity. But both Him, and the Son who came forth from Him and taught us these things, and the host of the other good angels who follow and are made like to Him,[2] and the prophetic Spirit, we worship and adore, knowing them in reason and truth, and declaring without grudging to every one who wishes to learn, as we have been taught.

CHAP. VII.—*Each Christian must be tried by his own life.*

But some one will say, Some have ere now been arrested and convicted as evil-doers. For you condemn many, many a time, after inquiring into the life of each of the accused severally, but not on account of those of whom we have been

[1] The word δαίμων means in Greek a god, but the Christians used the word to signify an evil spirit. Justin uses the same word here for god and demon. The connection which Justin and other Christian writers supposed to exist between evil spirits and the gods of the heathens will be apparent from Justin's own statements. The word διάβολος, devil, is not applied to these demons. There is but one devil, but many demons.

[2] This is the literal and obvious translation of Justin's words. But from c. 13, 16, and 61, it is evident that he did not desire to inculcate the worship of angels. We are therefore driven to adopt another translation of this passage, even though it be somewhat harsh. Two such translations have been proposed: the first connecting "us" and "the host of the other good angels" as the common object of the verb "taught;" the second connecting "these things" with "the host of," etc., and making these two together the subject taught. In the first case the translation would stand, "taught these things to us and to the host," etc.; in the second case the translation would be, "taught us about these things, and about the host of the others who follow Him, viz. the good angels."

speaking.[1] And this we acknowledge, that as among the Greeks those who teach such theories as please themselves are all called by the one name "Philosopher," though their doctrines be diverse, so also among the Barbarians this name on which accusations are accumulated is the common property of those who are and those who seem wise. For all are called Christians. Wherefore we demand that the deeds of all those who are accused to you be judged, in order that each one who is convicted may be punished as an evil-doer, and not as a Christian; and if it is clear that any one is blameless, that he may be acquitted, since by the mere fact of his being a Christian he does no wrong.[2] For we will not require that you punish our accusers;[3] they being sufficiently punished by their present wickedness and ignorance of what is right.

CHAP. VIII.—*Christians confess their faith in God.*

And reckon ye that it is for your sakes we have been saying these things; for it is in our power, when we are examined, to deny that we are Christians; but we would not live by telling a lie. For, impelled by the desire of the eternal and pure life, we seek the abode that is with God, the Father and Creator of all, and hasten to confess our faith, persuaded and convinced as we are that they who have proved to God[4] by their works that they followed Him, and loved to abide with Him where there is no sin to cause disturbance, can obtain these things. This, then, to speak shortly, is what we expect and have learned from Christ, and teach. And Plato, in like manner, used to say that Rhadamanthus and Minos would punish the wicked who came before them; and we say that the same thing will be done, but at the hand of Christ, and upon the wicked in the same bodies united again to their spirits which are now to

[1] *i.e.* according to Otto, "not on account of the sincere Christians of whom we have been speaking." According to Trollope, "not on account of (or at the instigation of) the demons before mentioned."

[2] Or, "as a Christian who has done no wrong."

[3] Compare the Rescript of Adrian appended to this Apology.

[4] Literally, "persuaded God."

undergo everlasting punishment; and not only, as Plato said, for a period of a thousand years. And if any one say that this is incredible or impossible, this error of ours is one which concerns ourselves only, and no other person, so long as you cannot convict us of doing any harm.

CHAP. IX.—*Folly of idol worship.*

And neither do we honour with many sacrifices and garlands of flowers such deities as men have formed and set in shrines and called gods; since we see that these are soulless and dead, and have not the form of God (for we do not consider that God has such a form as some say that they imitate to His honour), but have the names and forms of those wicked demons which have appeared. For why need we tell you who already know, into what forms the craftsmen, carving and cutting, casting and hammering, fashion the materials? And often out of vessels of dishonour, by merely changing the form, and making an image of the requisite shape, they make what they call a god; which we consider not only senseless, but to be even insulting to God, who, having ineffable glory and form, thus gets His name attached to things that are corruptible, and require constant service. And that the artificers of these are both intemperate, and, not to enter into particulars, are practised in every vice, you very well know; even their own girls who work along with them they corrupt. What infatuation! that dissolute men should be said to fashion and make gods for your worship, and that you should appoint such men the guardians of the temples where they are enshrined; not recognising that it is unlawful even to think or say that men are the guardians of gods.

CHAP. X.—*How God is to be served.*

But we have received by tradition that God does not need the material offerings which men can give, seeing, indeed, that He Himself is the provider of all things. And we have been taught, and are convinced, and do believe, that He accepts those only who imitate the excellences which reside in Him, temperance, and justice, and philanthropy, and as many virtues as are peculiar to a God who is called by no proper name. And we have been taught that He in the beginning did of His goodness, for man's sake, create all things out of unformed matter; and if men by their works show themselves worthy of this His design, they are deemed worthy, and so we have received—of reigning in company with Him, being delivered from corruption and suffering. For as in the beginning He created us when we were not, so do we consider that, in like manner, those who choose what is pleasing to Him are, on account of their choice, deemed worthy of incorruption and of fellowship with Him. For the coming into being at first was not in our own power; and in order that we may follow those things which please Him, choosing them by means of the rational faculties He has Himself endowed us with, He both persuades us and leads us to faith. And we think it for the advantage of all men that they are not restrained from learning these things, but are even urged thereto. For the restraint which human laws could not effect, the Word, inasmuch as He is divine, would have effected, had not the wicked demons, taking as their ally the lust of wickedness which is in every man, and which draws variously to all manner of vice, scattered many false and profane accusations, none of which attach to us.

Chap. xi.—*What kingdom Christians look for.*

And when you hear that we look for a kingdom, you suppose, without making any inquiry, that we speak of a human kingdom; whereas we speak of that which is with God, as appears also from the confession of their faith made by those who are charged with being Christians, though they know that death is the punishment awarded to him who so confesses. For if we looked for a human kingdom, we should also deny our Christ, that we might not be slain; and we should strive to escape detection, that we might obtain what we expect. But since our thoughts are not fixed on the present, we are not concerned when men cut us off; since also death is a debt which must at all events be paid.

CHAP. XII.—*Christians live as under God's eye.*

And more than all other men are we your helpers and allies in promoting peace, seeing that we hold this view, that it is alike impossible for the wicked, the covetous, the conspirator, and for the virtuous, to escape the notice of God, and that each man goes to everlasting punishment or salvation according to the value of his actions. For if all men knew this, no one would choose wickedness even for a little, knowing that he goes to the everlasting punishment of fire; but would by all means restrain himself, and adorn himself with virtue, that he might obtain the good gifts of God, and escape the punishments. For those who, on account of the laws and punishments you impose, endeavour to escape detection when they offend (and they offend, too, under the impression that it is quite possible to escape your detection, since you are but men), those persons, if they learned and were convinced that nothing, whether actually done or only intended, can escape the knowledge of God, would by all means live decently on account of the penalties threatened, as even you yourselves will admit. But you seem to fear lest all men become righteous, and you no longer have any to punish. Such would be the concern of public executioners, but not of good princes. But, as we before said, we are persuaded that these things are prompted by evil spirits, who demand sacrifices and service even from those who live unreasonably; but as for you, we presume that you who aim at [a reputation for] piety and philosophy will do nothing unreasonable. But if you also, like the foolish, prefer custom to truth, do what you have power to do. But just so much power have rulers who esteem opinion more than truth, as robbers have in a desert. And that you will not succeed is declared by the Word, than whom, after God who begat Him, we know there is no ruler more kingly and just. For as all shrink from succeeding to the poverty or sufferings or obscurity of their fathers, so whatever the Word forbids us to choose, the sensible man will not choose. That all these things should come to pass, I say, our Teacher foretold, He who is both Son and Apostle of God the Father of all and the Ruler, Jesus Christ; from whom also we have the name of Christians. Whence we become more assured of all the things He taught us, since whatever He beforehand foretold should come to pass, is seen in fact coming to pass; and this is the work of God, to tell of a thing before it happens, and as it was foretold so to show it happening. It were possible to pause here and add no more, reckoning that we demand what is just and true; but because we are well aware that it is not easy suddenly to change a mind possessed by ignorance, we intend to add a few things, for the sake of persuading those who love the truth, knowing that it is not impossible to put ignorance to flight by presenting the truth.

CHAP. XIII.—*Christians serve God rationally.*

What sober-minded man, then, will not acknowledge that we are not atheists, worshipping as we do the Maker of this universe, and declaring, as we have been taught, that He has no need of streams of blood and libations and incense; whom we praise to the utmost of our power by the exercise of prayer and thanksgiving for all things wherewith we are supplied, as we have been taught that the only honour that is worthy of Him is not to consume by fire what He has brought into being for our sustenance, but to use it for ourselves and those who need, and with gratitude to Him to offer thanks by invocations and hymns[1] for our creation, and for all the means of health, and for the various qualities of the different kinds of things, and for the changes of the seasons; and to present before Him petitions for our existing again in incorruption through faith in Him. Our teacher of these things is Jesus Christ, who also was born for this purpose, and was crucified under Pontius Pilate, procurator of Judæa, in the times of Tiberius Cæsar; and that we reasonably worship Him, having

[1] *πομπὰς καὶ ὕμνους.* "Grabe, and it should seem correctly, understands *πομπὰς* to be *solemn prayers*. . . . He also remarks, that the *ὕμνοι* were either psalms of David, or some of those psalms and songs made by the primitive Christians, which are mentioned in Eusebius, *H. E.* v. 28."—TROLLOPE.

learned that He is the Son of the true God Himself, and holding Him in the second place, and the prophetic Spirit in the third, we will prove. For they proclaim our madness to consist in this, that we give to a crucified man a place second to the unchangeable and eternal God, the Creator of all; for they do not discern the mystery that is herein, to which, as we make it plain to you, we pray you to give heed.

CHAP. XIV.—*The demons misrepresent Christian doctrine.*

For we forewarn you to be on your guard, lest those demons whom we have been accusing should deceive you, and quite divert you from reading and understanding what we say. For they strive to hold you their slaves and servants; and sometimes by appearances in dreams, and sometimes by magical impositions, they subdue all who make no strong opposing effort for their own salvation. And thus do we also, since our persuasion by the Word, stand aloof from them (*i.e.* the demons), and follow the only unbegotten God through His Son—we who formerly delighted in fornication, but now embrace chastity alone; we who formerly used magical arts, dedicate ourselves to the good and unbegotten God; we who valued above all things the acquisition of wealth and possessions, now bring what we have into a common stock, and communicate to every one in need; we who hated and destroyed one another, and on account of their different manners would not live[1] with men of a different tribe, now, since the coming of Christ, live familiarly with them, and pray for our enemies, and endeavour to persuade those who hate us unjustly to live conformably to the good precepts of Christ, to the end that they may become partakers with us of the same joyful hope of a reward from God the ruler of all. But lest we should seem to be reasoning sophistically, we consider it right, before giving you the promised[2] explanation, to cite a few precepts given by Christ Himself. And be it yours, as powerful rulers, to inquire whether we have been taught and do teach these things truly.

[1] Literally, "would not use the same hearth or fire."

[2] See the end of chap. xiii.

Brief and concise utterances fell from Him, for He was no sophist, but His word was the power of God.

CHAP. XV.—*What Christ Himself taught.*

Concerning chastity, He uttered such sentiments as these:[1] "Whosoever looketh upon a woman to lust after her, hath committed adultery with her already in his heart before God." And, "If thy right eye offend thee, cut it out; for it is better for thee to enter into the kingdom of heaven with one eye, than, having two eyes, to be cast into everlasting fire." And, "Whosoever shall marry her that is divorced from another husband, committeth adultery."[2] And, "There are some who have been made eunuchs of men, and some who were born eunuchs, and some who have made themselves eunuchs for the kingdom of heaven's sake; but all cannot receive this saying."[3] So that all who, by human law, are twice married,[4] are in the eye of our Master sinners, and those who look upon a woman to lust after her. For not only he who in act commits adultery is rejected by Him, but also he who desires to commit adultery: since not only our works, but also our thoughts, are open before God. And many, both men and women, who have been Christ's disciples from childhood, remain pure at the age of sixty or seventy years; and I boast that I could produce such from every race of men. For what shall I say, too, of the countless multitude of those who have reformed intemperate habits, and learned these things? For Christ called not the just nor the chaste to repentance, but the ungodly, and the licentious, and the unjust; His words being, "I came not to call the righteous,

[1] The reader will notice that Justin quotes from memory, so that there are some slight discrepancies between the words of Jesus as here cited, and the same sayings as recorded in our Gospels.

[2] Matt. v. 28, 29, 32. [3] Matt. xix. 12.

[4] διγαμίας ποιούμενοι, lit. contracting a double marriage. Of double marriages there are three kinds: the first, marriage with a second wife while the first is still alive and recognised as a lawful wife, or bigamy; the second, marriage with a second wife after divorce from the first; and third, marriage with a second wife after the death of the first. It is thought that Justin here refers to the second case.

but sinners to repentance."[1] For the heavenly Father desires rather the repentance than the punishment of the sinner. And of our love to all, He taught thus: "If ye love them that love you, what new thing do ye? for even fornicators do this. But I say unto you, Pray for your enemies, and love them that hate you, and bless them that curse you, and pray for them that despitefully use you."[2] And that we should communicate to the needy, and do nothing for glory, He said, "Give to him that asketh, and from him that would borrow turn not away; for if ye lend to them of whom ye hope to receive, what new thing do ye? even the publicans do this. Lay not up for yourselves treasure upon earth, where moth and rust doth corrupt, and where robbers break through; but lay up for yourselves treasure in heaven, where neither moth nor rust doth corrupt. For what is a man profited, if he shall gain the whole world, and lose his own soul? or what shall a man give in exchange for it? Lay up treasure, therefore, in heaven, where neither moth nor rust doth corrupt."[3] And, "Be ye kind and merciful, as your Father also is kind and merciful, and maketh His sun to rise on sinners, and the righteous, and the wicked. Take no thought what ye shall eat, or what ye shall put on: are ye not better than the birds and the beasts? And God feedeth them. Take no thought, therefore, what ye shall eat, or what ye shall put on; for your heavenly Father knoweth that ye have need of these things. But seek ye the kingdom of heaven, and all these things shall be added unto you. For where his treasure is, there also is the mind of a man."[4] And, "Do not these things to be seen of men; otherwise ye have no reward from your Father which is in heaven."[5]

1 Matt. ix. 13.
2 Matt. v. 46, 44; Luke vi. 28.
3 Luke vi. 30, 34; Matt. vi. 19, xvi. 26, vi. 20.
4 Luke vi. 36; Matt. v. 45, vi. 25, 26, 33, 21.
5 Matt. vi. 1.

CHAP. XVI.—*Concerning patience and swearing.*

And concerning our being patient of injuries, and ready to serve all, and free from anger, this is what He said: "To him that smiteth thee on the one cheek, offer also the other; and him that taketh away thy cloak or coat, forbid not. And whosoever shall be angry, is in danger of the fire. And every one that compelleth thee to go with him a mile, follow him two. And let your good works shine before men, that they, seeing them, may glorify your Father which is in heaven."[1] For we ought not to strive; neither has He desired us to be imitators of wicked men, but He has exhorted us to lead all men, by patience and gentleness, from shame and the love of evil. And this indeed is proved in the case of many who once were of your way of thinking, but have changed their violent and tyrannical disposition, being overcome either by the constancy which they have witnessed in their neighbours' lives,[2] or by the extraordinary forbearance they have observed in their fellow-travellers when defrauded, or by the honesty of those with whom they have transacted business.

And with regard to our not swearing at all, and always speaking the truth, He enjoined as follows: "Swear not at all; but let your yea be yea, and your nay, nay; for whatsoever is more than these cometh of evil."[3] And that we ought to worship God alone, He thus persuaded us: "The greatest commandment is, Thou shalt worship the Lord thy God, and Him only shalt thou serve, with all thy heart, and with all thy strength, the Lord God that made thee."[4] And when a certain man came to Him and said, "Good Master," He answered and said, "There is none good but God only, who made all things."[5] And let those who are not found living as He taught, be understood to be no Christians, even though they profess with the lip the precepts of Christ; for not those who make profession, but those who do the works, shall be saved, according to His word: "Not every one who

[1] Luke vi. 29; Matt. vi. 22, 41, 16.
[2] *i.e.* Christian neighbours.
[3] Matt. v. 34, 37.
[4] Mark xii. 30.
[5] Matt. xix. 6, 17.

saith to me, Lord, Lord, shall enter into the kingdom of heaven, but he that doeth the will of my Father which is in heaven. For whosoever heareth me, and doeth my sayings, heareth Him that sent me. And many will say unto me, Lord, Lord, have we not eaten and drunk in Thy name, and done wonders? And then will I say unto them, Depart from me, ye workers of iniquity. Then shall there be wailing and gnashing of teeth, when the righteous shall shine as the sun, and the wicked are sent into everlasting fire. For many shall come in my name, clothed outwardly in sheep's clothing, but inwardly being ravening wolves. By their works ye shall know them. And every tree that bringeth not forth good fruit, is hewn down and cast into the fire."[1] And as to those who are not living pursuant to these His teachings, and are Christians only in name, we demand that all such be punished by you.

Chap. xvii.—*Christ taught civil obedience.*

And everywhere we, more readily than all men, endeavour to pay to those appointed by you the taxes both ordinary and extraordinary,[2] as we have been taught by Him; for at that time some came to Him and asked Him, if one ought to pay tribute to Cæsar; and He answered, "Tell me, whose image does this coin bear?" And they said, "Cæsar's;" And again He answered them, "Render therefore to Cæsar the things that are Cæsar's, and to God the things that are God's."[3] Whence to God alone we render worship, but in other things we gladly serve you, acknowledging you as kings and rulers of men, and praying that with your kingly power you be found to possess also sound judgment. But if you pay no regard to our prayers and frank explanations, we shall suffer no loss, since we believe (or rather, indeed, are persuaded) that every man will suffer punishment in eternal fire according to the merit of his deed, and will render

[1] Matt. vii. 21, etc.; Luke xiii. 26; Matt. xiii. 42, vii. 15, 16, 19.

[2] φόρους καὶ εἰσφοράς. The former is the annual tribute; the latter, any occasional assessment. See Otto's Note, and Thucyd. iii 19.

[3] Matt. xxii. 17, 19, 20, 21.

account according to the power he has received from God, as Christ intimated when He said, "To whom God has given more, of him shall more be required."[1]

CHAP. XVIII.—*Proof of immortality and the resurrection.*

For reflect upon the end of each of the preceding kings, how they died the death common to all, which, if it issued in insensibility, would be a godsend[2] to all the wicked. But since sensation remains to all who have ever lived, and eternal punishment is laid up (*i.e.* for the wicked), see that ye neglect not to be convinced, and to hold as your belief, that these things are true. For let even necromancy, and the divinations you practise by immaculate children,[3] and the evoking of departed human souls,[4] and those who are called among the magi, Dream-senders and Assistant-spirits (Familiars),[5] and all that is done by those who are skilled in such matters—let these persuade you that even after death souls are in a state of sensation; and those who are seized and cast about by the spirits of the dead, whom all call dæmoniacs or madmen;[6] and what you repute as oracles, both of Amphi-

[1] Luke xii. 48.

[2] ἕρμαιον, a piece of unlooked-for luck, Hermes being the reputed giver of such gifts: *vid.* Liddell and Scott's *Lex.*; see also the Scholiast, quoted by Stallbaum in Plato's *Phaed.* p. 107, on a passage singularly analogous to this.

[3] Boys and girls, or even children, prematurely taken from the womb, were slaughtered, and their entrails inspected, in the belief that the souls of the victims (being still conscious, as Justin is arguing) would reveal things hidden and future. Instances are abundantly cited by Otto and Trollope.

[4] This form of spirit-rapping was familiar to the ancients, and Justin again (*Dial. c. Tryph.* c. 105) uses the invocation of Samuel by the witch of Endor as a proof of the immortality of the soul.

[5] Valesius (on Euseb. *H. E.* iv. 7) states that the magi had two kinds of familiars: the first, who were sent to inspire men with dreams which might give them intimations of things future; and the second, who were sent to watch over men, and protect them from diseases and misfortunes. The first, he says, they called (as here) ὀνειροπομπούς, and the second παρέδρους.

[6] Justin is not the only author in ancient or recent times who has classed dæmoniacs and maniacs together; neither does he stand alone

lochus, Dodona, Pytho, and as many other such as exist; and the opinions of your authors, Empedocles and Pythagoras, Plato and Socrates, and the pit of Homer,[1] and the descent of Ulysses to inspect these things, and all that has been uttered of a like kind. Such favour as you grant to these, grant also to us, who not less but more firmly than they believe in God; since we expect to receive again our own bodies, though they be dead and cast into the earth, for we maintain that with God nothing is impossible.

CHAP. XIX.—*The resurrection possible.*

And to any thoughtful person would anything appear more incredible, than, if we were not in the body, and some one were to say that it was possible that from a small drop of human seed bones and sinews and flesh be formed into a shape such as we see? For let this now be said hypothetically: if you yourselves were not such as you now are, and born of such parents [and causes], and one were to show you human seed and a picture of a man, and were to say with confidence that from such a substance such a being could be produced, would you believe before you saw the actual production? No one will dare to deny [that such a statement would surpass belief]. In the same way, then, you are now incredulous because you have never seen a dead man rise again. But as at first you would not have believed it possible that such persons could be produced from the small drop, and yet now you see them thus produced, so also judge ye that it is not impossible that the bodies of men, after they have been dissolved, and like seeds resolved into earth, should in God's appointed time rise again and put on incorruption. For what power worthy of God those imagine who say, that each thing returns to that from which it was produced, and that beyond this not even God Himself can do anything, we are

among the ancients in the opinion that dæmoniacs were possessed by the spirits of departed men. References will be found in Trollope's note.

[1] See the *Odyssey*, Book xi. line 25, where Ulysses is described as digging a pit or trench with his sword, and pouring libations, in order to collect around him the souls of the dead.

unable to conceive; but this we see clearly, that they would not have believed it possible that they could have become such and produced from such materials, as they now see both themselves and the whole world to be. And that it is better to believe even what is impossible to our own nature and to men, than to be unbelieving like the rest of the world, we have learned; for we know that our master Jesus Christ said, that "what is impossible with men is possible with God,"[1] and, "Fear not them that kill you, and after that can do no more; but fear Him who after death is able to cast both soul and body into hell."[2] And hell is a place where those are to be punished who have lived wickedly, and who do not believe that those things which God has taught us by Christ will come to pass.

CHAP. XX.—*Heathen analogies to Christian doctrine.*

And the Sibyl[3] and Hystaspes said that there should be a dissolution by God of things corruptible. And the philosophers called Stoics teach that even God Himself shall be resolved into fire, and they say that the world is to be formed anew by this revolution; but we understand that God, the creator of all things, is superior to the things that are to be changed. If, therefore, on some points we teach the same things as the poets and philosophers whom you honour, and on other points are fuller and more divine in our teaching, and if we alone afford proof of what we assert, why are we unjustly hated more than all others? For while we say that all things have been produced and arranged into a world by God, we shall seem to utter the doctrine of Plato; and while we say that there will be a burning up of all, we shall seem to utter the doctrine of the Stoics; and while we affirm that

[1] Matt. xix. 26. [2] Matt. x. 28.

[3] The Sibylline Oracles are now generally regarded as heathen fragments largely interpolated by unscrupulous men during the early ages of the church. For an interesting account of these somewhat perplexing documents, see Burton's *Lectures on the Ecclesiastical History of the First Three Centuries*, Lect. xvii. The prophecies of Hystaspes were also commonly appealed to as genuine by the early Christians.

the souls of the wicked, being endowed with sensation even after death, are punished, and that those of the good being delivered from punishment spend a blessed existence, we shall seem to say the same things as the poets and philosophers; and while we maintain that men ought not to worship the works of their hands, we say the very things which have been said by the comic poet Menander, and other similar writers, for they have declared that the workman is greater than the work.

Chap. XXI.—*Analogies to the history of Christ.*

And when we say also that the Word, who is the first-birth[1] of God, was produced without sexual union, and that He, Jesus Christ, our teacher, was crucified and died, and rose again, and ascended into heaven, we propound nothing different from what you believe regarding those whom you esteem sons of Jupiter. For you know how many sons your esteemed writers ascribe to Jupiter: Mercury, the interpreting word and teacher of all; Æsculapius, who, though he was a great physician, was struck by a thunderbolt, and so ascended to heaven; and Bacchus too, after he had been torn limb from limb; and Hercules, when he had committed himself to the flames to escape his toils; and the sons of Leda, the Dioscuri; and Perseus, son of Danae; and Bellerophon, who, though sprung from mortals, rose to heaven on the horse Pegasus. For what shall I say of Ariadne, and those who, like her, have been declared to be set among the stars? And what of the emperors who die among yourselves, whom you deem worthy of deification, and in whose behalf you produce some one who swears he has seen the burning Cæsar rise to heaven from the funeral pyre? And what kind of deeds are recorded of each of these reputed sons of Jupiter, it is needless to tell to those who already know. This only shall be said, that they are written for the advantage and encouragement[2] of youthful scholars; for all reckon it an honourable

[1] *i.e.* first-born.

[2] *διαφορὰν καὶ προτροπήν.* The irony here is so obvious as to make the proposed reading (*διαφθορὰν καὶ παρατροπήν*, corruption and depravation)

thing to imitate the gods. But far be such a thought concerning the gods from every well-conditioned soul, as to believe that Jupiter himself, the governor and creator of all things, was both a parricide and the son of a parricide, and that being overcome by the love of base and shameful pleasures, he came in to Ganymede and those many women whom he violated, and that his sons did like actions. But, as we said above, wicked devils perpetrated these things. And we have learned that those only are deified who have lived near to God in holiness and virtue; and we believe that those who live wickedly and do not repent are punished in everlasting fire.

Chap. xxii.—*Analogies to the Sonship of Christ.*

Moreover, the Son of God called Jesus, even if only a man by ordinary generation, yet, on account of His wisdom, is worthy to be called the Son of God; for all writers call God the Father of men and gods. And if we assert that the Word of God was born of God in a peculiar manner, different from ordinary generation, let this, as said above, be no extraordinary thing to you, who say that Mercury is the angelic word of God. But if any one objects that He was crucified, in this also He is on a par with those reputed sons of Jupiter of yours, who suffered as we have now enumerated. For their sufferings at death are recorded to have been not all alike, but diverse; so that not even by the peculiarity of His suffering does He seem to be inferior to them; but, on the contrary, as we promised in the preceding part of this discourse, we will now prove Him superior—or rather have already proved Him to be so—for the superior is revealed by His actions. And if we even affirm that He was born of a virgin, accept this in common with what you accept of Perseus. And in that we say that He made whole the lame, the paralytic, and those born blind, we seem to say what is very similar to the deeds said to have been done by Æsculapius.

unnecessary. Otto prefers the reading adopted above. Trollope, on the other hand, inclines to the latter reading, mainly on the score of the former expressions being unusual. See his very sensible note *in loc.*

CHAP. XXIII.—*The argument.*

And that this may now become evident to you—(firstly[1]) that whatever we assert in conformity with what has been taught us by Christ, and by the prophets who preceded Him, are alone true, and are older than all the writers who have existed; that we claim to be acknowledged, not because we say the same things as these writers said, but because we say true things: and (secondly) that Jesus Christ is the only proper Son who has been begotten by God, being His Word and first-begotten, and power; and, becoming man according to His will, He taught us these things for the conversion and restoration of the human race: and (thirdly) that before He became a man among men, some, influenced by the devils before mentioned, related beforehand, through the instrumentality of the poets, those circumstances as having really happened, which, having fictitiously devised, they narrated, in the same manner as they have caused to be fabricated the scandalous reports against us of infamous and impious actions,[2] of which there is neither witness nor proof—we shall bring forward the following proof.

CHAP. XXIV.—*Varieties of heathen worship.*

In the first place [we furnish proof], because, though we say things similar to what the Greeks say, we only are hated on account of the name of Christ, and though we do no wrong, are put to death as sinners; other men in other places worshipping trees and rivers, and mice and cats and crocodiles,

[1] The Benedictine editor, Maranus, Otto, and Trollope, here note that Justin in this chapter promises to make good three distinct positions: *1st*, That Christian doctrines alone are true, and are to be received, not on account of their resemblance to the sentiments of poets or philosophers, but on their own account; *2d*, that Jesus Christ is the incarnate Son of God, and our teacher; *3d*, that before His incarnation, the devils, having some knowledge of what He would accomplish, enabled the heathen poets and priests in some points to anticipate, though in a distorted form, the facts of the incarnation. The first he establishes in chap. xxiv.-xxix.; the second in chap. xxx.-liii.; and the third in chap. liv. et sq.

[2] We have here followed the reading and rendering of Trollope.

and many irrational animals. Nor are the same animals esteemed by all; but in one place one is worshipped, and another in another, so that all are profane in the judgment of one another, on account of their not worshipping the same objects. And this is the sole accusation you bring against us, that we do not reverence the same gods as you do, nor offer to the dead libations and the savour of fat, and crowns for their statues,[1] and sacrifices. For you very well know that the same animals are with some esteemed gods, with others wild beasts, and with others sacrificial victims.

Chap. xxv.—*False gods abandoned by Christians.*

And, secondly, because we—who, out of every race of men, used to worship Bacchus the son of Semele, and Apollo the son of Latona (who in their loves with men did such things as it is shameful even to mention), and Proserpine and Venus (who were maddened with love of Adonis, and whose mysteries also you celebrate), or Æsculapius, or some one or other of those who are called gods—have now, through Jesus Christ, learned to despise these, though we be threatened with death for it, and have dedicated ourselves to the unbegotten and impassible God; of whom we are persuaded that never was he goaded by lust of Antiope, or such other women, or of Ganymede, nor was rescued by that hundred-handed giant whose aid was obtained through Thetis, nor was anxious on this account[2] that her son Achilles should destroy many of the Greeks because of his concubine Briseis. Those who believe these things we pity, and those who invented them we know to be devils.

Chap. xxvi.—*Magicians not trusted by Christians.*

And, thirdly, because after Christ's ascension into heaven the devils put forward certain men who said that they themselves were gods; and they were not only not persecuted

[1] ἐν γραφαῖς στεφάνους. The only conjecture which seems at all probable is that of the Benedictine editor followed here.

[2] *i.e.* on account of the assistance gained for him by Thetis, and in return for it.

by you, but even deemed worthy of honours. There was a Samaritan, Simon, a native of the village called Gitto, who in the reign of Claudius Cæsar, and in your royal city of Rome, did mighty acts of magic, by virtue of the art of the devils operating in him. He was considered a god, and as a god was honoured by you with a statue, which statue was erected on the river Tiber, between the two bridges, and bore this inscription, in the language of Rome:

"Simoni Deo Sancto,"[1]
"To Simon the holy God."

And almost all the Samaritans, and a few even of other nations, worship him, and acknowledge him as the first god; and a woman, Helena, who went about with him at that time, and had formerly been a prostitute, they say is the first idea generated by him. And a man, Menander, also a Samaritan, of the town Capparetæa, a disciple of Simon, and inspired by devils, we know to have deceived many while he was in Antioch by his magical art. He persuaded those who adhered to him that they should never die, and even now there are some living who hold this opinion of his. And there is Marcion, a man of Pontus, who is even at this day alive, and teaching his disciples to believe in some other god greater than the Creator. And he, by the aid of the devils, has caused many of every nation to speak blasphemies, and to deny that God is the maker of this unvierse, and

[1] It is very generally supposed that Justin was mistaken in understanding this to have been a statue erected to Simon Magus. This supposition rests on the fact that in the year 1574 there was dug up in the island of the Tiber a fragment of marble, with the inscription "Semoni Sanco Deo," etc., being probably the base of a statue erected to the Sabine deity Semo Sancus. This inscription Justin is supposed to have mistaken for the one he gives above. This has always seemed to us very slight evidence on which to reject so precise a statement as Justin here makes; a statement which he would scarcely have hazarded in an apology addressed to Rome, where every person had the means of ascertaining its accuracy. If, as is supposed, he made a mistake, it must have been at once exposed, and other writers would not have so frequently repeated the story as they have done. See *Burton's Bampton Lectures*, p. 374.

to assert that some other, being greater than He, has done greater works. All who take their opinions from these men, are, as we before said,[1] called Christians; just as also those who do not agree with the philosophers in their doctrines, have yet in common with them the name of philosophers given to them. And whether they perpetrate those fabulous and shameful deeds[2]—the upsetting of the lamp, and promiscuous intercourse, and eating human flesh—we know not; but we do know that they are neither persecuted nor put to death by you, at least on account of their opinions. But I have a treatise against all the heresies that have existed already composed, which, if you wish to read it, I will give you.

CHAP. XXVII.—*Guilt of exposing children.*

But as for us, we have been taught that to expose newly-born children is the part of wicked men; and this we have been taught lest we should do any one an injury, and lest we should sin against God, first, because we see that almost all so exposed (not only the girls, but also the males) are brought up to prostitution. And as the ancients are said to have reared herds of oxen, or goats, or sheep, or grazing horses, so now we see you rear children only for this shameful use; and for this pollution a multitude of females and hermaphrodites, and those who commit unmentionable iniquities, are found in every nation. And you receive the hire of these, and duty and taxes from them, whom you ought to exterminate from your realm. And any one who uses such persons, besides the godless and infamous and impure intercourse, may possibly be having intercourse with his own child, or relative, or brother. And there are some who prostitute even their own children and wives, and some are openly mutilated for the purpose of sodomy; and they refer these mysteries to the mother of the gods, and along with each of those whom you esteem gods there is painted a serpent,[3] a great symbol

[1] See chap. vii.

[2] Which were commonly charged against the Christians.

[3] Thirlby remarks that the serpent was the symbol specially of eternity, of power, and of wisdom, and that there was scarcely any divine

and mystery. Indeed, the things which you do openly and with applause, as if the divine light were overturned and extinguished, these you lay to our charge; which, in truth, does no harm to us who shrink from doing any such things, but only to those who do them and bear false witness against us.

CHAP. XXVIII.—*God's care for men.*

For among us the prince of the wicked spirits is called the serpent, and Satan, and the devil, as you can learn by looking into our writings. And that he would be sent into the fire with his host, and the men who follow him, and would be punished for an endless duration, Christ foretold. For the reason why God has delayed to do this, is His regard for the human race. For He foreknows that some are to be saved by repentance, some even that are perhaps not yet born.[1] In the beginning He made the human race with the power of thought and of choosing the truth and doing right, so that all men are without excuse before God; for they have been born rational and contemplative. And if any one disbelieves that God cares for these things,[2] he will thereby either insinuate that God does not exist, or he will assert that though He exists He delights in vice, or exists like a stone, and that neither virtue nor vice are anything, but only in the opinion of men these things are reckoned good or evil. And this is the greatest profanity and wickedness.

CHAP. XXIX.—*Continence of Christians.*

And again [we fear to expose children], lest some of them be not picked up, but die, and we become murderers. But whether we marry, it is only that we may bring up children;

attribute to which the heathen did not find some likeness in this animal. See also Hardwick's *Christ and other Masters*, vol. ii. 146 (2d ed.).

[1] Literally, "For He foreknows some about to be saved by repentance, and some not yet perhaps born."

[2] Those things which concern the salvation of man; so Trollope and the other interpreters, except Otto, who reads τούτων masculine, and understands it of the men first spoken of.

or whether we decline marriage, we live continently. And that you may understand that promiscuous intercourse is not one of our mysteries, one of our number a short time ago presented to Felix the governor in Alexandria a petition, craving that permission might be given to a surgeon to make him an eunuch. For the surgeons there said that they were forbidden to do this without the permission of the governor. And when Felix absolutely refused to sign such a permission, the youth remained single, and was satisfied with his own approving conscience, and the approval of those who thought as he did. And it is not out of place, we think, to mention here Antinous, who was alive but lately, and whom all were prompt, through fear, to worship as a god, though they knew both who he was and what was his origin.[1]

CHAP. XXX.—*Was Christ not a magician?*

But lest any one should meet us with the question, What should prevent that He whom we call Christ, being a man born of men, performed what we call His mighty works by magical art, and by this appeared to be the Son of God? we will now offer proof, not trusting mere assertions, but being of necessity persuaded by those who prophesied [of Him] before these things came to pass, for with our own eyes we behold things that have happened and are happening just as they were predicted; and this will, we think, appear even to you the strongest and truest evidence.

CHAP. XXXI.—*Of the Hebrew prophets.*

There were, then, among the Jews certain men who were prophets of God, through whom the prophetic Spirit published beforehand things that were to come to pass, ere ever they happened. And their prophecies, as they were spoken and when they were uttered, the kings who happened to be reigning among the Jews at the several times carefully preserved in their possession, when they had been arranged in

[1] For a sufficient account of the infamous history here alluded to, and the extravagant grief of Hadrian, and the servility of the people, see Smith's *Dictionary of Biography:* "Antinous."

books by the prophets themselves in their own Hebrew language. And when Ptolemy king of Egypt formed a library, and endeavoured to collect the writings of all men, he heard also of these prophets, and sent to Herod, who was at that time king of the Jews,[1] requesting that the books of the prophets be sent to him. And Herod the king did indeed send them, written, as they were, in the foresaid Hebrew language. And when their contents were found to be unintelligible to the Egyptians, he again sent and requested that men be commissioned to translate them into the Greek language. And when this was done, the books remained with the Egyptians, where they are until now. They are also in the possession of all Jews throughout the world; but they, though they read, do not understand what is said, but count us foes and enemies; and, like yourselves, they kill and punish us whenever they have the power, as you can well believe. For in the Jewish war which lately raged, Barchochebas, the leader of the revolt of the Jews, gave orders that Christians alone should be led to cruel punishments, unless they would deny Jesus Christ and utter blasphemy. In these books, then, of the prophets we found Jesus our Christ foretold as coming, born of a virgin, growing up to man's estate, and healing every disease and every sickness, and raising the dead, and being hated, and unrecognised, and crucified, and dying, and rising again, and ascending into heaven, and being, and being called, the Son of God. We find it also predicted that certain persons should be sent by Him into every nation to publish these things, and that rather among the Gentiles [than among the Jews] men should believe on Him. And He was predicted before He appeared, first 5000 years before, and again 3000, then 2000, then 1000, and yet again 800; for in the succession of generations prophets after prophets arose.

[1] Some attribute this blunder in chronology to Justin, others to his transcribers: it was Eleazar the high priest to whom Ptolemy applied.

CHAP. XXXII.—*Christ predicted by Moses.*

Moses then, who was the first of the prophets, spoke in these very words: "The sceptre shall not depart from Judah, nor a lawgiver from between his feet, until He come for whom it is reserved; and He shall be the desire of the nations, binding His foal to the vine, washing His robe in the blood of the grape."[1] It is yours to make accurate inquiry, and ascertain up to whose time the Jews had a lawgiver and king of their own. Up to the time of Jesus Christ, who taught us, and interpreted the prophecies which were not yet understood, [they had a lawgiver] as was foretold by the holy and divine Spirit of prophecy through Moses, "that a ruler would not fail the Jews until He should come for whom the kingdom was reserved" (for Judah was the forefather of the Jews, from whom also they have their name of Jews); and after He (*i.e.* Christ) appeared, you began to rule the Jews, and gained possession of all their territory. And the prophecy, "He shall be the expectation of the nations," signified that there would be some of all nations who should look for Him to come again. And this indeed you can see for yourselves, and be convinced of by fact. For of all races of men there are some who look for Him who was crucified in Judæa, and after whose crucifixion the land was straightway surrendered to you as spoil of war. And the prophecy, "binding His foal to the vine, and washing His robe in the blood of the grape," was a significant symbol of the things that were to happen to Christ, and of what He was to do. For the foal of an ass stood bound to a vine at the entrance of a village, and He ordered His acquaintances to bring it to Him then; and when it was brought, He mounted and sat upon it, and entered Jerusalem, where was the vast temple of the Jews which was afterwards destroyed by you. And after this He was crucified, that the rest of the prophecy might be fulfilled. For this "washing His robe in the blood of the grape" was predictive of the passion He was to endure, cleansing by His blood those who believe on Him.

[1] Gen. xlix. 10.

For what is called by the Divine Spirit through the prophet "His robe," are those men who believe in Him in whom abideth the seed[1] of God, the Word. And what is spoken of as "the blood of the grape," signifies that He who should appear would have blood, though not of the seed of man, but of the power of God. And the first power after God the Father and Lord of all is the Word, who is also the Son; and of Him we will, in what follows, relate how He took flesh and became man. For as man did not make the blood of the vine, but God, so it was hereby intimated that the blood should not be of human seed, but of divine power, as we have said above. And Isaiah, another prophet, foretelling the same things in other words, spoke thus: "A star shall rise out of Jacob, and a flower shall spring from the root of Jesse; and in His arm shall the nations trust."[2] And a star of light has arisen, and a flower has sprung from the root of Jesse—this Christ. For by the power of God He was conceived by a virgin of the seed of Jacob, who was the father of Judah, who, as we have shown, was the father of the Jews; and Jesse was His forefather according to the oracle, and He was the son of Jacob and Judah according to lineal descent.

CHAP. XXXIII.—*Manner of Christ's birth predicted.*

And hear again how Isaiah in express words foretold that He should be born of a virgin; for he spoke thus: "Behold, a virgin shall conceive, and bring forth a son, and they shall say for His name, 'God with us.'"[3] For things which were incredible and seemed impossible with men, these God predicted by the Spirit of prophecy as about to come to pass, in order that, when they came to pass, there might be no unbelief, but faith, because of their prediction. But lest some, not understanding the prophecy now cited, should charge us with the very things we have been laying to the charge of the poets who say that Jupiter went in to women through lust, let us try to explain the words. This, then, "Behold, a

[1] Grabe would here read, not σπέρμα, but πνεῦμα, the spirit; but the Benedictine, Otto, and Trollope all think that no change should be made.
[2] Isa. xi. 1.
[3] Isa. vii. 14.

virgin shall conceive," signifies that a virgin should conceive without intercourse. For if she had had intercourse with any one whatever, she was no longer a virgin; but the power of God having come upon the virgin, overshadowed her, and caused her while yet a virgin to conceive. And the angel of God who was sent to the same virgin at that time brought her good news, saying, "Behold, thou shalt conceive of the Holy Ghost, and shalt bear a Son, and He shall be called the Son of the Highest, and thou shalt call His name Jesus; for He shall save His people from their sins,"[1]—as they who have recorded all that concerns our Saviour Jesus Christ have taught, whom we believed, since by Isaiah also, whom we have now adduced, the Spirit of prophecy declared that He should be born as we intimated before. It is wrong, therefore, to understand the Spirit and the power of God as anything else than the Word, who is also the first-born of God, as the foresaid prophet Moses declared; and it was this which, when it came upon the virgin and overshadowed her, caused her to conceive, not by intercourse, but by power. And the name Jesus in the Hebrew language means Σωτὴρ (Saviour) in the Greek tongue. Wherefore, too, the angel said to the virgin, "Thou shalt call His name Jesus, for He shall save His people from their sins." And that the prophets are inspired[2] by no other than the Divine Word, even you, as I fancy, will grant.

Chap. xxxiv.—*Place of Christ's birth foretold.*

And hear what part of earth He was to be born in, as another prophet, Micah, foretold. He spoke thus: "And thou, Bethlehem, the land of Judah, art not the least among the princes of Judah; for out of thee shall come forth a Governor, who shall feed my people."[3] Now there is a village in the land of the Jews, thirty-five stadia from Jerusalem, in which Jesus Christ was born, as you can

[1] Luke i. 32; Matt. i. 21.

[2] θεοφοροῦνται, lit. are borne by a god—a word used of those who were supposed to be wholly under the influence of a deity.

[3] Micah v. 2.

ascertain also from the registers of the taxing made under Cyrenius, your first procurator in Judæa.

CHAP. XXXV.—*Other fulfilled prophecies.*

And how Christ after He was born was to escape the notice of other men until He grew to man's estate, which also came to pass, hear what was foretold regarding this. There are the following predictions:[1]—"Unto us a child is born, and unto us a young man is given, and the government shall be upon His shoulders;"[2] which is significant of the power of the cross, for to it, when He was crucified, He applied His shoulders, as shall be more clearly made out in the ensuing discourse. And again the same prophet Isaiah, being inspired by the prophetic Spirit, said, "I have spread out my hands to a disobedient and gainsaying people, to those who walk in a way that is not good. They now ask of me judgment, and dare to draw near to God."[3] And again in other words, through another prophet, He says, "They pierced my hands and my feet, and for my vesture they cast lots."[4] And indeed David, the king and prophet, who uttered these things, suffered none of them; but Jesus Christ stretched forth His hands, being crucified by the Jews speaking against Him, and denying that He was the Christ. And as the prophet spoke, they tormented Him, and set Him on the judgment-seat, and said, Judge us. And the expression, "They pierced my hands and my feet," was used in reference to the nails of the cross which were fixed in His hands and feet. And after He was crucified they cast lots upon His vesture, and they that crucified Him parted it among them. And that these things did happen, you can ascertain from the Acts of Pontius Pilate.[5] And we will cite the prophetic utterances

1 These predictions have so little reference to the point Justin intends to make out, that some editors have supposed that a passage has here been lost. Others think the irrelevancy an insufficient ground for such a supposition.

2 Isa. ix. 6. 3 Isa. lxv. 2, lviii. 2. 4 Ps. xxii. 16.

5 ἄκτων. These Acts of Pontius Pilate, or regular accounts of his procedure sent by Pilate to the Emperor Tiberius, are supposed to have been destroyed at an early period, possibly in consequence of the unanswer-

of another prophet, Zephaniah,[1] to the effect that He was foretold expressly as to sit upon the foal of an ass and to enter Jerusalem. The words are these: "Rejoice greatly, O daughter of Zion; shout, O daughter of Jerusalem: behold, thy King cometh unto thee; lowly, and riding upon an ass, and upon a colt the foal of an ass."[2]

CHAP. XXXVI.—*Different modes of prophecy.*

But when you hear the utterances of the prophets spoken as it were personally, you must not suppose that they are spoken by the inspired themselves, but by the Divine Word who moves them. For sometimes He declares things that are to come to pass, in the manner of one who foretells the future; sometimes He speaks as from the person of God the Lord and Father of all; sometimes as from the person of Christ; sometimes as from the person of the people answering the Lord or His Father, just as you can see even in your own writers, one man being the writer of the whole, but introducing the persons who converse. And this the Jews who possessed the books of the prophets did not understand, and therefore did not recognise Christ even when He came, but even hate us who say that He has come, and who prove that, as was predicted, He was crucified by them.

CHAP. XXXVII.—*Utterances of the Father.*

And that this too may be clear to you, there were spoken from the person of the Father, through Isaiah the prophet, the following words: "The ox knoweth his owner, and the ass his master's crib; but Israel doth not know, and my people hath not understood. Woe, sinful nation, a people full of sins, a wicked seed, children that are transgressors, ye

able appeals which the Christians constantly made to them. There exists a forgery in imitation of these Acts. See Trollope.

[1] The reader will notice that these are not the words of Zephaniah, but of Zechariah (ix. 9), to whom also Justin himself refers them in the *Dial. Tryph.* c. 53.

[2] Zech. ix. 9.

have forsaken the Lord."[1] And again elsewhere, when the same prophet speaks in like manner from the person of the Father, "What is the house that ye will build for me? saith the Lord. The heaven is my throne, and the earth is my footstool."[2] And again, in another place, "Your new moons and your sabbaths my soul hateth; and the great day of the fast and of ceasing from labour I cannot away with; nor, if ye come to be seen of me, will I hear you: your hands are full of blood; and if ye bring fine flour, incense, it is abomination unto me: the fat of lambs and the blood of bulls I do not desire. For who hath required this at your hands? But loose every bond of wickedness, tear asunder the tight knots of violent contracts, cover the houseless and naked, deal thy bread to the hungry."[3] What kind of things are taught through the prophets from [the person of] God, you can now perceive.

CHAP. XXXVIII.—*Utterances of the Son.*

And when the Spirit of prophecy speaks from the person of Christ, the utterances are of this sort: "I have spread out my hands to a disobedient and gainsaying people, to those who walk in a way that is not good."[4] And again: "I gave my back to the scourges, and my cheeks to the buffetings; I turned not away my face from the shame of spittings; and the Lord was my helper: therefore was I not confounded: but I set my face as a firm rock; and I knew that I should not be ashamed, for He is near that justifieth me."[5] And again, when he says, "They cast lots upon my vesture, and pierced my hands and my feet. And I lay down and slept, and rose again, because the Lord sustained me."[6] And again, when he says, "They spake with their lips, they wagged the head, saying, Let him deliver himself."[7] And that all these things happened to Christ at the hands of the Jews, you can

[1] Isa. i. 3. This quotation varies only in one word from that of the LXX.

[2] Isa. lxvi. 1.

[3] Isa. i. 14, xviii. 6.

[4] Isa. lxv. 2.

[5] Isa. l. 6.

[6] Ps. xxii. 18, iii. 5.

[7] Ps. xxii. 7.

ascertain. For when He was crucified, they did shoot out the lip, and wagged their heads, saying, "Let him who raised the dead save himself."[1]

Chap. xxxix.—*Direct predictions by the Spirit.*

And when the Spirit of prophecy speaks as predicting things that are to come to pass, He speaks in this way: "For out of Zion shall go forth the law, and the word of the Lord from Jerusalem. And He shall judge among the nations, and shall rebuke many people; and they shall beat their swords into ploughshares, and their spears into pruning-hooks: nation shall not lift up sword against nation, neither shall they learn war any more."[2] And that it did so come to pass, we can convince you. For from Jerusalem there went out into the world, men, twelve in number, and these illiterate, of no ability in speaking: but by the power of God they proclaimed to every race of men that they were sent by Christ to teach to all the word of God; and we who formerly used to murder one another do not only now refrain from making war upon our enemies, but also, that we may not lie nor deceive our examiners, willingly die confessing Christ. For that saying, "The tongue has sworn, but the mind is unsworn,"[3] might be imitated by us in this matter. But if the soldiers enrolled by you, and who have taken the military oath, prefer their allegiance to their own life, and parents, and country, and all kindred, though you can offer them nothing incorruptible, it were verily ridiculous if we, who earnestly long for incorruption, should not endure all things, in order to obtain what we desire from Him who is able to grant it.

Chap. xl.—*Christ's advent foretold.*

And hear how it was foretold concerning those who published His doctrine and proclaimed His appearance, the above-mentioned prophet and king speaking thus by the Spirit of prophecy: "Day unto day uttereth speech, and night unto night showeth knowledge. There is no speech

[1] Comp. Matt. xxvii. 39. [2] Isa. ii. 3. [3] Eurip. *Hipp.* 608.

nor language where their voice is not heard. Their voice has gone out into all the earth, and their words to the ends of the world. In the sun hath He set His tabernacle, and he as a bridegroom going out of his chamber shall rejoice as a giant to run his course."[1] And we have thought it right and relevant to mention some other prophetic utterances of David besides these; from which you may learn how the Spirit of prophecy exhorts men to live, and how He foretold the conspiracy which was formed against Christ by Herod the king of the Jews, and the Jews themselves, and Pilate, who was your governor among them, with his soldiers; and how He should be believed on by men of every race; and how God calls Him His Son, and has declared that He will subdue all His enemies under Him; and how the devils, as much as they can, strive to escape the power of God the Father and Lord of all, and the power of Christ Himself; and how God calls all to repentance before the day of judgment comes. These things were uttered thus: "Blessed is the man who hath not walked in the counsel of the ungodly, nor stood in the way of sinners, nor sat in the seat of the scornful: but his delight is in the law of the Lord; and in His law will he meditate day and night. And he shall be like a tree planted by the rivers of waters, which shall give his fruit in his season; and his leaf shall not wither, and whatsoever he doeth shall prosper. The ungodly are not so, but are like the chaff which the wind driveth away from the face of the earth. Therefore the ungodly shall not stand in the judgment, nor sinners in the counsel of the righteous. For the Lord knoweth the way of the righteous; but the way of the ungodly shall perish. Why do the heathen rage, and the people imagine new things? The kings of the earth set themselves, and the rulers take counsel together, against the Lord, and against His Anointed, saying, Let us break their bands asunder, and cast their yoke from us. He that dwelleth in the heavens shall laugh at them, and the Lord shall have them in derision. Then shall He speak to them in His wrath, and vex them in His sore displeasure. Yet have I been set

[1] Ps. xix. 2, etc.

by Him a King on Zion His holy hill, declaring the decree of the Lord. The Lord said to me, Thou art my Son; this day have I begotten Thee. Ask of me, and I shall give Thee the heathen for Thine inheritance, and the uttermost parts of the earth as Thy possession. Thou shalt herd them with a rod of iron; as the vessels of a potter shalt Thou dash them in pieces. Be wise now, therefore, O ye kings; be instructed, all ye judges of the earth. Serve the Lord with fear, and rejoice with trembling. Embrace instruction, lest at any time the Lord be angry, and ye perish from the right way, when His wrath has been suddenly kindled. Blessed are all they that put their trust in Him."[1]

CHAP. XLI.—*The crucifixion predicted.*

And again, in another prophecy, the Spirit of prophecy, through the same David, intimated that Christ, after He had been crucified, should reign, and spoke as follows: "Sing to the Lord, all the earth, and day by day declare His salvation. For great is the Lord, and greatly to be praised, to be feared above all the gods. For all the gods of the nations are idols of devils; but God made the heavens. Glory and praise are before His face, strength and glorying are in the habitation of His holiness. Give glory to the Lord, the Father everlasting. Receive grace, and enter His presence, and worship in His holy courts. Let all the earth fear before His face; let it be established, and not shaken. Let them rejoice among the nations. The Lord hath reigned from the tree."[2]

CHAP. XLII.—*Prophecy using the past tense.*

But when the Spirit of prophecy speaks of things that are about to come to pass as if they had already taken place,—as may be observed even in the passages already cited by me,—that this circumstance may afford no excuse to readers [for misinterpreting them], we will make even this also quite

[1] Ps. i. ii.

[2] Ps. xcvi. 1, etc. This last clause, which is not extant in our copies either of the LXX. or of the Hebrew, Justin charged the Jews with erasing. See *Dial. Tryph.* c. 73.

plain. The things which He absolutely knows will take place, He predicts as if already they had taken place. And that the utterances must be thus received, you will perceive, if you give your attention to them. The words cited above, David uttered 1500[1] years before Christ became a man and was crucified; and no one of those who lived before Him, nor yet of His contemporaries, afforded joy to the Gentiles by being crucified. But our Jesus Christ, being crucified and dead, rose again, and having ascended to heaven, reigned; and by those things which were published in His name among all nations by the apostles, there is joy afforded to those who expect the immortality promised by Him.

CHAP. XLIII.—*Responsibility asserted.*

But lest some suppose, from what has been said by us, that we say that whatever happens, happens by a fatal necessity, because it is foretold as known beforehand, this too we explain. We have learned from the prophets, and we hold it to be true, that punishments, and chastisements, and good rewards, are rendered according to the merit of each man's actions. Since if it be not so, but all things happen by fate, neither is anything at all in our own power. For if it be fated that this man, *e.g.*, be good, and this other evil, neither is the former meritorious nor the latter to be blamed. And again, unless the human race have the power of avoiding evil and choosing good by free choice, they are not accountable for their actions, of whatever kind they be. But that it is by free choice they both walk uprightly and stumble, we thus demonstrate. We see the same man making a transition to opposite things. Now, if it had been fated that he were to be either good or bad, he could never have been capable of both the opposites, nor of so many transitions. But not even would some be good and others bad, since we thus make fate the cause of evil, and exhibit her as acting in opposition to herself; or that which has been already stated would seem to be true, that neither virtue nor vice is anything, but that things are only

[1] A chronological error, whether of the copyist or of Justin himself cannot be known.

reckoned good or evil by opinion; which, as the true word shows, is the greatest impiety and wickedness. But this we assert is inevitable fate, that they who choose the good have worthy rewards, and they who choose the opposite have their merited awards. For not like other things, as trees and quadrupeds, which cannot act by choice, did God make man: for neither would he be worthy of reward or praise did he not of himself choose the good, but were created for this end;[1] nor, if he were evil, would he be worthy of punishment, not being evil of himself, but being able to be nothing else than what he was made.

Chap. xliv.—*Not nullified by prophecy.*

And the holy Spirit of prophecy taught us this, telling us by Moses that God spoke thus to the man first created: "Behold, before thy face are good and evil: choose the good."[2] And again, by the other prophet Isaiah, that the following utterance was made as if from God the Father and Lord of all: "Wash you, make you clean; put away evils from your souls; learn to do well; judge the orphan, and plead for the widow: and come and let us reason together, saith the Lord: And if your sins be as scarlet, I will make them white as wool; and if they be red like as crimson, I will make them white as snow. And if ye be willing and obey me, ye shall eat the good of the land; but if ye do not obey me, the sword shall devour you: for the mouth of the Lord hath spoken it."[3] And that expression, "The sword shall devour you," does not mean that the disobedient shall be slain by the sword, but the sword of God is fire, of which they who choose to do wickedly become the fuel. Wherefore He says, "The sword shall devour you: for the mouth of the Lord hath spoken it." And if He had spoken concerning a sword that cuts and at once despatches, He would not have said, shall *devour*. And so, too, Plato, when he says, "The blame is his who chooses, and God is blameless,"[4] took this from the prophet Moses

[1] Or, "but were made so." The words are, *ἀλλὰ τοῦτο γενόμενος*, and the meaning of Justin is sufficiently clear.

[2] Deut. xxx. 15, 19.

[3] Isa. i. 16, etc.

[4] Plato, *Rep.* x.

and uttered it. For Moses is more ancient than all the Greek writers. And whatever both philosophers and poets have said concerning the immortality of the soul, or punishments after death, or contemplation of things heavenly, or doctrines of the like kind, they have received such suggestions from the prophets as have enabled them to understand and interpret these things. And hence there seem to be seeds of truth among all men; but they are charged with not accurately understanding [the truth] when they assert contradictories. So that what we say about future events being foretold, we do not say it as if they came about by a fatal necessity; but God foreknowing all that shall be done by all men, and it being His decree that the future actions of men shall all be recompensed according to their several value, He foretells by the Spirit of prophecy that He will bestow meet rewards according to the merit of the actions done, always urging the human race to effort and recollection, showing that He cares and provides for men. But by the agency of the devils death has been decreed against those who read the books of Hystaspes, or of the Sibyl, or of the prophets, that through fear they may prevent men who read them from receiving the knowledge of the good, and may retain them in slavery to themselves; which, however, they could not always effect. For not only do we fearlessly read them, but, as you see, bring them for your inspection, knowing that their contents will be pleasing to all. And if we persuade even a few, our gain will be very great; for, as good husbandmen, we shall receive the reward from the Master.

CHAP. XLV.—*Christ's session in heaven foretold.*

And that God the Father of all would bring Christ to heaven after He had raised Him from the dead, and would keep Him there[1] until He has subdued His enemies the devils, and until the number of those who are foreknown by Him as good and virtuous is complete, on whose account He has still

[1] So Thirlby, Otto, and Trollope seem all to understand the word κατέχειν; yet it seems worth considering whether Justin has not borrowed both the sense and the word from 2 Thess. ii. 6, 7.

delayed the consummation—hear what was said by the prophet David. These are his words: "The Lord said unto my Lord, Sit Thou at my right hand, until I make Thine enemies Thy footstool. The Lord shall send to Thee the rod of power out of Jerusalem; and rule Thou in the midst of Thine enemies. With Thee is the government in the day of Thy power, in the beauties of Thy saints: from the womb of morning[1] have I begotten Thee."[2] That which he says, "He shall send to Thee the rod of power out of Jerusalem," is predictive of the mighty word, which His apostles, going forth from Jerusalem, preached everywhere; and though death is decreed against those who teach or at all confess the name of Christ, we everywhere both embrace and teach it. And if you also read these words in a hostile spirit, ye can do no more, as I said before, than kill us; which indeed does no harm to us, but to you and all who unjustly hate us, and do not repent, brings eternal punishment by fire.

CHAP. XLVI.—*The Word in the world before Christ.*

But lest some should, without reason, and for the perversion of what we teach, maintain that we say that Christ was born one hundred and fifty years ago under Cyrenius, and subsequently, in the time of Pontius Pilate, taught what we say He taught; and should cry out against us as though all men who were born before Him were irresponsible—let us anticipate and solve the difficulty. We have been taught that Christ is the first-born of God, and we have declared above that He is the Word of whom every race of men were partakers; and those who lived reasonably[3] are Christians, even though they have been thought atheists; as, among the Greeks, Socrates and Heraclitus, and men like them; and among the barbarians, Abraham, and Ananias, and Azarias, and Misael, and Elias, and many others whose actions and names we now decline to recount, because we know it would be tedious. So that even they who lived before Christ, and lived without reason, were wicked and hostile to Christ, and

[1] Or, "before the morning star." [2] Ps. cx. 1, etc.

[3] μετὰ λόγου, "with reason," or "the Word."

slew those who lived reasonably. But why, through the power of the Word, according to the will of God the Father and Lord of all, He was born of a virgin as a man, and was named Jesus, and was crucified, and died, and rose again, and ascended into heaven, an intelligent man will be able to comprehend from what has been already so largely said. And we, since the proof of this subject is less needful now, will pass for the present to the proof of those things which are urgent.

CHAP. XLVII.—*Desolation of Judæa foretold.*

That the land of the Jews, then, was to be laid waste, hear what was said by the Spirit of prophecy. And the words were spoken as if from the person of the people wondering at what had happened. They are these: "Sion is a wilderness, Jerusalem a desolation. The house of our sanctuary has become a curse, and the glory which our fathers blessed is burned up with fire, and all its glorious things are laid waste: and Thou refrainest Thyself at these things, and hast held Thy peace, and hast humbled us very sore."[1] And ye are convinced that Jerusalem has been laid waste, as was predicted. And concerning its desolation, and that no one should be permitted to inhabit it, there was the following prophecy by Isaiah: "Their land is desolate, their enemies consume it before them, and none of them shall dwell therein."[2] And that it is guarded by you lest any one dwell in it, and that death is decreed against a Jew apprehended entering it, you know very well.

CHAP. XLVIII.—*Christ's work and death foretold.*

And that it was predicted that our Christ should heal all diseases and raise the dead, hear what was said. There are these words: "At His coming the lame shall leap as an hart, and the tongue of the stammerer shall be clear speaking: the blind shall see, and the lepers shall be cleansed; and the dead shall rise, and walk about."[3] And that He did those things, you can learn from the Acts of Pontius Pilate. And how it

[1] Isa. lxiv. 10-12. [2] Isa. i. 7. [3] Isa. xxxv. 6.

was predicted by the Spirit of prophecy that He and those who hoped in Him should be slain, hear what was said by Isaiah. These are the words: "Behold now the righteous perisheth, and no man layeth it to heart; and just men are taken away, and no man considereth. From the presence of wickedness is the righteous man taken, and his burial shall be in peace: he is taken from our midst."[1]

CHAP. XLIX.—*His rejection by the Jews foretold.*

And again, how it was said by the same Isaiah, that the Gentile nations who were not looking for Him should worship Him, but the Jews who always expected Him should not recognise Him when He came. And the words are spoken as from the person of Christ; and they are these: "I was manifest to them that asked not for me; I was found of them that sought me not: I said, Behold me, to a nation that called not on my name. I spread out my hands to a disobedient and gainsaying people, to those who walked in a way that is not good, but follow after their own sins; a people that provoketh me to anger to my face."[2] For the Jews having the prophecies, and being always in expectation of the Christ to come, did not recognise Him; and not only so, but even treated Him shamefully. But the Gentiles, who had never heard anything about Christ, until the apostles set out from Jerusalem and preached concerning Him, and gave them the prophecies, were filled with joy and faith, and cast away their idols, and dedicated themselves to the Unbegotten God through Christ. And that it was foreknown that these infamous things should be uttered against those who confessed Christ, and that those who slandered Him, and said that it was well to preserve the ancient customs, should be miserable, hear what was briefly said by Isaiah; it is this: "Woe unto them that call sweet bitter, and bitter sweet."[3]

CHAP. L.—*His humiliation predicted.*

But that, having become man for our sakes, He endured to suffer and to be dishonoured, and that He shall come again

[1] Isa. lvii. 1. [2] Isa. lxv. 1–3. [3] Isa. v. 20.

with glory, hear the prophecies which relate to this; they are these: "Because they delivered His soul unto death, and He was numbered with the transgressors, He has borne the sin of many, and shall make intercession for the transgressors. For, behold, my servant shall deal prudently, and shall be exalted, and shall be greatly extolled. As many were astonished at Thee, so marred shall Thy form be before men, and so hidden from them Thy glory; so shall many nations wonder, and the kings shall shut their mouths at Him. For they to whom it was not told concerning Him, and they who have not heard, shall understand. O Lord, who hath believed our report? and to whom is the arm of the Lord revealed? We have declared before Him as a child, as a root in a dry ground. He had no form, nor glory; and we saw Him, and there was no form nor comeliness: but His form was dishonoured and marred more than the sons of men. A man under the stroke, and knowing how to bear infirmity, because His face was turned away: He was despised, and of no reputation. It is He who bears our sins, and is afflicted for us; yet we did esteem Him smitten, stricken, and afflicted. But He was wounded for our transgressions, He was bruised for our iniquities, the chastisement of peace was upon Him, by His stripes we are healed. All we, like sheep, have gone astray; every man has wandered in his own way. And He delivered Him for our sins; and He opened not His mouth for all His affliction. He was brought as a sheep to the slaughter, and as a lamb before his shearer is dumb, so He openeth not His mouth. In His humiliation, His judgment was taken away."[1] Accordingly, after He was crucified, even all His acquaintances forsook Him, having denied Him; and afterwards, when He had risen from the dead and appeared to them, and had taught them to read the prophecies in which all these things were foretold as coming to pass, and when they had seen Him ascending into heaven, and had believed, and had received power sent thence by Him upon them, and went to every race of men, they taught these things, and were called apostles.

[1] Isa. lii. 13–15, liii. 1-8.

CHAP. LI.—*The majesty of Christ.*

And that the Spirit of prophecy might signify to us that He who suffers these things has an ineffable origin, and rules His enemies, He spake thus: "His generation who shall declare? because His life is cut off from the earth: for their transgressions He comes to death. And I will give the wicked for His burial, and the rich for His death; because He did no violence, neither was any deceit in His mouth. And the Lord is pleased to cleanse Him from the stripe. If He be given for sin, your soul shall see His seed prolonged in days. And the Lord is pleased to deliver His soul from grief, to show Him light, and to form Him with knowledge, to justify the righteous who richly serveth many. And He shall bear our iniquities. Therefore He shall inherit many, and He shall divide the spoil of the strong; because His soul was delivered to death: and He was numbered with the transgressors; and He bare the sins of many, and He was delivered up for their transgressions."[1] Hear, too, how He was to ascend into heaven according to prophecy. It was thus spoken: "Lift up the gates of heaven; be ye opened, that the King of glory may come in. Who is this King of glory? The Lord, strong and mighty."[2] And how also He should come again out of heaven with glory, hear what was spoken in reference to this by the prophet Jeremiah.[3] His words are: "Behold, as the Son of man He cometh in the clouds of heaven, and His angels with Him."[4]

CHAP. LII.—*Certain fulfilment of prophecy.*

Since, then, we prove that all things which have already happened had been predicted by the prophets before they came to pass, we must necessarily believe also that those things which are in like manner predicted, but are yet to come to pass, shall certainly happen. For as the things which have already taken place came to pass when fore-

[1] Isa. liii. 8–12. [2] Ps. xxiv. 7.
[3] This prophecy occurs not in Jeremiah, but in Dan. vii. 13.
[4] Dan. vii. 13.

told, and even though unknown, so shall the things that remain, even though they be unknown and disbelieved, yet come to pass. For the prophets have proclaimed two advents of His: the one, that which is already past, when He came as a dishonoured and suffering man; but the second, when, according to prophecy, He shall come from heaven with glory, accompanied by His angelic host, when also He shall raise the bodies of all men who have lived, and shall clothe those of the worthy with immortality, and shall send those of the wicked, endued with eternal sensibility, into everlasting fire with the wicked devils. And that these things also have been foretold as yet to be, we will prove. By Ezekiel the prophet it was said: "Joint shall be joined to joint, and bone to bone, and flesh shall grow again; and every knee shall bow to the Lord, and every tongue shall confess Him."[1] And in what kind of sensation and punishment the wicked are to be, hear from what was said in like manner with reference to this; it is as follows: "Their worm shall not rest, and their fire shall not be quenched;"[2] and then shall they repent, when it profits them not. And what the people of the Jews shall say and do, when they see Him coming in glory, has been thus predicted by Zechariah the prophet: "I will command the four winds to gather the scattered children; I will command the north wind to bring them, and the south wind, that it keep not back. And then in Jerusalem there shall be great lamentation, not the lamentation of mouths or of lips, but the lamentation of the heart; and they shall rend not their garments, but their hearts. Tribe by tribe they shall mourn, and then they shall look on Him whom they have pierced; and they shall say, Why, O Lord, hast Thou made us to err from Thy way? The glory which our fathers blessed, has for us been turned into shame."[3]

[1] Ezek. xxxvii. 7, 8; Isa. xlv. 24.
[2] Isa. lxvi. 24.
[3] Zech. xii. 3-14; Isa. lxiii. 17, lxiv. 11.

CHAP. LIII.—*Summary of the prophecies.*

Though we could bring forward many other prophecies, we forbear, judging these sufficient for the persuasion of those who have ears to hear and understand; and considering also that those persons are able to see that we do not make mere assertions without being able to produce proof, like those fables that are told of the so-called sons of Jupiter. For with what reason should we believe of a crucified man that He is the first-born of the Unbegotten God, and Himself will pass judgment on the whole human race, unless we had found testimonies concerning Him published before He came and was born as man, and unless we saw that things had happened accordingly—the devastation of the land of the Jews, and men of every race persuaded by His teaching through the apostles, and rejecting their old habits, in which, being deceived, they had had their conversation; yea, seeing ourselves too, and knowing that the Christians from among the Gentiles are both more numerous and more true than those from among the Jews and Samaritans? For all the other human races are called Gentiles by the Spirit of prophecy; but the Jewish and Samaritan races are called the tribe of Israel, and the house of Jacob. And the prophecy in which it was predicted that there should be more believers from the Gentiles than from the Jews and Samaritans, we will produce: it ran thus: "Rejoice, O barren, thou that dost not bear; break forth and shout, thou that dost not travail, because many more are the children of the desolate than of her that hath an husband."[1] For all the Gentiles were "desolate" of the true God, serving the works of their hands; but the Jews and Samaritans, having the word of God delivered to them by the prophets, and always expecting the Christ, did not recognise Him when He came, except some few, of whom the Spirit of prophecy by Isaiah had predicted that they should be saved. He spoke as from their person: "Except the Lord had left us a seed, we should have been as Sodom and Gomorrah."[2] For Sodom

[1] Isa. liv. 1.

[2] Isa. i. 9.

and Gomorrah are related by Moses to have been cities of ungodly men, which God burned with fire and brimstone, and overthrew, no one of their inhabitants being saved except a certain stranger, a Chaldæan by birth, whose name was Lot; with whom also his daughters were rescued. And those who care may yet see their whole country desolate and burned, and remaining barren. And to show how those from among the Gentiles were foretold as more true and more believing, we will cite what was said by Isaiah[1] the prophet; for he spoke as follows: "Israel is uncircumcised in heart, but the Gentiles are uncircumcised in the flesh." So many things, therefore, as these, when they are seen with the eye, are enough to produce conviction and belief in those who embrace the truth, and are not bigoted in their opinions, nor are governed by their passions.

CHAP. LIV.—*Origin of heathen mythology.*

But those who hand down the myths which the poets have made, adduce no proof to the youths who learn them; and we proceed to demonstrate that they have been uttered by the influence of the wicked demons, to deceive and lead astray the human race. For having heard it proclaimed through the prophets that the Christ was to come, and that the ungodly among men were to be punished by fire, they put forward many to be called sons of Jupiter, under the impression that they would be able to produce in men the idea that the things which were said with regard to Christ were mere marvellous tales, like the things which were said by the poets. And these things were said both among the Greeks and among all nations where they [the demons] heard the prophets foretelling that Christ would specially be believed in; but that in hearing what was said by the prophets they did not accurately understand it, but imitated what was said of our Christ, like men who are in error, we will make plain. The prophet Moses, then, was, as we have already said, older than all writers; and by him, as we have also said before, it was thus predicted: "There shall not fail a prince from Judah,

[1] The following words are found, not in Isaiah, but in Jer. ix. 26.

nor a lawgiver from between his feet, until He come for whom it is reserved; and He shall be the desire of the Gentiles, binding His foal to the vine, washing His robe in the blood of the grape."[1] The devils, accordingly, when they heard these prophetic words, said that Bacchus was the son of Jupiter, and gave out that he was the discoverer of the vine, and they number wine[2] [or, the ass] among his mysteries; and they taught that, having been torn in pieces, he ascended into heaven. And because in the prophecy of Moses it had not been expressly intimated whether He who was to come was the Son of God, and whether He would, riding on the foal, remain on earth or ascend into heaven, and because the name of "foal" could mean either the foal of an ass or the foal of a horse, they, not knowing whether He who was foretold would bring the foal of an ass or of a horse as the sign of His coming, nor whether He was the Son of God, as we said above, or of man, gave out that Bellerophon, a man born of man, himself ascended to heaven on his horse Pegasus. And when they heard it said by the other prophet Isaiah, that He should be born of a virgin, and by his own means ascend into heaven, they pretended that Perseus was spoken of. And when they knew what was said, as has been cited above, in the prophecies written aforetime, "Strong as a giant to run his course,"[3] they said that Hercules was strong, and had journeyed over the whole earth. And when, again, they learned that it had been foretold that He should heal every sickness, and raise the dead, they produced Æsculapius.

CHAP. LV.—*Symbols of the cross.*

But in no instance, not even in any of those called sons of Jupiter, did they imitate the being crucified; for it was not

[1] Gen. xlix. 10.

[2] In the MSS. the reading is *οἶνον* (wine); but as Justin's argument seems to require *ὄνον* (an ass), Sylburg inserted this latter word in his edition; and this reading is approved by Grabe and Thirlby, and adopted by Otto and Trollope. It may be added, that *ἀναγράφουσι* is much more suitable to *ὄνον* than to *οἶνον*.

[3] Ps. xix. 5.

understood by them, all the things said of it having been put symbolically. And this, as the prophet foretold, is the greatest symbol of His power and rule; as is also proved by the things which fall under our observation. For consider all the things in the world, whether without this form they could be administered or have any community. For the sea is not traversed except that trophy which is called a sail abide safe in the ship; and the earth is not ploughed without it: diggers and mechanics do not their work, except with tools which have this shape. And the human form differs from that of the irrational animals in nothing else than in its being erect and having the hands extended, and having on the face extending from the forehead what is called the nose, through which there is respiration for the living creature; and this shows no other form than that of the cross. And so it was said by the prophet, "The breath before our face is the Lord Christ."[1] And the power of this form is shown by your own symbols on what are called "vexilla" [banners] and trophies, with which all your state processions are made, using these as the insignia of your power and government, even though you do so unwittingly. And with this form you consecrate the images of your emperors when they die, and you name them gods by inscriptions. Since, therefore, we have urged you both by reason and by an evident form, and to the utmost of our ability, we know that now we are blameless even though you disbelieve; for our part is done and finished.

CHAP. LVI.—*The demons still mislead men.*

But the evil spirits were not satisfied with saying, before Christ's appearance, that those who were said to be sons of Jupiter were born of him; but after He had appeared and been born among men, and when they learned how He had been foretold by the prophets, and knew that He should be believed on and looked for by every nation, they again, as was said above, put forward other men, the Samaritans Simon and Menander, who did many mighty works by magic,

[1] From Lam. iv. 20 (Sept.).

and deceived many, and still keep them deceived. For even among yourselves, as we said before, Simon was in the royal city Rome in the reign of Claudius Cæsar, and so greatly astonished the sacred senate and people of the Romans, that he was considered a god, and honoured, like the others whom you honour as gods, with a statue. Wherefore we pray that the sacred senate and your people may, along with yourselves, be arbiters of this our memorial, in order that if any one be entangled by that man's doctrines, he may learn the truth, and so be able to escape error; and as for the statue, if you please, destroy it.

CHAP. LVII.—*And cause persecution.*

Nor can the devils persuade men that there will be no conflagration for the punishment of the wicked; as they were unable to effect that Christ should be hidden after He came. But this only can they effect, that they who live irrationally, and were brought up licentiously in wicked customs, and are prejudiced in their own opinions, should kill and hate us; whom we not only do not hate, but, as is proved, pity and endeavour to lead to repentance. For we do not fear death, since it is acknowledged we must surely die; and there is nothing new, but all things continue the same in this administration of things; and if satiety overtakes those who enjoy even one year of these things, they ought to give heed to our doctrines, that they may live eternally free both from suffering and from want. But if they believe that there is nothing after death, but declare that those who die pass into insensibility, then they become our benefactors when they set us free from the sufferings and necessities of this life, and prove themselves to be wicked, and inhuman, and bigoted. For they kill us with no intention of delivering us, but cut us off that we may be deprived of life and pleasure.

CHAP. LVIII.—*And raise up heretics.*

And, as we said before, the devils put forward Marcion of Pontus, who is even now teaching men to deny that God is the maker of all things in heaven and on earth, and that the

Christ predicted by the prophets is His Son, and preaches another god besides the Creator of all, and likewise another son. And this man many have believed, as if he alone knew the truth, and laugh at us, though they have no proof of what they say, but are carried away irrationally as lambs by a wolf, and become the prey of atheistical doctrines, and of devils. For they who are called devils attempt nothing else than to seduce men from God who made them, and from Christ His first-begotten; and those who are unable to raise themselves above the earth they have riveted, and do now rivet, to things earthly, and to the works of their own hands; but those who devote themselves to the contemplation of things divine, they secretly beat back; and if they have not a wise sober-mindedness, and a pure and passionless life, they drive them into godlessness.

CHAP. LIX.—*Plato's obligation to Moses.*

And that you may learn that it was from our teachers—we mean the account given through the prophets—that Plato borrowed his statement that God, having altered matter which was shapeless, made the world, hear the very words spoken through Moses, who, as above shown, was the first prophet, and of greater antiquity than the Greek writers; and through whom the Spirit of prophecy, signifying how and from what materials God at first formed the world, spake thus: "In the beginning God created the heaven and the earth. And the earth was invisible and unfurnished, and darkness was upon the face of the deep; and the Spirit of God moved over the waters. And God said, Let there be light; and it was so." So that both Plato and they who agree with him, and we ourselves, have learned, and you also can be convinced, that by the word of God the whole world was made out of the substance spoken of before by Moses. And that which the poets call Erebus, we know was spoken of formerly by Moses.[1]

[1] Comp. Deut. xxxii. 22.

CHAP. LX.—*Plato's doctrine of the Cross.*

And the physiological discussion[1] concerning the Son of God in the *Timæus* of Plato, where he says, "He placed him crosswise[2] in the universe," he borrowed in like manner from Moses; for in the writings of Moses it is related how at that time, when the Israelites went out of Egypt and were in the wilderness, they fell in with poisonous beasts, both vipers and asps, and every kind of serpent, which slew the people; and that Moses, by the inspiration and influence of God, took brass, and made it into the figure of a cross, and set it in the holy tabernacle, and said to the people, "If ye look to this figure, and believe, ye shall be saved thereby."[3] And when this was done, it is recorded that the serpents died, and it is handed down that the people thus escaped death. Which things Plato reading, and not accurately understanding, and not apprehending that it was the figure of the cross, but taking it to be a placing crosswise, he said that the power next to the first God was placed crosswise in the universe. And as to his speaking of a third, he did this because he read, as we said above, that which was spoken by Moses, "that the Spirit of God moved over the waters." For he gives the second place to the Logos which is with God, who he said was placed crosswise in the universe; and the third place to the Spirit who was said to be borne upon the water, saying, "And the third around the third."[4] And hear how the Spirit of prophecy signified through Moses that there should be a conflagration. He spoke thus: "Everlasting fire shall descend, and shall devour to the pit beneath."[5] It is not, then, that we hold the same opinions as others, but that all speak in imitation of ours. Among us these things can be heard and learned from persons who do not even know the forms of the letters, who

[1] Literally, "that which is treated physiologically."

[2] "He impressed him as a χίασμα, *i.e.* in the form of the letter χ, upon the universe." Plato is speaking of the soul of the universe.

[3] Num. xxi. 8.

[4] Τὰ δὲ τρίτα περὶ τὸν τρίτον.

[5] Deut. xxxii. 22.

are uneducated and barbarous in speech, though wise and believing in mind; some, indeed, even maimed and deprived of eyesight; so that you may understand that these things are not the effect of human wisdom, but are uttered by the power of God.

CHAP. LXI.—*Christian baptism.*

I will also relate the manner in which we dedicated ourselves to God when we had been made new through Christ; lest, if we omit this, we seem to be unfair in the explanation we are making. As many as are persuaded and believe that what we teach and say is true, and undertake to be able to live accordingly, are instructed to pray and to entreat God with fasting, for the remission of their sins that are past, we praying and fasting with them. Then they are brought by us where there is water, and are regenerated in the same manner in which we were ourselves regenerated. For, in the name of God, the Father and Lord of the universe, and of our Saviour Jesus Christ, and of the Holy Spirit, they then receive the washing with water. For Christ also said, "Except ye be born again, ye shall not enter into the kingdom of heaven."[1] Now, that it is impossible for those who have once been born to enter into their mothers' wombs, is manifest to all. And how those who have sinned and repent shall escape their sins, is declared by Esaias the prophet, as I wrote above;[2] he thus speaks: "Wash you, make you clean; put away the evil of your doings from your souls; learn to do well; judge the fatherless, and plead for the widow: and come and let us reason together, saith the Lord. And though your sins be as scarlet, I will make them white like wool; and though they be as crimson, I will make them white as snow. But if ye refuse and rebel, the sword shall devour you: for the mouth of the Lord hath spoken it."[3]

And for this [rite] we have learned from the apostles this reason. Since at our birth we were born without our own knowledge or choice, by our parents coming together, and were brought up in bad habits and wicked training; in

[1] John iii. 5. [2] Chap. xliv. [3] Isa. i. 16–20.

order that we may not remain the children of necessity and of ignorance, but may become the children of choice and knowledge, and may obtain in the water the remission of sins formerly committed, there is pronounced over him who chooses to be born again, and has repented of his sins, the name of God the Father and Lord of the universe; he who leads to the laver the person that is to be washed calling him by this name alone. For no one can utter the name of the ineffable God; and if any one dare to say that there is a name, he raves with a hopeless madness. And this washing is called illumination, because they who learn these things are illuminated in their understandings. And in the name of Jesus Christ, who was crucified under Pontius Pilate, and in the name of the Holy Ghost, who through the prophets foretold all things about Jesus, he who is illuminated is washed.

CHAP. LXII.—*Its imitation by demons.*

And the devils, indeed, having heard this washing published by the prophet, instigated those who enter their temples, and are about to approach them with libations and burnt-offerings, also to sprinkle themselves; and they cause them also to wash themselves entirely, as they depart [from the sacrifice], before they enter into the shrines in which their images are set. And the command, too, given by the priests to those who enter and worship in the temples, that they take off their shoes, the devils, learning what happened to the above-mentioned prophet Moses, have given in imitation of these things. For at that juncture, when Moses was ordered to go down into Egypt and lead out the people of the Israelites who were there, and while he was tending the flocks of his maternal uncle[1] in the land of Arabia, our Christ conversed with him under the appearance of fire from a bush, and said, "Put off thy shoes, and draw near and hear." And he, when he had put off his shoes and drawn near, heard that he was to go down into Egypt and lead out the people of the Israelites there; and he received mighty

[1] Thirlby conjectures that Justin here confused in his mind the histories of Moses and Jacob.

power from Christ, who spoke to him in the appearance of fire, and went down and led out the people, having done great and marvellous things; which, if you desire to know, you will learn them accurately from his writings.

CHAP. LXIII.—*How God appeared to Moses.*

And all the Jews even now teach that the nameless God spake to Moses; whence the Spirit of prophecy, accusing them by Isaiah the prophet mentioned above, said, "The ox knoweth his owner, and the ass his master's crib; but Israel doth not know me, and my people do not understand."[1] And Jesus the Christ, because the Jews knew not what the Father was, and what the Son, in like manner accused them; and Himself said, "No one knoweth the Father, but the Son; nor the Son, but the Father, and they to whom the Son revealeth Him."[2] Now the Word of God is His Son, as we have before said. And He is called Angel and Apostle; for He declares whatever we ought to know, and is sent forth to declare whatever is revealed; as our Lord Himself says, "He that heareth me, heareth Him that sent me."[3] From the writings of Moses also this will be manifest; for thus it is written in them, "And the angel of God spake to Moses, in a flame of fire out of the bush, and said, I am that I am, the God of Abraham, the God of Isaac, the God of Jacob, the God of thy fathers; go down into Egypt, and bring forth my people."[4] And if you wish to learn what follows, you can do so from the same writings; for it is impossible to relate the whole here. But so much is written for the sake of proving that Jesus the Christ is the Son of God and His Apostle, being of old the Word, and appearing sometimes in the form of fire, and sometimes in the likeness of angels; but now, by the will of God, having become man for the human race, He endured all the sufferings which the devils instigated the senseless Jews to inflict upon Him; who, though they have it expressly affirmed in the writings of Moses, "And the angel of God spake to Moses in a flame

[1] Isa. i. 3.
[2] Matt. xi. 27.
[3] Luke x. 16.
[4] Ex. iii. 6.

of fire in a bush, and said, I am that I am, the God of Abraham, and the God of Isaac, and the God of Jacob," yet maintain that He who said this was the Father and Creator of the universe. Whence also the Spirit of prophecy rebukes them, and says, "Israel doth not know me, my people hath not understood me."[1] And again, Jesus, as we have already shown, while He was with them, said, "No one knoweth the Father, but the Son; nor the Son, but the Father, and those to whom the Son will reveal Him."[2] The Jews, accordingly, being throughout of opinion that it was the Father of the universe who spake to Moses, though He who spake to him was indeed the Son of God, who is called both Angel and Apostle, are justly charged, both by the Spirit of prophecy and by Christ Himself, with knowing neither the Father nor the Son. For they who affirm that the Son is the Father, are proved neither to have become acquainted with the Father, nor to know that the Father of the universe has a Son; who also, being the first-begotten Word of God, is even God. And of old He appeared in the shape of fire and in the likeness of an angel to Moses and to the other prophets; but now in the times of your reign, having, as we before said, become man by a virgin, according to the counsel of the Father, for the salvation of those who believe on Him, He endured both to be set at nought and to suffer, that by dying and rising again He might conquer death. And that which was said out of the bush to Moses, "I am that I am, the God of Abraham, and the God of Isaac, and the God of Jacob, and the God of your fathers,"[3] this signified that they, even though dead, are yet in existence, and are men belonging to Christ Himself. For they were the first of all men to busy themselves in the search after God; Abraham being the father of Isaac, and Isaac of Jacob, as Moses wrote.

CHAP. LXIV.—*Further misrepresentations of the truth.*

From what has been already said, you can understand how the devils, in imitation of what was said by Moses, asserted that Proserpine was the daughter of Jupiter, and instigated

1 Isa. i. 3. 2 Matt. xi. 27. 3 Ex. iii. 6.

the people to set up an image of her under the name of Kore [Cora, *i.e.* the maiden or daughter] at the spring-heads. For, as we wrote above,[1] Moses said, "In the beginning God made the heaven and the earth. And the earth was without form, and unfurnished: and the Spirit of God moved upon the face of the waters." In imitation, therefore, of what is here said of the Spirit of God moving on the waters, they said that Proserpine [or Cora] was the daughter of Jupiter.[2] And in like manner also they craftily feigned that Minerva was the daughter of Jupiter, not by sexual union, but, knowing that God conceived and made the world by the Word, they say that Minerva is the first conception [ἔννοια]; which we consider to be very absurd, bringing forward the form of the conception in a female shape. And in like manner the actions of those others who are called sons of Jupiter sufficiently condemn them.

CHAP. LXV.—*Administration of the sacraments.*

But we, after we have thus washed him who has been convinced and has assented to our teaching, bring him to the place where those who are called brethren are assembled, in order that we may offer hearty prayers in common for ourselves and for the baptized [illuminated] person, and for all others in every place, that we may be counted worthy, now that we have learned the truth, by our works also to be found good citizens and keepers of the commandments, so that we may be saved with an everlasting salvation. Having ended the prayers, we salute one another with a kiss.[3] There is then brought to the president of the brethren[4] bread and

[1] Chap. lix.

[2] And therefore caused her to preside over the waters, as above.

[3] The kiss of charity, the kiss of peace, or "the peace" (ἡ εἰρήνη), was enjoined by the Apostle Paul in his epistles to the Corinthians, Thessalonians, and Romans, and thence passed into a common Christian usage. It was continued in the Western Church, under regulations to prevent its abuse, until the thirteenth century. Stanley remarks (*Corinthians*, i. 414), "It is still continued in the worship of the Coptic Church."

[4] τῷ προεστῶτι τῶν ἀδελφῶν. This expression may quite legitimately be translated, "to that one of the brethren who was presiding."

a cup of wine mixed with water; and he taking them, gives praise and glory to the Father of the universe, through the name of the Son and of the Holy Ghost, and offers thanks at considerable length for our being counted worthy to receive these things at His hands. And when he has concluded the prayers and thanksgivings, all the people present express their assent by saying Amen. This word Amen answers in the Hebrew language to γένοιτο [so be it]. And when the president has given thanks, and all the people have expressed their assent, those who are called by us deacons give to each of those present to partake of the bread and wine mixed with water over which the thanksgiving was pronounced, and to those who are absent they carry away a portion.

Chap. lxvi.—*Of the Eucharist.*

And this food is called among us *Εὐχαριστία* [1] [the Eucharist], of which no one is allowed to partake but the man who believes that the things which we teach are true, and who has been washed with the washing that is for the remission of sins, and unto regeneration, and who is so living as Christ has enjoined. For not as common bread and common drink do we receive these; but in like manner as Jesus Christ our Saviour, having been made flesh by the word of God, had both flesh and blood for our salvation, so likewise have we been taught that the food which is blessed by the prayer of His word, and from which our blood and flesh by transmutation are nourished, is the flesh and blood of that Jesus who was made flesh.[2] For the apostles, in the memoirs composed by them, which are called Gospels, have thus delivered unto us what was enjoined upon them; that Jesus took bread, and when He had given thanks, said, "This do ye in

[1] Literally, thanksgiving. See Matt. xxvi. 27.

[2] This passage is claimed alike by Calvinists, Lutherans, and Romanists; and, indeed, the language is so inexact, that each party may plausibly maintain that their own opinion is advocated by it. The expression "the prayer of His word," or of the word we have from Him, seems to signify the prayer pronounced over the elements, in imitation of our Lord's thanksgiving before breaking the bread.

remembrance of me,[1] this is my body;" and that, after the same manner, having taken the cup and given thanks, He said, "This is my blood;" and gave it to them alone. Which the wicked devils have imitated in the mysteries of Mithras, commanding the same thing to be done. For, that bread and a cup of water are placed with certain incantations in the mystic rites of one who is being initiated, you either know or can learn.

CHAP. LXVII.—*Weekly worship of the Christians.*

And we afterwards continually remind each other of these things. And the wealthy among us help the needy; and we always keep together; and for all things wherewith we are supplied, we bless the Maker of all through His Son Jesus Christ, and through the Holy Ghost. And on the day called Sunday,[2] all who live in cities or in the country gather together to one place, and the memoirs of the apostles or the writings of the prophets are read, as long as time permits; then, when the reader has ceased, the president verbally instructs, and exhorts to the imitation of these good things. Then we all rise together and pray, and, as we before said, when our prayer is ended, bread and wine and water are brought, and the president in like manner offers prayers and thanksgivings, according to his ability,[3] and the people assent, saying Amen; and there is a distribution to each, and a participation of that over which thanks have been given,[4] and to those who are absent a portion is sent by the deacons. And they who are well to do, and willing, give what each thinks fit; and what is collected is deposited with the president, who succours the orphans and widows, and those who, through sickness or any other cause, are in want, and those who are in bonds, and the strangers sojourning among us, and in a word takes care of

[1] Luke xxii. 19.

[2] τῇ τοῦ Ἡλίου λεγομένῃ ἡμέρᾳ.

[3] ὅση δύναμις αὐτῷ,—a phrase over which there has been much contention, but which seems to admit of no other meaning than that given above.

[4] Or, of the eucharistic elements.

all who are in need. But Sunday is the day on which we all hold our common assembly, because it is the first day on which God, having wrought a change in the darkness and matter, made the world; and Jesus Christ our Saviour on the same day rose from the dead. For He was crucified on the day before that of Saturn (Saturday); and on the day after that of Saturn, which is the day of the Sun, having appeared to His apostles and disciples, He taught them these things, which we have submitted to you also for your consideration.

CHAP. LXVIII.—*Conclusion.*

And if these things seem to you to be reasonable and true, honour them; but if they seem nonsensical, despise them as nonsense, and do not decree death against those who have done no wrong, as you would against enemies. For we forewarn you, that you shall not escape the coming judgment of God, if you continue in your injustice; and we ourselves will invite you to do that which is pleasing to God. And though from the letter of the greatest and most illustrious Emperor Adrian, your father, we could demand that you order judgment to be given as we have desired, yet we have made this appeal and explanation, not on the ground of Adrian's decision, but because we know that what we ask is just. And we have subjoined the copy of Adrian's epistle, that you may know that we are speaking truly about this. And the following is the copy:—

EPISTLE OF ADRIAN[1] IN BEHALF OF THE CHRISTIANS.

I have received the letter addressed to me by your predecessor Serenius Granianus, a most illustrious man; and this communication I am unwilling to pass over in silence, lest innocent persons be disturbed, and occasion be given to the informers for practising villany. Accordingly, if the inhabitants of your province will so far sustain this petition of theirs as to accuse the Christians in some court of law, I

[1] Addressed to Minucius Fundanus.

do not prohibit them from doing so. But I will not suffer them to make use of mere entreaties and outcries. For it is far more just, if any one desires to make an accusation, that you give judgment upon it. If, therefore, any one makes the accusation, and furnishes proof that the said men do anything contrary to the laws, you shall adjudge punishments in proportion to the offences. And this, by Hercules, you shall give special heed to, that if any man shall, through mere calumny, bring an accusation against any of these persons, you shall award to him more severe punishments in proportion to his wickedness.

EPISTLE OF ANTONINUS TO THE COMMON ASSEMBLY OF ASIA.

The Emperor Cæsar Titus Ælius Adrianus Antoninus Augustus Pius, Supreme Pontiff, in the fifteenth year of his tribuneship, consul for the third time, father of the fatherland, to the common assembly of Asia, greeting: I should have thought that the gods themselves would see to it that such offenders should not escape. For if they had the power, they themselves would much rather punish those who refuse to worship them; but it is you who bring trouble on these persons, and accuse as the opinion of atheists that which they hold, and lay to their charge certain other things which we are unable to prove. But it would be advantageous to them that they should be thought to die for that of which they are accused, and they conquer you by being lavish of their lives rather than yield that obedience which you require of them. And regarding the earthquakes which have already happened and are now occurring, it is not seemly that you remind us of them, losing heart whenever they occur, and thus set your conduct in contrast with that of these men; for they have much greater confidence towards God than you yourselves have. And you, indeed, seem at such times to ignore the gods, and you neglect the temples, and make no recognition of the worship of God. And hence you are jealous of those who do serve Him, and persecute them to the death. Concerning such persons, some others also of the governors of provinces wrote to my most divine father; to whom he replied that they should not at all disturb such persons, unless they were found to be attempting anything against the Roman government. And to myself many have sent intimations regarding such persons, to whom I also replied in pursuance of my father's judgment. But if any one has a matter to bring against any person of this class merely as such a person,[1] let the accused be acquitted of the charge, even though he should be found to be such an one; but let the accuser be amenable to justice.

EPISTLE OF MARCUS AURELIUS TO THE SENATE, IN WHICH HE TESTIFIES THAT THE CHRISTIANS WERE THE CAUSE OF HIS VICTORY.

The Emperor Cæsar Marcus Aurelius Antoninus, Germanicus, Parthicus, Sarmaticus, to the people of Rome, and to the sacred senate, greeting: I explained to you my grand design, and what advantages I gained on the confines of Germany, with much labour and suffering, in consequence of the circumstance that I was surrounded by the enemy; I myself being shut up in Carnuntum by seventy-four cohorts, nine miles off. And the enemy being at hand, the scouts pointed out to us, and our general Pompeianus showed us that there was close on us a mass of a mixed multitude of 977,000 men, which indeed we saw; and I was shut up by this vast host, having with me only a battalion composed of the first, tenth, double and marine legions. Having then examined my own position, and my host, with respect to the vast mass of barbarians and of the enemy, I quickly betook myself to prayer to the gods of my country. But being disregarded by them, I summoned those who among us go by the name of Christians. And having made inquiry, I discovered a great number and vast host of them, and raged against them, which was by no means becoming; for afterwards I learned

[1] That is, if any one accuses a Christian merely on the ground of his being a Christian.

their power. Wherefore they began the battle, not by preparing weapons, nor arms, nor bugles; for such preparation is hateful to them, on account of the God they bear about in their conscience. Therefore it is probable that those whom we suppose to be atheists, have God as their ruling power entrenched in their conscience. For having cast themselves on the ground, they prayed not only for me, but also for the whole army as it stood, that they might be delivered from the present thirst and famine. For during five days we had got no water, because there was none; for we were in the heart of Germany, and in the enemy's territory. And simultaneously with their casting themselves on the ground, and praying to God (a God of whom I am ignorant), water poured from heaven, upon us most refreshingly cool, but upon the enemies of Rome a withering[1] hail. And immediately we recognised the presence of God following on the prayer—a God unconquerable and indestructible. Founding upon this, then, let us pardon such as are Christians, lest they pray for and obtain such a weapon against ourselves. And I counsel that no such person be accused on the ground of his being a Christian. But if any one be found laying to the charge of a Christian that he is a Christian, I desire that it be made manifest that he who is accused as a Christian, and acknowledges that he is one, is accused of nothing else than only this, that he is a Christian; but that he who arraigns him be burned alive. And I further desire, that he who is entrusted with the government of the province shall not compel the Christian, who confesses and certifies such a matter, to retract; neither shall he commit him. And I desire that these things be confirmed by a decree of the senate. And I command this my edict to be published in the Forum of Trajan, in order that it may be read. The prefect Vitrasius Pollio will see that it be transmitted to all the provinces round about, and that no one who wishes to make use of or to possess it be hindered from obtaining a copy from the document I now publish.

[1] Literally, "fiery."

THE SECOND APOLOGY OF JUSTIN

FOR THE CHRISTIANS.

ADDRESSED TO THE ROMAN SENATE.

Chap. I.—*Introduction.*

ROMANS, the things which have recently[1] happened in your city under Urbicus, and the things which are likewise being everywhere unreasonably done by the governors, have compelled me to frame this composition for your sakes, who are men of like passions, and brethren, though ye know it not, and though ye be unwilling to acknowledge it on account of your glorying in what you esteem dignities. For everywhere, whoever is corrected by father, or neighbour, or child, or friend, or brother, or husband, or wife, for a fault, for being hard to move, for loving pleasure and being hard to urge to what is right (except those who have been persuaded that the unjust and intemperate shall be punished in eternal fire, but that the virtuous and those who lived like Christ shall dwell with God in a state that is free from suffering,—we mean, those who have become Christians), and the evil demons, who hate us, and who keep such men as these subject to themselves, and serving them in the capacity of judges, incite them, as rulers actuated by evil spirits, to put us to death. But that the cause of all that has taken place under Urbicus may become quite plain to you, I will relate what has been done.

[1] Literally, "both yesterday and the day before."

CHAP. II.—*Urbicus condemns the Christians to death.*

A certain woman lived with an intemperate[1] husband; she herself, too, having formerly been intemperate. But when she came to the knowledge of the teachings of Christ she became sober-minded, and endeavoured to persuade her husband likewise to be temperate, citing the teaching of Christ, and assuring him that there shall be punishment in eternal fire inflicted upon those who do not live temperately and conformably to right reason. But he, continuing in the same excesses, alienated his wife from him by his actions. For she, considering it wicked to live any longer as a wife with a husband who sought in every way means of indulging in pleasure contrary to the law of nature, and in violation of what is right, wished to be divorced from him. And when she was over-persuaded by her friends, who advised her still to continue with him, in the idea that some time or other her husband might give hope of amendment, she did violence to her own feeling and remained with him. But when her husband had gone into Alexandria, and was reported to be conducting himself worse than ever, she—that she might not, by continuing in matrimonial connection with him, and by sharing his table and his bed, become a partaker also in his wickednesses and impieties—gave him what you call a bill of divorce,[2] and was separated from him. But this noble husband of hers,—while he ought to have been rejoicing that those actions which formerly she unhesitatingly committed with the servants and hirelings, when she delighted in drunkenness and every vice, she had now given up, and desired that he too should give up the same,—when she had gone from him without his desire, brought an accusation against her, affirming that she was a Christian. And she presented a paper to thee, the Emperor, requesting that first she be permitted to arrange her affairs, and afterwards to make her defence against the accusation, when her affairs

[1] *ἀκολασταίνοντι*, which word includes unchastity, as well as the other forms of intemperance.

[2] *ῥεπούδιον*, *i.e.* "repudium," a bill of repudiation.

were set in order. And this you granted. And her quondam husband, since he was now no longer able to prosecute her, directed his assaults against a man, Ptolemæus, whom Urbicus punished, and who had been her teacher in the Christian doctrines. And this he did in the following way. He persuaded a centurion—who had cast Ptolemæus into prison, and who was friendly to himself—to take Ptolemæus and interrogate him on this sole point: whether he were a Christian? And Ptolemæus, being a lover of truth, and not of a deceitful or false disposition, when he confessed himself to be a Christian, was bound by the centurion, and for a long time punished in the prison. And, at last, when the man[1] came to Urbicus, he was asked this one question only: whether he was a Christian? And again, being conscious of his duty, and the nobility of it through the teaching of Christ, he confessed his discipleship in the divine virtue. For he who denies anything, either denies it because he condemns the thing itself, or he shrinks from confession because he is conscious of his own unworthiness or alienation from it; neither of which cases is that of the true Christian. And when Urbicus ordered him to be led away to punishment, one Lucius, who was also himself a Christian, seeing the unreasonable judgment that had thus been given, said to Urbicus: "What is the ground of this judgment? Why have you punished this man, not as an adulterer, nor fornicator, nor murderer, nor thief, nor robber, nor convicted of any crime at all, but who has only confessed that he is called by the name of Christian? This judgment of yours, O Urbicus, does not become the Emperor Pius, nor the philosopher, the son of Cæsar, nor the sacred senate."[2] And he said nothing else in answer to Lucius than this: "You also seem to me to be such an one." And when Lucius answered, "Most certainly I am," he again ordered him also to be led away. And he professed his thanks, knowing that he was delivered from such wicked rulers, and was going to the Father and King of the heavens.

[1] *i.e.* Ptolemæus.

[2] On this passage, see Donaldson's *Critical History*, *etc.*, vol. ii. p. 79.

And still a third having come forward, was condemned to be punished.

Chap. III.—*Justin accuses Crescens of ignorant prejudice against the Christians.*

I too, therefore, expect to be plotted against and fixed to the stake, by some of those I have named, or perhaps by Crescens, that lover of bravado and boasting; for the man is not worthy of the name of philosopher who publicly bears witness against us in matters which he does not understand, saying that the Christians are atheists and impious, and doing so to win favour with the deluded mob, and to please them. For if he assails us without having read the teachings of Christ, he is thoroughly depraved, and far worse than the illiterate, who often refrain from discussing or bearing false witness about matters they do not understand. Or, if he has read them and does not understand the majesty that is in them, or, understanding it, acts thus that he may not be suspected of being such [a Christian], he is far more base and thoroughly depraved, being conquered by illiberal and unreasonable opinion and fear. For I would have you to know that I proposed to him certain questions on this subject, and interrogated him, and found most convincingly that he, in truth, knows nothing. And to prove that I speak the truth, I am ready, if these disputations have not been reported to you, to conduct them again in your presence. And this would be an act worthy of a prince. But if my questions and his answers have been made known to you, you are already aware that he is acquainted with none of our matters; or, if he is acquainted with them, but, through fear of those who might hear him, does not dare to speak out, like Socrates, he proves himself, as I said before, no philosopher, but an opinionative man;[2] at least he does not regard that Socratic and most admirable saying: "But a man must in no wise be

[1] Words resembling "philosopher" in sound, viz. *φιλοψόφου καὶ φιλοκόμπου.*

[2] *φιλόδοξος*, which may mean a lover of vainglory.

honoured before the truth."[1] But it is impossible for a Cynic, who makes indifference his end, to know any good but indifference.

CHAP. IV.—*Why the Christians do not kill themselves.*

But lest some one say to us, "Go then all of you and kill yourselves, and pass even now to God, and do not trouble us," I will tell you why we do not so, but why, when examined, we fearlessly confess. We have been taught that God did not make the world aimlessly, but for the sake of the human race; and we have before stated that He takes pleasure in those who imitate His properties, and is displeased with those that embrace what is worthless either in word or deed. If, then, we all kill ourselves, we shall become the cause, as far as in us lies, why no one should be born, or instructed in the divine doctrines, or even why the human race should not exist; and we shall, if we so act, be ourselves acting in opposition to the will of God. But when we are examined, we make no denial, because we are not conscious of any evil, but count it impious not to speak the truth in all things, which also we know is pleasing to God, and because we are also now very desirous to deliver you from an unjust prejudice.

CHAP. V.—*How the angels transgressed.*

But if this idea take possession of some one, that if we acknowledge God as our helper, we should not, as we say, be oppressed and persecuted by the wicked; this, too, I will solve. God, when He had made the whole world, and subjected things earthly to man, and arranged the heavenly elements for the increase of fruits and rotation of the seasons, and appointed this divine law—for these things also He evidently made for man—committed the care of men and of all things under heaven to angels whom He appointed over them. But the angels transgressed this appointment, and were captivated by love of women, and begat children who are those that are called demons; and besides, they afterwards

[1] See Plato, *Rep.* p. 595.

subdued the human race to themselves, partly by magical writings, and partly by fears and the punishments they occasioned, and partly by teaching them to offer sacrifices, and incense, and libations, of which things they stood in need after they were enslaved by lustful passions; and among men they sowed murders, wars, adulteries, intemperate deeds, and all wickedness. Whence also the poets and mythologists, not knowing that it was the angels and those demons who had been begotten by them that did these things to men, and women, and cities, and nations, which they related, ascribed them to God Himself, and to those who were accounted to be His very offspring, and to the offspring of those who were called His brothers, Neptune and Pluto, and to the children again of these their offspring. For whatever name each of the angels had given to himself and his children, by that name they called them.

CHAP. VI.—*Names of God and of Christ, their meaning and power.*

But to the Father of all, who is unbegotten, there is no name given. For by whatever name He be called, He has as His elder the person who gives Him the name. But these words, Father, and God, and Creator, and Lord, and Master, are not names, but appellations derived from His good deeds and functions. And His Son, who alone is properly called Son, the Word, who also was with Him and was begotten before the works, when at first He created and arranged all things by Him, is called Christ, in reference to His being anointed and God's ordering all things through Him; this name itself also containing an unknown significance; as also the appellation "God" is not a name, but an opinion implanted in the nature of men of a thing that can hardly be explained. But "Jesus," His name as man and Saviour, has also significance. For He was made man also, as we before said, having been conceived according to the will of God the Father, for the sake of believing men, and for the destruction of the demons. And now you can learn this from what is under your own observation. For numberless demoniacs throughout the whole world, and in your city, many of our Christian men exorcising them in the name of Jesus Christ, who was crucified under Pontius Pilate, have healed and do heal, rendering helpless and driving the possessing devils out of the men, though they could not be cured by all the other exorcists, and those who used incantations and drugs.

CHAP. VII.—*The world preserved for the sake of Christians. Man's responsibility.*

Wherefore God delays causing the confusion and destruction of the whole world, by which the wicked angels and demons and men shall cease to exist, because of the seed of the Christians, who know that they are the cause of preservation in nature.[1] Since, if it were not so, it would not have been possible for you to do these things, and to be impelled by evil spirits; but the fire of judgment would descend and utterly dissolve all things, even as formerly the flood left no one but him only with his family who is by us called Noah, and by you Deucalion, from whom again such vast numbers have sprung, some of them evil and others good. For so we say that there will be the conflagration, but not as the Stoics, according to their doctrine of all things being changed into one another, which seems most degrading. But neither do we affirm that it is by fate that men do what they do, or suffer what they suffer, but that each man by free choice acts rightly or sins; and that it is by the influence of the wicked demons that earnest men, such as Socrates and the like, suffer persecution and are in bonds, while Sardanapalus, Epicurus, and the like, seem to be blessed in abundance and glory. The Stoics, not observing this, maintained that all things take place according to the necessity of fate. But since God in the beginning made the race of angels and men with free-will, they will justly suffer in eternal fire the punishment of whatever sins they have committed. And this is the nature of all that is made, to be capable of vice and virtue. For neither would any of them be praiseworthy unless there were

[1] This is Dr Donaldson's rendering of a clause on which the editors differ both as to reading and rendering.

power to turn to both [virtue and vice]. And this also is shown by those men everywhere who have made laws and philosophized according to right reason, by their prescribing to do some things and refrain from others. Even the Stoic philosophers, in their doctrine of morals, steadily honour the same things, so that it is evident that they are not very felicitous in what they say about principles and incorporeal things. For if they say that human actions come to pass by fate, they will maintain either that God is nothing else than the things which are ever turning, and altering, and dissolving into the same things, and will appear to have had a comprehension only of things that are destructible, and to have looked on God Himself as emerging both in part and in whole in every wickedness;[1] or that neither vice nor virtue is anything; which is contrary to every sound idea, reason, and sense.

CHAP. VIII.—*All have been hated in whom the Word has dwelt.*

And those of the Stoic school—since, so far as their moral teaching went, they were admirable, as were also the poets in some particulars, on account of the seed of reason [the Logos] implanted in every race of men—were, we know, hated and put to death,—Heraclitus for instance, and, among those of our own time, Musonius and others. For, as we intimated, the devils have always effected, that all those who anyhow live a reasonable and earnest life, and shun vice, be hated. And it is nothing wonderful if the devils are proved to cause those to be much worse hated who live not according to a part only of the word diffused [among men], but by the knowledge and contemplation of the whole Word, which is Christ. And they, having been shut up in eternal fire, shall suffer their just punishment and penalty. For if they are even now overthrown by men through the name of Jesus Christ, this is an intimation of the punishment in eternal fire which is to be inflicted on themselves and those who serve them. For thus did both all the prophets foretell, and our own teacher Jesus teach.

[1] Literally, "becoming (γινόμενον) both through the parts and through the whole in every wickedness."

CHAP. IX.—*Eternal punishment not a mere threat.*

And that no one may say what is said by those who are deemed philosophers, that our assertions that the wicked are punished in eternal fire are big words and bugbears, and that we wish men to live virtuously through fear, and not because such a life is good and pleasant; I will briefly reply to this, that if this be not so, God does not exist; or, if He exist, He cares not for men, and neither virtue nor vice is anything, and, as we said before, lawgivers unjustly punish those who transgress good commandments. But since these are not unjust, and their Father teaches them by the word to do the same things as Himself, they who agree with them are not unjust. And if one object that the laws of men are diverse, and say that with some, one thing is considered good, another evil, while with others what seemed bad to the former is esteemed good, and what seemed good is esteemed bad, let him listen to what we say to this. We know that the wicked angels appointed laws conformable to their own wickedness, in which the men who are like them delight; and the right Reason,[1] when He came, proved that not all opinions nor all doctrines are good, but that some are evil, while others are good. Wherefore, I will declare the same and similar things to such men as these, and, if need be, they shall be spoken of more at large. But at present I return to the subject.

CHAP. X.—*Christ compared with Socrates.*

Our doctrines, then, appear to be greater than all human teaching; because Christ, who appeared for our sakes, became the whole rational being, both body, and reason, and soul. For whatever either lawgivers or philosophers uttered well, they elaborated by finding and contemplating some part of the Word. But since they did not know the whole of the Word, which is Christ, they often contradicted themselves. And those who by human birth were more ancient than Christ, when they attempted to consider and prove things by

[1] These words can be taken of the Logos as well as of the right reason diffused among men by Him.

reason, were brought before the tribunals as impious persons and busybodies. And Socrates, who was more zealous in this direction than all of them, was accused of the very same crimes as ourselves. For they said that he was introducing new divinities, and did not consider those to be gods whom the state recognised. But he cast out from the state both Homer[1] and the rest of the poets, and taught men to reject the wicked demons and those who did the things which the poets related; and he exhorted them to become acquainted with the God who was to them unknown, by means of the investigation of reason, saying, "That it is neither easy to find the Father and Maker of all, nor, having found Him, is it safe to declare Him to all."[2] But these things our Christ did through His own power. For no one trusted in Socrates so as to die for this doctrine, but in Christ, who was partially known even by Socrates (for He was and is the Word who is in every man, and who foretold the things that were to come to pass both through the prophets and in His own person when He was made of like passions, and taught these things), not only philosophers and scholars believed, but also artisans and people entirely uneducated, despising both glory, and fear, and death; since He is a power of the ineffable Father, and not the mere instrument of human reason.

CHAP. XI.—*How Christians view death.*

But neither should we be put to death, nor would wicked men and devils be more powerful than we, were not death a debt due by every man that is born. Wherefore we give thanks when we pay this debt. And we judge it right and opportune to tell here, for the sake of Crescens and those who rave as he does, what is related by Xenophon. Hercules, says Xenophon, coming to a place where three ways met, found Virtue and Vice, who appeared to him in the form of women: Vice, in a luxurious dress, and with a seductive expression rendered blooming by such ornaments, and her

[1] Plato, *Rep.* x. c. i. p. 595.

[2] Plat. *Timæus*, p. 28, C. (but "possible," and not "safe," is the word used by Plato).

eyes of a quickly melting tenderness,[1] said to Hercules that if he would follow her, she would always enable him to pass his life in pleasure and adorned with the most graceful ornaments, such as were then upon her own person; and Virtue, who was of squalid look and dress, said, But if you obey me, you shall adorn yourself not with ornament nor beauty that passes away and perishes, but with everlasting and precious graces. And we are persuaded that every one who flees those things that seem to be good, and follows hard after what are reckoned difficult and strange, enters into blessedness. For Vice, when by imitation of what is incorruptible (for what is really incorruptible she neither has nor can produce) she has thrown around her own actions, as a disguise, the properties of Virtue, and qualities which are really excellent, leads captive earthly-minded men, attaching to Virtue her own evil properties. But those who understand the excellences which belong to that which is real, are also uncorrupt in virtue. And this every sensible person ought to think both of Christians and of the athletes, and of those who did what the poets relate of the so-called gods, concluding as much from our contempt of death, even when it could be escaped.[2]

CHAP. XII.—*Christians proved innocent by their contempt of death.*

For I myself, too, when I was delighting in the doctrines of Plato, and heard the Christians slandered, and saw them fearless of death, and of all other things which are counted fearful, perceived that it was impossible that they could be living in wickedness and pleasure. For what sensual or intemperate man, or who that counts it good to feast on human flesh,[3] could welcome death that he might be deprived

[1] Another reading is πρὸς τὰς ὄψεις, referring to the eyes of the beholder; and which may be rendered, "speedily fascinating to the sight."

[2] Καὶ φευκτοῦ θανάτου may also be rendered, "even of death *which men flee from*."

[3] Alluding to the common accusation against the Christians.

of his enjoyments, and would not rather continue always the present life, and attempt to escape the observation of the rulers; and much less would he denounce himself when the consequence would be death? This also the wicked demons have now caused to be done by evil men. For having put some to death on account of the accusations falsely brought against us, they also dragged to the torture our domestics, either children or weak women, and by dreadful torments forced them to admit those fabulous actions which they themselves openly perpetrate; about which we are the less concerned, because none of these actions are really ours, and we have the unbegotten and ineffable God as witness both of our thoughts and deeds. For why did we not even publicly profess that these were the things which we esteemed good, and prove that these are the divine philosophy, saying that the mysteries of Saturn are performed when we slay a man, and that when we drink our fill of blood, as it is said we do, we are doing what you do before that idol you honour, and on which you sprinkle the blood not only of irrational animals, but also of men, making a libation of the blood of the slain by the hand of the most illustrious and noble man among you? And imitating Jupiter and the other gods in sodomy and shameless intercourse with women, might we not bring as our apology the writings of Epicurus and the poets? But because we persuade men to avoid such instruction, and all who practise them and imitate such examples, as now in this discourse we have striven to persuade you, we are assailed in every kind of way. But we are not concerned, since we know that God is a just observer of all. But would that even now some one would mount a lofty rostrum, and shout with a loud voice,[1] "Be ashamed, be ashamed, ye who charge the guiltless with those deeds which yourselves openly commit, and ascribe things which apply to yourselves and to your gods to those who have not even the slightest sympathy with them. Be ye converted; become wise."

[1] Literally, "with a tragic voice,"—the loud voice in which the Greek tragedies were recited through the mask.

CHAP. XIII.—*How the Word has been in all men.*

For I myself, when I discovered the wicked disguise which the evil spirits had thrown around the divine doctrines of the Christians, to turn aside others from joining them, laughed both at those who framed these falsehoods, and at the disguise itself, and at popular opinion; and I confess that I both boast and with all my strength strive to be found a Christian; not because the teachings of Plato are different from those of Christ, but because they are not in all respects similar, as neither are those of the others, stoics, and poets, and historians. For each man spoke well in proportion to the share he had of the spermatic word,[1] seeing what was related to it. But they who contradict themselves on the more important points appear not to have possessed the heavenly[2] wisdom, and the knowledge which cannot be spoken against. Whatever things were rightly said among all men, are the property of us Christians. For next to God, we worship and love the Word who is from the Unbegotten and Ineffable God, since also He became man for our sakes, that, becoming a partaker of our sufferings, He might also bring us healing. For all the writers were able to see realities darkly through the sowing of the implanted word that was in them. For the seed and imitation imparted according to capacity is one thing, and quite another is the thing itself, of which there is the participation and imitation according to the grace which is from Him.

CHAP. XIV.—*Justin prays that this appeal be published.*

And we therefore pray you to publish this little book, appending what you think right, that our opinions may be known to others, and that these persons may have a fair chance of being freed from erroneous notions and ignorance of good, who by their own fault are become subject to punishment; that so these things may be published to men, because it is in the nature of man to know good and evil; and by their

[1] The word disseminated among men.

[2] Literally, dimly seen at a distance.

condemning us, whom they do not understand, for actions which they say are wicked, and by delighting in the gods who did such things, and even now require similar actions from men, and by inflicting on us death or bonds or some other such punishment, as if we were guilty of these things, they condemn themselves, so that there is no need of other judges.

Chap. xv.—*Conclusion.*

And I despised the wicked and deceitful doctrine of Simon of my own nation. And if you give this book your authority, we will expose him before all, that, if possible, they may be converted. For this end alone did we compose this treatise. And our doctrines are not shameful, according to a sober judgment, but are indeed more lofty than all human philosophy; and if not so, they are at least unlike the doctrines of the Sotadists, and Philænidians, and Dancers, and Epicureans, and such other teachings of the poets, which all are allowed to acquaint themselves with, both as acted and as written. And henceforth we shall be silent, having done as much as we could, and having added the prayer that all men everywhere may be counted worthy of the truth. And would that you also, in a manner becoming piety and philosophy, would for your own sakes judge justly!

DIALOGUE OF JUSTIN,

PHILOSOPHER AND MARTYR,

WITH

TRYPHO, A JEW.

Chap. i.—*Introduction.*

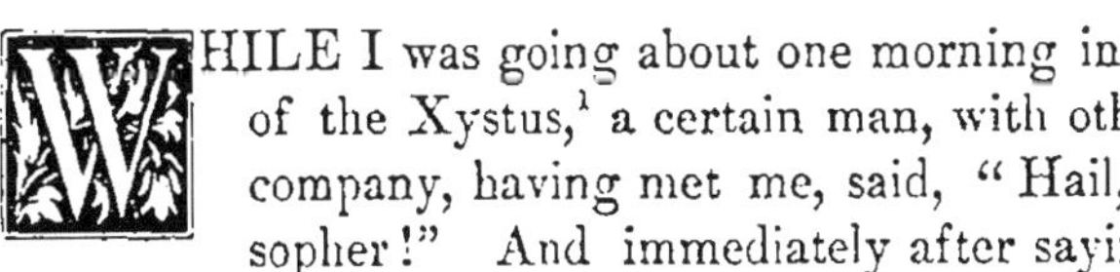

WHILE I was going about one morning in the walks of the Xystus,[1] a certain man, with others in his company, having met me, said, "Hail, O philosopher!" And immediately after saying this, he turned round and walked along with me; his friends likewise followed him. And I in turn having addressed him, said, "What is there important?"

And he replied, "I was instructed," says he, "by Corinthus the Socratic in Argos, that I ought not to despise or treat with indifference those who array themselves in this dress,[2] but to show them all kindness, and to associate with them, as perhaps some advantage would spring from the intercourse either to some such man or to myself. It is good, moreover, for both, if either the one or the other be benefited. On this account, therefore, whenever I see any one in such costume, I gladly approach him, and now, for the same reason, have I willingly accosted you; and these accompany me, in the expectation of hearing for themselves something profitable from you."

[1] This Xystus, on the authority of Euseb. (iv. 18), was at Ephesus. There, Philostratus mentions, Apollonius was wont to have disputations. —*Otto.*

[2] Euseb. (iv. 11): "Justin, in philosopher's garb, preached the word of God."

"But who are you, most excellent man?" So I replied to him in jest.[1]

Then he told me frankly both his name and his family. "Trypho," says he, "I am called; and I am a Hebrew of the circumcision, and having escaped from the war[2] lately carried on there, I am spending my days in Greece, and chiefly at Corinth."

"And in what," said I, "would you be profited by philosophy so much as by your own lawgiver and the prophets?"

"Why not?" he replied. "Do not the philosophers turn every discourse on God? and do not questions continually arise to them about His unity and providence? Is not this truly the duty of philosophy, to investigate the Deity?"

"Assuredly," said I, "so we too have believed. But the most[3] have not taken thought of this, whether there be one or more gods, and whether they have a regard for each one of us or no, as if this knowledge contributed nothing to our happiness; nay, they moreover attempt to persuade us that God takes care of the universe with its genera and species, but not of me and you, and each individually, since otherwise we would surely not need to pray to Him night and day. But it is not difficult to understand the upshot of this; for fearlessness and licence in speaking result to such as maintain these opinions, doing and saying whatever they choose, neither dreading punishment nor hoping for any benefit from God. For how could they? They affirm that the same things shall always happen; and, further, that I and you shall again live in like manner, having become neither better men nor worse. But there are some others,[4] who, having supposed the soul to be immortal and immaterial, believe that though they have committed evil they will not suffer punishment (for that which is immaterial is insensible), and that the soul, in consequence of its immortality, needs nothing from God."

And he, smiling gently, said, "Tell us your opinion of

[1] In jest, no doubt, because quoting a line from Homer, *Il.* ii. 123, τίς δὲ σύ ἐσσι, φέριστε, καταθνητῶν ἀνθρώπων.

[2] The war instigated by Bar Cochba.

[3] The opinions of Stoics.—*Otto.*

[4] The Platonists.

these matters, and what idea you entertain respecting God, and what your philosophy is."

CHAP. II.—*Justin describes his studies in philosophy.*

"I will tell you," said I, "what seems to me; for philosophy is, in fact, the greatest possession, and most honourable before God,[1] to whom it leads us and alone commends us; and these are truly holy men who have bestowed attention on philosophy. What philosophy is, however, and the reason why it has been sent down to men, have escaped the observation of most; for there would be neither Platonists, nor Stoics, nor Peripatetics, nor Theoretics,[2] nor Pythagoreans, this knowledge being *one.*[3] I wish to tell you why it has become many-headed. It has happened that those who first handled it [*i.e.* philosophy], and who were therefore esteemed illustrious men, were succeeded by those who made no investigations concerning truth, but only admired the perseverance and self-discipline of the former, as well as the novelty of the doctrines; and each thought that to be true which he learned from his teacher: then, moreover, those latter persons handed down to *their* successors such things, and others similar to them; and this system was called by the name of him who was styled the father of the doctrine. Being at first desirous of personally conversing with one of these men, I surrendered myself to a certain Stoic; and having spent a considerable time with him, when I had not acquired any further knowledge of God (for he did not know himself, and said such instruction was unnecessary), I left him and betook myself to another, who was called a Peripatetic, and as *he* fancied, shrewd. And this man, after having entertained me for the first few days, requested

[1] ᾧ some omit, and put θεῷ of prev. cl. in this cl., reading so: "Philosophy is the greatest possession, and most honourable, and introduces us to God," etc.

[2] Maranus thinks that those who are different from the masters of practical philosophy are called *Theoretics.* I do not know whether they may be better designated *Sceptics* or *Pyrrhonists.—Otto.*

[3] Julian, *Orat.* vi., says: "Let no one divide our philosophy into many parts, or cut it into many parts, and especially let him not make many out of *one:* for as truth is one, so also is philosophy."

me to settle the fee, in order that our intercourse might not be unprofitable. Him, too, for this reason I abandoned, believing him to be no philosopher at all. But when my soul was eagerly desirous to hear the peculiar and choice philosophy, I came to a Pythagorean, very celebrated—a man who thought much of his own wisdom. And then, when I had an interview with him, willing to become his hearer and disciple, he said, 'What then? Are you acquainted with music, astronomy, and geometry? Do you expect to perceive any of those things which conduce to a happy life, if you have not been first informed on those points which wean the soul from sensible objects, and render it fitted for objects which appertain to the mind, so that it can contemplate that which is honourable in its essence and that which is good in its essence?' Having commended many of these branches of learning, and telling me that they were necessary, he dismissed me when I confessed to him my ignorance. Accordingly I took it rather impatiently, as was to be expected when I failed in my hope, the more so because I deemed the man had some knowledge; but reflecting again on the space of time during which I would have to linger over those branches of learning, I was not able to endure longer procrastination. In my helpless condition it occurred to me to have a meeting with the Platonists, for their fame was great. I thereupon spent as much of my time as possible with one who had lately settled in our city,[1]—a sagacious man, holding a high position among the Platonists,—and I progressed, and made the greatest improvements daily. And the perception of immaterial things quite overpowered me, and the contemplation of ideas furnished my mind with wings,[2] so that in a little while I supposed that I had become wise; and such was my stupidity, I expected forthwith to look upon God, for this is the end of Plato's philosophy.

[1] Either Flavia Neapolis is indicated, or Ephesus.—*Otto.*

[2] Narrating his progress in the study of Platonic philosophy, he elegantly employs this trite phrase of Plato's.—*Otto.*

CHAP. III.—*Justin narrates the manner of his conversion.*

"And while I was thus disposed, when I wished at one period to be filled with great quietness, and to shun the path of men, I used to go into a certain field not far from the sea. And when I was near that spot one day, which having reached I purposed to be by myself, a certain old man, by no means contemptible in appearance, exhibiting meek and venerable manners, followed me at a little distance. And when I turned round to him, having halted, I fixed my eyes rather keenly on him.

"And he said, 'Do you know me?'

"I replied in the negative.

"'Why, then,' said he to me, 'do you so look at me?'

"'I am astonished,' I said, 'because you have chanced to be in my company in the same place; for I had not expected to see any man here.'

"And he says to me, 'I am concerned about some of my household. These are gone away from me; and therefore have I come to make personal search for them, if, perhaps, they shall make their appearance somewhere. But why are you here?' said he to me.

"'I delight,' said I, 'in such walks, where my attention is not distracted, for converse with myself is uninterrupted; and such places are most fit for philology.'[1]

"'Are you, then, a philologian,'[2] said he, 'but no lover of deeds or of truth? and do you not aim at being a practical man so much as being a sophist?'

"'What greater work,' said I, 'could one accomplish than this, to show the reason which governs all, and having laid hold of it, and being mounted upon it, to look down on the errors of others, and their pursuits? But without philosophy and right reason, prudence would not be present to any man. Wherefore it is necessary for every man to philosophize, and

[1] Philology, used here to denote the exercise of the *reason*.

[2] Philology, used here to denote the exercise of *speech*. The twofold use of λόγος—*oratio* and *ratio*—ought to be kept in view. The old man uses it in the former, Justin in the latter sense.

to esteem this the greatest and most honourable work; but other things only of second-rate or third-rate importance, though, indeed, if they be made to depend on philosophy, they are of moderate value, and worthy of acceptance; but deprived of it, and not accompanying it, they are vulgar and coarse to those who pursue them.'

"'Does philosophy, then, make happiness?' said he, interrupting.

"'Assuredly,' I said, 'and it alone.'

"'What, then, is philosophy?' he says; 'and what is happiness? Pray tell me, unless something hinders you from saying.'

"'Philosophy, then,' said I, 'is the knowledge of that which really exists, and a clear perception of the truth; and happiness is the reward of such knowledge and wisdom.'

"'But what do you call God?' said he.

"'That which always maintains the same nature, and in the same manner, and is the cause of all other things—that, indeed, is God.' So I answered him; and he listened to me with pleasure, and thus again interrogated me:

"'Is not knowledge a term common to different matters? For in arts of all kinds, he who knows any one of them is called a skilful man, in the art of generalship, or of ruling, or of healing equally. But in divine and human affairs it is not so. Is there a knowledge which affords understanding of human and divine things, and then a thorough acquaintance with the divinity and the righteousness of them?'

"'Assuredly,' I replied.

"'What, then? Is it in the same way we know man and God, as we know music, and arithmetic, and astronomy, or any other similar branch?'

"'By no means,' I replied.

"'You have not answered me correctly, then,' he said; 'for some [branches of knowledge] come to us by learning, or by some employment, while of others we have knowledge by sight. Now, if one were to tell you that there exists in India an animal with a nature unlike all others, but of such and such a kind, multiform and various, you would not know it before you saw it; but neither would you be competent to give any account of it, unless you should hear from one who had seen it.'

"'Certainly not,' I said.

"'How then,' he said, 'should the philosophers judge correctly about God, or speak any truth, when they have no knowledge of Him, having neither seen Him at any time, nor heard Him?'

"'But, father,' said I, 'the Deity cannot be seen merely by the eyes, as other living beings can, but is discernible to the mind alone, as Plato says; and I believe him.'

CHAP. IV.—*The soul of itself cannot see God.*

"'Is there then,' says he, 'such and so great power in our mind? Or can a man not perceive by sense sooner? Will the mind of man see God at any time, if it is uninstructed by the Holy Spirit?'

"'Plato indeed says,' replied I, 'that the mind's eye is of such a nature, and has been given for this end, that we may see that very Being when the mind is pure itself, who is the cause of all discerned by the mind, having no colour, no form, no greatness—nothing, indeed, which the bodily eye looks upon; but It is something of this sort, he goes on to say, that is beyond all essence, unutterable and inexplicable, but alone honourable and good, coming suddenly into souls well-dispositioned, on account of their affinity to and desire of seeing Him.'

"'What affinity, then,' replied he, 'is there between us and God? Is the soul also divine and immortal, and a part of that very regal mind? And even as that sees God, so also is it attainable by us to conceive of the Deity in our mind, and thence to become happy?'

"'Assuredly,' I said.

"'And do all the souls of all living beings comprehend Him?' he asked; 'or are the souls of men of one kind, and the souls of horses and of asses of another kind?'

"'No; but the souls which are in all are similar,' I answered.

"'Then,' says he, 'shall both horses and asses see, or have they seen at some time or other, God?'

"'No,' I said; 'for the majority of men will not, saving such as shall live justly, purified by righteousness, and by every other virtue.'

"'It is not, therefore,' said he, 'on account of his affinity, that a man sees God, nor because he has a mind, but because he is temperate and righteous?'

"'Yes,' said I; 'and because he has that whereby he perceives God.'

"'What then? Do goats or sheep injure any one?'

"'No one in any respect,' I said.

"'Therefore these animals will see [God] according to your account,' says he.

"'No; for their body being of such a nature, is an obstacle to them.'

"He rejoined, 'If these animals could assume speech, be well assured that they would with greater reason ridicule our body; but let us now dismiss this subject, and let it be conceded to you as you say. Tell me, however, this: Does the soul see [God] so long as it is in the body, or after it has been removed from it?'

"'So long as it is in the form of a man, it is possible for it,' I continue, 'to attain to this by means of the mind; but especially when it has been set free from the body, and being apart by itself, it gets possession of that which it was wont continually and wholly to love.'

"'Does it remember this, then [the sight of God], when it is again in the man?'

"'It does not appear to me so,' I said.

"'What, then, is the advantage to those who have seen [God]? or what has he who has seen more than he who has not seen, unless he remember this fact, that he *has* seen?'

"'I cannot tell,' I answered.

"'And what do those suffer who are judged to be unworthy of this spectacle?' said he.

"'They are imprisoned in the bodies of certain wild beasts, and this is their punishment.'

"'Do they know, then, that it is for this reason they are in such forms, and that they have committed some sin?'

"'I do not think so.'

"'Then these reap no advantage from their punishment, as it seems: moreover, I would say that they are not punished unless they are conscious of the punishment.'

"'No indeed.'

"'Therefore souls neither see God nor transmigrate into other bodies; for they would know that so they are punished, and they would be afraid to commit even the most trivial sin afterwards. But that they can perceive that God exists, and that righteousness and piety are honourable, I also quite agree with you,' said he.

"'You are right,' I replied.

CHAP. V.—*The soul is not in its own nature immortal.*

"'Those philosophers know nothing, then, about these things; for they cannot tell what a soul is.'

"'It does not appear so.'

"'Nor ought it to be called immortal; for if it is immortal, it is plainly unbegotten.'

"'It is both unbegotten and immortal, according to some who are styled Platonists.'

"'Do you say that the world is also unbegotten?'

"'Some say so. I do not, however, agree with them.'

"'You are right; for what reason has one for supposing that a body so solid, possessing resistance, composite, changeable, decaying, and renewed every day, has not arisen from some cause? But if the world is begotten, souls also are necessarily begotten; and perhaps at one time they were not in existence, for they were made on account of men and other living creatures, if you will say that they have been begotten wholly apart, and not along with their respective bodies.'

"'This seems to be correct.'

"'They are not, then, immortal?'

"'No; since the world has appeared to us to be begotten.'

"'But I do not say, indeed, that all souls die; for that were truly a piece of good fortune to the evil. What then? The souls of the pious remain in a better place, while those of the unjust and wicked are in a worse, waiting for the time of judgment. Thus some which have appeared worthy of God never die; but others are punished so long as God wills them to exist and to be punished.'

" 'Is what you say, then, of a like nature with that which Plato in *Timæus* hints about the world, when he says that it is indeed subject to decay, inasmuch as it has been created, but that it will neither be dissolved nor meet with the fate of death on account of the will of God? Does it seem to you the very same can be said of the soul, and generally of all things? For those things which exist after[1] God, or shall at any time exist,[2] these have the nature of decay, and are such as may be blotted out and cease to exist; for God alone is unbegotten and incorruptible, and therefore He is God, but all other things after Him are created and corruptible. For this reason souls both die and are punished: since, if they were unbegotten, they would neither sin, nor be filled with folly, nor be cowardly, and again ferocious; nor would they willingly transform into swine, and serpents, and dogs; and it would not indeed be just to compel them, if they be unbegotten. For that which is unbegotten is similar to, equal to, and the same with that which is unbegotten; and neither in power nor in honour should the one be preferred to the other, and hence there are not many things which are unbegotten: for if there were some difference between them, you would not discover the cause of the difference, though you searched for it; but after letting the mind ever wander to infinity, you would at length, wearied out, take your stand on one Unbegotten, and say that this is the Cause of all. Did such escape the observation of Plato and Pythagoras, those wise men,' I said, 'who have been as a wall and fortress of philosophy to us?'

[1] "Beside."

[2] Otto says: If the old man begins to speak here, then ἔχει must be read for ἔχειν. The received text makes it appear that Justin continues a quotation, or the substance of it, from Plato.

CHAP. VI.—*These things were unknown to Plato and other philosophers.*

"'It makes no matter to me,' said he, 'whether Plato or Pythagoras, or, in short, any other man, held such opinions. For the truth is so; and you would perceive it from this. The soul assuredly is or has life. If, then, it is life, it would cause something else, and not itself, to live, even as motion would move something else than itself. Now, that the soul lives, no one would deny. But if it lives, it lives not as being life, but as the partaker of life; but that which partakes of anything, is different from that of which it does partake. Now the soul partakes of life, since God wills it to live. Thus, then, it will not even partake [of life] when God does not will it to live. For to live is not its attribute, as it is God's; but as a man does not live always, and the soul is not for ever conjoined with the body, since, whenever this harmony must be broken up, the soul leaves the body, and the man exists no longer; even so, whenever the soul must cease to exist, the spirit of life is removed from it, and there is no more soul, but it goes back to the place from whence it was taken.'

CHAP. VII.—*The knowledge of truth to be sought from the prophets alone.*

"'Should any one, then, employ a teacher?' I say, 'or whence may any one be helped, if not even in them there is truth?'

"'There existed, long before this time, certain men more ancient than all those who are esteemed philosophers, both righteous and beloved by God, who spoke by the Divine Spirit, and foretold events which would take place, and which are now taking place. They are called prophets. These alone both saw and announced the truth to men, neither reverencing nor fearing any man, not influenced by a desire for glory, but speaking those things alone which they saw and which they heard, being filled with the Holy Spirit. Their writings are still extant, and he who has read them is very much helped in his knowledge of the beginning and end of things, and of those matters which the philosopher ought to know, provided he has believed them. For they did not use demonstration in their treatises, seeing that they were witnesses to the truth above all demonstration, and worthy of belief; and those events which have happened, and those which are happening, compel you to assent to the utterances made by them, although, indeed, they were entitled to credit on account of the miracles which they performed, since they both glorified the Creator, the God and Father of all things, and proclaimed His Son, the Christ [sent] by Him: which, indeed, the false prophets, who are filled with the lying unclean spirit, neither have done nor do, but venture to work certain wonderful deeds for the purpose of astonishing men, and glorify the spirits and demons of error. But pray that, above all things, the gates of light may be opened to you; for these things cannot be perceived or understood by all, but only by the man to whom God and His Christ have imparted wisdom.'

CHAP. VIII.—*Justin by his colloquy is kindled with love to Christ.*

"When he had spoken these and many other things, which there is no time for mentioning at present, he went away, bidding me attend to them; and I have not seen him since. But straightway a flame was kindled in my soul; and a love of the prophets, and of those men who are friends of Christ, possessed me; and whilst revolving his words in my mind, I found this philosophy alone to be safe and profitable. Thus, and for this reason, I am a philosopher. Moreover, I would wish that all, making a resolution similar to my own, do not keep themselves away from the words of the Saviour. For they possess a terrible power in themselves, and are sufficient to inspire those who turn aside from the path of rectitude with awe; while the sweetest rest is afforded those who make a diligent practice of them. If, then, you have any concern for yourself, and if you are eagerly looking for salvation, and if you believe in God, you may—since you are not indifferent to the matter[1]—become acquainted with the Christ of God, and, after being initiated,[2] live a happy life."

When I had said this, my beloved friend,[3] those who were with Trypho laughed; but he, smiling, says, "I approve of your other remarks, and admire the eagerness with which you study divine things; but it were better for you still to abide in the philosophy of Plato, or of some other man, cultivating endurance, self-control, and moderation, rather than be deceived by false words, and follow the opinions of men of no reputation. For if you remain in that mode of philosophy, and live blamelessly, a hope of a better destiny were left to you; but when you have forsaken God, and reposed confidence in man, what safety still awaits you? If, then, you are willing to listen to me (for I have already considered you a friend), first be circumcised, then observe what ordinances have been enacted with respect to the Sabbath, and the feasts, and the new moons of God; and, in a word, do all things which have been written in the law: and then perhaps you shall obtain mercy from God. But Christ—if He has indeed been born, and exists anywhere—is unknown, and does not even know Himself, and has no power until Elias come to anoint Him, and make Him manifest to all. And you, having accepted a groundless report, invent a Christ for yourselves, and for his sake are inconsiderately perishing."

CHAP. IX.—*The Christians have not believed groundless stories.*

"I excuse and forgive you, my friend," I said. "For you know not what you say, but have been persuaded by teachers who do not understand the Scriptures; and you speak, like a diviner, whatever comes into your mind. But if you are willing to listen to an account of Him, how we have not

1 According to one interpretation, this clause is applied to God: "If you believe in God, seeing He is not indifferent to the matter," etc. Maranus says that it means: A Jew who reads so much of Christ in the Old Testament, cannot be indifferent to the things which pertain to Him.

2 Literally: having become perfect. Some refer the words to perfection of character; some to initiation by baptism.

3 Latin version, "beloved Pompeius."

been deceived, and shall not cease to confess Him,—although men's reproaches be heaped upon us, although the most terrible tyrant compel us to deny Him,—I shall prove to you as you stand here that we have not believed empty fables, or words without any foundation, but words filled with the Spirit of God, and big with power, and flourishing with grace."

Then again those who were in his company laughed, and shouted in an unseemly manner. Then I rose up and was about to leave; but he, taking hold of my garment, said I should not accomplish that[1] until I had performed what I promised. "Let not, then, your companions be so tumultuous, or behave so disgracefully," I said. "But if they wish, let them listen in silence; or, if some better occupation prevent them, let them go away; while we, having retired to some spot, and resting there, may finish the discourse." It seemed good to Trypho that we should do so; and accordingly, having agreed upon it, we retired to the middle space of the Xystus. Two of his friends, when they had ridiculed and made game of our zeal, went off. And when we were come to that place, where there are stone seats on both sides, those with Trypho, having seated themselves on the one side, conversed with each other, some one of them having thrown in a remark about the war waged in Judæa.

CHAP. X.—*Trypho blames the Christians for this alone—the non-observance of the law.*

And when they ceased, I again addressed them thus:

"Is there any other matter, my friends, in which we are blamed, than this, that we live not after the law, and are not circumcised in the flesh as your forefathers were, and do not observe sabbaths as you do? Are our lives and customs also slandered among you? And I ask this: have you also believed concerning us, that we eat men; and that after the feast, having extinguished the lights, we engage in promiscuous concubinage? Or do you condemn us in this alone, that we adhere to such tenets, and believe in an opinion, untrue, as you think?"

[1] According to another reading, "I did not *leave*."

"This is what we are amazed at," said Trypho, "but those things about which the multitude speak are not worthy of belief; for they are most repugnant to human nature. Moreover, I am aware that your precepts in the so-called Gospel are so wonderful and so great, that I suspect no one can keep them; for I have carefully read them. But this is what we are most at a loss about: that you, professing to be pious, and supposing yourselves better than others, are not in any particular separated from them, and do not alter your mode of living from the nations, in that you observe no festivals or sabbaths, and do not have the rite of circumcision; and further, resting your hopes on a man that was crucified, you yet expect to obtain some good thing from God, while you do not obey His commandments. Have you not read, that that soul shall be cut off from his people who shall not have been circumcised on the eighth day? And this has been ordained for strangers and for slaves equally. But you, despising this covenant rashly, reject the consequent duties, and attempt to persuade yourselves that you know God, when, however, you perform none of those things which they do who fear God. If, therefore, you can defend yourself on these points, and make it manifest in what way you hope for anything whatsoever, even though you do not observe the law, this we would very gladly hear from you, and we shall make other similar investigations."[1]

CHAP. XI.—*The law abrogated; the new testament promised and given by God.*

"There will be no other God, O Trypho, nor was there from eternity any other existing" (I thus addressed him), "but He who made and disposed all this universe. Nor do we think that there is one God for us, another for you, but that He alone is God who led your fathers out from Egypt with a strong hand and a high arm. Nor have we trusted in any other (for there is no other), but in Him in whom you also have trusted, the God of Abraham, and of Isaac, and of Jacob. But we do not trust through Moses or through the law; for then we would do the same as yourselves. But now[1]—(for I have read that there shall be a final law, and a covenant, the chiefest of all, which it is now incumbent on all men to observe, as many as are seeking after the inheritance of God. For the law promulgated on Horeb is now old, and belongs to yourselves alone; but *this* is for all universally. Now, law placed against law has abrogated that which is before it, and a covenant which comes after in like manner has put an end to the previous one; and an eternal and final law—namely, Christ—has been given to us, and the covenant is trustworthy, after which there shall be no law, no commandment, no ordinance. Have you not read this which Isaiah says: 'Hearken unto me, hearken unto me, my people; and, ye kings, give ear unto me: for a law shall go forth from me, and my judgment shall be for a light to the nations. My righteousness approaches swiftly, and my salvation shall go forth, and nations shall trust in mine arm?'[2] And by Jeremiah, concerning this same new covenant, He thus speaks: 'Behold, the days come, saith the Lord, that I will make a new covenant with the house of Israel and with the house of Judah; not according to the covenant which I made with their fathers, in the day that I took them by the hand, to bring them out of the land of Egypt'[3]). If, therefore, God proclaimed a new covenant which was to be instituted, and this for a light of the nations, we see and are persuaded that men approach God, leaving their idols and other unrighteousness, through the name of Him who was crucified, Jesus Christ, and abide by their confession even unto death, and maintain piety. Moreover, by the works and by the attendant miracles, it is possible for all to understand that He is the new law, and the new covenant, and the expectation of those who out of every people wait for the good things of God. For the true spiritual Israel, and descendants of Judah, Jacob, Isaac, and Abraham (who in uncir-

[1] Editors suppose that Justin inserts a long parenthesis here, from "for" to "Egypt." It is more natural to take this as an anacoluthon. Justin was going to say "But now we trust through Christ," but feels that such a statement requires a preliminary explanation.

[2] According to the LXX., Isa. li. 4, 5.

[3] Jer. xxxi. 31, 32.

cumcision was approved of and blessed by God on account of his faith, and called the father of many nations), are we who have been led to God through this crucified Christ, as shall be demonstrated while we proceed.

CHAP. XII.—*The Jews violate the eternal law, and interpret ill that of Moses.*

I also adduced another passage in which Isaiah exclaims: "'Hear my words, and your soul shall live; and I will make an everlasting covenant with you, even the sure mercies of David. Behold, I have given Him for a witness to the people: nations which know not Thee shall call on Thee; peoples who know not Thee shall escape to Thee, because of thy God, the Holy One of Israel; for He has glorified Thee.'[1] This same law you have despised, and His new holy covenant you have slighted; and now you neither receive it, nor repent of your evil deeds. 'For your ears are closed, your eyes are blinded, and the heart is hardened,' Jeremiah[2] has cried; yet not even then do you listen. The Lawgiver is present, yet you do not see Him; to the poor the gospel is preached, the blind see, yet you do not understand. You have now need of a second circumcision, though you glory greatly in the flesh. The new law requires you to keep perpetual sabbath, and you, because you are idle for one day, suppose you are pious, not discerning why this has been commanded you; and if you eat unleavened bread, you say the will of God has been fulfilled. The Lord our God does not take pleasure in such observances: if there is any perjured person or a thief among you, let him cease to be so; if any adulterer, let him repent; then he has kept the sweet and true sabbaths of God. If any one has impure hands, let him wash and be pure.

CHAP. XIII.—*Isaiah teaches that sins are forgiven through Christ's blood.*

"For Isaiah did not send you to a bath, there to wash

[1] Isa. lv. 3 ff. according to LXX.

[2] Not in Jeremiah; some would insert, in place of Jeremiah, Isaiah or John.

away murder and other sins, which not even all the water of the sea were sufficient to purge; but, as might have been expected, this was that saving bath of the olden time which followed[1] those who repented, and who no longer were purified by the blood of goats and of sheep, or by the ashes of an heifer, or by the offerings of fine flour, but by faith through the blood of Christ, and through His death, who died for this very reason, as Isaiah himself said, when he spake thus: 'The Lord shall make bare His holy arm in the eyes of all the nations, and all the nations and the ends of the earth shall see the salvation of God. Depart ye, depart ye, depart ye,[2] go ye out from thence, and touch no unclean thing; go ye out of the midst of her, be ye clean that bear the vessels of the Lord, for[3] ye go not with haste. For the Lord shall go before you; and the Lord, the God of Israel, shall gather you together. Behold, my servant shall deal prudently; and He shall be exalted, and be greatly glorified. As many were astonished at Thee, so Thy form and Thy glory shall be marred more than men. So shall many nations be astonished at Him, and the kings shall shut their mouths; for that which had not been told them concerning Him shall they see, and that which they had not heard shall they consider. Lord, who hath believed our report? and to whom is the arm of the Lord revealed? We have announced Him as a child before Him, as a root in a dry ground. He hath no form or comeliness, and when we saw Him He had no form or beauty; but His form is dishonoured, and fails more than the sons of men. He is a man in affliction, and acquainted with bearing sickness, because His face has been turned away; He was despised, and we esteemed Him not. He bears our sins, and is distressed for us; and we esteemed Him to be in toil and in affliction, and in evil treatment. But He was wounded for our transgressions, He was bruised for our iniquities; the chastisement of our peace was upon Him. With His stripes

[1] Cor. x. 4. Otto reads: which he mentioned and which was for those who repented.

[2] Three times in Justin, not in LXX.

[3] Deviating slightly from LXX., omitting a clause.

we are healed. All we, like sheep, have gone astray. Every man has turned to his own way; and the Lord laid on Him our iniquities, and by reason of His oppression He opens not His mouth. He was brought as a sheep to the slaughter; and as a lamb before her shearer is dumb, so He openeth not His mouth. In His humiliation His judgment was taken away. And who shall declare His generation? For His life is taken from the earth. Because of the transgressions of my people He came unto death. And I will give the wicked for His grave, and the rich for His death, because He committed no iniquity, and deceit was not found in His mouth. And the Lord wills to purify Him from affliction. If He has been given for sin, your soul shall see a long-lived seed. And the Lord wills to take His soul away from trouble, to show Him light, and to form Him in understanding, to justify the righteous One who serves many well. And He shall bear our sins; therefore He shall inherit many, and shall divide the spoil of the strong, because His soul was delivered to death; and He was numbered with the transgressors, and He bare the sins of many, and was delivered for their transgression. Sing, O barren, who bearest not; break forth and cry aloud, thou who dost not travail in pain: for more are the children of the desolate than the children of the married wife. For the Lord said, Enlarge the place of thy tent and of thy curtains; fix them, spare not, lengthen thy cords, and strengthen thy stakes; stretch forth to thy right and thy left; and thy seed shall inherit the Gentiles, and thou shalt make the desolate cities to be inhabited. Fear not because thou art ashamed, neither be thou confounded because thou hast been reproached; for thou shalt forget everlasting shame, and shalt not remember the reproach of thy widowhood, because the Lord has made a name for Himself, and He who has redeemed thee shall be called through the whole earth the God of Israel. The Lord has called thee as[1] a woman forsaken and grieved in spirit, as[1] a woman hated from her youth.'[2]

[1] LXX. "*not* as," etc.

[2] Isa. lii. 10 ff. following the LXX. on to liv. 6.

CHAP. XIV.—*Righteousness is not placed in Jewish rites, but in the conversion of the heart given in baptism by Christ.*

"By reason, therefore, of this laver of repentance and knowledge of God, which has been ordained on account of the transgression of God's people, as Isaiah cries, we have believed, and testify that that very baptism which he announced is alone able to purify those who have repented; and this is the water of life. But the cisterns which you have dug for yourselves are broken and profitless to you. For what is the use of that baptism which cleanses the flesh and body alone? Baptize the soul from wrath and from covetousness, from envy, and from hatred; and, lo! the body is pure. For this is the symbolic significance of unleavened bread, that you do not commit the old deeds of wicked leaven. But you have understood all things in a carnal sense, and you suppose it to be piety if you do such things, while your souls are filled with deceit, and, in short, with every wickedness. Accordingly, also, after the seven days of eating unleavened bread, God commanded them to mingle new leaven, that is, the performance of other works, and not the imitation of the old and evil works. And because this is what this new Lawgiver demands of you, I shall again refer to the words which have been quoted by me, and to others also which have been passed over. They are related by Isaiah to the following effect: 'Hearken to me, and your soul shall live; and I will make with you an everlasting covenant, even the sure mercies of David. Behold, I have given Him for a witness to the people, a leader and commander to the nations. Nations which know not Thee shall call on Thee; and peoples who know not Thee shall escape unto Thee, because of Thy God, the Holy One of Israel, for He has glorified Thee. Seek ye God; and when you find Him, call on Him, so long as He may be nigh you. Let the wicked forsake his ways, and the unrighteous man his thoughts; and let him return unto the Lord, and he will obtain mercy, because He will abundantly pardon your sins. For my thoughts are not as your thoughts, neither are my ways as your ways; but as far removed as the heavens are from the earth, so far is my way removed from your way, and your thoughts from my thoughts. For as the snow or the rain descends from heaven, and shall not return till it waters the earth, and makes it bring forth and bud, and gives seed to the sower and bread for food, so shall my word be that goeth forth out of my mouth: it shall not return until it shall have accomplished all that I desired, and I shall make my commandments prosperous. For ye shall go out with joy, and be taught with gladness. For the mountains and the hills shall leap while they expect you, and all the trees of the fields shall applaud with their branches: and instead of the thorn shall come up the cypress, and instead of the brier shall come up the myrtle. And the Lord shall be for a name, and for an everlasting sign, and He shall not fail!'[1] Of these and such like words written by the prophets, O Trypho," said I, "some have reference to the first advent of Christ, in which He is preached as inglorious, obscure, and of mortal appearance; but others had reference to His second advent, when He shall appear in glory and above the clouds; and your nation shall see and know Him whom they have pierced, as Hosea, one of the twelve prophets, and Daniel, foretold.

CHAP. XV.—*In what the true fasting consists.*

"Learn, therefore, to keep the true fast of God, as Isaiah says, that you may please God. Isaiah has cried thus: 'Shout vehemently, and do not spare: lift up thy voice as with a trumpet, and show my people their transgressions, and the house of Jacob their sins. They seek me from day to day, and desire to know my ways, as a nation that did righteousness, and forsook not the judgment of God. They ask of me now righteous judgment, and desire to draw near to God, saying, Wherefore have we fasted, and Thou seest not? and afflicted our souls, and Thou hast not known? Because in the days of your fasting you find your own pleasure, and oppress all those who are subject to you. Behold, ye fast

[1] Isa. lv. 3 to end.

for strifes and debates, and smite the humble with your fists. Why do ye fast for me, as to-day, so that your voice is heard aloud? This is not the fast which I have chosen, the day in which a man shall afflict his soul. And not even if you bend your neck like a ring, or clothe yourself in sackcloth and ashes, shall you call this a fast, and a day acceptable to the Lord. This is not the fast which I have chosen, saith the Lord; but loose every unrighteous bond, dissolve the terms of wrongous covenants, let the oppressed go free, and avoid every iniquitous contract. Deal thy bread to the hungry, and lead the homeless poor under thy dwelling; if thou seest the naked, clothe him; and do not hide thyself from thine own flesh. Then shall thy light break forth as the morning, and thy garments[1] shall rise up quickly: and thy righteousness shall go before thee, and the glory of God shall envelope thee. Then shalt thou cry, and the Lord shall hear thee: while thou art speaking, He will say, Behold, I am here. And if thou take away from thee the yoke, and the stretching out of the hand, and the word of murmuring: and shalt give heartily thy bread to the hungry, and shalt satisfy the afflicted soul; then shall thy light arise in the darkness, and thy darkness shall be as the noon-day: and thy God shall be with thee continually, and thou shalt be satisfied according as thy soul desireth, and thy bones shall become fat, and shall be as a watered garden, and as a fountain of water, or as a land where water fails not.'[2] Circumcise, therefore, the foreskin of your heart, as the words of God in all these passages demand.

CHAP. XVI.—*Circumcision given as a sign, that the Jews might be driven away for their evil deeds done to Christ and the Christians.*

"And God himself proclaimed by Moses, speaking thus: 'And circumcise the hardness of your hearts, and no longer stiffen the neck. For the Lord your God is both Lord of lords, and a great, mighty, and terrible God, who regardeth

[1] ἱμάτια; some read ἰάματα, as in LXX., "thy health," the better reading probably.
[2] Isa. lviii. 1–12.

not persons, and taketh not rewards.'[1] And in Leviticus: 'Because they have transgressed against me, and despised me, and because they have walked contrary to me, I also walked contrary to them, and I shall cut them off in the land of their enemies. Then shall their uncircumcised heart be turned.'[2] For the circumcision according to the flesh, which is from Abraham, was given for a sign; that you may be separated from other nations, and from us; and that you alone may suffer that which you now justly suffer; and that your land may be desolate, and your cities burned with fire; and that strangers may eat your fruit in your presence, and not one of you may go up to Jerusalem.[3] For you are not recognised among the rest of men by any other mark than your fleshly circumcision. For none of you, I suppose, will venture to say that God neither did nor does foresee the events which are future, nor fore-ordained his deserts for each one. Accordingly, these things have happened to you in fairness and justice, for you have slain the Just One, and His prophets before Him; and now you reject those who hope in Him, and in Him who sent Him—God the Almighty and Maker of all things—cursing in your synagogues those that believe on Christ. For you have not the power to lay hands upon us, on account of those who now have the mastery. But as often as you could, you did so. Wherefore God, by Isaiah, calls to you, saying, 'Behold how the righteous man perished, and no one regards it. For the righteous man is taken away from before iniquity. His grave shall be in peace, he is taken away from the midst. Draw near hither, ye lawless children, seed of the adulterers, and children of the whore. Against whom have you sported yourselves, and against whom have you opened the mouth, and against whom have you loosened the tongue?'[4]

[1] Deut. x. 16 f. [2] Lev. xxvi. 40, 41.

[3] See *Apol.* i. 47. The Jews were prohibited by law from entering Jerusalem on pain of death. And so Justin sees in circumcision their own punishment.

[4] Isa. lvii. 1–4.

CHAP. XVII.—*The Jews sent persons through the whole earth to spread calumnies on Christians.*

"For other nations have not inflicted on us and on Christ this wrong to such an extent as you have, who in very deed are the authors of the wicked prejudice against the Just One, and us who hold by Him. For after that you had crucified Him, the only blameless and righteous Man,—through whose stripes those who approach the Father by Him are healed,—when you knew that He had risen from the dead and ascended to heaven, as the prophets foretold He would, you not only did not repent of the wickedness which you had committed, but at that time you selected and sent out from Jerusalem chosen men through all the land to tell that the godless heresy of the Christians had sprung up, and to publish those things which all they who knew us not speak against us. So that you are the cause not only of your own unrighteousness, but in fact of that of all other men. And Isaiah cries justly: 'By reason of you, my name is blasphemed among the Gentiles.'[1] And: 'Woe unto their soul! because they have devised an evil device against themselves, saying, Let us bind the righteous, for he is distasteful to us. Therefore they shall eat the fruit of their doings. Woe unto the wicked! evil shall be rendered to him according to the works of his hands.' And again, in other words:[2] 'Woe unto them that draw their iniquity as with a long cord, and their transgressions as with the harness of a heifer's yoke: who say, Let his speed come near; and let the counsel of the Holy One of Israel come, that we may know it. Woe unto them that call evil good, and good evil; that put light for darkness, and darkness for light; that put bitter for sweet, and sweet for bitter!'[3] Accordingly, you displayed great zeal in publishing throughout all the land bitter and dark and unjust things against the only blameless and righteous Light sent by God. For He appeared distasteful to you when He cried among you, 'It is written, My house is the house of prayer; but ye have made it a den of thieves!'[4]

[1] Isa. lii. 5. [2] Isa. iii. 9 ff. [3] Isa. v. 18, 20. [4] Matt. xxi. 13.

He overthrew also the tables of the money-changers in the temple, and exclaimed, 'Woe unto you, scribes and Pharisees, hypocrites! because ye pay tithe of mint and rue, but do not observe the love of God and justice. Ye whited sepulchres! appearing beautiful outward, but are within full of dead men's bones.'[1] And to the scribes, 'Woe unto you, scribes! for ye have the keys, and ye do not enter in yourselves, and them that are entering in ye hinder; ye blind guides!'

CHAP. XVIII.—*Christians would observe the law, if they did not know why it was instituted.*

"For since you have read, O Trypho, as you yourself admitted, the doctrines taught by our Saviour, I do not think that I have done foolishly in adding some short utterances of His to the prophetic statements. Wash therefore, and be now clean, and put away iniquity from your souls, as God bids you be washed in this laver, and be circumcised with the true circumcision. For we too would observe the fleshly circumcision, and the Sabbaths, and in short all the feasts, if we did not know for what reason they were enjoined you,—namely, on account of your transgressions and the hardness of your hearts. For if we patiently endure all things contrived against us by wicked men and demons, so that even amid cruelties unutterable, death and torments, we pray for mercy to those who inflict such things upon us, and do not wish to give the least retort to any one, even as the new Lawgiver commanded us: how is it, Trypho, that we would not observe those rites which do not harm us,—I speak of fleshly circumcision, and Sabbaths, and feasts?"

CHAP. XIX.—*Circumcision unknown before Abraham. The law was given by Moses on account of the hardness of their hearts.*

"It is this about which we are at a loss, and with reason, because, while you endure such things, you do not observe all the other customs which we are now discussing."

[1] This and following quotation taken promiscuously from Matt. xxiii. and Luke xi.

"This circumcision is not, however, necessary for all men, but for you alone, in order that, as I have already said, you may suffer these things which you now justly suffer. Nor do we receive that useless baptism of cisterns, for it has nothing to do with this baptism of life. Wherefore also God has announced that you have forsaken Him, the living fountain, and digged for yourselves broken cisterns which can hold no water. Even you, who are the circumcised according to the flesh, have need of our circumcision; but we, having the latter, do not require the former. For if it were necessary, as you suppose, God would not have made Adam uncircumcised; would not have had respect to the gifts of Abel when, being uncircumcised, he offered sacrifice; and would not have been pleased with the uncircumcision of Enoch, who was not found, because God had translated him. Lot, being uncircumcised, was saved from Sodom, the angels themselves and the Lord sending him out. Noah was the beginning of our race; yet, uncircumcised, along with his children he went into the ark. Melchizedek, the priest of the Most High, was uncircumcised; to whom also Abraham, the first who received circumcision after the flesh, gave tithes, and he blessed him: after whose order God declared, by the mouth of David, that He would establish the everlasting priest. Therefore to you alone this circumcision was necessary, in order that the people may be no people, and the nation no nation; as also Hosea,[1] one of the twelve prophets, declares. Moreover, all those righteous men already mentioned, though they kept no Sabbaths, were pleasing to God; and after them Abraham with all his descendants until Moses, under whom your nation appeared unrighteous and ungrateful to God, making a calf in the wilderness: wherefore God, accommodating himself to that nation, enjoined them also to offer sacrifices, as if to His name, in order that you might not serve idols. Which precept, however, you have not observed; nay, you sacrificed your children to demons. And you were commanded to keep Sabbaths, that you might retain the memorial of God. For His word makes this announcement,

[1] Hos. i. and ii.

saying, 'That ye may know that I am God who redeemed you.'[1]

CHAP. XX.—*Why choice of meats was prescribed.*

"Moreover, you were commanded to abstain from certain kinds of food, in order that you might keep God before your eyes while you ate and drank, seeing that you were prone and very ready to depart from His knowledge, as Moses also affirms: 'The people ate and drank, and rose up to play.'[2] And again: 'Jacob ate, and was satisfied, and waxed fat; and he who was beloved kicked: he waxed fat, he grew thick, he was enlarged, and he forsook God who had made him.'[3] For it was told you by Moses in the book of Genesis, that God granted to Noah, being a just man, to eat of every animal, but not of flesh with the blood, which is *dead*."[4] And as he was ready to say, "as the green herbs," I anticipated him: "Why do you not receive this statement, 'as the green herbs,' in the sense in which it was given by God, to wit, that just as God has granted the herbs for sustenance to man, even so has He given the animals for the diet of flesh? But, you say, a distinction was laid down thereafter to Noah, because we do not eat certain herbs. As you interpret it, the thing is incredible. And first I shall not occupy myself with this, though able to say and to hold that every vegetable is food, and fit to be eaten. But although we discriminate between green herbs, not eating all, we refrain from eating some, not because they are common or unclean, but because they are bitter, or deadly, or thorny. But we lay hands on and take of all herbs which are sweet, very nourishing and good, whether they are marine or land plants. Thus also God by the mouth of Moses commanded you to abstain from unclean and improper[5] and violent animals: when, moreover, though you were eating manna

[1] Ezek. xx. 12. [2] Ex. xxxii. 6. [3] Deut. xxxii. 15.

[4] *νεκριμαῖον*, or "dieth of itself;" com. reading was *ἐκριμαῖον*, which was supposed to be derived from *ἐκρίπτω*, and to mean "which ought to be cast out:" the above was suggested by H. Stephanus.

[5] *ἄδικος καὶ παράνομος.*

in the desert, and were seeing all those wondrous acts wrought for you by God, you made and worshipped the golden calf.[1] Hence he cries continually, and justly, 'They are foolish children, in whom is no faith.'[2]

CHAP. XXI.—*Sabbaths were instituted on account of the people's sins, and not for a work of righteousness.*

"Moreover, that God enjoined you to keep the Sabbath, and imposed on you other precepts for a sign, as I have already said, on account of your unrighteousness, and that of your fathers,—as He declares that for the sake of the nations, lest His name be profaned among them, therefore He permitted some of you to remain alive,—these words of His can prove to you: they are narrated by Ezekiel thus: 'I am the Lord your God; walk in my statutes, and keep my judgments, and take no part in the customs of Egypt; and hallow my Sabbaths; and they shall be a sign between me and you, that ye may know that I am the Lord your God. Notwithstanding ye rebelled against me, and your children walked not in my statutes, neither kept my judgments to do them: which if a man do, he shall live in them. But they polluted my Sabbaths. And I said that I would pour out my fury upon them in the wilderness, to accomplish my anger upon them; yet I did it not; that my name might not be altogether profaned in the sight of the heathen. I led them out before their eyes, and I lifted up mine hand unto them in the wilderness, that I would scatter them among the heathen, and disperse them through the countries; because they had not executed my judgments, but had despised my statutes, and polluted my Sabbaths, and their eyes were after the devices of their fathers. Wherefore I gave them also statutes which were not good, and judgments whereby they

[1] "The reasoning of S. Justin is not quite clear to interpreters. As we abstain from some herbs, not because they are forbidden by law, but because they are deadly; so the law of abstinence from improper and violent animals was imposed not on Noah, but on you as a yoke on account of your sins."—*Maranus.*

[2] Deut. xxxii. 6, 20.

shall not live. And I shall pollute them in their own gifts, that I may destroy all that openeth the womb, when I pass through them.'[1]

CHAP. XXII.—*So also were sacrifices and oblations.*

"And that you may learn that it was for the sins of your own nation, and for their idolatries, and not because there was any necessity for such sacrifices, that they were likewise enjoined, listen to the manner in which He speaks of these by Amos, one of the twelve, saying: 'Woe unto you that desire the day of the Lord! to what end is this day of the Lord for you? It is darkness and not light, as when a man flees from the face of a lion, and a bear meets him; and he goes into his house, and leans his hands against the wall, and the serpent bites him. Shall not the day of the Lord be darkness and not light, even very dark, and no brightness in it? I have hated, I have despised your feast-days, and I will not smell in your solemn assemblies: wherefore, though ye offer me your burnt-offerings and sacrifices, I will not accept them; neither will I regard the peace-offerings of your presence. Take thou away from me the multitude of thy songs and psalms; I will not hear thine instruments. But let judgment be rolled down as water, and righteousness as an impassable torrent. Have ye offered unto me victims and sacrifices in the wilderness, O house of Israel? saith the Lord. And have ye taken up the tabernacle of Moloch, and the star of your god Raphan, the figures which ye made for yourselves? And I will carry you away beyond Damascus, saith the Lord, whose name is the Almighty God. Woe to them that are at ease in Zion, and trust in the mountain of Samaria: those who are named among the chiefs have plucked away the first-fruits of the nations: the house of Israel have entered for themselves. Pass all of you unto Calneh, and see; and from thence go ye unto Hamath the great, and go down thence to Gath of the strangers, the noblest of all these kingdoms, if their boundaries are greater than your boundaries. Ye who come to the evil day, who

[1] Ezek. xx. 19-26.

are approaching, and who hold to false Sabbaths; who lie on beds of ivory, and are at ease upon their couches; who eat the lambs out of the flock, and the sucking calves out of the midst of the herd; who applaud at the sound of the musical instruments; they reckon them as stable, and not as fleeting, who drink wine in bowls, and anoint themselves with the chief ointments, but they are not grieved for the affliction of Joseph. Wherefore now they shall be captives, among the first of the nobles who are carried away; and the house of evil-doers shall be removed, and the neighing of horses shall be taken away from Ephraim.'[1] And again by Jeremiah: 'Collect your flesh, and sacrifices, and eat: for concerning neither sacrifices nor libations did I command your fathers in the day in which I took them by the hand to lead them out of Egypt.'[2] And again by David, in the forty-ninth Psalm, He thus said: 'The God of gods, the Lord, hath spoken, and called the earth, from the rising of the sun unto the going down thereof. Out of Zion is the perfection of His beauty. God, even our God, shall come openly, and shall not keep silence. Fire shall burn before Him, and it shall be very tempestuous round about Him. He shall call to the heavens above, and to the earth, that He may judge His people. Assemble to Him His saints; those that have made a covenant with Him by sacrifices. And the heavens shall declare His righteousnes, for God is judge. Hear, O my people, and I will speak to thee; O Israel, and I will testify to thee: I am God, even thy God. I will not reprove thee for thy sacrifices; thy burnt-offerings are continually before me. I will take no bullocks out of thy house, nor he-goats out of thy folds: for all the beasts of the field are mine, the herds and the oxen on the mountains. I know all the fowls of the heavens, and the beauty of the field is mine. If I were hungry, I would not tell thee; for the world is mine, and the fulness thereof. Will I eat the flesh of bulls, or drink the blood of goats? Offer unto God the sacrifice of praise, and pay thy vows unto the Most High, and call upon me in the day of trouble, and I will deliver thee, and thou

[1] Amos v. 18 to end, vi. 1–7. [2] Jer. vii. 21 f.

shalt glorify me. But unto the wicked God saith, What hast thou to do to declare my statutes, and to take my covenant into thy mouth? But thou hast hated instruction, and cast my words behind thee. When thou sawest a thief, thou consentedst with him; and hast been partaker with the adulterer. Thy mouth has framed evil, and thy tongue has enfolded deceit. Thou sittest and speakest against thy brother; thou slanderest thine own mother's son. These things hast thou done, and I kept silence; thou thoughtest that I would be like thyself in wickedness. I will reprove thee, and set thy sins in order before thine eyes. Now consider this, ye that forget God, lest He tear you in pieces, and there be none to deliver. The sacrifice of praise shall glorify me; and there is the way in which I shall show him my salvation.'[1] Accordingly He neither takes sacrifices from you, nor commanded them at first to be offered because they are needful to Him, but because of your sins. For indeed the temple, which is called the temple in Jerusalem, He admitted to be His house or court, not as though He needed it, but in order that you, in this view of it, giving yourselves to Him, might not worship idols. And that this is so, Isaiah says: 'What house have ye built me? saith the Lord. Heaven is my throne, and earth is my footstool.'[2]

Chap. XXIII.—*The opinion of the Jews regarding the law does an injury to God.*

"But if we do not admit this, we shall be liable to fall into foolish opinions, as if it were not the same God who existed in the times of Enoch and all the rest, who neither were circumcised after the flesh, nor observed Sabbaths, nor any other rites, seeing that Moses enjoined such observances; or that God has not wished each race of mankind continually to perform the same righteous actions: to admit which, seems to be ridiculous and absurd. Therefore we must confess that He, who is ever the same, has commanded these and such like institutions on account of sinful men, and we must declare Him to be benevolent, foreknowing, needing

[1] Ps. l. (in E. V.).
[2] Isa. lxvi. 1.

nothing, righteous and good. But if this be not so, tell me, sir, what you think of those matters which we are investigating." And when no one responded: "Wherefore, Trypho, I will proclaim to you, and to those who wish to become proselytes, the divine message which I heard from that man.[1] Do you see that the elements are not idle, and keep no Sabbaths? Remain as you were born. For if there was no need of circumcision before Abraham, or of the observance of Sabbaths, of feasts and sacrifices, before Moses; no more need is there of them now, after that, according to the will of God, Jesus Christ the Son of God has been born without sin, of a virgin sprung from the stock of Abraham. For when Abraham himself was in uncircumcision, he was justified and blessed by reason of the faith which he reposed in God, as the Scripture tells. Moreover, the Scriptures and the facts themselves compel us to admit that He received circumcision for a sign, and not for righteousness. So that it was justly recorded concerning the people, that the soul which shall not be circumcised on the eighth day shall be cut off from his family. And, furthermore, the inability of the female sex to receive fleshly circumcision, proves that this circumcision has been given for a sign, and not for a work of righteousness. For God has given likewise to women the ability to observe all things which are righteous and virtuous; but we see that the bodily form of the male has been made different from the bodily form of the female; yet we know that neither of them is righteous or unrighteous merely for this cause, but [is considered righteous] by reason of piety and righteousness.

CHAP. XXIV.—*The Christians' circumcision far more excellent.*

"Now, sirs," I said, "it is possible for us to show how the eighth day possessed a certain mysterious import, which the seventh day did not possess, and which was promulgated by God through these rites. But lest I appear now to diverge to other subjects, understand what I say: the

[1] The man he met by the sea-shore.

blood of that circumcision is obsolete, and we trust in the blood of salvation; there is now another covenant, and another law has gone forth from Zion. Jesus Christ circumcises all who will—as was declared above—with knives of stone;[1] that they may be a righteous nation, a people keeping faith, holding to the truth, and maintaining peace. Come then with me, all who fear God, who wish to see the good of Jerusalem. Come, let us go to the light of the Lord; for He has liberated His people, the house of Jacob. Come, all nations; let us gather ourselves together at Jerusalem, no longer plagued by war for the sins of her people. 'For I was manifest to them that sought me not; I was found of them that asked not for me;'[2] He exclaims by Isaiah: 'I said, Behold me, unto nations which were not called by my name. I have spread out my hands all the day unto a disobedient and gainsaying people, which walked in a way that was not good, but after their own sins. It is a people that provoketh me to my face.'[2]

CHAP. XXV.—*The Jews boast in vain that they are sons of Abraham.*

"Those who justify themselves, and say they are sons of Abraham, shall be desirous even in a small degree to receive the inheritance along with you;[3] as the Holy Spirit, by the mouth of Isaiah, cries, speaking thus while he personates them: 'Return from heaven, and behold from the habitation of Thy holiness and glory. Where is Thy zeal and strength? Where is the multitude of Thy mercy? for Thou hast sustained us, O Lord. For Thou art our Father, because Abraham is ignorant of us, and Israel has not recognised us. But Thou, O Lord, our Father, deliver us: from the beginning Thy name is upon us. O Lord, why hast Thou made us to err from Thy way? and hardened our hearts, so that we do not fear Thee? Return for Thy servants' sake, the tribes of Thine inheritance, that we may inherit for a little Thy holy mountain. We were as from the beginning, when

[1] Josh. v. 2; Isa. xxvi. 2, 3. [2] Isa. lxv. 1-3.
[3] Other edd. have, "with us."

Thou didst not bear rule over us, and when Thy name was not called upon us. If Thou wilt open the heavens, trembling shall seize the mountains before Thee: and they shall be melted, as wax melts before the fire; and fire shall consume the adversaries, and Thy name shall be manifest among the adversaries; the nations shall be put into disorder before Thy face. When Thou shalt do glorious things, trembling shall seize the mountains before Thee. From the beginning we have not heard, nor have our eyes seen a God besides Thee: and Thy works,[1] the mercy which Thou shalt show to those who repent. He shall meet those who do righteousness, and they shall remember Thy ways. Behold, Thou art wroth, and we were sinning. Therefore we have erred and become all unclean, and all our righteousness is as the rags of a woman set apart: and we have faded away like leaves by reason of our iniquities; thus the wind will take us away. And there is none that calleth upon Thy name, or remembers to take hold of Thee; for Thou hast turned away Thy face from us, and hast given us up on account of our sins. And now return, O Lord, for we are all Thy people. The city of Thy holiness has become desolate. Zion has become as a wilderness, Jerusalem a curse; the house, our holiness, and the glory which our fathers blessed, has been burned with fire; and all the glorious nations[2] have fallen along with it. And in addition to these [misfortunes], O Lord, Thou hast refrained Thyself, and art silent, and hast humbled us very much.' "[3]

And Trypho remarked, "What is this you say? that none of us shall inherit anything on the holy mountain of God?"

Chap. xxvi.—*No salvation to the Jews except through Christ.*

And I replied, "I do not say so; but those who have persecuted and do persecute Christ, if they do not repent,

[1] Otto reads: "Thy works which Thou shalt do to those who wait for mercy."

[2] Some suppose the correct reading to be, "our glorious *institutions* have," etc., ἔθη for ἔθνη.

[3] Isa. lxiii. 15 to end, and lxiv.

shall not inherit anything on the holy mountain. But the Gentiles, who have believed on Him, and have repented of the sins which they have committed, they shall receive the inheritance along with the patriarchs and the prophets, and the just men who are descended from Jacob, even although they neither keep the Sabbath, nor are circumcised, nor observe the feasts. Assuredly they shall receive the holy inheritance of God. For God speaks by Isaiah thus: 'I, the Lord God, have called Thee in righteousness, and will hold Thine hand, and will strengthen Thee; and I have given Thee for a covenant of the people, for a light of the Gentiles, to open the eyes of the blind, to bring out them that are bound from the chains, and those who sit in darkness from the prison-house.'[1] And again: 'Lift up a standard[2] for the people; for, lo, the Lord has made it heard unto the end of the earth. Say ye to the daughters of Zion, Behold, thy Saviour has come; having His reward, and His work before His face: and He shall call it a holy nation, redeemed by the Lord. And thou shalt be called a city sought out, and not forsaken. Who is this that cometh from Edom? in red garments from Bosor? This that is beautiful in apparel, going up with great strength? I speak righteousness, and the judgment of salvation. Why are Thy garments red, and Thine apparel as from the trodden wine-press? Thou art full of the trodden grape. I have trodden the wine-press all alone, and of the people there is no man with me; and I have trampled them in fury, and crushed them to the ground, and spilled their blood on the earth. For the day of retribution has come upon them, and the year of redemption is present. And I looked, and there was none to help; and I considered, and none assisted: and my arm delivered; and my fury came on them, and I trampled them in my fury, and spilled their blood on the earth.' "[3]

[1] Isa. xlii. 6, 7.

[2] συσσεισμόν, "a shaking," is the original reading; but LXX. has σύσσημον, a standard or signal, and this most edd. adopt.

[3] Isa lxii. 10 to end, lxiii. 1–6

CHAP. XXVII.—*Why God taught the same things by the prophets as by Moses.*

And Trypho said, "Why do you select and quote whatever you wish from the prophetic writings, but do not refer to those which expressly command the Sabbath to be observed? For Isaiah thus speaks: 'If thou shalt turn away thy foot from the Sabbaths, so as not to do thy pleasure on the holy day, and shalt call the Sabbaths the holy delights of thy God; if thou shalt not lift thy foot to work, and shalt not speak a word from thine own mouth; then thou shalt trust in the Lord, and He shall cause thee to go up to the good things of the land; and He shall feed thee with the inheritance of Jacob thy father: for the mouth of the Lord hath spoken it.'"[1]

And I replied, "I have passed them by, my friends, not because such prophecies were contrary to me, but because you have understood, and do understand, that although God commands you by all the prophets to do the same things which He also commanded by Moses, it was on account of the hardness of your hearts, and your ingratitude towards Him, that He continually proclaims them, in order that, even in this way, if you repented, you might please Him, and neither sacrifice your children to demons, nor be partakers with thieves, nor lovers of gifts, nor hunters after revenge, nor fail in doing judgment for orphans, nor be inattentive to the justice due to the widow, nor have your hands full of blood. 'For the daughters of Zion have walked with a high neck, both sporting by winking with their eyes, and sweeping along their dresses.[2] For they are all gone aside,' He exclaims, 'they are all become useless. There is none that understands, there is not so much as one. With their tongues they have practised deceit, their throat is an open sepulchre, the poison of asps is under their lips, destruction and misery are in their paths, and the way of peace they have not known.'[3] So that, as in the beginning, these things were enjoined you because of your wickedness, in like manner

[1] Isa. lviii. 13, 14. [2] Isa. iii. 16.

[3] Various passages strung together; comp. Rom. iii. 10, and foll. verses.

because of your stedfastness in it, or rather your increased proneness to it, by means of the same precepts He calls you to a remembrance or knowledge of it. But you are a people hard-hearted and without understanding, both blind and lame, children in whom is no faith, as He Himself says, honouring Him only with your lips, far from Him in your hearts, teaching doctrines that are your own and not His. For, tell me, did God wish the priests to sin when they offer the sacrifices on the Sabbaths? or those to sin, who are circumcised and do circumcise on the Sabbaths; since He commands that on the eighth day—even though it happen to be a Sabbath—those who are born shall be always circumcised? or could not the infants be operated upon one day previous or one day subsequent to the Sabbath, if He knew that it is a sinful act upon the Sabbaths? Or why did He not teach those—who are called righteous and pleasing to Him, who lived before Moses and Abraham, who were not circumcised in their foreskin, and observed no Sabbaths—to keep these institutions?"

CHAP. XXVIII.—*True righteousness is obtained by Christ.*

And Trypho replied, "We heard you adducing this consideration a little ago, and we have given it attention: for, to tell the truth, it is worthy of attention; and that answer which pleases most—namely, that so it seemed good to Him—does not satisfy me. For this is ever the shift to which those have recourse who are unable to answer the question."

Then I said, "Since I bring from the Scriptures and the facts themselves both the proofs and the inculcation of them, do not delay or hesitate to put faith in me, although I am an uncircumcised man; so short a time is left you in which to become proselytes. If Christ's coming shall have anticipated you, in vain you will repent, in vain you will weep; for He will not hear you. 'Break up your fallow ground,' Jeremiah has cried to the people, 'and sow not among thorns. Circumcise yourselves to the Lord, and circumcise the foreskin of your heart.'[1] Do not sow, therefore, among thorns, and in untilled ground, whence you can have no fruit. Know

[1] Jer. iv. 3.

Christ; and behold the fallow ground, good, good and fat, is in your hearts. 'For, behold, the days come, saith the Lord, that I will visit all them that are circumcised in their foreskins; Egypt, and Judah,[1] and Edom, and the sons of Moab. For all the nations are uncircumcised, and all the house of Israel are uncircumcised in their hearts.'[2] Do you see how that God does not mean this circumcision which is given for a sign? For it is of no use to the Egyptians, or the sons of Moab, or the sons of Edom. But though a man be a Scythian or a Persian, if he has the knowledge of God and of His Christ, and keeps the everlasting righteous decrees, he is circumcised with the good and useful circumcision, and is a friend of God, and God rejoices in his gifts and offerings. But I will lay before you, my friends, the very words of God, when He said to the people by Malachi, one of the twelve prophets, 'I have no pleasure in you, saith the Lord; and I shall not accept your sacrifices at your hands: for from the rising of the sun unto its setting my name shall be glorified among the Gentiles; and in every place a sacrifice is offered unto my name, even a pure sacrifice: for my name is honoured among the Gentiles, saith the Lord; but ye profane it.'[3] And by David He said, 'A people whom I have not known, served me; at the hearing of the ear they obeyed me.'[4]

CHAP. XXIX.—*Christ is useless to those who observe the law.*

"Let us glorify God, all nations gathered together; for He has also visited us. Let us glorify Him by the King of glory, by the Lord of hosts. For He has been gracious towards the Gentiles also; and our sacrifices He esteems more grateful than yours. What need, then, have I of circumcision, who have been witnessed to by God? What need have I of that other baptism, who have been baptized with the Holy Ghost? I think that while I mention this I would persuade even those who are possessed of scanty intelligence. For these words have neither been prepared by me, nor

[1] So in A. V., but supposed to be Idumæa.
[2] Jer. ix. 25 f.
[3] Mal. i. 10, etc.
[4] Ps. xviii. 43.

embellished by the art of man; but David sung them, Isaiah preached them, Zechariah proclaimed them, and Moses wrote them. Are you acquainted with them, Trypho? They are contained in your Scriptures, or rather not yours, but ours. For we believe them; but you, though you read them, do not catch the spirit that is in them. Be not offended at, or reproach us with, the bodily uncircumcision with which God has created us; and think it not strange that we drink hot water on the Sabbaths, since God directs the government of the universe on this day equally as on all others; and the priests, as on other days, so on this, are ordered to offer sacrifices; and there are so many righteous men who have performed none of these legal ceremonies, and yet are witnessed to by God Himself.

CHAP. XXX.—*Christians possess the true righteousness.*

"But impute it to your own wickedness, that God even can be accused by those who have no understanding, of not having always instructed all in the same righteous statutes. For such institutions seemed to be unreasonable and unworthy of God to many men, who had not received grace to know that your nation were called to conversion and repentance of spirit,[1] while they were in a sinful condition and labouring under spiritual disease; and that the prophecy which was announced subsequent to the death of Moses is everlasting. And this is mentioned in the Psalm,[2] my friends. And that we, who have been made wise by them, confess that the statutes of the Lord are sweeter than honey and the honey-comb, is manifest from the fact that, though threatened with death, we do not deny His name. Moreover, it is also manifest to all, that we who believe in Him pray to be kept by Him from strange, *i.e.* from wicked and deceitful, spirits; as the word of prophecy, personating one of those who believe in Him, figuratively declares. For we do con-

[1] Or, "repentance of the Father;" *πατρός* for *πνεύματος*. Maranus explains the confusion on the ground of the similarity between the contractions for the words, *πρς* and *πνς*.

[2] Ps. xix.

tinually beseech God by Jesus Christ to preserve us from the demons which are hostile to the worship of God, and whom we of old time served, in order that, after our conversion by Him to God, we may be blameless. For we call Him Helper and Redeemer, the power of whose name even the demons do fear; and at this day, when they are exorcised in the name of Jesus Christ, crucified under Pontius Pilate, governor of Judæa, they are overcome. And thus it is manifest to all, that His Father has given Him so great power, by virtue of which demons are subdued to His name, and to the dispensation of His suffering.

CHAP. XXXI.—*If Christ's power be now so great, how much greater at the second advent!*

"But if so great a power is shown to have followed and to be still following the dispensation of His suffering, how great shall that be which shall follow His glorious advent! For He shall come on the clouds as the Son of man, so Daniel foretold, and His angels shall come with Him. These are the words: 'I beheld till the thrones were set; and the Ancient of days did sit, whose garment was white as snow, and the hair of His head like the pure wool. His throne was like a fiery flame, His wheels as burning fire. A fiery stream issued and came forth from before Him. Thousand thousands ministered unto Him, and ten thousand times ten thousand stood before Him. The books were opened, and the judgment was set. I beheld then the voice of the great words which the horn speaks: and the beast was beat down, and his body destroyed, and given to the burning flame. And the rest of the beasts were taken away from their dominion, and a period of life was given to the beasts until a season and time. I saw in the vision of the night, and, behold, one like the Son of man coming with the clouds of heaven; and He came to the Ancient of days, and stood before Him. And they who stood by brought Him near; and there were given Him power and kingly honour, and all nations of the earth by their families, and all glory, serve Him. And His dominion is an everlasting dominion, which shall not be taken away; and His kingdom shall not be destroyed. And my spirit was chilled within my frame, and the visions of my head troubled me. I came near unto one of them that stood by, and inquired the precise meaning of all these things. In answer he speaks to me, and showed me the judgment of the matters: These great beasts are four kingdoms, which shall perish from the earth, and shall not receive dominion for ever, even for ever and ever. Then I wished to know exactly about the fourth beast, which destroyed all [the others] and was very terrible, its teeth of iron, and its nails of brass; which devoured, made waste, and stamped the residue with its feet: also about the ten horns upon its head, and of the one which came up, by means of which three of the former fell. And that horn had eyes, and a mouth speaking great things; and its countenance excelled the rest. And I beheld that horn waging war against the saints, and prevailing against them, until the Ancient of days came; and He gave judgment for the saints of the Most High. And the time came, and the saints of the Most High possessed the kingdom. And it was told me concerning the fourth beast: There shall be a fourth kingdom upon earth, which shall prevail over all these kingdoms, and shall devour the whole earth, and shall destroy and make it thoroughly waste. And the ten horns are ten kings that shall arise; and one shall arise after them;[1] and he shall surpass the first in evil deeds, and he shall subdue three kings, and he shall speak words against the Most High, and shall overthrow the rest of the saints of the Most High, and shall expect to change the seasons and the times. And it shall be delivered into his hands for a time, and times, and half a time. And the judgment sat, and they shall take away his dominion, to consume and to destroy it unto the end. And the kingdom, and the power, and the great places of the kingdoms under the heavens, were given to the holy people of the Most High, to reign in an everlasting kingdom: and all powers shall be subject to Him, and shall obey Him. Hitherto is the end of the matter. I, Daniel, was

[1] Literally, "And the ten horns, ten kings shall arise after them."

possessed with a very great astonishment, and my speech was changed in me; yet I kept the matter in my heart.' "[1]

CHAP. XXXII.—*Trypho objecting that Christ is described as glorious by Daniel, Justin distinguishes two advents.*

And when I had ceased, Trypho said, "These and such like scriptures, sir, compel us to wait for Him who, as Son of man, receives from the Ancient of days the everlasting kingdom. But this so-called Christ of yours was dishonourable and inglorious, so much so that the last curse contained in the law of God fell on him, for he was crucified."

Then I replied to him, "If, sirs, it were not said by the scriptures which I have already quoted, that His form was inglorious, and His generation not declared, and that for His death the rich would suffer death, and with His stripes we should be healed, and that He would be led away like a sheep; and if I had not explained that there would be two advents of His,—one in which He was pierced by you; a second, when you shall know Him whom you have pierced, and your tribes shall mourn, each tribe by itself, the women apart, and the men apart,—then I must have been speaking dubious and obscure things. But now, by means of the contents of those Scriptures esteemed holy and prophetic amongst you, I attempt to prove all [that I have adduced], in the hope that some one of you may be found to be of that remnant which has been left by the grace of the Lord of Sabaoth for the eternal salvation. In order, therefore, that the matter inquired into may be plainer to you, I will mention to you other words also spoken by the blessed David, from which you will perceive that the Lord is called the Christ by the Holy Spirit of prophecy; and that the Lord, the Father of all, has brought Him again from the earth, setting Him at His own right hand, until He makes His enemies His footstool; which indeed happens from the time that our Lord Jesus Christ ascended to heaven, after He rose again from the dead, the times now running on to their consummation; and he whom Daniel foretells would have dominion for a

[1] Dan. vii. 9–28.

time, and times, and an half, is even already at the door, about to speak blasphemous and daring things against the Most High. But you, being ignorant of how long he will have dominion, hold another opinion. For you interpret the 'time' as being a hundred years. But if this is so, the man of sin must, at the shortest, reign three hundred and fifty years, in order that we may compute that which is said by the holy Daniel—'and times'—to be *two* times only. All this I have said to you in digression, in order that you at length may be persuaded of what has been declared against you by God, that you are foolish sons; and of this, 'Therefore, behold, I will proceed to take away this people, and shall take them away; and I will strip the wise of their wisdom, and will hide the understanding of their prudent men;'[1] and may cease to deceive yourselves and those who hear you, and may learn of us, who have been taught wisdom by the grace of Christ. The words, then, which were spoken by David, are these:[2] 'The Lord said unto my Lord, Sit Thou at my right hand, until I make Thine enemies Thy footstool. The Lord shall send the rod of Thy strength out of Sion: rule Thou also in the midst of Thine enemies. With Thee shall be, in the day, the chief of Thy power, in the beauties of Thy saints. From the womb, before the morning star, have I begotten Thee. The Lord hath sworn, and will not repent: Thou art a priest for ever after the order of Melchizedek. The Lord is at Thy right hand: He has crushed kings in the day of His wrath: He shall judge among the heathen, He shall fill [with] the dead bodies.[3] He shall drink of the brook in the way; therefore shall He lift up the head.'

CHAP. XXXIII.—*Ps.* cx. *is not spoken of Hezekiah. He proves that Christ was first humble, then shall be glorious.*

"And," I continued, "I am not ignorant that you venture to expound this psalm as if it referred to king Hezekiah; but

[1] Isa. xxix. 14. [2] Ps. cx.

[3] πληρώσει πτώματα; Lat. version, *implebit ruinas.* Thirlby suggested that an omission has taken place in the MSS. by the transcriber's fault.

that you are mistaken, I shall prove to you from these very words forthwith. 'The Lord hath sworn, and will not repent,' it is said; and, 'Thou art a priest for ever, after the order of Melchizedek,' with what follows and precedes. Not even you will venture to object that Hezekiah was either a priest, or is the everlasting priest of God; but that this is spoken of our Jesus, these expressions show. But your ears are shut up, and your hearts are made dull.[1] For by this statement, 'The Lord hath sworn, and will not repent: Thou art a priest for ever, after the order of Melchizedek,' with an oath God has shown Him (on account of your unbelief) to be the High Priest after the order of Melchizedek; *i.e.* as Melchizedek was described by Moses as the priest of the Most High, and he was a priest of those who were in uncircumcision, and blessed the circumcised Abraham who brought him tithes, so God has shown that His everlasting Priest, called also by the Holy Spirit Lord, would be Priest of those in uncircumcision. Those too in circumcision who approach Him, that is, believing Him and seeking blessings from Him, He will both receive and bless. And that He shall be first humble as a man, and then exalted, these words at the end of the Psalm show: 'He shall drink of the brook in the way,' and then, 'Therefore shall He lift up the head.'

CHAP. XXXIV.—*Nor does Ps.* lxxii. *apply to Solomon, whose faults Christians shudder at.*

"Further, to persuade you that you have not understood anything of the Scriptures, I will remind you of another psalm, dictated to David by the Holy Spirit, which you say refers to Solomon, who was also your king. But it refers also to our Christ. But you deceive yourselves by the ambiguous forms of speech. For where it is said, 'The law of the Lord is perfect,' you do not understand it of the law which was to be after Moses, but of the law which was given by Moses, although God declared that He would establish a new law and a new covenant. And where it has been said,

[1] πεπήρωνται. Maranus thinks πεπώρονται more probable, "hardened."

'O God, give Thy judgment to the king,' since Solomon was king, you say that the Psalm refers to him, although the words of the Psalm expressly proclaim that reference is made to the everlasting King, *i.e.* to Christ. For Christ is King, and Priest, and God, and Lord, and angel, and man, and captain, and stone, and a Son born, and first made subject to suffering, then returning to heaven, and again coming with glory, and He is preached as having the everlasting kingdom: so I prove from all the Scriptures. But that you may perceive what I have said, I quote the words of the Psalm; they are these: 'O God, give Thy judgment to the king, and Thy righteousness unto the king's son, to judge Thy people with righteousness, and Thy poor with judgment. The mountains shall take up peace to the people, and the little hills righteousness. He shall judge the poor of the people, and shall save the children of the needy, and shall abase the slanderer. He shall co-endure with the sun, and before the moon unto all generations. He shall come down like rain upon the fleece, as drops falling on the earth. In His days shall righteousness flourish, and abundance of peace until the moon be taken away. And He shall have dominion from sea to sea, and from the rivers unto the ends of the earth. Ethiopians shall fall down before Him, and His enemies shall lick the dust. The kings of Tarshish and the isles shall offer gifts; the kings of Arabia and Seba shall offer gifts; and all the kings of the earth shall worship Him, and all the nations shall serve Him: for He has delivered the poor from the man of power, and the needy that hath no helper. He shall spare the poor and needy, and shall save the souls of the needy: He shall redeem their souls from usury and injustice, and His name shall be honourable before them. And He shall live, and to Him shall be given of the gold of Arabia, and they shall pray continually for Him: they shall bless Him all the day. And there shall be a foundation on the earth, it shall be exalted on the tops of the mountains: His fruit shall be on Lebanon, and they of the city shall flourish like grass of the earth. His name shall be blessed for ever. His name shall endure before the sun; and all tribes of the earth shall be blessed in Him, all nations shall call Him blessed. Blessed be the Lord, the God of Israel, who only doeth wondrous things; and blessed be His glorious name for ever, and for ever and ever; and the whole earth shall be filled with His glory. Amen, amen.'[1] And at the close of this Psalm which I have quoted, it is written, 'The hymns of David the son of Jesse are ended.' Moreover, that Solomon was a renowned and great king, by whom the temple called that at Jerusalem was built, I know; but that none of those things mentioned in the Psalm happened to him, is evident. For neither did all kings worship him; nor did he reign to the ends of the earth; nor did his enemies, falling before him, lick the dust. Nay, also, I venture to repeat what is written in the book of Kings as committed by him, how through a woman's influence he worshipped the idols of Sidon, which those of the Gentiles who know God, the Maker of all things through Jesus the crucified, do not venture to do, but abide every torture and vengeance even to the extremity of death, rather than worship idols, or eat meat offered to idols."

CHAP. XXXV.—*Heretics confirm the catholics in the faith.*

And Trypho said, "I believe, however, that many of those who say that they confess Jesus, and are called Christians, eat meats offered to idols, and declare that they are by no means injured in consequence." And I replied, "The fact that there are such men confessing themselves to be Christians, and admitting the crucified Jesus to be both Lord and Christ, yet not teaching His doctrines, but those of the spirits of error, causes us who are disciples of the true and pure doctrine of Jesus Christ, to be more faithful and stedfast in the hope announced by Him. For what things He predicted would take place in His name, these we do see being actually accomplished in our sight. For He said, 'Many shall come in my name, clothed outwardly in sheep's clothing, but inwardly they are ravening wolves.'[2] And, 'There shall be schisms and heresies.'[3] And, 'Beware of

[1] Ps. lxxii. [2] Matt. vii. 15. [3] 1 Cor. xi. 19.

false prophets, who shall come to you clothed outwardly in sheep's clothing, but inwardly they are ravening wolves.'[1] And, 'Many false Christs and false apostles shall arise, and shall deceive many of the faithful.'[2] There are, therefore, and there were many, my friends, who, coming forward in the name of Jesus, taught both to speak and act impious and blasphemous things; and these are called by us after the name of the men from whom each doctrine and opinion had its origin. (For some in one way, others in another, teach to blaspheme the Maker of all things, and Christ, who was foretold by Him as coming, and the God of Abraham, and of Isaac, and of Jacob, with whom we have nothing in common, since we know them to be atheists, impious, unrighteous, and sinful, and confessors of Jesus in name only, instead of worshippers of Him. Yet they style themselves Christians, just as certain among the Gentiles inscribe the name of God upon the works of their own hands, and partake in nefarious and impious rites.) Some are called Marcians, and some Valentinians, and some Basilidians, and some Saturnilians, and others by other names; each called after the originator of the individual opinion, just as each one of those who consider themselves philosophers, as I said before, thinks he must bear the name of the philosophy which he follows, from the name of the father of the particular doctrine. So that, in consequence of these events, we know that Jesus foreknew what would happen after Him, as well as in consequence of many other events which He foretold would befall those who believed on and confessed Him, the Christ. For all that we suffer, even when killed by friends, He foretold would take place; so that it is manifest no word or act of His can be found fault with. Wherefore we pray for you and for all other men who hate us; in order that you, having repented along with us, may not blaspheme Him who, by His works, by the mighty deeds even now wrought through His name, by the words He taught, by the prophecies announced concerning Him, is the blameless, and in all things irreproachable, Christ Jesus; but, believing on

[1] Matt. vii. 15. [2] Matt. xxiv. 11.

Him, may be saved in His second glorious advent, and may not be condemned to fire by Him."

CHAP. XXXVI.—*He proves that Christ is called Lord of hosts.*

Then he replied, "Let these things be so as you say—namely, that it was foretold Christ would suffer, and be called a stone; and after His first appearance, in which it had been announced He would suffer, would come in glory, and be Judge finally of all, and eternal King and Priest. Now show if this man be He of whom these prophecies were made."

And I said, "As you wish, Trypho, I shall come to these proofs which you seek in the fitting place; but now you will permit me first to recount the prophecies, which I wish to do in order to prove that Christ is called both God and Lord of hosts, and Jacob, in parable by the Holy Spirit; and your interpreters, as God says, are foolish, since they say that reference is made to Solomon and not to Christ, when he bore the ark of testimony into the temple which he built. The Psalm of David is this: 'The earth is the Lord's, and the fulness thereof; the world, and all that dwell therein. He hath founded it upon the seas, and prepared it upon the floods. Who shall ascend into the hill of the Lord? or who shall stand in His holy place? He that is clean of hands and pure of heart: who has not received his soul in vain, and has not sworn guilefully to his neighbour: he shall receive blessing from the Lord, and mercy from God his Saviour. This is the generation of them that seek the Lord, that seek the face of the God of Jacob.[1] Lift up your gates, ye rulers; and be ye lift up, ye everlasting doors; and the King of glory shall come in. Who is this King of glory? The Lord strong and mighty in battle. Lift up your gates, ye rulers; and be ye lift up, ye everlasting doors; and the King of glory shall come in. Who is this King of glory? The Lord of hosts, He is the King of glory.'[2] Accordingly, it is shown that

[1] Maranus remarks from Thirlby: "As Justin wrote a little before, 'and is called Jacob in parable,' it seems to convince us that Justin wrote, 'thy face, O Jacob.'"

[2] Ps. xxiv.

Solomon is not the Lord of hosts; but when our Christ rose from the dead and ascended to heaven, the rulers in heaven, under appointment of God, are commanded to open the gates of heaven, that He who is King of glory may enter in, and having ascended, may sit on the right hand of the Father until He make the enemies His footstool, as has been made manifest by another Psalm. For when the rulers of heaven saw Him of uncomely and dishonoured appearance, and inglorious, not recognising Him, they inquired, 'Who is this King of glory?' And the Holy Spirit, either from the person of His Father, or from His own person, answers them, 'The Lord of hosts, He is this King of glory.' For every one will confess that not one of those who presided over the gates of the temple at Jerusalem would venture to say concerning Solomon, though he was so glorious a king, or concerning the ark of testimony, 'Who is this King of glory?'

CHAP. XXXVII.—*The same is proved from other Psalms.*

"Moreover, in the diapsalm of the forty-sixth Psalm, reference is thus made to Christ: 'God went up with a shout, the Lord with the sound of a trumpet. Sing ye to our God, sing ye: sing to our King, sing ye; for God is King of all the earth: sing with understanding. God has ruled over the nations. God sits upon His holy throne. The rulers of the nations were assembled along with the God of Abraham, for the strong ones of God are greatly exalted on the earth.'[1] And in the ninety-eighth Psalm, the Holy Spirit reproaches you, and predicts Him whom you do not wish to be king to be King and Lord, both of Samuel, and of Aaron, and of Moses, and, in short, of all the others. And the words of the Psalm are these: 'The Lord has reigned, let the nations be angry: [it is] He who sits upon the cherubim, let the earth be shaken. The Lord is great in Zion, and He is high above all the nations. Let them confess Thy great name, for it is fearful and holy, and the honour of the King loves judgment. Thou hast prepared equity; judgment and righteousness hast Thou performed in Jacob. Exalt the Lord

[1] Ps. xlvii. 6-10.

our God, and worship the footstool of His feet; for He is holy. Moses and Aaron among His priests, and Samuel among those who call upon His name. They called (says the Scripture) on the Lord, and He heard them. In the pillar of the cloud He spake to them; for[1] they kept His testimonies, and the commandment which He gave them. O Lord our God, Thou heardest them: O God, Thou wert propitious to them, and [yet] taking vengeance on all their inventions. Exalt the Lord our God, and worship at His holy hill; for the Lord our God is holy.'"[2]

CHAP. XXXVIII.—*It is an annoyance to the Jew that Christ is said to be adored. Justin confirms it, however, from Ps.* xlv.

And Trypho said, "Sir, it were good for us if we obeyed our teachers, who laid down a law that we should have no intercourse with any of you, and that we should not have even any communication with you on these questions. For you utter many blasphemies, in that you seek to persuade us that this crucified man was with Moses and Aaron, and spoke to them in the pillar of the cloud; then that he became man, was crucified, and ascended up to heaven, and comes again to earth, and ought to be worshipped."

Then I answered, "I know that, as the word of God says, this great wisdom of God, the Maker of all things, and the Almighty, is hid from you. Wherefore, in sympathy with you, I am striving to the utmost that you may understand these matters which to you are paradoxical; but if not, that I myself may be innocent in the day of judgment. For you shall hear other words which appear still more paradoxical; but be not confounded, nay, rather remain still more zealous hearers and investigators, despising the tradition of your teachers, since they are convicted by the Holy Spirit of inability to perceive the truths taught by God, and of preferring to teach their own doctrines. Accordingly, in the forty-fourth [forty-fifth] Psalm, these words are in like manner referred to Christ: 'My heart has brought forth a good matter; I tell my works to the King. My tongue is the pen

[1] "For" wanting in both Codd.

[2] Ps. xcix.

of a ready writer. Fairer in beauty than the sons of men: grace is poured forth into Thy lips: therefore hath God blessed Thee for ever. Gird Thy sword upon Thy thigh, O mighty One. Press on in Thy fairness and in Thy beauty, and prosper and reign, because of truth, and of meekness, and of righteousness: and Thy right hand shall instruct Thee marvellously. Thine arrows are sharpened, O mighty One; the people shall fall under Thee; in the heart of the enemies of the King [the arrows are fixed]. Thy throne, O God, is for ever and ever: a sceptre of equity is the sceptre of Thy kingdom. Thou hast loved righteousness, and hast hated iniquity; therefore thy God[1] hath anointed Thee with the oil of gladness above Thy fellows. [He hath anointed Thee] with myrrh, and oil,[2] and cassia, from Thy garments; from the ivory palaces, whereby they made Thee glad. Kings' daughters are in Thy honour. The queen stood at Thy right hand, clad in garments[3] embroidered with gold. Hearken, O daughter, and behold, and incline thine ear, and forget thy people and the house of thy father: and the King shall desire thy beauty; because He is thy Lord, they shall worship Him also. And the daughter of Tyre [shall be there] with gifts. The rich of the people shall entreat Thy face. All the glory of the King's daughter [is] within, clad in embroidered garments of needlework. The virgins that follow her shall be brought to the King; her neighbours shall be brought unto Thee: they shall be brought with joy and gladness: they shall be led into the King's shrine. Instead of thy fathers, thy sons have been born: Thou shalt appoint them rulers over all the earth. I shall remember Thy name in every generation: therefore the people shall confess Thee for ever, and for ever and ever.'

CHAP. XXXIX.—*The Jews hate the Christians who believe this. How great the distinction is between both!*

"Now it is not surprising," I continued, "that you hate us who hold these opinions, and convict you of a continual

[1] Or, "God, thy God."

[2] στακτή.

[3] Literally, "garments of gold, variegated."

hardness of heart.[1] For indeed Elijah, conversing with God concerning you, speaks thus: 'Lord, they have slain Thy prophets, and digged down Thine altars: and I am left alone, and they seek my life.' And He answers him: 'I have still seven thousand men who have not bowed the knee to Baal.'[2] Therefore, just as God did not inflict His anger on account of those seven thousand men, even so He has now neither yet inflicted judgment, nor does inflict it, knowing that daily some [of you] are becoming disciples in the name of Christ, and quitting the path of error; who are also receiving gifts, each as he is worthy, illumined through the name of this Christ. For one receives the spirit of understanding, another of counsel, another of strength, another of healing, another of foreknowledge, another of teaching, and another of the fear of God."

To this Trypho said to me, "I wish you knew that you are beside yourself, talking these sentiments."

And I said to him, "Listen, O friend,[3] for I am not mad or beside myself; but it was prophesied that, after the ascent of Christ to heaven, He would deliver[4] us from error and give us gifts. The words are these: 'He ascended up on high; He led captivity captive; He gave gifts to men.'[5] Accordingly, we who have received gifts from Christ, who has ascended up on high, prove from the words of prophecy that you, 'the wise in yourselves, and the men of understanding in your own eyes,'[6] are foolish, and honour God and His Christ by lip only. But we, who are instructed in the whole truth,[7] honour Them both in acts, and in knowledge, and in heart, even unto death. But you hesitate to confess that He is Christ, as the Scriptures and the events witnessed and done in His name prove, perhaps for this reason, lest you be persecuted by the rulers, who, under the influence of the wicked and deceitful spirit, the serpent, will not cease putting to death and persecuting those who confess the name of Christ until

[1] Literally, "of a hard-hearted opinion."
[2] 1 Kings xix. 14, 18.
[3] ὦ οὗτος.
[4] Literally, "carry us captive."
[5] Ps. lxviii. 19.
[6] Isa. v. 21.
[7] Contrasting either catholics with heretics, or Christians with Jews.

He come again, and destroy them all, and render to each his deserts."

And Trypho replied, "Now, then, render us the proof that this man who you say was crucified and ascended into heaven is the Christ of God. For you have sufficiently proved by means of the scriptures previously quoted by you, that it is declared in the Scriptures that Christ must suffer, and come again with glory, and receive the eternal kingdom over all the nations, every kingdom being made subject to Him: now show us that this man is He."

And I replied, "It has been already proved, sirs, to those who have ears, even from the facts which have been conceded by you; but that you may not think me at a loss, and unable to give proof of what you ask, as I promised, I shall do so at a fitting place. At present, I resume the consideration of the subject which I was discussing.

CHAP. XL.—*He returns to the Mosaic laws, and proves that they were figures of the things which pertain to Christ.*

"The mystery, then, of the lamb which God enjoined to be sacrificed as the passover, was a type of Christ; with whose blood, in proportion to their faith in Him, they anoint their houses, *i.e.* themselves, who believe on Him. For that the creation which God created—to wit, Adam—was a house for the spirit which proceeded from God, you all can understand. And that this injunction was temporary, I prove thus. God does not permit the lamb of the passover to be sacrificed in any other place than where His name was named; knowing that the days will come, after the suffering of Christ, when even the place in Jerusalem shall be given over to your enemies, and all the offerings, in short, shall cease; and that lamb which was commanded to be wholly roasted was a symbol of the suffering of the cross which Christ would undergo. For the lamb,[1] which is roasted, is roasted and dressed up in the form of the cross. For one spit is transfixed right through from the lower parts up to the head, and one across the

[1] Some think this particularly refers to the paschal lamb, others to any lamb which is roasted.

back, to which are attached the legs of the lamb. And the two goats which were ordered to be offered during the fast, of which one was sent away as the scape [goat], and the other sacrificed, were similarly declarative of the two appearances of Christ: the first, in which the elders of your people, and the priests, having laid hands on Him and put Him to death, sent Him away as the scape [goat]; and His second appearance, because in the same place in Jerusalem you shall recognise Him whom you have dishonoured, and who was an offering for all sinners willing to repent, and keeping the fast which Isaiah speaks of, loosening the terms[1] of the violent contracts, and keeping the other precepts, likewise enumerated by him, and which I have quoted,[2] which those believing in Jesus do. And further, you are aware that the offering of the two goats, which were enjoined to be sacrificed at the fast, was not permitted to take place similarly anywhere else, but only in Jerusalem.

Chap. XLI.—*The oblation of fine flour was a figure of the Eucharist.*

"And the offering of fine flour, sirs," I said, "which was prescribed to be presented on behalf of those purified from leprosy, was a type of the bread of the Eucharist, the celebration of which our Lord Jesus Christ prescribed, in remembrance of the suffering which He endured on behalf of those who are purified in soul from all iniquity, in order that we may at the same time thank God for having created the world, with all things therein, for the sake of man, and for delivering us from the evil in which we were, and for utterly overthrowing[3] principalities and powers by Him who suffered according to His will. Hence God speaks by the mouth of Malachi, one of the twelve [prophets], as I said before,[4] about the sacrifices at that time presented by you: 'I have no pleasure in you, saith the Lord; and I will not accept your sacrifices at your hands: for, from the rising of the sun unto the going down of the same, my name has been glorified

[1] Literally, "cords."
[2] Chap. xv.
[3] Literally, "overthrowing with a perfect overthrow."
[4] Chap. xxviii.

among the Gentiles, and in every place incense is offered to my name, and a pure offering: for my name is great among the Gentiles, saith the Lord: but ye profane it.'[1] [So] He then speaks of those Gentiles, namely us, who in every place offer sacrifices to Him, *i.e.* the bread of the Eucharist, and also the cup of the Eucharist, affirming both that we glorify His name, and that you profane [it]. The command of circumcision, again, bidding [them] always circumcise the children on the eighth day, was a type of the true circumcision, by which we are circumcised from deceit and iniquity through Him who rose from the dead on the first day after the Sabbath, [namely through] our Lord Jesus Christ. For the first day after the Sabbath, remaining the first[2] of all the days, is called, however, the eighth, according to the number of all the days of the cycle, and [yet] remains the first.

CHAP. XLII.—*The bells on the priest's robe were a figure of the apostles.*

"Moreover, the prescription that twelve bells[3] be attached to the [robe] of the high priest, which hung down to the feet, was a symbol of the twelve apostles, who depend on the power of Christ, the eternal Priest; and through their voice it is that all the earth has been filled with the glory and grace of God and of His Christ. Wherefore David also says: 'Their sound has gone forth into all the earth, and their words to the ends of the world.'[4] And Isaiah speaks as if he were personating the apostles, when they say to Christ that they believe not in their own report, but in the power of Him who sent them. And so he says: 'Lord, who hath believed our report? and to whom is the arm of the Lord revealed? We have preached before Him as if [He were] a child, as if a root in a dry ground.'[5] (And what follows in order of the prophecy already quoted.[6]) But when the pas-

[1] Mal. i. 10-12. [2] Or, "being the first."

[3] Ex. xxviii. 33 gives no definite number of bells. Otto presumes Justin to have confounded the bells and the gems, which were twelve in number.

[4] Ps. xix. 4. [5] Isa. liii. 1, 2. [6] Chap. xiii.

sage speaks as from the lips of many, 'We have preached before Him,' and adds, 'as if a child,' it signifies that the wicked shall become subject to Him, and shall obey His command, and that all shall become as one child. Such a thing as you may witness in the body: although the members are enumerated as many, all are called *one*, and are a *body*. For, indeed, a commonwealth and a church,[1] though many individuals in number, are in fact as one, called and addressed by one appellation. And in short, sirs," said I, "by enumerating all the other appointments of Moses, I can demonstrate that they were types, and symbols, and declarations of those things which would happen to Christ, of those who it was foreknown were to believe in Him, and of those things which would also be done by Christ Himself. But since what I have now enumerated appears to me to be sufficient, I revert again to the order of the discourse.[2]

CHAP. XLIII.—*He concludes that the law had an end in Christ, who was born of the Virgin.*

"As, then, circumcision began with Abraham, and the Sabbath and sacrifices and offerings and feasts with Moses, and it has been proved they were enjoined on account of the hardness of your people's heart, so it was necessary, in accordance with the Father's will, that they should have an end in Him who was born of a virgin, of the family of Abraham and tribe of Judah, and of David; in Christ the Son of God, who was proclaimed as about to come to all the world, to be the everlasting law and the everlasting covenant, even as the forementioned prophecies show. And we, who have approached God through Him, have received not carnal, but spiritual circumcision, which Enoch and those like him observed. And we have received it through baptism, since we were sinners, by God's mercy; and all men may equally obtain it. But since the mystery of His birth now demands our attention, I shall speak of it. Isaiah then asserted in regard to the generation of Christ, that it could not be de-

[1] ἐκκλησία. Lat. vers. has *conventus*.

[2] Literally, "to the discourse in order."

clared by man, in words already quoted:[1] 'Who shall declare His generation? for His life is taken from the earth: for the transgressions of my people was He led[2] to death.'[3] The Spirit of prophecy thus affirmed that the generation of Him who was to die, that we sinful men might be healed by His stripes, was such as could not be declared. Furthermore, that the men who believe in Him may possess the knowledge of the manner in which He came into the world,[4] the Spirit of prophecy by the same Isaiah foretold how it would happen thus: 'And the Lord spoke again to Ahaz, saying, Ask for thyself a sign from the Lord thy God, in the depth, or in the height. And Ahaz said, I will not ask, neither will I tempt the Lord. And Isaiah said, Hear then, O house of David; Is it a small thing for you to contend with men, and how do you contend with the Lord? Therefore the Lord Himself will give you a sign. Behold, the virgin shall conceive, and shall bear a son, and his name shall be called Immanuel. Butter and honey shall he eat, before he knows or prefers the evil, and chooses out the good;[5] for before the child knows good or ill, he rejects evil[6] by choosing out the good. For before the child knows how to call father or mother, he shall receive the power of Damascus and the spoil of Samaria in presence of the king of Assyria. And the land shall be forsaken,[7] which thou shalt with difficulty endure in consequence of the presence of its two kings.[8] But God shall bring on thee, and on thy people, and on the house of thy father, days which have not yet come upon thee since the day in which Ephraim took away from Judah the king of

[1] Chap. xiii. [2] Or, "was I led." [3] Isa. liii. 8.

[4] Literally, "He was in the world, being born."

[5] See chap. lxvi.

[6] Literally, "disobeys evil" (*ἀπειθεῖ πονηρά*). Conjectured: *ἀπωθεῖ*; and *ἀπειθεῖ πονηρία*.

[7] The MSS. of Justin read, "shall be taken:" *καταληφθήσεται*. This is plainly a mistake for *καταλειφθήσεται*; but whether the mistake is Justin's or the transcribers', it would be difficult to say, as Thirlby remarks.

[8] The rendering of this is doubtful: literally, "from the face of the two kings," and the words might go with "shall be forsaken."

Assyria.'[1] Now it is evident to all, that in the race of Abraham according to the flesh no one has been born of a virgin, or is said to have been born [of a virgin], save this our Christ. But since you and your teachers venture to affirm that in the prophecy of Isaiah it is not said, 'Behold, the virgin shall conceive,' but, 'Behold, the young woman shall conceive, and bear a son;' and [since] you explain the prophecy as if [it referred] to Hezekiah, who was your king, I shall endeavour to discuss shortly this point in opposition to you, and to show that reference is made to Him who is acknowledged by us as Christ.

CHAP. XLIV.—*The Jews in vain promise themselves salvation, which cannot be obtained except through Christ.*

"For thus, so far as you are concerned, I shall be found in all respects innocent, if I strive earnestly to persuade you by bringing forward demonstrations. But if you remain hard-hearted, or weak in [forming] a resolution, on account of death, which is the lot of the Christians, and are unwilling to assent to the truth, you shall appear as the authors of your own [evils]. And you deceive yourselves while you fancy that, because you are the seed of Abraham after the flesh, therefore you shall fully inherit the good things announced to be bestowed by God through Christ. For no one, not even of them,[2] has anything to look for, but only those who in mind are assimilated to the faith of Abraham, and who have recognised all the mysteries: for I say,[3] that some injunctions were laid on you in reference to the worship of

[1] Isa. vii. 10-17 with Isa. viii. 4 inserted. The last clause may also be translated, "in which He took away from Judah Ephraim, even the king of Assyria."

[2] *i.e.* of Abraham's seed.

[3] Justin distinguishes between such essential acts as related to God's worship and the establishment of righteousness, and such ceremonial observances as had a mere temporary significance. The recognition of this distinction he alleges to be necessary to salvation: necessary in this sense, that justification must be placed not on the latter, but on the former; and without such recognition, a Jew would, as Justin says, rest his hopes on his noble descent from Abraham.

God and practice of righteousness; but some injunctions and acts were likewise mentioned in reference to the mystery of Christ, on account of[1] the hardness of your people's hearts. And that this is so, God makes known in Ezekiel, [when] He said concerning it: 'If Noah and Jacob[2] and Daniel should beg either sons or daughters, the request would not be granted them.'[3] And in Isaiah, of the very same matter He spake thus: 'The Lord God said, they shall both go forth and look on the members [of the bodies] of the men that have transgressed. For their worm shall not die, and their fire shall not be quenched, and they shall be a gazing-stock to all flesh.'[4] So that it becomes you to eradicate this hope from your souls, and hasten to know in what way forgiveness of sins, and a hope of inheriting the promised good things, shall be yours. But there is no other [way] than this,—to become acquainted with this Christ, to be washed in the fountain[5] spoken of by Isaiah for the remission of sins; and for the rest, to live sinless lives."

CHAP. XLV.—*Those who were righteous before and under the law shall be saved by Christ.*

And Trypho said, "If I seem to interrupt these matters, which you say must be investigated, yet the question which I mean to put is urgent. Suffer me first."

And I replied, "Ask whatever you please, as it occurs to you; and I shall endeavour, after questions and answers, to resume and complete the discourse."

Then he said, "Tell me, then, shall those who lived according to the law given by Moses, live in the same manner with Jacob, Enoch, and Noah, in the resurrection of the dead, or not?"

I replied to him, "When I quoted, sir, the words spoken

[1] More probably, "or on account of," etc.

[2] In Bible, "Job;" Maranus prefers "Jacob," and thinks the mention of his name very suitable to disprove the arrogant claims of Jacob's posterity.

[3] Ezek. xiv. 20.

[4] Isa. lxvi. 24.

[5] Some refer this to Christ's baptism. See Cyprian, *Adv. Jud.* i. 24.—*Otto.*

by Ezekiel, that 'even if Noah and Daniel and Jacob were to beg sons and daughters, the request would not be granted them,' but that each one, that is to say, shall be saved by his own righteousness, I said also, that those who regulated their lives by the law of Moses would in like manner be saved. For what in the law of Moses is naturally good, and pious, and righteous, and has been prescribed to be done by those who obey it;[1] and what was appointed to be performed by reason of the hardness of the people's hearts; was similarly recorded, and done also by those who were under the law. Since those who did that which is universally, naturally, and eternally good are pleasing to God, they shall be saved through this Christ in the resurrection equally with those righteous men who were before them, namely Noah, and Enoch, and Jacob, and whoever else there be, along with those who have known[2] this Christ, Son of God, who was before the morning star and the moon, and submitted to become incarnate, and be born of this virgin of the family of David, in order that, by this dispensation, the serpent that sinned from the beginning, and the angels like him, may be destroyed, and that death may be contemned, and for ever quit, at the second coming of the Christ Himself, those who believe in Him and live acceptably,—and be no more: when some are sent to be punished unceasingly into judgment and condemnation of fire; but others shall exist in freedom from suffering, from corruption, and from grief, and in immortality."

CHAP. XLVI.—*Trypho asks whether a man who keeps the law even now will be saved. Justin proves that it contributes nothing to righteousness.*

"But if some, even now, wish to live in the observance of the institutions given by Moses, and yet believe in this Jesus who was crucified, recognising Him to be the Christ of God, and that it is given to Him to be absolute Judge of all, and that His is the everlasting kingdom, can they also be saved?" he inquired of me.

[1] It, *i.e.* the law, or "what in the law," etc.
[2] Those who live after Christ.

And I replied, "Let us consider that also together, whether one may now observe all the Mosaic institutions."

And he answered, "No. For we know that, as you said, it is not possible either anywhere to sacrifice the lamb of the passover, or to offer the goats ordered for the fast; or, in short, [to present] all the other offerings."

And I said, "Tell [me] then yourself, I pray, some things which can be observed; for you will be persuaded that, though a man does not keep or has not performed the eternal[1] decrees, he may assuredly be saved."

Then he replied, "To keep the Sabbath, to be circumcised, to observe months, and to be washed if you touch anything prohibited by Moses, or after sexual intercourse."

And I said, "Do you think that Abraham, Isaac, Jacob, Noah, and Job, and all the rest before or after them equally righteous, also Sarah the wife of Abraham, Rebekah the wife of Isaac, Rachel the wife of Jacob, and Leah, and all the rest of them, until the mother of Moses the faithful servant, who observed none of these [statutes], will be saved?"

And Trypho answered, "Were not Abraham and his descendants circumcised?"

And I said, "I know that Abraham and his descendants were circumcised. The reason why circumcision was given to them I stated at length in what has gone before; and if what has been said does not convince you,[2] let us again search into the matter. But you are aware that, up to Moses, no one in fact who was righteous observed any of these rites at all of which we are talking, or received one commandment to observe, except that of circumcision, which began from Abraham."

And he replied, "We know it, and admit that they are saved."

Then I returned answer, "You perceive that God by Moses laid all such ordinances upon you on account of the hardness of your people's hearts, in order that, by the large number of them, you might keep God continually, and in

[1] "Eternal," *i.e.* as the Jew thinks.

[2] Literally, "put you out of countenance."

every action, before your eyes, and never begin to act unjustly or impiously. For He enjoined you to place around you [a fringe] of purple dye,[1] in order that you might not forget God; and He commanded you to wear a phylactery,[2] certain characters, which indeed we consider holy, being engraved on very thin parchment; and by these means stirring you up[3] to retain a constant remembrance of God: at the same time, however, convincing you, that in your hearts you have not even a faint remembrance of God's worship. Yet not even so were you dissuaded from idolatry: for in the times of Elijah, when [God] recounted the number of those who had not bowed the knee to Baal, He said the number was seven thousand; and in Isaiah He rebukes you for having sacrificed your children to idols. But we, because we refuse to sacrifice to those to whom we were of old accustomed to sacrifice, undergo extreme penalties, and rejoice in death,—believing that God will raise us up by His Christ, and will make us incorruptible, and undisturbed, and immortal; and we know that the ordinances imposed by reason of the hardness of your people's hearts, contribute nothing to the performance of righteousness and of piety."

CHAP. XLVII.—*Justin communicates with Christians who observe the law. Not a few catholics do otherwise.*

And Trypho again inquired, "But if some one, knowing that this is so, after he recognises that this man is Christ, and has believed in and obeys Him, wishes, however, to observe these [institutions], will he be saved?"

I said, "In my opinion, Trypho, such an one will be saved, if he does not strive in every way to persuade other men,—I mean those Gentiles who have been circumcised from error by Christ, to observe the same things as himself, telling them that they will not be saved unless they do so. This you did yourself at the commencement of the discourse, when you declared that I would not be saved unless I observe these institutions."

Then he replied, "Why then have you said, 'In my

[1] Num. xv. 38. [2] Deut. vi. 6. [3] Literally, "importuning."

opinion, such an one will be saved,' unless there are some[1] who affirm that such will not be saved?"

"There are such people, Trypho," I answered; "and these do not venture to have any intercourse with or to extend hospitality to such persons; but I do not agree with them. But if some, through weak-mindedness, wish to observe such institutions as were given by Moses, from which they expect some virtue, but which we believe were appointed by reason of the hardness of the people's hearts, along with their hope in this Christ, and [wish to perform] the eternal and natural acts of righteousness and piety, yet choose to live with the Christians and the faithful, as I said before, not inducing them either to be circumcised like themselves, or to keep the Sabbath, or to observe any other such ceremonies, then I hold that we ought to join ourselves to such, and associate with them in all things as kinsmen and brethren. But if, Trypho," I continued, "some of your race, who say they believe in this Christ, compel those Gentiles who believe in this Christ to live in all respects according to the law given by Moses, or choose not to associate so intimately with them, I in like manner do not approve of them. But I believe that even those, who have been persuaded by them to observe the legal dispensation along with their confession of God in Christ, shall probably be saved. And I hold, further, that such as have confessed and known this man to be Christ, yet who have gone back from some cause to the legal dispensation, and have denied that this man is Christ, and have repented not before death, shall by no means be saved. Further, I hold that those of the seed of Abraham who live according to the law, and do not believe in this Christ before death, shall likewise not be saved, and especially those who have anathematized and do anathematize this very Christ in the synagogues, and everything by which they might obtain salvation and escape the vengeance of fire.[2] For the goodness and the loving-kindness of God, and His boundless riches, hold

[1] Or, "Are there not some," etc.

[2] The text seems to be corrupt. Otto reads: "Do anathematize those who put their trust in this very Christ so as to obtain salvation," etc.

righteous and sinless the man who, as Ezekiel[1] tells, repents of sins; and reckons sinful, unrighteous, and impious the man who falls away from piety and righteousness to unrighteousness and ungodliness. Wherefore also our Lord Jesus Christ said, 'In whatsoever things I shall take you, in these I shall judge you.'"[2]

CHAP. XLVIII.—*Before the divinity of Christ is proved, he [Trypho] demands that it be settled that he is Christ.*

And Trypho said, "We have heard what you think of these matters. Resume the discourse where you left off, and bring it to an end. For some of it appears to me to be paradoxical, and wholly incapable of proof. For when you say that this Christ existed as God before the ages, then that he submitted to be born and become man, yet that he is not man of man, this [assertion] appears to me to be not merely paradoxical, but also foolish."

And I replied to this, "I know that the statement does appear to be paradoxical, especially to those of your race, who are ever unwilling to understand or to perform the [requirements] of God, but [ready to perform] those of your teachers, as God Himself declares.[3] Now assuredly, Trypho," I continued, "[the proof] that this man[4] is the Christ of God does not fail, though I be unable to prove that He existed formerly as Son of the Maker of all things, being God, and was born a man by the Virgin. But since I have certainly proved that this man is the Christ of God, whoever He be, even if I do not prove that He pre-existed, and submitted to be born a man of like passions with us, having a body, according to the Father's will; in this last matter alone is it just to say that I have erred, and not to deny that He is the Christ, though it should appear that He was born man of men, and [nothing more] is proved [than this], that He has become Christ by election. For there are some, my friends," I said,

[1] Ezek. xxxiii. 11-20.

[2] Grabius thinks this taken from the Gospel according to the Hebrews. It is not in the New or Old Testament.

[3] Comp. Isa. xxix. 13.

[4] Or, "such a man."

"of our race,[1] who admit that He is Christ, while holding Him to be man of men; with whom I do not agree, nor would I,[2] even though most of those who have [now] the same opinions as myself should say so; since we were enjoined by Christ Himself to put no faith in human doctrines, but in those proclaimed by the blessed prophets and taught by Himself."

CHAP. XLIX.—*To those who object that Elijah has not yet come, he replies that he is the precursor of the first advent.*

And Trypho said, "Those who affirm him to have been a man, and to have been anointed by election, and then to have become Christ, appear to me to speak more plausibly than you who hold those opinions which you express. For we all expect that Christ will be a man [born] of men, and that Elijah when he comes will anoint him. But if this man appear to be Christ, he must certainly be known as man [born] of men; but from the circumstance that Elijah has not yet come, I infer that this man is not He [the Christ]."

Then I inquired of him, "Does not Scripture, in the book of Zechariah,[3] say that Elijah shall come before the great and terrible day of the Lord?"

And he answered, "Certainly."

"If therefore Scripture compels you to admit that two advents of Christ were predicted to take place,—one in which He would appear suffering, and dishonoured, and without comeliness; but the other in which He would come glorious, and Judge of all, as has been made manifest in many of the fore-cited passages,—shall we not suppose that the word of God has proclaimed that Elijah shall be the pre-

[1] Some read, "of *your* race," referring to the *Ebionites*. Maranus believes the reference is to the Ebionites, and supports in a long note the reading "our," inasmuch as Justin would be more likely to associate these Ebionites with Christians than with Jews, even though they were heretics.

[2] Langus translates: "Nor would, indeed, many who are of the same opinion as myself say so."

[3] Mal. iv. 5.

cursor of the great and terrible day, that is, of His second advent?"

"Certainly," he answered.

"And, accordingly, our Lord in His teaching," I continued, "proclaimed that this very thing would take place, saying that Elijah would also come. And we know that this shall take place when our Lord Jesus Christ shall come in glory from heaven; whose first manifestation the Spirit of God who was in Elijah preceded as herald in [the person of] John, a prophet among your nation; after whom no other prophet appeared among you. He cried, as he sat by the river Jordan: 'I baptize you with water to repentance; but He that is stronger than I shall come, whose shoes I am not worthy to bear: He shall baptize you with the Holy Ghost and with fire: whose fan is in His hand, and He will thoroughly purge His floor, and will gather the wheat into the barn; but the chaff He will burn up with unquenchable fire.'[1] And this very prophet your king Herod had shut up in prison; and when his birth-day was celebrated, and the niece[2] of the same Herod by her dancing had pleased him, he told her to ask whatever she pleased. Then the mother of the maiden instigated her to ask the head of John, who was in prison; and having asked it, [Herod] sent and ordered the head of John to be brought in on a charger. Wherefore also our Christ said, [when He was] on earth, to those who were affirming that Elijah must come before Christ: 'Elijah shall come, and restore all things; but I say unto you, that Elijah has already come, and they knew him not, but have done to him whatsoever they chose.'[3] And it is written, 'Then the disciples understood that He spake to them about John the Baptist.'"

And Trypho said, "This statement also seems to me paradoxical; namely, that the prophetic Spirit of God, who was in Elijah, was also in John."

To this I replied, "Do you not think that the same thing happened in the case of Joshua the son of Nave (Nun), who succeeded to the command of the people after Moses, when

[1] Matt. iii. 11, 12. [2] Literally, "cousin." [3] Matt. xvii. 12.

Moses was commanded to lay his hands on Joshua, and God said to him, 'I will take of the spirit which is in thee, and put it on him?'"[1]

And he said, "Certainly."

"As therefore," I say, "while Moses was still among men, God took of the spirit which was in Moses and put it on Joshua, even so God was able to cause [the spirit] of Elijah to come upon John; in order that, as Christ at His first coming appeared inglorious, even so the first coming of the spirit, which remained always pure in Elijah[2] like that of Christ, might be perceived to be inglorious. For the Lord said He would wage war against Amalek with concealed hand; and you will not deny that Amalek fell. But if it is said that only in the glorious advent of Christ war will be waged with Amalek, how great will the fulfilment[3] of Scripture be which says, 'God will wage war against Amalek with concealed hand!' You can perceive that the concealed power of God was in Christ the crucified, before whom demons, and all the principalities and powers of the earth, tremble."

CHAP. L.—*It is proved from Isaiah that John is the precursor of Christ.*

And Trypho said, "You seem to me to have come out of a great conflict with many persons about all the points we have been searching into, and therefore quite ready to return answers to all questions put to you. Answer me then, first, how you can show that there is another God besides the Maker of all things; and then you will show, [further], that He submitted to be born of the Virgin."

I replied, "Give me permission first of all to quote certain passages from the prophecy of Isaiah, which refer to the office of forerunner discharged by John the Baptist and prophet before this our Lord Jesus Christ."

[1] Num. xi. 17, spoken of the seventy elders. Justin confuses what is said here with Num. xxvii. 18 and Deut. xxxiv. 9.

[2] The meaning is, that no division of person took place. Elijah remained the same after as before his spirit was shed on John.

[3] Literally, "fruit."

"I grant it," said he.

Then I said, "Isaiah thus foretold John's forerunning: 'And Hezekiah said to Isaiah, Good is the word of the Lord which He spake: Let there be peace and righteousness in my days.'[1] And, 'Encourage the people; ye priests, speak to the heart of Jerusalem, and encourage her, because her humiliation is accomplished. Her sin is annulled; for she has received of the Lord's hand double for her sins. A voice of one crying in the wilderness, Prepare the ways of the Lord; make straight the paths of our God. Every valley shall be filled up, and every mountain and hill shall be brought low: and the crooked shall be made straight, and the rough way shall be plain ways; and the glory of the Lord shall be seen, and all flesh shall see the salvation of God: for the Lord hath spoken it. A voice of one saying, Cry; and I said, What shall I cry? All flesh is grass, and all the glory of man as the flower of grass. The grass has withered, and the flower of it has fallen away; but the word of the Lord endureth for ever. Thou that bringest good tidings to Zion, go up to the high mountain; thou that bringest good tidings to Jerusalem, lift up thy voice with strength. Lift ye up, be not afraid; tell the cities of Judah, Behold your God! Behold, the Lord comes with strength, and [His] arm comes with authority. Behold, His reward is with Him, and His work before Him. As a shepherd He will tend His flock, and will gather the lambs with [His] arm, and cheer on her that is with young. Who has measured the water with [his] hand, and the heaven with a span, and all the earth with [his] fist? Who has weighed the mountains, and [put] the valleys into a balance? Who has known the mind of the Lord? And who has been His counsellor, and who shall advise Him? Or with whom did He take counsel, and he instructed Him? Or who showed Him judgment? Or who made Him to know the way of understanding? All the nations are reckoned as a drop of a bucket, and as a turning of a balance, and shall be reckoned as spittle. But Lebanon is not sufficient to burn, nor the beasts sufficient for a burnt-offer-

[1] Isa. xxxix. 8.

ing; and all the nations are considered nothing, and for nothing.'"[1]

CHAP. LI.—*It is proved that this prophecy has been fulfilled.*

And when I ceased, Trypho said, "All the words of the prophecy you repeat, sir, are ambiguous, and have no force in proving what you wish to prove." Then I answered, "If the prophets had not ceased, so that there were no more in your nation, Trypho, after this John, it is evident that what I say in reference to Jesus Christ might be regarded perhaps as ambiguous. But if John came first calling on men to repent, and Christ, while [John] still sat by the river Jordan, having come, put an end to his prophesying and baptizing, and preached also Himself, saying that the kingdom of heaven is at hand, and that He must suffer many things from the scribes and Pharisees, and be crucified, and on the third day rise again, and would appear again in Jerusalem, and would again eat and drink with His disciples; and foretold that in the interval between His [first and second] advent, as I previously said,[2] priests and false prophets would arise in His name, which things do actually appear; then how can they be ambiguous, when you may be persuaded by the facts? Moreover, He referred to the fact that there would be no longer in your nation any prophet, and to the fact that men recognised how that the New Testament, which God formerly announced [His intention of] promulgating, was then present, *i.e.* Christ Himself; and in the following terms: 'The law and the prophets were until John the Baptist; from that time the kingdom of heaven suffereth violence, and the violent take it by force. And if you can[3] receive it, he is Elijah, who was to come. He that hath ears to hear, let him hear.'[4]

CHAP. LII.—*Jacob predicted two advents of Christ.*

"And it was prophesied by Jacob the patriarch that there would be two advents of Christ, and that in the first

[1] Isa. xl. 1–17.
[2] Chap. xxv.
[3] "Are willing."
[4] Matt. xi. 12–15.

He would suffer, and that after He came there would be neither prophet nor king in your nation (I proceeded), and that the nations who believe in the suffering Christ would look for His future appearance. And for this reason the Holy Spirit had uttered these truths in a parable, and obscurely: for," I added, "it is said, 'Judah, thy brethren have praised thee: thy hands [shall be] on the neck of thine enemies; the sons of thy father shall worship thee. Judah is a lion's whelp; from the germ, my son, thou art sprung up. Reclining, he lay down like a lion, and like [a lion's] whelp: who shall raise him up? A ruler shall not depart from Judah, or a leader from his thighs, until that which is laid up in store for him shall come; and he shall be the desire of nations, binding his foal to the vine, and the foal of his ass to the tendril of the vine. He shall wash his garments in wine, and his vesture in the blood of the grape. His eyes shall be bright with[1] wine, and his teeth white like milk.'[2] Moreover, that in your nation there never failed either prophet or ruler, from the time when they began until the time when this Jesus Christ appeared and suffered, you will not venture shamelessly to assert, nor can you prove it. For though you affirm that Herod, after[3] whose [reign] He suffered, was an Ashkelonite, nevertheless you admit that there was a high priest in your nation; so that you then had one who presented offerings according to the law of Moses, and observed the other legal ceremonies; also [you had] prophets in succession until John, (even then, too, when your nation was carried captive to Babylon, when your land was ravaged by war, and the sacred vessels carried off); there never failed to be a prophet among you, who was lord, and leader, and ruler of your nation. For the Spirit which was in the prophets anointed your kings, and established them. But after the manifestation and death of our Jesus Christ in your nation, there was and is nowhere any prophet: nay, further, you ceased to exist under your own king, your land was laid

[1] Or, "in comparison of."

[2] Gen. xlix. 8–12.

[3] *ἀφ' οὗ*; many translated "under whom," as if *ἐφ' οὗ*. This would be erroneous. Conjectured also *ἔφυγε* for *ἔπαθεν*.

waste, and forsaken like a lodge in a vineyard; and the statement of Scripture, in the mouth of Jacob, 'And He shall be the desire of nations,' meant symbolically His two advents, and that the nations would believe in Him; which facts you may now at length discern. For those out of all the nations who are pious and righteous through the faith of Christ, look for His future appearance.

CHAP. LIII.—*Jacob predicted that Christ would ride on an ass, and Zechariah confirms it.*

"And that expression, 'binding his foal to the vine, and the ass's foal to the vine tendril,' was a declaring beforehand both of the works wrought by Him at His first advent, and also of that belief in Him which the nations would repose. For they were like an unharnessed foal, which was not bearing a yoke on its neck, until this Christ came, and sent His disciples to instruct them; and they bore the yoke of His word, and yielded the neck to endure all [hardships], for the sake of the good things promised by Himself, and expected by them. And truly our Lord Jesus Christ, when He intended to go into Jerusalem, requested His disciples to bring Him a certain ass, along with its foal, which was bound in an entrance of a village called Bethphage; and having seated Himself on it, He entered into Jerusalem. And as this was done by Him in the manner in which it was prophesied in precise terms that it would be done by the Christ, and as the fulfilment was recognised, it became a clear proof that He was the Christ. And though all this happened and is proved from Scripture, you are still hard-hearted. Nay, it was prophesied by Zechariah, one of the twelve [prophets], that such would take place, in the following words: 'Rejoice greatly, daughter of Zion; shout, and declare, daughter of Jerusalem; behold, thy King shall come to thee, righteous, bringing salvation, meek, and lowly, riding on an ass, and the foal of an ass.'[1] Now, that the Spirit of prophecy, as well as the patriarch Jacob, mentioned both an ass and its foal, which would be used by Him; and, further, that He, as I

[1] Zech. ix. 9.

previously said, requested His disciples to bring both beasts; [this fact] was a prediction that you of the synagogue, along with the Gentiles, would believe in Him. For as the unharnessed colt was a symbol of the Gentiles, even so the harnessed ass was a symbol of your nation. For you possess the law which was imposed [upon you] by the prophets. Moreover, the prophet Zechariah foretold that this same Christ would be smitten, and His disciples scattered: which also took place. For after His crucifixion, the disciples that accompanied Him were dispersed, until He rose from the dead, and persuaded them that so it had been prophesied concerning Him, that He would suffer; and being thus persuaded, they went into all the world, and taught these truths. Hence also we are strong in His faith and doctrine, since we have [this our] persuasion both from the prophets, and from those who throughout the world are seen to be worshippers of God in the name of that crucified One. The following is said, too, by Zechariah: 'O sword, rise up against my Shepherd, and against the man of my people, saith the Lord of hosts. Smite the Shepherd, and His flock shall be scattered.'[1]

CHAP. LIV.—*What the blood of the grape signifies.*

"And that expression which was committed to writing[2] by Moses, and prophesied by the patriarch Jacob, namely, 'He shall wash His garments with wine, and His vesture with the blood of the grape,' signified that He would wash those that believe in Him with His own blood. For the Holy Spirit called those who receive remission of sins through Him, His garments; amongst whom He is always present in power, but will be manifestly present at His second coming. That the Scripture mentions the blood of the grape has been evidently designed, because Christ derives blood not from the seed of man, but from the power of God. For as God, and not man, has produced the blood of the vine, so also [the Scripture] has predicted that the blood of Christ would be not of the seed of man, but of the power of God. But this prophecy, sirs, which I repeated, proves

[1] Zech. xiii. 7. [2] Literally, "inquired into."

that Christ is not man of men, begotten in the ordinary course of humanity."

CHAP. LV.—*Trypho asks that Christ be proved God, but without metaphor. Justin promises to do so.*

And Trypho answered, "We shall remember this your exposition, if you strengthen [your solution of] this difficulty by other arguments: but now resume the discourse, and show us that the Spirit of prophecy admits another God besides the Maker of all things, taking care not to speak of the sun and moon, which, it is written,[1] God has given to the nations to worship as gods; and oftentimes the prophets, employing[2] this manner of speech, say that 'thy God is a God of gods, and a Lord of lords,' adding frequently, 'the great and strong and terrible [God].' For such expressions are used, not as if they really were gods, but because the Scripture is teaching us that the true God, who made all things, is Lord alone of those who are reputed gods and lords. And in order that the Holy Spirit may convince [us] of this, He said by the holy David, 'The gods of the nations, reputed gods, are idols of demons, and not gods;'[3] and He denounces a curse on those who make and those who worship them."

And I replied, "I would not bring forward these proofs, Trypho, by which I am aware those who worship these [idols] and such like are condemned, but such [proofs] as no one could find any objection to. They will appear strange to you, although you read them every day; so that even from this fact we[4] understand that, because of your wickedness, God has withheld from you the ability to discern the wisdom of His Scriptures; yet [there are] some exceptions, to whom, according to the grace of His long-suffering, as Isaiah said, He has left a seed of[5] salvation, lest your race be utterly destroyed, like Sodom and Gomorrah. Pay attention, there-

[1] Deut iv. 19, an apparent misinterpretation of the passage.
[2] Or, "misusing."
[3] Ps. xcvi. 5.
[4] Com. reading, "you;" evidently wrong.
[5] Literally, "for."

fore, to what I shall record out of the holy Scriptures, which[1] do not need to be expounded, but only listened to.

CHAP. LVI.—*God who appeared to Moses is distinguished from God the Father.*

"Moses, then, the blessed and faithful servant of God, declares that He who appeared to Abraham under the oak in Mamre is God, sent with the two angels in His company to judge Sodom by Another who remains ever in the super-celestial places, invisible to all men, holding personal intercourse with none, whom we believe to be Maker and Father of all things; for he speaks thus: 'God appeared to him under the oak in Mamre, as he sat at his tent-door at noon-tide. And lifting up his eyes, he saw, and behold, three men stood before him; and when he saw them, he ran to meet them from the door of his tent; and he bowed himself toward the ground, and said;'"[2] (and so on till;)[3] "'Abraham gat up early in the morning to the place where he stood before the Lord: and he looked toward Sodom and Gomorrah, and toward the adjacent country, and beheld, and, lo, a flame went up from the earth, like the smoke of a furnace.'" And when I had made an end of quoting these words, I asked them if they had understood them.

And they said they had understood them, but that the passages adduced brought forward no proof that there is any other God or Lord, or that the Holy Spirit says so, besides the Maker of all things.

Then I replied, "I shall attempt to persuade you, since you have understood the Scriptures, [of the truth] of what I say, that there is, and that there is said to be, another God and Lord subject to[4] the Maker of all things; who is also called an Angel, because He announces to men whatsoever the

[1] Two constructions, "which" referring either to Scriptures as whole, or to what he records from them. Last more probable.

[2] Gen. xviii. 1, 2.

[3] Gen. xix. 27, 28; "and so on" inserted probably not by Justin, but by some copyist, as is evident from succeeding words.

[4] Some, "besides;" but probably as above.

Maker of all things—above whom there is no other God—wishes to announce to them." And quoting once more the previous passage, I asked Trypho, "Do you think that God appeared to Abraham under the oak in Mamre, as the Scripture asserts?"

He said, "Assuredly."

"Was He one of those three," I said, "whom Abraham saw, and whom the Holy Spirit of prophecy describes as men?"

He said, "No; but God appeared to him, before the vision of the three. Then those three whom the Scripture calls men, were angels; two of them sent to destroy Sodom, and one to announce the joyful tidings to Sarah, that she would bear a son; for which cause he was sent, and having accomplished his errand, went away."[1]

"How then," said I, "does the one of the three, who was in the tent, and who said, 'I shall return to thee hereafter, and Sarah shall have a son,'[2] appear to have returned when Sarah had begotten a son, and to be there declared, by the prophetic word, God? But that you may clearly discern what I say, listen to the words expressly employed by Moses; they are these: 'And Sarah saw the son of Hagar the Egyptian bond-woman, whom she bore to Abraham, sporting with Isaac her son, and said to Abraham, Cast out this bond-woman and her son; for the son of this bond-woman shall not share the inheritance of my son Isaac. And the matter seemed very grievous in Abraham's sight, because of his son. But God said to Abraham, Let it not be grievous in thy sight because of the son, and because of the bond-woman. In all that Sarah hath said unto thee, hearken to her voice; for in Isaac shall thy seed be called.'[3] Have you perceived, then, that He who said under the oak that He would return, since He knew it would be necessary to advise Abraham to do what Sarah wished him, came back as it is written; and is God, as the words declare, when they so speak: 'God said to Abraham, Let it not be grievous in thy sight because of

[1] Or, "going away, departed." [2] Gen. xviii. 10.
[3] Gen. xxi. 9–12.

the son, and because of the bond-woman?' " I inquired. And Trypho said, "Certainly; but you have not proved from this that there is another God besides Him who appeared to Abraham, and who also appeared to the other patriarchs and prophets. You have proved, however, that we were wrong in believing that the three who were in the tent with Abraham were all angels."

I replied again, "If I could not have proved to you from the Scriptures that one of those three is God, and is called Angel,[1] because, as I already said, He brings messages to those to whom God the Maker of all things wishes [messages to be brought], then in regard to Him who appeared to Abraham on earth in human form in like manner as the two angels who came with Him, and who was God even before the creation of the world, it were reasonable for you to entertain the same belief as is entertained by the whole of your nation."

"Assuredly," he said, "for up to this moment this has been our belief."

Then I replied, "Reverting to the Scriptures, I shall endeavour to persuade you, that He who is said to have appeared to Abraham, and to Jacob, and to Moses, and who is called God, is distinct from Him who made all things,—numerically, I mean, not [distinct] in will. For I affirm that He has never at any time done[2] anything which He who made the world—above whom there is no other God—has not wished Him both to do and to engage Himself with."

And Trypho said, "Prove now that this is the case, that we also may agree with you. For we do not understand you to affirm that He has done or said anything contrary to the will of the Maker of all things."

[1] Or, "Messenger." In the various passages in which Justin assigns the reason for Christ being called angel or messenger, Justin uses also the verb ἀγγέλλω, to convey messages, to announce. The similarity between ἄγγελος and ἀγγέλλω cannot be retained in English, and therefore the point of Justin's remarks is lost to the English reader.

[2] Some supply, "or said."

Then I said, "The scripture just quoted by me will make this plain to you. It is thus: 'The sun was risen on the earth, and Lot entered into Segor (Zoar); and the Lord rained on Sodom sulphur and fire from the Lord out of heaven, and overthrew these cities and all the neighbourhood.'"[1]

Then the fourth of those who had remained with Trypho said, "It[2] must therefore necessarily be said that one of the two angels who went to Sodom, and is named by Moses in the Scripture Lord, is different from Him who also is God, and appeared to Abraham."[3]

"It is not on this ground solely," I said, "that it must be admitted absolutely that some other one is called Lord by the Holy Spirit besides Him who is considered Maker of all things; not solely [for what is said] by Moses, but also [for what is said] by David. For there is written by him: 'The Lord says to my Lord, Sit on my right hand, until I make Thine enemies Thy footstool,'[4] as I have already quoted. And again, in other words: 'Thy throne, O God, is for ever and ever. A sceptre of equity is the sceptre of Thy kingdom: Thou hast loved righteousness and hated iniquity: therefore God, even Thy God, hath anointed Thee with the oil of gladness above Thy fellows.'[5] If, therefore, you assert that the Holy Spirit calls some other one God and Lord, besides the Father of all things and His Christ, answer me; for I undertake to prove to you from Scriptures themselves, that He whom the Scripture calls Lord is not one of the two angels that went to Sodom, but He who was with them, and is called God, that appeared to Abraham."

And Trypho said, "Prove this; for, as you see, the day advances, and we are not prepared for such perilous replies;

[1] Gen. xix. 23.

[2] Or, "We must of necessity think that, besides the one of the two angels who came down to Sodom, and whom the Scripture by Moses calls Lord, God Himself appeared to Abraham."

[3] This passage is rather confused; the translation is necessarily free, but, it is believed, correct. Justin's friend wishes to make out that *two* distinct individuals are called *Lord* or *God* in the narrative.

[4] Ps. cx. 1.

[5] Ps. xlv. 6, 7.

since never yet have we heard any man investigating, or searching into, or proving these matters; nor would we have tolerated your conversation, had you not referred everything to the Scriptures: for you are very zealous in adducing proofs from them; and you are of opinion that there is no God above the Maker of all things."

Then I replied, "You are aware, then, that the Scripture says, 'And the Lord said to Abraham, Why did Sarah laugh, saying, Shall I truly conceive? for I am old. Is anything impossible with God? At the time appointed shall I return to thee according to the time of life, and Sarah shall have a son.'[1] And after a little interval: 'And the men rose up from thence, and looked towards Sodom and Gomorrah; and Abraham went with them, to bring them on the way. And the Lord said, I will not conceal from Abraham, my servant, what I do.'[2] And again, after a little, it thus says: 'The Lord said, The cry of Sodom and Gomorrah is great,[3] and their sins are very grievous. I will go down now, and see whether they have done altogether according to their cry which has come unto me; and if not, that I may know. And the men turned away thence, and went to Sodom. But Abraham was standing before the Lord; and Abraham drew near, and said, Wilt Thou destroy the righteous with the wicked?'"[4] (and so on,[5] for I do not think fit to write over again the same words, having written them all before, but shall of necessity give those by which I established the proof to Trypho and his companions. Then I proceeded to what follows, in which these words are recorded:) "'And the Lord went His way as soon as He had left communing with Abraham; and [Abraham] went to his place. And there came two angels to Sodom at even. And Lot sat in the gate of Sodom;'[6] and what follows until, 'But the men put forth their hands, and pulled Lot into the house to them, and shut to the door of the house;'[7] and what follows till, 'And the angels laid hold

[1] Gen. xviii. 13, 14.
[2] Gen. xviii. 16, 17.
[3] Literally, "is multiplied."
[4] Gen. xviii. 20-23.
[5] Comp. Note 3, p. 158.
[6] Gen. xviii. 33, xix. 1.
[7] Gen. xix. 10.

on his hand, and on the hand of his wife, and on the hands of his daughters, the Lord being merciful to him. And it came to pass, when they had brought them forth abroad, that they said, Save, save thy life. Look not behind thee, nor stay in all the neighbourhood; escape to the mountain, lest thou be taken along with [them]. And Lot said to them, I beseech [Thee], O Lord, since Thy servant hath found grace in Thy sight, and Thou hast magnified Thy righteousness, which Thou showest towards me in saving my life; but I cannot escape to the mountain, lest evil overtake me, and I die. Behold, this city is near to flee unto, and it is small: there I shall be safe, since it is small; and my soul shall live. And He said to him, Behold, I have accepted thee[1] also in this matter, so as not to destroy the city for which thou hast spoken. Make haste to save thyself there; for I shall not do anything till thou be come thither. Therefore he called the name of the city Segor (Zoar). The sun was risen upon the earth; and Lot entered into Segor (Zoar). And the Lord rained on Sodom and Gomorrah sulphur and fire from the Lord out of heaven; and He overthrew these cities, and all the neighbourhood.'"[2] And after another pause I added: "And now have you not perceived, my friends, that one of the three, who is both God and Lord, and ministers to Him who is in the heavens, is Lord of the two angels? For when [the angels] proceeded to Sodom, He remained behind, and communed with Abraham in the words recorded by Moses; and when He departed after the conversation, Abraham went back to his place. And when he came [to Sodom], the two angels no longer converse with Lot, but Himself, as the Scripture makes evident; and He is the Lord who received commission from the Lord who [remains] in the heavens, *i.e.* the Maker of all things, to inflict upon Sodom and Gomorrah the [judgments] which the Scripture describes in these terms: 'The Lord rained upon Sodom and Gomorrah sulphur and fire from the Lord out of heaven.'"

[1] Literally, "I have admired thy face."
[2] Gen. xix. 16–25.

CHAP. LVII.—*The Jew objects, Why is he said to have eaten, if he be God? Answer of Justin.*

Then Trypho said when I was silent, "That Scripture compels us to admit this, is manifest; but there is a matter about which we are deservedly at a loss—namely, about what was said to the effect that [the Lord] ate what was prepared and placed before Him by Abraham; and you would admit this."

I answered, "It is written that they ate; and if we believe[1] that it is said the three ate, and not the two alone—who were really angels, and are nourished in the heavens, as is evident to us, even though they are not nourished by food similar to that which mortals use—(for, concerning the sustenance of manna which supported your fathers in the desert, Scripture speaks thus, that they ate angels' food): [if we believe that three ate], then I would say that the scripture which affirms they ate bears the same meaning as when we would say about fire that it has devoured all things; yet it is not certainly understood that they ate, masticating with teeth and jaws. So that not even here should we be at a loss about anything, if we are acquainted even slightly with figurative modes of expression, and able to rise above them."

And Trypho said, "It is possible that [the question] about the mode of eating may be thus explained: [the mode, that is to say,] in which it is written, they took and ate what had been prepared by Abraham: so that you may now proceed to explain to us how this God who appeared to Abraham, and is minister to God the Maker of all things, being born of the Virgin, became man, of like passions with all, as you said previously."

Then I replied, "Permit me first, Trypho, to collect some other proofs on this head, so that you, by the large number of them, may be persuaded of [the truth of] it, and thereafter I shall explain what you ask."

And he said, "Do as seems good to you; for I shall be thoroughly pleased."

[1] Literally, "hear."

CHAP. LVIII.—*The same is proved from the visions which appeared to Jacob.*

Then I continued, "I purpose to quote to you scriptures, not that I am anxious to make merely an artful display of words; for I possess no such faculty, but God's grace alone has been granted to me to the understanding of His Scriptures, of which grace I exhort all to become partakers freely and bounteously, in order that they may not, through want of it,[1] incur condemnation in the judgment which God the Maker of all things shall hold through my Lord Jesus Christ."

And Trypho said, "What you do is worthy of the worship of God; but you appear to me to feign ignorance when you say that you do not possess a store of artful words."

I again replied, "Be it so, since you think so; yet I am persuaded that I speak the truth.[2] But give me your attention, that I may now rather adduce the remaining proofs."

"Proceed," said he.

And I continued: "It is again written by Moses, my brethren, that He who is called God and appeared to the patriarchs is called both Angel and Lord, in order that from this you may understand Him to be minister to the Father of all things, as you have already admitted, and may remain firm, persuaded by additional arguments. The word of God, therefore, [recorded] by Moses, when referring to Jacob the grandson of Abraham, speaks thus: 'And it came to pass, when the sheep conceived, that I saw them with my eyes in the dream: And, behold, the he-goats and the rams which leaped upon the sheep and she-goats were spotted with white, and speckled and sprinkled with a dun colour. And the Angel of God said to me in the dream, Jacob, Jacob. And I said, What is it, Lord? And He said, Lift up thine eyes, and see that the he-goats and rams leaping on the sheep and she-goats are spotted with white, speckled, and sprinkled with a dun colour. For I have seen what Laban doeth unto thee. I am the God who appeared

[1] Literally, "for this sake."
[2] Or, "speak otherwise."

to thee in Bethel,[1] where thou anointedst a pillar and vowedst a vow unto me. Now therefore arise, and get thee out of this land, and depart to the land of thy birth, and I shall be with thee.'[2] And again, in other words, speaking of the same Jacob, it thus says: 'And having risen up that night, he took the two wives, and the two women-servants, and his eleven children, and passed over the ford Jabbok; and he took them and went over the brook, and sent over all his belongings. But Jacob was left behind alone, and an Angel[3] wrestled with him until morning. And He saw that He is not prevailing against him, and He touched the broad part of his thigh; and the broad part of Jacob's thigh grew stiff while he wrestled with Him. And He said, Let me go, for the day breaketh. But he said, I will not let Thee go, except Thou bless me. And He said to him, What is thy name? And he said, Jacob. And He said, Thy name shall be called no more Jacob, but Israel shall be thy name; for thou hast prevailed with God, and with men shalt be powerful. And Jacob asked Him, and said, Tell me Thy name. But He said, Why dost thou ask after my name? And He blessed him there. And Jacob called the name of that place Peniel,[4] for I saw God face to face, and my soul rejoiced.'[5] And again, in other terms, referring to the same Jacob, it says the following: 'And Jacob came to Luz, in the land of Canaan, which is Bethel, he and all the people that were with him. And there he built an altar, and called the name of that place Bethel; for there God appeared to him when he fled from the face of his brother Esau. And Deborah, Rebekah's nurse, died, and was buried beneath Bethel under an oak: and Jacob called the name of it The Oak of Sorrow. And God appeared again to Jacob in Luz, when he came out from Mesopotamia in Syria, and He blessed him. And God said to him, Thy name shall be no more called Jacob, but Israel shall be thy name.'[6] He is called God, and He is and shall be God." And when all had agreed on these grounds,

[1] Literally, "in the place of God."
[2] Gen. xxxi. 10-13.
[3] Some read, "a man."
[4] Literally, "the face of God."
[5] Gen. xxxii. 22-30.
[6] Gen. xxxv. 6-10.

I continued: "Moreover, I consider it necessary to repeat to you the words which narrate how He who is both Angel and God and Lord, and who appeared as a man to Abraham, and who wrestled in human form with Jacob, was seen by him when he fled from his brother Esau. They are as follows: 'And Jacob went out from the well of the oath,[1] and went toward Charran.[2] And he lighted on a spot, and slept there, for the sun was set; and he gathered of the stones of the place, and put them under his head. And he slept in that place; and he dreamed, and, behold, a ladder was set up on the earth, whose top reached to heaven; and the angels of God ascended and descended upon it. And the Lord stood[3] above it, and He said, I am the Lord, the God of Abraham thy father, and of Isaac; be not afraid: the land whereon thou liest, to thee will I give it, and to thy seed; and thy seed shall be as the dust of the earth, and shall be extended to the west, and south, and north, and east: and in thee, and in thy seed, shall all families of the earth be blessed. And, behold, I am with thee, keeping thee in every way wherein thou goest, and will bring thee again into this land; for I will not leave thee, until I have done all that I have spoken to thee of. And Jacob awaked out of his sleep, and said, Surely the Lord is in this place, and I knew it not. And he was afraid, and said, How dreadful is this place! this is none other than the house of God, and this is the gate of heaven. And Jacob rose up in the morning, and took the stone which he had placed under his head, and he set it up for a pillar, and poured oil upon the top of it; and Jacob called the name of the place The House of God, and the name of the city formerly was Ulammaus.'"[4]

CHAP. LIX.—*God distinct from the Father conversed with Moses.*

When I had spoken these words, I continued: "Permit me, further, to show you from the book of Exodus how this same One, who is both Angel, and God, and Lord, and man, and

[1] Or, "Beersheba."
[2] So LXX. and N. T.; Heb. "Haran."
[3] Literally, "was set up."
[4] Gen. xxviii. 10–19.

who appeared in human form to Abraham and Isaac,[1] appeared in a flame of fire from the bush, and conversed with Moses." And after they said they would listen cheerfully, patiently, and eagerly, I went on: "These words are in the book which bears the title of Exodus: 'And after many days the king of Egypt died, and the children of Israel groaned by reason of the works;'[2] and so on until, 'Go and gather the elders of Israel, and thou shalt say unto them, The Lord God of your fathers, the God of Abraham, the God of Isaac, and the God of Jacob, hath appeared to me, saying, I am surely beholding you, and the things which have befallen you in Egypt.'"[3] In addition to these words, I went on: "Have you perceived, sirs, that this very God whom Moses speaks of as an Angel that talked to him in the flame of fire, declares to Moses that He is the God of Abraham, of Isaac, and of Jacob?"

CHAP. LX.—*Opinions of the Jews with regard to Him who appeared in the bush.*

Then Trypho said, "We do not perceive this from the passage quoted by you, but [only this], that it was an angel who appeared in the flame of fire, but God who conversed with Moses; so that there were really two persons in company with each other, an angel and God, that appeared in that vision."

I again replied, "Even if this were so, my friends, that an angel and God were together in the vision seen by Moses, yet, as has already been proved to you by the passages previously quoted, it will not be the Creator of all things that is the God that said to Moses that He was the God of Abraham, and the God of Isaac, and the God of Jacob, but it will be He who has been proved to you to have appeared to Abraham, ministering to the will of the Maker of all things, and likewise carrying into execution His counsel in the judgment of Sodom; so that, even though it be as you say, that there were two—an angel and God—he who has but the smallest

[1] Some conjecture "Jacob," others insert "Jacob" after "Isaac."
[2] Ex. ii. 23.
[3] Ex. iii. 16.

intelligence will not venture to assert that the Maker and Father of all things, having left all supercelestial matters, was visible on a little portion of the earth."

And Trypho said, "Since it has been previously proved that He who is called God and Lord, and appeared to Abraham, received from the Lord, who is in the heavens, that which He inflicted on the land of Sodom, even although an angel had accompanied the God who appeared to Moses, we shall perceive that the God who communed with Moses from the bush was not the Maker of all things, but He who has been shown to have manifested Himself to Abraham and to Isaac and to Jacob; who also is called and is perceived to be the Angel of God the Maker of all things, because He publishes to men the commands of the Father and Maker of all things."

And I replied, "Now assuredly, Trypho, I shall show that, in the vision of Moses, this same One alone who is called an Angel, and who is God, appeared to and communed with Moses. For the Scripture says thus: 'The Angel of the Lord appeared to him in a flame of fire from the bush; and he sees that the bush burns with fire, but the bush was not consumed. And Moses said, I will turn aside and see this great sight, for the bush is not burnt. And when the Lord saw that he is turning aside to behold, the Lord called to him out of the bush.'[1] In the same manner, therefore, in which the Scripture calls Him who appeared to Jacob in the dream an Angel, then [says] that the same Angel who appeared in the dream spoke to him,[2] saying, 'I am the God that appeared to thee when thou didst flee from the face of Esau thy brother;' and [again] says that, in the judgment which befell Sodom in the days of Abraham, the Lord had inflicted the punishment[3] of the Lord who [dwells] in the heavens;—even so here, the Scripture, in announcing that the angel of the Lord appeared to Moses, and in afterwards declaring him to be Lord and God, speaks of the same One, whom it declares by the many testimonies already quoted to be minister to God, who is above the world, above whom there is no other [God].

[1] Ex. iii. 2-4. [2] Gen. xxxv. 7. [3] Literally, "judgment."

CHAP. LXI.—*Wisdom is begotten of the Father, as fire from fire.*

"I shall give you another testimony, my friends," said I, "from the Scriptures, that God begat before all creatures a Beginning,[1] [who was] a certain rational power [proceeding] from Himself, who is called by the Holy Spirit, now the Glory of the Lord, now the Son, again Wisdom, again an Angel, then God, and then Lord and Logos; and on another occasion He calls Himself Captain, when He appeared in human form to Joshua the son of Nave (Nun). For He can be called by all those names, since He ministers to the Father's will, and since He was begotten of the Father by an act of will;[2] just as we see[3] happening among ourselves: for when we give out some word, we beget the word; yet not by abscission, so as to lessen the word[4] [which remains] in us, when we give it out: and just as we see also happening in the case of a fire, which is not lessened when it has kindled [another], but remains the same; and that which has been kindled by it likewise appears to exist by itself, not diminishing that from which it was kindled. The Word of Wisdom, who is Himself this God begotten of the Father of all things, and Word, and Wisdom, and Power, and the Glory of the Begetter, will bear evidence to me, when He speaks by Solomon the following: 'If I shall declare to you what happens daily, I shall call to mind events from everlasting, and review them. The Lord made me the beginning of His ways for His works. From everlasting He established me in the beginning, before He had made the earth, and before He had made the deeps, before the springs of the waters had issued forth, before the mountains had been

[1] Or, "in the beginning, before all creatures."

[2] The act of will or volition is on the part of the Father.

[3] Or, "Do we not see," etc.

[4] The word λόγος, translated "word," means both the thinking power or reason which produces ideas and the expression of these ideas. And Justin passes here from the one meaning to the other. When we utter a thought, the utterance of it does not diminish the power of thought in us, though in one sense the thought has gone away from us.

established. Before all the hills He begets me. God made the country, and the desert, and the highest inhabited places under the sky. When He made ready the heavens, I was along with Him, and when He set up His throne on the winds: when He made the high clouds strong, and the springs of the deep safe, when He made the foundations of the earth, I was with Him arranging. I was that in which He rejoiced; daily and at all times I delighted in His countenance, because He delighted in the finishing of the habitable world, and delighted in the sons of men. Now, therefore, O son, hear me. Blessed is the man who shall listen to me, and the mortal who shall keep my ways, watching[1] daily at my doors, observing the posts of my ingoings. For my outgoings are the outgoings of life, and [my] will has been prepared by the Lord. But they who sin against me, trespass against their own souls; and they who hate me love death.'[2]

CHAP. LXII.—*The words "Let us make man" agree with the testimony of Proverbs.*

"And the same sentiment was expressed, my friends, by the word of God [written] by Moses, when it indicated to us, with regard to Him whom it has pointed out,[3] that God speaks in the creation of man with the very same design, in the following words: 'Let us make man after our image and likeness. And let them have dominion over the fish of the sea, and over the fowl of the heaven, and over the cattle, and over all the earth, and over all the creeping things that creep on the earth. And God created man: after the image of God did He create him; male and female

[1] The MSS. of Justin read "sleeping," but this is regarded as the mistake of some careless transcriber.

[2] Prov. viii. 21 ff.

[3] Justin, since he is of opinion that the Word is the beginning of the universe, thinks that by these words, "in the beginning," Moses indicated the Word, like many other writers. Hence also he says in Ap. i. 23, that Moses declares the Word "to be begotten first by God." If this explanation does not satisfy, read, "with regard to Him whom I have pointed out" (Maranus).

created He them. And God blessed them, and said, Increase and multiply, and fill the earth, and have power over it.'[1] And that you may not change the [force of the] words just quoted, and repeat what your teachers assert,—either that God said to Himself, 'Let us make,' just as we, when about to do something, oftentimes say to ourselves, 'Let us make;' or that God spoke to the elements, to wit, the earth and other similar substances of which we believe man was formed, 'Let us make,'—I shall quote again the words narrated by Moses himself, from which we can indisputably learn that [God] conversed with some one who was numerically distinct from Himself, and also a rational being. These are the words: 'And God said, Behold, Adam has become as one of us, to know good and evil.'[2] In saying, therefore, 'as one of us,' [Moses] has declared that [there is a certain] number of persons associated with one another, and that they are at least two. For I would not say that the dogma of that heresy[3] which is said to be among you[4] is true, or that the teachers of it can prove that [God] spoke to angels, or that the human frame was the workmanship of angels. But this Offspring, which was truly brought forth from the Father, was with the Father before all the creatures, and the Father communed with Him; even as the Scripture by Solomon has made clear, that He whom Solomon calls Wisdom, was begotten as a Beginning before all His creatures and as Offspring by God, who has also declared this same thing in the revelation made to Joshua the son of Nave (Nun). Listen, therefore, to the following from the book of Joshua,

[1] Gen. i. 26, 28. [2] Gen. iii. 22. [3] Heresy or sect.

[4] Or, "among us." Maranus pronounces against this latter reading for the following reasons: (1.) The Jews had their own heresies which supplied many things to the Christian heresies, especially to Menander and Saturninus. (2.) The sect which Justin here refutes was of opinion that God spoke to angels. But those angels, as Menander and Saturninus invented, "exhorted themselves, saying, Let us make," etc. (3.) The expression διδάσκαλοι suits the rabbins well. So Justin frequently calls them. (4.) Those teachers seem for no other cause to have put the words in the angels' mouths, than to eradicate the testimony by which they proved divine persons.

that what I say may become manifest to you; it is this: 'And it came to pass, when Joshua was near Jericho, he lifted up his eyes, and sees a man standing over against him. And Joshua approached to Him, and said, Art thou for us, or for our adversaries? And He said to him, I am Captain of the Lord's host: now have I come. And Joshua fell on his face on the ground, and said to Him, Lord, what commandest Thou Thy servant? And the Lord's Captain says to Joshua, Loose the shoes off thy feet; for the place whereon thou standest is holy ground. And Jericho was shut up and fortified, and no one went out of it. And the Lord said to Joshua, Behold, I give into thine hand Jericho, and its king, [and] its mighty men.' "[1]

CHAP. LXIII.—*It is proved that this God was incarnate.*

And Trypho said, "This point has been proved to me forcibly, and by many arguments, my friend. It remains, then, to prove that He submitted to become man by the Virgin, according to the will of His Father; and to be crucified, and to die. Prove also clearly, that after this He rose again and ascended to heaven."

I answered, "This, too, has been already demonstrated by me in the previously quoted words of the prophecies, my friends; which, by recalling and expounding for your sakes, I shall endeavour to lead you to agree with me also about this matter. The passage, then, which Isaiah records, 'Who shall declare His generation? for His life is taken away from the earth,'[2]—does it not appear to you to refer to One who, not having descent from men, was said to be delivered over to death by God for the transgressions of the people?—of whose blood, Moses (as I mentioned before), when speaking in parable, said, that He would wash His garments in the blood of the grape; since His blood did not spring from the seed of man, but from the will of God. And then, what is said by David, 'In the splendours of Thy holiness have I begotten Thee from the womb, before the morning star. The Lord hath sworn, and will not repent, Thou art a priest for

[1] Josh. v. 13 ad fin., and vi. 1, 2.
[2] Isa. liii. 8.

ever, after the order of Melchizedek,'[1]—does this not declare to you[2] that [He was] from of old,[3] and that the God and Father of all things intended Him to be begotten by a human womb? And speaking in other words, which also have been already quoted, [he says]: 'Thy throne, O God, is for ever and ever: a sceptre of rectitude is the sceptre of Thy kingdom. Thou hast loved righteousness, and hast hated iniquity: therefore God, even Thy God, hath anointed Thee with the oil of gladness above Thy fellows. [He hath anointed Thee] with myrrh, and oil, and cassia from Thy garments, from the ivory palaces, whereby they made Thee glad. Kings' daughters are in Thy honour. The queen stood at Thy right hand, clad in garments embroidered with gold.[4] Hearken, O daughter, and behold, and incline thine ear, and forget thy people and the house of thy father; and the King shall desire thy beauty: because He is thy Lord, and thou shalt worship Him.'[5] Therefore these words testify explicitly that He is witnessed to by Him who established these things,[6] as deserving to be worshipped, as God and as Christ. Moreover, that the word of God speaks to those who believe in Him as being one soul, and one synagogue, and one church, as to a daughter; that it thus addresses the church which has sprung from His name and partakes of His name (for we are all called Christians), is distinctly proclaimed in like manner in the following words, which teach us also to forget [our] old ancestral customs, when they speak thus:[7] 'Hearken, O daughter, and behold, and incline thine ear; forget thy people and the house of thy father, and the King shall desire thy beauty: because He is thy Lord, and thou shalt worship Him.'"

[1] Ps. cx. 3, 4.

[2] Or, "to us."

[3] ἄνωθεν; in Lat. vers. *antiquitus*, which Maranus prefers.

[4] Literally, "garments of gold, variegated."

[5] Ps. xlv. 6–11.

[6] The incarnation, etc.

[7] "Being so" literally.

CHAP. LXIV.—*Justin adduces other proofs to the Jew, who denies that he needs this Christ.*

Here Trypho said, "Let Him be recognised as Lord and Christ and God, as the Scriptures declare, by you of the Gentiles, who have from His name been all called Christians; but we who are servants of God that made this same [Christ], do not require to confess or worship Him."

To this I replied, "If I were to be quarrelsome and light-minded like you, Trypho, I would no longer continue to converse with you, since you are prepared not to understand what has been said, but only to return some captious answer;[1] but now, since I fear the judgment of God, I do not state an untimely opinion concerning any one of your nation, as to whether or not some of them may be saved by the grace of the Lord of Sabaoth. Therefore, although you act wrongfully, I shall continue to reply to any proposition you shall bring forward, and to any contradiction which you make; and, in fact, I do the very same to all men of every nation, who wish to examine along with me, or make inquiry at me, regarding this subject. Accordingly, if you had bestowed attention on the scriptures previously quoted by me, you would already have understood, that those who are saved of your own nation are saved through this [man], and partake of His lot; and you would not certainly have asked me about this matter. I shall again repeat the words of David previously quoted by me, and beg of you to comprehend them, and not to act wrongfully, and stir each other up to give merely some contradiction. The words which David speaks, then, are these: 'The Lord has reigned; let the nations be angry: [it is] He who sits upon the cherubim; let the earth be shaken. The Lord is great in Zion; and He is high above all the nations. Let them confess Thy great name, for it is fearful and holy; and the honour of the king loves judgment. Thou hast prepared equity; judgment and righteousness hast Thou performed in Jacob. Exalt the Lord our God, and worship the footstool of His feet; for He

[1] Literally, "but only sharpen yourselves to say something."

is holy. Moses and Aaron among His priests, and Samuel among them that call upon His name; they called on the Lord, and He heard them. In the pillar of the cloud He spake to them; for they kept His testimonies and His commandments which He gave them.'[1] And from the other words of David, also previously quoted, which you foolishly affirm refer to Solomon, [because] inscribed for Solomon, it can be proved that they do not refer to Solomon, and that this [Christ] existed before the sun, and that those of your nation who are saved shall be saved through Him. [The words] are these: 'O God, give Thy judgment to the king, and Thy righteousness unto the king's son. He shall judge[2] Thy people with righteousness, and Thy poor with judgment. The mountains shall take up peace to the people, and the little hills righteousness. He shall judge the poor of the people, and shall save the children of the needy, and shall abase the slanderer: and He shall co-endure with the sun, and before the moon unto all generations;' and so on until, 'His name endureth before the sun, and all tribes of the earth shall be blessed in Him. All nations shall call Him blessed. Blessed be the Lord, the God of Israel, who only doeth wondrous things: and blessed be His glorious name for ever and ever: and the whole earth shall be filled with His glory. Amen, amen.'[3] And you remember from other words also spoken by David, and which I have mentioned before, how it is declared that He would come forth from the highest heavens, and again return to the same places, in order that you may recognise Him as God coming forth from above, and man living among men; and [how it is declared] that He will again appear, and they who pierced Him shall see Him, and shall bewail Him. [The words] are these: 'The heavens declare the glory of God, and the firmament showeth His handiwork. Day unto day uttereth speech, and night unto night showeth knowledge. They are not speeches or words whose voices are heard. Their sound has gone out through all the earth, and their words to the ends of the world. In

[1] Ps. xcix. 1-7.
[2] Or, "to judge," as in chap. xxxiv.
[3] Ps. lxxii. 1, etc.

the sun has he set his habitation; and he, like a bridegroom going forth from his chamber, will rejoice as a giant to run his race: from the highest heaven is his going forth, and he returns to the highest heaven, and there is not one who shall be hidden from his heat.' "[1]

CHAP. LXV.—*The Jew objects that God does not give His glory to another. Justin explains the passage.*

And Trypho said, "Being shaken[2] by so many scriptures, I know not what to say about the scripture which Isaiah writes, in which God says that He gives not His glory to another, speaking thus: 'I am the Lord God; this is my name; my glory will I not give to another, nor my virtues.' "[3]

And I answered, "If you spoke these words, Trypho, and then kept silence in simplicity and with no ill intent, neither repeating what goes before nor adding what comes after, you must be forgiven; but if [you have done so] because you imagined that you could throw doubt on the passage, in order that I might say the scriptures contradicted each other, you have erred. But I shall not venture to suppose or to say such a thing; and if a scripture which appears to be of such a kind be brought forward, and if there be a pretext [for saying] that it is contrary [to some other], since I am entirely convinced that no scripture contradicts another, I shall admit rather that I do not understand what is recorded, and shall strive to persuade those who imagine that the scriptures are contradictory, to be rather of the same opinion as myself. With what intent, then, you have brought forward the difficulty, God knows. But I shall remind you of what the passage says, in order that you may recognise even from this very [place] that God gives glory to His Christ alone. And I shall take up some short passages, sirs, those which are in connection with what has been said by Trypho, and those which are also joined on in consecutive order. For I will not repeat those of another section, but those which are joined together in one. Do you also give me your attention. [The words] are these: 'Thus saith the

[1] Ps. xix. 1–6. [2] Literally, "importuned." [3] Isa. xlii. 8.

Lord, the God that created the heavens, and made[1] them fast, that established the earth, and that which is in it; and gave breath to the people upon it, and spirit to them who walk therein: I the Lord God have called Thee in righteousness, and will hold Thine hand, and will strengthen Thee; and I have given Thee for a covenant of the people, for a light of the Gentiles, to open the eyes of the blind, to bring out them that are bound from the chains, and those who sit in darkness from the prison-house. I am the Lord God; this is my name: my glory will I not give to another, nor my virtues to graven images. Behold, the former things are come to pass; new things which I announce, and before they are announced they are made manifest to you. Sing unto the Lord a new song: His sovereignty [is] from the end of the earth. [Sing], ye who descend into the sea, and continually sail[2] [on it]; ye islands, and inhabitants thereof. Rejoice, O wilderness, and the villages thereof, and the houses; and the inhabitants of Cedar shall rejoice, and the inhabitants of the rock shall cry aloud from the top of the mountains: they shall give glory to God; they shall publish His virtues among the islands. The Lord God of hosts shall go forth, He shall destroy war utterly, He shall stir up zeal, and He shall cry aloud to the enemies with strength.'"[3] And when I repeated this, I said to them, "Have you perceived, my friends, that God says He will give Him whom He has established as a light of the Gentiles, glory, and to no other; and not, as Trypho said, that God was retaining the glory to Himself?"

Then Trypho answered, "We have perceived this also; pass on therefore to the remainder of the discourse."

CHAP. LXVI.—*He proves from Isaiah that God was born from a virgin.*

And I, resuming the discourse where I had left off[4] at a previous stage, when proving that He was born of a virgin, and that His birth of a virgin had been predicted by Isaiah,

[1] Literally, "fixed."
[2] Or, "ye islands which sail on it;" or without "continually."
[3] Isa. xlii. 5–13.
[4] Chap. xliii.

quoted again the same prophecy. It is as follows: 'And the Lord spoke again to Ahaz, saying, Ask for thyself a sign from the Lord thy God, in the depth or in the height. And Ahaz said, I will not ask, neither will I tempt the Lord. And Isaiah said, Hear then, O house of David; Is it no small thing for you to contend with men? And how do you contend with the Lord? Therefore the Lord Himself will give you a sign; Behold, the virgin shall conceive, and shall bear a son, and they shall call his name Immanuel. Butter and honey shall he eat; before he knows or prefers the evil he will choose out the good. For before the child knows ill or good, he rejects evil by choosing out the good. For before the child knows how to call father or mother, he shall receive the power of Damascus, and the spoil of Samaria, in presence of the king of Assyria. And the land shall be forsaken, which[1] thou shalt with difficulty endure in consequence of the presence of its two kings. But God shall bring on thee, and on thy people, and on the house of thy father, days which have not yet come upon thee since the day in which Ephraim took away from Judah the king of Assyria.'"[2] And I continued: "Now it is evident to all, that in the race of Abraham according to the flesh no one has been born of a virgin, or is said to have been born [of a virgin], save this our Christ."

CHAP. LXVII.—*Trypho compares Jesus with Perseus; and would prefer [to say] that He was elected [to be Christ] on account of observance of the law. Justin speaks of the law as formerly.*

And Trypho answered, "The Scripture has not, 'Behold, the virgin shall conceive, and bear a son,' but, 'Behold, the young woman shall conceive, and bear a son,' and so on, as you quoted. But the whole prophecy refers to Hezekiah, and it is proved that it was fulfilled in him, according to the terms of this prophecy. Moreover, in the fables of those

[1] ἥν, which is in chap. xliii., is here omitted, but ought to be inserted without doubt.

[2] Isa. vii. 10–17, with Isa. viii. 4 inserted between vers. 16 and 17.

who are called Greeks, it is written that Perseus was begotten of Danae, who was a virgin; he who was called among them Zeus having descended on her in the form of a golden shower. And you ought to feel ashamed when you make assertions similar to theirs, and rather [should] say that this Jesus was born man of men. And if you prove from the Scriptures that He is the Christ, and that on account of having led a life conformed to the law, and perfect, He deserved the honour of being elected to be Christ, [it is well]; but do not venture to tell monstrous phenomena, lest you be convicted of talking foolishly like the Greeks."

Then I said to this, "Trypho, I wish to persuade you, and all men in short, of this, that even though you talk worse things in ridicule and in jest, you will not move me from my fixed design; but I shall always adduce from the words which you think can be brought forward [by you] as proof [of your own views], the demonstration of what I have stated along with the testimony of the Scriptures. You are not, however, acting fairly or truthfully in attempting to undo those things in which there has been constantly agreement between us; namely, that certain commands were instituted by Moses on account of the hardness of your people's hearts. For you said that, by reason of His living conformably to law, He was elected and became Christ, if indeed He were proved to be so."

And Trypho said, "You admitted[1] to us that He was both circumcised, and observed the other legal ceremonies ordained by Moses."

And I replied, "I have admitted it, and do admit it: yet I have admitted that He endured all these not as if He were justified by them, but completing the dispensation which His Father, the Maker of all things, and Lord and God, wished Him [to complete]. For I admit that He endured crucifixion and death, and the incarnation, and the suffering of as

[1] We have not seen that Justin admitted this; but it is not to be supposed that the passage where he did admit it has been lost, as Perionius suspected; for sometimes Justin refers to passages at other places, which he did not relate in their own place.—*Maranus.*

many inflictions as your nation put upon Him. But since again you dissent from that to which you but lately assented, Trypho, answer me: Are those righteous patriarchs who lived before Moses, who observed none of those [ordinances] which, the Scripture shows, received the commencement of [their] institution from Moses, saved, [and have they attained to] the inheritance of the blessed?"

And Trypho said, "The Scriptures compel me to admit it."

"Likewise I again ask you," said I, "did God enjoin your fathers to present the offerings and sacrifices because He had need of them, or because of the hardness of their hearts and tendency to idolatry?"

"The latter," said he, "the Scriptures in like manner compel us to admit."

"Likewise," said I, "did not the Scriptures predict that God promised to dispense a new covenant besides that which [was dispensed] in the mountain Horeb?"

This, too, he replied, had been predicted.

Then I said again, "Was not the old covenant laid on your fathers with fear and trembling, so that they could not give ear to God?"

He admitted it.

"What then?" said I: "God promised that there would be another covenant, not like that old one, and said that it would be laid on them without fear, and trembling, and lightnings, and that it would be such as to show what kind of commands and deeds God knows to be eternal and suited to every nation, and what commandments He has given, suiting them to the hardness of your people's hearts, as He exclaims also by the prophets."

"To this also," said he, "those who are lovers of truth and not lovers of strife must assuredly assent."

Then I replied, "I know not how you speak of persons very fond of strife, [since] you yourself oftentimes were plainly acting in this very manner, frequently contradicting what you had agreed to."

CHAP. LXVIII.—*He complains of the obstinacy of Trypho; he answers his objection; he convicts the Jews of bad faith.*

And Trypho said, "You endeavour to prove an incredible and well-nigh impossible thing; [namely], that God endured to be born and become man."

"If I undertook," said I, "to prove this by doctrines or arguments of man, you should not bear with me. But if I quote frequently scriptures, and so many of them, referring to this point, and ask you to comprehend them, you are hard-hearted in the recognition of the mind and will of God. But if you wish to remain for ever so, I would not be injured at all; and for ever retaining the same [opinions] which I had before I met with you, I shall leave you."

And Trypho said, "Look, my friend, you made yourself master of these [truths] with much labour and toil. And we accordingly must diligently scrutinize all that we meet with, in order to give our assent to those things which the Scriptures compel us [to believe]."

Then I said to this, "I do not ask you not to strive earnestly by all means, in making an investigation of the matters inquired into; but [I ask you], when you have nothing to say, not to contradict those things which you said you had admitted."

And Trypho said, "So we shall endeavour to do."

I continued again: "In addition to the questions I have just now put to you, I wish to put more: for by means of these questions I shall strive to bring the discourse to a speedy termination."

And Trypho said, "Ask the questions."

Then I said, "Do you think that any other one is said to be worthy of worship and called Lord and God in the Scriptures, except the Maker of all, and Christ, who by so many scriptures was proved to you to have become man?"

And Trypho replied, "How can we admit this, when we have instituted so great an inquiry as to whether there is any other than the Father alone?"

Then I again said, "I must ask you this also, that I may

know whether or not you are of a different opinion from that which you admitted some time ago."[1]

He replied, "It is not, sir."

Then again I, "Since you certainly admit these things, and since Scripture says, 'Who shall declare His generation?' ought you not now to suppose that He is not the seed of a human race?"

And Trypho said, "How then does the Word say to David, that of his loins God shall take to Himself a Son, and shall establish His kingdom, and shall set Him on the throne of His glory?"

And I said, "Trypho, if the prophecy which Isaiah uttered, 'Behold, the virgin shall conceive,' is said not to the house of David, but to another house of the twelve tribes, perhaps the matter would have some difficulty; but since this prophecy refers to the house of David, Isaiah has explained how that which was spoken by God to David in mystery would take place. But perhaps you are not aware of this, my friends, that there were many sayings written obscurely, or parabolically, or mysteriously, and symbolical actions, which the prophets who lived after the persons who said or did them expounded."

"Assuredly," said Trypho.

"If, therefore, I shall show that this prophecy of Isaiah refers to our Christ, and not to Hezekiah, as you say, shall I not in this matter, too, compel you not to believe your teachers, who venture to assert that the explanation which your seventy elders that were with Ptolemy the king of the Egyptians gave, is untrue in certain respects? For some statements in the Scriptures, which appear explicitly to convict them of a foolish and vain opinion, these they venture to assert have not been so written. But other statements, which they fancy they can distort and harmonize with human actions,[2] these, they say, refer not to this Jesus Christ of ours, but to him of whom they are pleased to explain them. Thus, for instance, they have taught you that this scripture which

[1] τέως: Vulg. παρὰ Θεῷ, *vitiose.—Otto.*

[2] The text is corrupt, and various emendations have been proposed.

we are now discussing refers to Hezekiah, in which, as I promised, I shall show they are wrong. And since they are compelled, they agree that some scriptures which we mention to them, and which expressly prove that Christ was to suffer, to be worshipped, and [to be called] God, and which I have already recited to you, do refer indeed to Christ, but they venture to assert that this man is not Christ. But they admit that He will come to suffer, and to reign, and to be worshipped, and to be God;[1] and this opinion I shall in like manner show to be ridiculous and silly. But since I am pressed to answer first to what was said by you in jest, I shall make answer to it, and shall afterwards give replies to what follows.

CHAP. LXIX.—*The devil, since he emulates the truth, has invented fables about Bacchus, Hercules, and Æsculapius.*

"Be well assured, then, Trypho," I continued, "that I am established in the knowledge of and faith in the Scriptures by those counterfeits which he who is called the devil is said to have performed among the Greeks; just as some were wrought by the Magi in Egypt, and others by the false prophets in Elijah's days. For when they tell that Bacchus, son of Jupiter, was begotten by [Jupiter's] intercourse with Semele, and that he was the discoverer of the vine; and when they relate, that being torn in pieces, and having died, he rose again, and ascended to heaven; and when they introduce wine[2] into his mysteries, do I not perceive that [the devil] has imitated the prophecy announced by the patriarch Jacob, and recorded by Moses? And when they tell that Hercules was strong, and travelled over all the world, and was begotten by Jove of Alcmene, and ascended to heaven when he died, do I not perceive that the scripture which speaks of Christ, 'strong as a giant to run his race,'[3] has been in like manner imitated? And when he [the devil] brings forward Æscu-

[1] Or, "and to be worshipped as God."

[2] Or, "an ass." The ass was sacred to Bacchus; and many fluctuate between οἶνον and ὄνον.

[3] Ps. xix. 5.

lapius as the raiser of the dead and healer of all diseases, may I not say that in this matter likewise he has imitated the prophecies about Christ? But since I have not quoted to you such scripture as tells that Christ will do these things, I must necessarily remind you of one such: from which you can understand, how that to those destitute of a knowledge of God, I mean the Gentiles, who, 'having eyes, saw not, and having a heart, understood not,' worshipping the images of wood, [how even to them] Scripture prophesied that they would renounce these [vanities], and hope in this Christ. It is thus written: 'Rejoice, thirsty wilderness: let the wilderness be glad, and blossom as the lily: the deserts of the Jordan shall both blossom and be glad: and the glory of Lebanon was given to it, and the honour of Carmel. And my people shall see the exaltation of the Lord, and the glory of God. Be strong, ye careless hands and enfeebled knees. Be comforted, ye faint in soul: be strong, fear not. Behold, our God gives, and will give, retributive judgment. He shall come and save us. Then the eyes of the blind shall be opened, and the ears of the deaf shall hear. Then the lame shall leap as an hart, and the tongue of the stammerers shall be distinct: for water has broken forth in the wilderness, and a valley in the thirsty land; and the parched ground shall become pools, and a spring of water shall [rise up] in the thirsty land.'[1] The spring of living water which gushed forth from God in the land destitute of the knowledge of God, namely the land of the Gentiles, was this Christ, who also appeared in your nation, and healed those who were maimed, and deaf, and lame in body from their birth, causing them to leap, to hear, and to see, by His word. And having raised the dead, and causing them to live, by His deeds He compelled the men who lived at that time to recognise Him. But though they saw such works, they asserted it was magical art. For they dared to call Him a magician, and a deceiver of the people. Yet He wrought such works, and persuaded those who were [destined to] believe on Him; for even if any one be labouring under a defect of body, yet be an

[1] Isa. xxxv. 1–7.

observer of the doctrines delivered by Him, He shall raise him up at His second advent perfectly sound, after He has made him immortal, and incorruptible, and free from grief.

CHAP. LXX.—*So also the mysteries of Mithras are distorted from the prophecies of Daniel and Isaiah.*

"And when those who record the mysteries of Mithras say that he was begotten of a rock, and call the place where those who believe in him are initiated a cave, do I not perceive here that the utterance of Daniel, that a stone without hands was cut out of a great mountain, has been imitated by them, and that they have attempted likewise to imitate the whole of Isaiah's[1] words?[2] For they[3] contrived that the words of righteousness be quoted also by them.[4] But I must repeat to you the words of Isaiah referred to, in order that from them you may know that these things are so. They are these: 'Hear, ye that are far off, what I have done; those that are near shall know my might. The sinners in Zion are removed; trembling shall seize the impious. Who shall announce to you the everlasting place? The man who walks in righteousness, speaks in the right way, hates sin and unrighteousness, and keeps his hands pure from bribes, stops the ears from hearing the unjust judgment of blood, closes the eyes from seeing unrighteousness: he shall dwell in the lofty

[1] The text here has *ταῦτα ποιῆσαι ὁμοίως*. Maranus suggests Ἡσαΐου for *ποιῆσαι*; and so we have translated.

[2] Maranus says: Justin says that the priests of Mithras imitated all the words of Isaiah about to be quoted; and to prove it, is content with a single example, namely, the precepts of righteousness, which they were wont to relate to him, as in these words of Isaiah: "He who walks in righteousness," etc. Justin omitted many other passages, as easy and obvious. For since Mithras is the same as fire, it manifestly answers to the fire of which Isaiah speaks. And since Justin reminded them who are initiated, that they are said to be initiated by Mithras himself, it was not necessary to remind them that the words of Isaiah are imitated in this: "You shall see the King with glory." Bread and water are referred to by Isaiah: so also in these mysteries of Mithras, Justin testifies that bread and a cup of water are placed before them (Apol. i.).

[3] *i.e.* the devils.

[4] *i.e.* the priests of Mithras.

cave of the strong rock. Bread shall be given to him, and his water [shall be] sure. Ye shall see the King with glory, and your eyes shall look far off. Your soul shall pursue diligently the fear of the Lord. Where is the scribe? where are the counsellors? where is he that numbers those who are nourished,—the small and great people? with whom they did not take counsel, nor knew the depth of the voices, so that they heard not. The people are become depreciated, and there is no understanding in him who hears.'[1] Now it is evident, that in this prophecy [allusion is made] to the bread which our Christ gave us to eat,[2] in remembrance of His being made flesh for the sake of His believers, for whom also He suffered; and to the cup which He gave us to drink,[2] in remembrance of His own blood, with giving of thanks. And this prophecy proves that we shall behold this very King with glory; and the very terms of the prophecy declare loudly, that the people foreknown to believe in Him were foreknown to pursue diligently the fear of the Lord. Moreover, these scriptures are equally explicit in saying, that those who are reputed to know the writings of the Scriptures, and who hear the prophecies, have no understanding. And when I hear, Trypho," said I, "that Perseus was begotten of a virgin, I understand that the deceiving serpent counterfeited also this.

CHAP. LXXI.—*The Jews reject the interpretation of the LXX., from which, moreover, they have taken away some passages.*

"But I am far from putting reliance in your teachers, who refuse to admit that the interpretation made by the seventy elders who were with Ptolemy [king] of the Egyptians is a correct one; and they attempt to frame another. And I wish you to observe, that they have altogether taken away many scriptures from the translations effected by those seventy elders who were with Ptolemy, and by which this very man who was crucified is proved to have been set forth expressly as God, and man, and as being crucified, and as dying; but since I am aware that this is denied by all of your

[1] Isa. xxxiii. 13-19. [2] Literally, "to do," ποιεῖν.

nation, I do not address myself to these points, but I proceed[1] to carry on my discussions by means of those passages which are still admitted by you. For you assent to those which I have brought before your attention, except that you contradict the statement, 'Behold, the virgin shall conceive,' and say it ought to be read, 'Behold, the young woman shall conceive.' And I promised to prove that the prophecy referred, not, as you were taught, to Hezekiah, but to this Christ of mine: and now I shall go to the proof."

Here Trypho remarked, "We ask you first of all to tell us some of the scriptures which you allege have been completely cancelled."

CHAP. LXXII.—*Passages have been removed by the Jews from Esdras and Jeremiah.*

And I said, "I shall do as you please. From the statements, then, which Esdras made in reference to the law of the passover, they have taken away the following: 'And Esdras said to the people, This passover is our Saviour and our refuge. And if you have understood, and your heart has taken it in, that we shall humble Him on a standard, and[2] thereafter hope in Him, then this place shall not be forsaken for ever, says the God of hosts. But if you will not believe Him, and will not listen to His declaration, you shall be a laughing-stock to the nations.'[3] And from the sayings of Jeremiah they have cut out the following: 'I [was] like a lamb that is brought to the slaughter: they devised a device against me, saying, Come, let us lay on wood on His bread, and let us blot Him out from the land of the living; and His name shall no more be remembered.'[4] And since this passage from the sayings of Jeremiah is still written in some copies [of the Scriptures] in the synagogues of the Jews (for it is only a short time since they were cut out), and since from these words it is demonstrated that the Jews deliberated about the Christ Himself, to crucify and put Him to

[1] Or, "profess."
[2] Or, "even if we."
[3] It is not known where this passage comes from.
[4] Jer. xi. 19.

death, He Himself is both declared to be led as a sheep to the slaughter, as was predicted by Isaiah, and is here represented as a harmless lamb; but being in a difficulty about them, they give themselves over to blasphemy. And again, from the sayings of the same Jeremiah these have been cut out: 'The Lord God remembered His dead people of Israel who lay in the graves; and He descended to preach to them His own salvation.' [1]

Chap. lxxiii. [*The words*] "*from the wood*" *have been cut out of Ps.* xcvi.

"And from the ninety-fifth (ninety-sixth) Psalm they have taken away this short saying of the words of David: 'From the wood.' [2] For when the passage said, 'Tell ye among the nations, the Lord hath reigned from the wood,' they have left, 'Tell ye among the nations, the Lord hath reigned.' Now no one of your people has ever been said to have reigned as God and Lord among the nations, with the exception of Him only who was crucified, of whom also the Holy Spirit affirms in the same Psalm that He was raised again, and freed from [the grave], declaring that there is none like Him among the gods of the nations: for they are idols of demons. But I shall repeat the whole Psalm to you, that you may perceive what has been said. It is thus: 'Sing unto the Lord a new song; sing unto the Lord, all the earth. Sing unto the Lord, and bless His name; show forth His salvation from day to day. Declare His glory among the nations, His wonders among all people. For the Lord is great, and greatly to be praised: He is to be feared above all the gods. For all the gods of the nations are demons; but the Lord made the heavens. Confession and beauty are in His presence; holiness and magnificence are in His sanctuary. Bring to the Lord, O ye countries of the nations, bring to the Lord glory and honour, bring to the Lord glory in His name. Take

[1] This is wanting in our Scriptures: it is cited by Iren. iii. 20 under the name of Isaiah, and in iv. 22 under that of Jeremiah.—*Maranus.*

[2] These words were not taken away by the Jews, but added by some Christian.—*Otto.*

sacrifices, and go into His courts; worship the Lord in His holy temple. Let the whole earth be moved before Him: tell ye among the nations, the Lord hath reigned.[1] For He hath established the world, which shall not be moved; He shall judge the nations with equity. Let the heavens rejoice, and the earth be glad; let the sea and its fulness shake. Let the fields and all therein be joyful. Let all the trees of the wood be glad before the Lord: for He comes, for He comes to judge the earth. He shall judge the world with righteousness, and the people with His truth.' "

Here Trypho remarked, "Whether [or not] the rulers of the people have erased any portion of the Scriptures, as you affirm, God knows; but it seems incredible."

"Assuredly," said I, "it does seem incredible. For it is more horrible than the calf which they made, when satisfied with manna on the earth; or than the sacrifice of children to demons; or than the slaying of the prophets. But," said I, "you appear to me not to have heard the scriptures which I said they had stolen away. For such as have been quoted are more than enough to prove the points in dispute, besides those which are retained by us,[2] and shall yet be brought forward."

CHAP. LXXIV.—*The beginning of Ps.* xcvi. *is attributed to the Father [by Trypho]. But [it refers] to Christ by these words: "Tell ye among the nations that the Lord," etc.*

Then Trypho said, "We know that you quoted these because we asked you. But it does not appear to me that this Psalm which you quoted last from the words of David refers to any other than the Father and Maker of the heavens and earth. You, however, asserted that it referred to Him who suffered, whom you also are eagerly endeavouring to prove to be Christ."

And I answered, "Attend to me, I beseech you, while I

[1] It is strange that "from the wood" is not added; but the audacity of the copyists in such matters is well known.—*Maranus.*

[2] Many think, "you."

speak of the statement which the Holy Spirit gave utterance to in this Psalm; and you shall know that I speak not sinfully, and that we[1] are not really bewitched; for so you shall be enabled of yourselves to understand many other statements made by the Holy Spirit. 'Sing unto the Lord a new song; sing unto the Lord, all the earth: sing unto the Lord, and bless His name; show forth His salvation from day to day, His wonderful works among all people.' He bids the inhabitants of all the earth, who have known the mystery of this salvation, *i.e.* the suffering of Christ, by which He saved them, sing and give praises to God the Father of all things, and recognise that He is to be praised and feared, and that He is the Maker of heaven and earth, who effected this salvation in behalf of the human race, who also was crucified and was dead, and who was deemed worthy by Him (God) to reign over all the earth. As [is clearly seen[2]] also by the land into which [He said] He would bring [your fathers]; [for He thus speaks]:[3] 'This people [shall go a whoring after other gods], and shall forsake me, and shall break my covenant which I made with them in that day; and I will forsake them, and will turn away my face from them; and they shall be devoured,[4] and many evils and afflictions shall find them out; and they shall say in that day, Because the Lord my God is not amongst us, these misfortunes have found us out. And I shall certainly turn away my face from them in that day, on account of all the evils which they have committed, in that they have turned to other gods.'[5]

CHAP. LXXV.—*It is proved that Jesus was the name of God in the book of Exodus.*

"Moreover, in the book of Exodus we have also perceived that the name of God Himself, which, He says, was not revealed to Abraham or to Jacob, was Jesus, and was declared

1 In text, "you." Maranus suggests, as far better, "we."

2 Something is here awanting; the suggested reading of Maranus has been adopted.

3 Deut. xxxi. 16–18.

4 Literally, "for food."

5 The first conference seems to have ended hereabout.

mysteriously through Moses. Thus it is written: 'And the Lord spake to Moses, Say to this people, Behold, I send my angel before thy face, to keep thee in the way, to bring thee into the land which I have prepared for thee. Give heed to Him, and obey Him; do not disobey Him. For He will not draw back from you; for my name is in Him.'[1] Now understand that He who led your fathers into the land is called by this name Jesus, and first called Auses (Oshea). For if you shall understand this, you shall likewise perceive that the name of Him who said to Moses, 'for my name is in Him,' was Jesus. For, indeed, He was also called Israel, and Jacob's name was changed to this also. Now Isaiah shows that those prophets who are sent to publish tidings from God are called His angels and apostles. For Isaiah says in a certain place, 'Send me.'[2] And that the prophet whose name was changed, Jesus [Joshua], was strong and great, is manifest to all. If, then, we know that God revealed Himself in so many forms to Abraham, and to Jacob, and to Moses, how are we at a loss, and do not believe that, according to the will of the Father of all things, it was possible for Him to be born man of the Virgin, especially after we have such[3] scriptures, from which it can be plainly perceived that He became so according to the will of the Father?

CHAP. LXXVI.—*From other passages the same majesty and government of Christ are proved.*

"For when Daniel speaks of 'one like unto the Son of man' who received the everlasting kingdom, does he not hint at this very thing? For he declares that, in saying 'like unto the Son of man,' He appeared, and was man, but not of human seed. And the same thing he proclaimed in mystery when he speaks of this stone which was cut out without hands. For the expression 'it was cut out without hands' signified that it is not a work of man, but [a work] of the will of the Father and God of all things, who brought Him forth. And when Isaiah says, 'Who shall declare His generation?'

[1] Ex. xxiii. 20, 21. [2] Isa. vi. 8. [3] Or, "so many."

he meant that His descent could not be declared. Now no one who is a man of men has a descent that cannot be declared. And when Moses says that He will wash His garments in the blood of the grape, does not this signify what I have now often told you is an obscure prediction, namely, that He had blood, but not from men; just as not man, but God, has begotten the blood of the vine? And when Isaiah calls Him the angel of mighty counsel, did he not foretell Him to be the teacher of those truths which He did teach when He came [to earth]? For He alone taught openly those mighty counsels which the Father designed both for all those who have been and shall be well-pleasing to Him, and also for those who have rebelled against His will, whether men or angels, when He said: 'They shall come from the east [and from the west[1]], and shall sit down with Abraham, and Isaac, and Jacob, in the kingdom of heaven: but the children of the kingdom shall be cast out into outer darkness.'[2] And, 'Many shall say to me in that day, Lord, Lord, have we not eaten, and drunk, and prophesied, and cast out demons in Thy name? And I will say to them, Depart from me.'[3] Again, in other words, by which He shall condemn those who are unworthy of salvation, He said, 'Depart into outer darkness, which the Father has prepared for Satan and his angels.'[4] And again, in other words, He said, 'I give unto you power to tread on serpents, and on scorpions, and on scolopendras, and on all the might of the enemy.'[5] And now we, who believe on our Lord Jesus, who was crucified under Pontius Pilate, when we exorcise all demons and evil spirits, have them subjected to us. For if the prophets declared obscurely that Christ would suffer, and thereafter be Lord of all, yet that [declaration] could not be understood by any man until He Himself persuaded the apostles that such statements were expressly related in the Scriptures. For He exclaimed before His crucifixion: 'The Son of man must suffer many things, and be rejected by the scribes and Pharisees, and be crucified, and on the third day rise again.'[6] And David predicted that

[1] Not in all edd. [2] Matt. viii. 11. [3] Matt. vii. 22.
[4] Matt. xxv. 41. [5] Luke x. 19. [6] Luke ix. 22.

He would be born from the womb before sun and moon,[1] according to the Father's will, and made Him known, being Christ, as God strong and to be worshipped."

CHAP. LXXVII.—*He returns to explain the prophecy of Isaiah.*

Then Trypho said, "I admit that such and so great arguments are sufficient to persuade one; but I wish [you] to know that I ask you for the proof which you have frequently proposed to give me. Proceed then to make this plain to us, that we may see how you prove that that [passage] refers to this Christ of yours. For we assert that the prophecy relates to Hezekiah." And I replied, "I shall do as you wish. But show me yourselves first of all how it is said of Hezekiah, that before he knew how to call father or mother, he received the power of Damascus and the spoils of Samaria in the presence of the king of Assyria. For it will not be conceded to you, as you wish to explain it, that Hezekiah waged war with the inhabitants of Damascus and Samaria in presence of the king of Assyria. 'For before the child knows how to call father or mother,' the prophetic word said, 'He shall take the power of Damascus and spoils of Samaria in presence of the king of Assyria.' For if the Spirit of prophecy had not made the statement with an addition, 'Before the child knows how to call father or mother, he shall take the power of Damascus and spoils of Samaria,' but had only said, 'And shall bear a son, and he shall take the power of Damascus and spoils of Samaria,' then you might say that God foretold that he would take these things, since He foreknew it. But now the prophecy has stated it with this addition: 'Before the child knows how to call father or mother, he shall take the power of Damascus and spoils of Samaria.' And you cannot prove that such a thing ever happened to any one among the Jews. But we are able to prove that it happened in the case of our Christ. For at the

[1] Justin puts "sun and moon" instead of "Lucifer." Maranus says, David did predict, not that Christ would be born of Mary before sun and moon, but that it would happen before sun and moon that He would be born of a virgin.

time of His birth, Magi who came from Arabia worshipped Him, coming first to Herod, who then was sovereign in your land, and whom the Scripture calls king of Assyria on account of his ungodly and sinful character. For you know," continued I, "that the Holy Spirit oftentimes announces such events by parables and similitudes; just as He did towards all the people in Jerusalem, frequently saying to them, 'Thy father is an Amorite, and thy mother a Hittite.'[1]

Chap. lxxviii.—*He proves that this prophecy harmonizes with Christ alone, from what is afterwards written.*

"Now this king Herod, at the time when the Magi came to him from Arabia, and said they knew from a star which appeared in the heavens that a King had been born in your country, and that they had come to worship Him, learned from the elders of your people that it was thus written regarding Bethlehem in the prophet: 'And thou, Bethlehem, in the land of Judah, art by no means least among the princes of Judah; for out of thee shall go forth the leader who shall feed my people.'[2] Accordingly the Magi from Arabia came to Bethlehem and worshipped the child, and presented Him with gifts, gold and frankincense, and myrrh; but returned not to Herod, being warned in a revelation after worshipping the child in Bethlehem. And Joseph, the spouse of Mary, who wished at first to put away his betrothed Mary, supposing her to be pregnant by intercourse with a man, *i.e.* from fornication, was commanded in a vision not to put away his wife; and the angel who appeared to him told him that what is in her womb is of the Holy Ghost. Then he was afraid, and did not put her away; but on the occasion of the first census which was taken in Judæa, under Cyrenius, he went up from Nazareth, where he lived, to Bethlehem, to which he belonged, to be enrolled; for his family was of the tribe of Judah, which then inhabited that region. Then along with Mary he is ordered to proceed into Egypt, and remain there with the child until another revelation warn them to return into Judæa. But when the child was born in

[1] Ezek. xvi. 3. [2] Mic. v. 2.

Bethlehem, since Joseph could not find a lodging in that village, he took up his quarters in a certain cave near the village; and while they were there Mary brought forth the Christ and placed Him in a manger, and here the Magi who came from Arabia found Him. I have repeated to you," I continued, "what Isaiah foretold about the sign which foreshadowed the cave; but for the sake of those who have come with us to-day, I shall again remind you of the passage." Then I repeated the passage from Isaiah which I have already written, adding that, by means of those words, those who presided over the mysteries of Mithras were stirred up by the devil to say that in a place, called among them a cave, they were initiated by him.[1] "So Herod, when the Magi from Arabia did not return to him, as he had asked them to do, but had departed by another way to their own country, according to the commands laid on them; and when Joseph, with Mary and the child, had now gone into Egypt, as it was revealed to them to do; as he did not know the child whom the Magi had gone to worship, ordered simply the whole of the children then in Bethlehem to be massacred. And Jeremiah prophesied that this would happen, speaking by the Holy Ghost thus: 'A voice was heard in Ramah, lamentation and much wailing, Rachel weeping for her children; and she would not be comforted, because they are not.'[2] Therefore, on account of the voice which would be heard from Ramah, *i.e.* from Arabia (for there is in Arabia at this very time a place called Rama), wailing would come on the place where Rachel the wife of Jacob called Israel, the holy patriarch, has been buried, *i.e.* on Bethlehem; while the women weep for their own slaughtered children, and have no consolation by reason of what has happened to them. For that expression of Isaiah, 'He shall take the power of Damascus and spoils of Samaria,' foretold that the power of the evil demon that dwelt in Damascus should be

[1] Text has, by "them;" but Maranus says the artifice lay in the priest's compelling the initiated to say that Mithras himself was the initiator in the cave.

[2] Jer. xxxi. 15.

overcome by Christ as soon as He was born; and this is proved to have happened. For the Magi, who were held in bondage[1] for the commission of all evil deeds through the power of that demon, by coming to worship Christ, show that they have revolted from that dominion which held them captive; and this [dominion] the Scripture has showed us to reside in Damascus. Moreover, that sinful and unjust power is termed well in parable, Samaria.[2] And none of you can deny that Damascus was, and is, in the region of Arabia, although now it belongs to what is called Syrophœnicia. Hence it would be becoming for you, sirs, to learn what you have not perceived, from those who have received grace from God, namely, from us Christians; and not to strive in every way to maintain your own doctrines, dishonouring those of God. Therefore also this grace has been transferred to us, as Isaiah says, speaking to the following effect: 'This people draws near to me, they honour me with their lips, but their heart is far from me; but in vain they worship me, teaching the commands and doctrines of men. Therefore, behold, I will proceed[3] to remove this people, and I shall remove them; and I shall take away the wisdom of their wise men, and bring to nothing the understanding of the prudent men.'"[4]

CHAP. LXXIX.—*He proves against Trypho that the wicked angels have revolted from God.*

On this, Trypho, who was somewhat angry, but respected the Scriptures, as was manifest from his countenance, said to me, "The utterances of God are holy, but your expositions are mere contrivances, as is plain from what has been explained by you; nay, even blasphemies, for you assert that angels sinned and revolted from God."

And I, wishing to get him to listen to me, answered in milder tones, thus: "I admire, sir, this piety of yours; and I

1 Literally, "spoiled."

2 Justin thinks the "spoils of Samaria" denote spoils of Satan; Tertull. thinks that they are spoils of Christ.

3 Literally, "add."

4 Isa. xxix. 13, 14.

pray that you may entertain the same disposition towards Him to whom angels are recorded to minister, as Daniel says; for [one] like the Son of man is led to the Ancient of days, and every kingdom is given to Him for ever and ever. But that you may know, sir," continued I, "that it is not our audacity which has induced us to adopt this exposition, which you reprehend, I shall give you evidence from Isaiah himself; for he affirms that evil angels have dwelt and do dwell in Tanis, in Egypt. These are [his] words: 'Woe to the rebellious children! Thus saith the Lord, You have taken counsel, but not through me; and [made] agreements, but not through my Spirit, to add sins to sins; who have sinned[1] in going down to Egypt (but they have not inquired at me), that they may be assisted by Pharaoh, and be covered with the shadow of the Egyptians. For the shadow of Pharaoh shall be a disgrace to you, and a reproach to those who trust in the Egyptians; for the princes in Tanis[2] are evil angels. In vain will they labour for a people which will not profit them by assistance, but [will be] for a disgrace and a reproach [to them].'[3] And, further, Zechariah tells, as you yourself have related, that the devil stood on the right hand of Joshua the priest, to resist him; and [the Lord] said, 'The Lord, who has taken[4] Jerusalem, rebuke thee.'[5] And again, it is written in Job,[6] as you said yourself, how that the angels came to stand before the Lord, and the devil came with them. And we have it recorded by Moses in the beginning of Genesis, that the serpent beguiled Eve, and was cursed. And we know that in Egypt there were magicians who emulated[7] the mighty power displayed by God through the faithful servant Moses. And you are aware that David said, 'The gods of the nations are demons.'"[8]

[1] LXX. "who walk," *πορευόμενοι* for *πονηρευόμενοι*.

[2] In E. V. "Zoan."

[3] Isa. xxx. 1-5.

[4] *ἐκδεξάμενος*; in chap. cxv. *inf.* it is *ἐκλεξάμενος*.

[5] Zech. iii. 1.

[6] Job i. 6.

[7] Maranus suggests the insertion of *ἐποίησαν* or *ἐπείρασαν* before *ἐξισοῦσθαι*.

[8] Ps. xcvi. 5.

CHAP. LXXX.—*The opinion of Justin with regard to the reign of a thousand years. Several catholics reject it.*

And Trypho to this replied, "I remarked to you, sir, that you are very anxious to be safe in all respects, since you cling to the Scriptures. But tell me, do you really admit that this place, Jerusalem, shall be rebuilt; and do you expect your people to be gathered together, and made joyful with Christ and the patriarchs, and the prophets, both the men of our nation, and other proselytes who joined them before your Christ came? or have you given way, and admitted this in order to have the appearance of worsting us in the controversies?"

Then I answered, "I am not so miserable a fellow, Trypho, as to say one thing and think another. I admitted to you formerly,[1] that I and many others are of this opinion, and [believe] that such will take place, as you assuredly are aware;[2] but, on the other hand, I signified to you that many who belong to the pure and pious faith, and are true Christians, think otherwise. Moreover, I pointed out to you that some who are called Christians, but are godless, impious heretics, teach doctrines that are in every way blasphemous, atheistical, and foolish. But that you may know that I do not say this before you alone, I shall draw up a statement, so far as I can, of all the arguments which have passed between us; in which I shall record myself as admitting the very same things which I admit to you. For I choose to follow not men or men's doctrines, but God and the doctrines [delivered] by Him. For if you have fallen in with some who are called Christians, but who do not admit this [truth],[3] and venture to blaspheme the God of Abraham, and the God of Isaac, and the God of Jacob; who say there is no resurrection of the dead, and that their souls, when they die, are taken to

[1] Justin made no previous allusion to this point, so far as we know from the writing preserved.

[2] Or, "so as to thoroughly believe that such will take place" (after "opinion").

[3] *i.e.* resurrection.

heaven; do not imagine that they are Christians, even as one, if he would rightly consider it, would not admit that the Sadducees, or similar sects of Genistæ, Meristæ,[1] Galilæans, Hellenists,[2] Pharisees, Baptists, are Jews (do not hear me impatiently when I tell you what I think), but are [only] called Jews and children of Abraham, worshipping God with the lips, as God Himself declared, but the heart was far from Him. But I and others, who are right-minded Christians on all points, are assured that there will be a resurrection of the dead, and a thousand years[3] in Jerusalem, which will then be built, adorned, and enlarged, [as] the prophets Ezekiel and Isaiah and others declare.

CHAP. LXXXI.—*He endeavours to prove this opinion from Isaiah and the Apocalypse.*

"For Isaiah spake thus concerning this space of a thousand years: 'For there shall be the new heaven and the new earth, and the former shall not be remembered, or come into their heart; but they shall find joy and gladness in it, which things I create. For, behold, I make Jerusalem a rejoicing, and my people a joy; and I shall rejoice over Jerusalem, and be glad over my people. And the voice of weeping shall be no more heard in her, or the voice of crying. And there shall be no

[1] Maranus says, Hieron. thinks the *Genistæ* were so called because they were sprung from Abraham (γένος), the *Meristæ* so called because they separated the Scriptures. Josephus bears testimony to the fact that the sects of the Jews differed in regard to fate and providence; the Pharisees submitting all things indeed to God, with the exception of human wills; the Essenes making no exceptions, and submitting all to God. I believe therefore that the *Genistæ* were so called because they believed the world to be in general governed by God; the *Meristæ*, because they believed that a fate or providence belonged to each man.

[2] Otto says, the author and chief of this sect of *Galilæans* was Judas Galilæus, who, after the exile of king Archelaus, when the Romans wished to raise a tax in Judæa, excited his countrymen to the retaining of their former liberty.—The *Hellenists*, or rather *Hellenæans*. No one mentions this sect but Justin; perhaps *Herodians* or *Hillelæans* (from R. Hillel).

[3] We have translated the text of Justin as it stands. Commentators make the sense, "and that there will be a thousand years in Jerusalem," or "that the saints will live a thousand years in Jerusalem."

more there a person of immature years, or an old man who shall not fulfil his days.[1] For the young man shall be an hundred years old;[2] but the sinner who dies an hundred years old,[2] he shall be accursed. And they shall build houses, and shall themselves inhabit them; and they shall plant vines, and shall themselves eat the produce of them, and drink the wine. They shall not build, and others inhabit; they shall not plant, and others eat. For according to the days of the tree of life shall be the days of my people; the works of their toil shall abound.[3] Mine elect shall not toil fruitlessly, or beget children to be cursed; for they shall be a seed righteous and blessed by the Lord, and their offspring with them. And it shall come to pass, that before they call I will hear; while they are still speaking, I shall say, What is it? Then shall the wolves and the lambs feed together, and the lion shall eat straw like the ox; but the serpent [shall eat] earth as bread. They shall not hurt or maltreat each other on the holy mountain, saith the Lord.'[4] Now we have understood that the expression used among these words, 'According to the days of the tree [of life[5]] shall be the days of my people; the works of their toil shall abound,' obscurely predicts a thousand years. For as Adam was told that in the day he ate of the tree he would die, we know that he did not complete a thousand years. We have perceived, moreover, that the expression, 'The day of the Lord is as a thousand years,'[6] is connected with this subject. And further, there was a certain man with us, whose name was John, one of the apostles of Christ, who prophesied, by a revelation that was made to him, that those who believed in our Christ would dwell[7] a thousand years in Jerusalem; and that thereafter the general, and, in short, the eternal resurrection and judgment of all men would likewise take place. Just as our Lord also said,

[1] Literally, "time."

[2] Literally, "the son of an hundred years."

[3] Or, as in margin of A. V., "they shall make the works of their toil continue long," so reading παλαιώσουσιν for πλεονάσουσιν: thus also LXX.

[4] Isa. lxv. 17 to end.

[5] These words are not found in the MSS.

[6] Ps. xc. 4; 2 Pet. iii. 8.

[7] Literally, "make."

'They shall neither marry nor be given in marriage, but shall be equal to the angels, the children of the God of the resurrection.'[1]

CHAP. LXXXII.—*The prophetical gifts of the Jews were transferred to the Christians.*

"For the prophetical gifts remain with us, even to the present time. And hence you ought to understand that [the gifts] formerly among your nation have been transferred to us. And just as there were false prophets contemporaneous with your holy prophets, so are there now many false teachers amongst us, of whom our Lord forewarned us to beware; so that in no respect are we deficient, since we know that He foreknew all that would happen to us after His resurrection from the dead and ascension to heaven. For He said we would be put to death, and hated for His name's sake; and that many false prophets and false Christs would appear in His name, and deceive many: and so has it come about. For many have taught godless, blasphemous, and unholy doctrines, forging them in His name; have taught, too, and even yet are teaching, those things which proceed from the unclean spirit of the devil, and which were put into their hearts. Therefore we are most anxious that you be persuaded not to be misled by such persons, since we know that every one who can speak the truth, and yet speaks it not, shall be judged by God, as God testified by Ezekiel, when He said, 'I have made thee a watchman to the house of Judah. If the sinner sin, and thou warn him not, he himself shall die in his sin; but his blood will I require at thine hand. But if thou warn him, thou shalt be innocent.'[2] And on this account we are, through fear, very earnest in desiring to converse [with men] according to the Scriptures, but not from love of money, or of glory, or of pleasure. For no man can convict us of any of these [vices]. No more do we wish to live like the rulers of your people, whom God reproaches when He says, 'Your rulers are companions of thieves, lovers of bribes, followers of the rewards.'[3] Now, if you know

[1] Luke xx. 35 f. [2] Ezek. iii. 17, 18, 19. [3] Isa. i. 23.

certain amongst us to be of this sort, do not for their sakes blaspheme the Scriptures and Christ, and do not assiduously strive to give falsified interpretations.

CHAP. LXXXIII.—*It is proved that the Psalm, "The Lord said to my Lord," etc., does not suit Hezekiah.*

"For your teachers have ventured to refer the passage, 'The Lord says to my Lord, Sit at my right hand, till I make Thine enemies Thy footstool,' to Hezekiah; as if he were requested to sit on the right side of the temple, when the king of Assyria sent to him and threatened him; and he was told by Isaiah not to be afraid. Now we know and admit that what Isaiah said took place; that the king of Assyria desisted from waging war against Jerusalem in Hezekiah's days, and the angel of the Lord slew about 185,000 of the host of the Assyrians. But it is manifest that the Psalm does not refer to him. For thus it is written, 'The Lord says to my Lord, Sit at my right hand, till I make Thine enemies Thy footstool. He shall send forth a rod of power over[1] Jerusalem, and it shall rule in the midst of Thine[2] enemies. In the splendour of the saints before the morning star have I begotten Thee. The Lord hath sworn, and will not repent, Thou art a priest for ever after the order of Melchizedek.' Who does not admit, then, that Hezekiah is no priest for ever after the order of Melchizedek? And who does not know that he is not the redeemer of Jerusalem? And who does not know that he neither sent a rod of power into Jerusalem, nor ruled in the midst of his enemies; but that it was God who averted from him the enemies, after he mourned and was afflicted? But our Jesus, who has not yet come in glory, has sent into Jerusalem a rod of power, namely, the word of calling and repentance [meant] for all nations over which demons held sway, as David says, 'The gods of the nations are demons.' And His strong word has

1 *ἐπί*, but afterwards *εἰς*. Maranus thinks that *ἐπί* is the insertion of some copyist.

2 Or better, "His." This quotation from Ps. cx. is put very differently from the previous quotation of the same Psalm in chap. xxxii.

prevailed on many to forsake the demons whom they used to serve, and by means of it to believe in the Almighty God because the gods of the nations are demons.[1] And we mentioned formerly that the statement, 'In the splendour of the saints before the morning star have I begotten Thee from the womb,' is made to Christ.

CHAP. LXXXIV.—*That prophecy, "Behold, a virgin," etc., suits Christ alone.*

"Moreover, the prophecy, 'Behold, the virgin shall conceive, and bear a son,' was uttered respecting Him. For if He to whom Isaiah referred was not to be begotten of a virgin, of whom[2] did the Holy Spirit declare, 'Behold, the Lord Himself shall give us a sign: behold, the virgin shall conceive, and bear a son?' For if He also were to be begotten of sexual intercourse, like all other first-born sons, why did God say that He would give a sign which is not common to all the first-born sons? But that which is truly a sign, and which was to be made trustworthy to mankind,—namely, that the first-begotten of all creation should become incarnate by the Virgin's womb, and be a child,—this he anticipated by the Spirit of prophecy, and predicted it, as I have repeated to you, in various ways; in order that, when the event should take place, it might be known as the operation of the power and will of the Maker of all things; just as Eve was made from one of Adam's ribs, and as all living beings were created in the beginning by the word of God. But you in these matters venture to pervert the expositions which your elders that were with Ptolemy king of Egypt gave forth, since you assert that the scripture is not so as they have expounded it, but says, 'Behold, the young woman shall conceive,' as if great events were to be inferred if a woman should beget from sexual intercourse: which indeed all young women, with the exception of the barren, do; but even these, God, if He wills, is able to cause [to bear]. For Samuel's mother, who was barren, brought forth by the will of God;

[1] This last clause is thought to be an interpolation.
[2] Or, "why was it."

and so also the wife of the holy patriarch Abraham; and Elisabeth, who bore John the Baptist, and other such. So that you must not suppose that it is impossible for God to do anything He wills. And especially when it was predicted that this would take place, do not venture to pervert or misinterpret the prophecies, since you will injure yourselves alone, and will not harm God.

Chap. lxxxv.—*He proves that Christ is the Lord of hosts from Ps.* xxiv., *and from His authority over demons.*

"Moreover, some of you venture to expound the prophecy which runs, 'Lift up your gates, ye rulers; and be ye lift up, ye everlasting doors, that the King of glory may enter,'[1] as if it referred likewise to Hezekiah, and others of you [expound it] of Solomon; but neither to the latter nor to the former, nor, in short, to any of your kings, can it be proved to have reference, but to this our Christ alone, who appeared without comeliness, and inglorious, as Isaiah and David and all the scriptures said; who is the Lord of hosts, by the will of the Father who conferred on Him [the dignity]; who also rose from the dead, and ascended to heaven, as the Psalm and the other scriptures manifested when they announced Him to be Lord of hosts; and of this you may, if you will, easily be persuaded by the occurrences which take place before your eyes. For every demon, when exorcised in the name of this very Son of God—who is the First-born of every creature, who became man by the Virgin, who suffered, and was crucified under Pontius Pilate by your nation, who died, who rose from the dead, and ascended into heaven—is overcome and subdued. But though you exorcise any demon in the name of any of those who were amongst you—either kings, or righteous men, or prophets, or patriarchs—it will not be subject to you. But if any of you exorcise it in [the name of] the God of Abraham, and the God of Isaac, and the God of Jacob, it will perhaps be subject to you. Now assuredly your exorcists, I have said,[2] make use of craft when they exorcise, even as the Gentiles do, and employ

[1] Ps. xxiv. 7. [2] Chap. lxxvi.

fumigations and incantations.[1] But that they are angels and powers whom the word of prophecy by David [commands] to lift up the gates, that He who rose from the dead, Jesus Christ, the Lord of hosts, according to the will of the Father, might enter, the word of David has likewise showed; which I shall again recall to your attention for the sake of those who were not with us yesterday, for whose benefit, moreover, I sum up many things I said yesterday. And now, if I say this to you, although I have repeated it many times, I know that it is not absurd so to do. For it is a ridiculous thing to see the sun, and the moon, and the other stars, continually keeping the same course, and bringing round the different seasons; and to see the computer who may be asked how many are twice two, because he has frequently said that they are four, not ceasing to say again that they are four; and equally so other things, which are confidently admitted, to be continually mentioned and admitted in like manner; yet that he who founds his discourse on the prophetic scriptures should leave them and abstain from constantly referring to the same scriptures, because it is thought he can bring forth something better than Scripture. The passage, then, by which I proved that God reveals that there are both angels and hosts in heaven is this: 'Praise the Lord from the heavens: praise Him in the highest. Praise Him, all His angels: praise Him, all His hosts.'"[2]

Then one of those who had come with them on the second day, whose name was Mnaseas, said, "We are greatly pleased that you undertake to repeat the same things on our account."

And I said, "Listen, my friends, to the scripture which induces me to act thus. Jesus commanded [us] to love even [our] enemies, as was predicted by Isaiah in many passages,

[1] *κατάδεσμοι*, by some thought to be verses by which evil spirits, once expelled, were kept from returning. Plato (*Rep.*) speaks of incantations by which demons were summoned to the help of those who practised such rites; but Justin refers to them only as being expelled. Others regard them as drugs.

[2] Ps. cxlviii. 1, 2.

in which also is contained the mystery of our own regeneration, as well, in fact, as the regeneration of all who expect that Christ will appear in Jerusalem, and by their works endeavour earnestly to please Him. These are the words spoken by Isaiah: 'Hear the word of the Lord, ye that tremble at His word. Say, our brethren, to them that hate you and detest you, that the name of the Lord has been glorified. He has appeared to your joy, and they shall be ashamed. A voice of noise from the city, a voice from the temple,[1] a voice of the Lord who rendereth recompense to the proud. Before she that travailed brought forth, and before the pains of labour came, she brought forth a male child. Who hath heard such a thing? and who hath seen such a thing? has the earth brought forth in one day? and has she produced a nation at once? for Zion has travailed and borne her children. But I have given such an expectation even to her that does not bring forth, said the Lord. Behold, I have made her that begetteth, and her that is barren, saith the Lord. Rejoice, O Jerusalem, and hold a joyous assembly, all ye that love her. Be glad, all ye that mourn for her, that ye may suck and be filled with the breast of her consolation, that having suck ye may be delighted with the entrance of His glory.'"[2]

CHAP. LXXXVI.—*There are various figures in the Old Testament of the wood of the cross by which Christ reigned.*

And when I had quoted this, I added, "Hear, then, how this man, of whom the Scriptures declare that He will come again in glory after His crucifixion, was symbolized both by the tree of life, which was said to have been planted in paradise, and by those events which should happen to all the just. Moses was sent with a rod to effect the redemption of the people; and with this in his hands at the head of the people, he divided the sea. By this he saw the water gushing out of the rock; and when he cast a tree into the waters of Marah, which were bitter, he made them sweet. Jacob, by putting rods into the water-troughs, caused the sheep of

[1] In both MSS. "people."

[2] Isa. lxvi. 5–11.

his uncle to conceive, so that he should obtain their young. With his rod the same Jacob boasts that he had crossed the river. He said he had seen a ladder, and the Scripture has declared that God stood above it. But that this was not the Father, we have proved from the Scriptures. And Jacob, having poured oil on a stone in the same place, is testified to by the very God who appeared to him, that he had anointed a pillar to the God who appeared to him. And that the stone symbolically proclaimed Christ, we have also proved by many scriptures; and that the unguent, whether it was of oil, or of stacte, or of any other compounded sweet balsams, had reference to Him, we have also proved,[1] inasmuch as the word says: 'Therefore God, even Thy God, hath anointed Thee with the oil of gladness above Thy fellows.'[2] For indeed all kings and anointed persons obtained from Him their share in the names of kings and anointed: just as He Himself received from the Father the titles of King, and Christ, and Priest, and Angel, and such like other titles which He bears or did bear. Aaron's rod, which blossomed, declared him to be the high priest. Isaiah prophesied that a rod would come forth from the root of Jesse, [and this was] Christ. And David says that the righteous man is 'like the tree that is planted by the channels of waters, which should yield its fruit in its season, and whose leaf should not fade.'[3] Again, the righteous is said to flourish like the palm-tree. God appeared from a tree to Abraham, as it is written, near the oak in Mamre. The people found seventy willows and twelve springs after crossing the Jordan.[4] David affirms that God comforted him with a rod and staff. Elisha, by casting a stick[5] into the river Jordan, recovered the iron part of the axe with which the sons of the prophets had gone to cut down trees to build the house in which they wished to read and study the law and commandments of God; even as our Christ, by being crucified on the tree, and by purifying [us] with water, has redeemed us, though plunged in the direst offences

[1] In chap. lxiii. probably, where the same Psalm is quoted.

[2] Ps. xlv. 7.

[3] Ps. i. 3.

[4] The Red Sea, not the Jordan.

[5] Literally, "a tree"

which we have committed, and has made [us] a house of prayer and adoration. Moreover, it was a rod that pointed out Judah to be the father of Tamar's sons by a great mystery."

CHAP. LXXXVII.—*Trypho maintains in objection these words: "And shall rest on him," etc. They are explained by Justin.*

Hereupon Trypho, after I had spoken these words, said, "Do not now suppose that I am endeavouring, by asking what I do ask, to overturn the statements you have made; but I wish to receive information respecting those very points about which I now inquire. Tell me, then, how, when the Scripture asserts by Isaiah, 'There shall come forth a rod from the root of Jesse; and a flower shall grow up from the root of Jesse; and the Spirit of God shall rest upon Him, the spirit of wisdom and understanding, the spirit of counsel and might, the spirit of knowledge and piety: and the spirit of the fear of the Lord shall fill Him:'[1] (now you admitted to me," continued he, "that this referred to Christ, and you maintain Him to be pre-existent God, and having become incarnate by God's will, to be born man by the Virgin:) how He can be demonstrated to have been pre-existent, who is filled with the powers of the Holy Ghost, which the Scripture by Isaiah enumerates, as if He were in lack of them?"

Then I replied, "You have inquired most discreetly and most prudently, for truly there does seem to be a difficulty; but listen to what I say, that you may perceive the reason of this also. The Scripture says that these enumerated powers of the Spirit have come on Him, not because He stood in need of them, but because they would rest in Him, *i.e.* would find their accomplishment in Him, so that there would be no more prophets in your nation after the ancient custom: and this fact you plainly perceive. For after Him no prophet has arisen among you. Now, that [you may know that] your prophets, each receiving some one or two powers from God, did and spoke the things which we have learned from the Scriptures, attend to the following remarks of mine. Solomon

[1] Isa. xi. 1 ff.

possessed the spirit of wisdom, Daniel that of understanding and counsel, Moses that of might and piety, Elijah that of fear, and Isaiah that of knowledge; and so with the others: each possessed one power, or one joined alternately with another; also Jeremiah, and the twelve [prophets], and David, and, in short, the rest who existed amongst you. Accordingly He[1] rested, *i.e.* ceased, when *He* came, after whom, in the times of this dispensation wrought out by Him amongst men,[2] it was requisite that such gifts should cease from you; and having received their rest in Him, should again, as had been predicted, become gifts which, from the grace of His Spirit's power, He imparts to those who believe in Him, according as He deems each man worthy thereof. I have already said, and do again say, that it had been prophesied that this would be done by Him after His ascension to heaven. It is accordingly said,[3] 'He ascended on high, He led captivity captive, He gave gifts unto the sons of men.' And again, in another prophecy it is said: 'And it shall come to pass after this, I will pour out my Spirit on all flesh, and on my servants, and on my handmaids, and they shall prophesy.'[4]

CHAP. LXXXVIII.—*Christ has not received the Holy Spirit on account of poverty.*

"Now, it is possible to see amongst us women and men who possess gifts of the Spirit of God; so that it was prophesied that the powers enumerated by Isaiah would come upon Him, not because He needed power, but because these would not continue after Him. And let this be a proof to you, namely, what I told you was done by the Magi from Arabia, who as soon as the child was born came to worship Him, for even at His birth He was in possession of His power; and as He grew up like all other men, by using the fitting means, He assigned its own [requirements] to each development, and was sustained by all kinds of nourishment,

[1] He, that is, the Spirit. The following "He" is Christ.
[2] Or, "wrought out amongst His people." So Otto.
[3] Literally, "He said accordingly." Ps. lxviii. 18.
[4] Joel ii. 28 f.

and waited for thirty years, more or less, until John appeared before Him as the herald of His approach, and preceded Him in the way of baptism, as I have already shown. And then, when Jesus had gone to the river Jordan, where John was baptizing, and when He had stepped into the water, a fire[1] was kindled in the Jordan; and when He came out of the water, the Holy Ghost lighted on Him like a dove, [as] the apostles of this very Christ of ours wrote. Now, we know that He did not go to the river because He stood in need of baptism, or of the descent of the Spirit like a dove; even as He submitted to be born and to be crucified, not because He needed such things, but because of the human race, which from Adam had fallen under the power of death and the guile of the serpent, and each one of which had committed personal transgression. For God, wishing both angels and men, who were endowed with free-will, and at their own disposal, to do whatever He had strengthened each to do, made them so, that if they chose the things acceptable to Himself, He would keep them free from death and from punishment; but that if they did evil, He would punish each as He sees fit. For it was not His entrance into Jerusalem sitting on an ass, which we have showed was prophesied, that empowered Him to be Christ, but it furnished men with a proof that He is the Christ; just as it was necessary in the time of John that men have proof, that they might know who is Christ. For when John remained[2] by the Jordan, and preached the baptism of repentance, wearing only a leathern girdle and a vesture made of camels' hair, eating nothing but locusts and wild honey, men supposed him to be Christ; but he cried to them, 'I am not the Christ, but the voice of one crying; for He that is stronger than I shall come, whose shoes I am not worthy to bear.'[3]

[1] Justin learned this either from tradition or from apocryphal books. Mention is made of a fire both in the Ebionite Gospel and in another publication called *Pauli prædicatio*, the readers and users of which denied that the rite of baptism had been duly performed, unless *quam mox in aquam descenderunt, statim super aquam ignis appareat.*

[2] Literally, "sat."

[3] Isa. i. 27.

And when Jesus came to the Jordan, He was considered to be the son of Joseph the carpenter; and He appeared without comeliness, as the Scriptures declared; and He was deemed a carpenter (for He was in the habit of working as a carpenter when among men, making ploughs and yokes; by which He taught the symbols of righteousness and an active life); but then the Holy Ghost, and for man's sake, as I formerly stated, lighted on Him in the form of a dove, and there came at the same instant from the heavens a voice, which was uttered also by David when he spoke, personating Christ, what the Father would say to Him: 'Thou art my Son: this day have I begotten Thee;'[1] [the Father] saying that His generation would take place for men, at the time when they would become acquainted with Him: 'Thou art my Son; this day have I begotten Thee.'"[2]

CHAP. LXXXIX.—*The cross alone is offensive to Trypho on account of the curse, yet it proves that Jesus is Christ.*

Then Trypho remarked, "Be assured that all our nation waits for Christ; and we admit that all the scriptures which you have quoted refer to Him. Moreover, I do also admit that the name of Jesus, by which the son of Nave (Nun) was called, has inclined me very strongly to adopt this view. But whether Christ should be so shamefully crucified, this we are in doubt about. For whosoever is crucified is said in the law to be accursed, so that I am exceedingly incredulous on this point. It is quite clear, indeed, that the Scriptures announce that Christ had to suffer; but we wish to learn if you can prove it to us whether it was by the suffering cursed in the law."

I replied to him, "If Christ was not to suffer, and the prophets had not foretold that He would be led to death on account of the sins of the people, and be dishonoured and scourged, and reckoned among the transgressors, and as a sheep be led to the slaughter, whose generation, the prophet says, no man can declare, then you would have good cause to wonder. But if these are to be characteristic of Him and mark Him out to all, how is it possible for us to do anything

[1] Ps. ii. 7.

[2] The repetition seems quite superfluous.

else than believe in Him most confidently? And will not as many as have understood the writings of the prophets, whenever they hear merely that He was crucified, say that this is He and no other?"

CHAP. XC.—*The stretched-out hands of Moses signified beforehand the cross.*

"Bring us on, then," said [Trypho], "by the Scriptures, that we may also be persuaded by you; for we know that He should suffer and be led as a sheep. But prove to us whether He must be crucified and die so disgracefully and so dishonourably by the death cursed in the law. For we cannot bring ourselves even to think of this."

"You know," said I, "that what the prophets said and did they veiled by parables and types, as you admitted to us; so that it was not easy for all to understand the most [of what they said], since they concealed the truth by these means, that those who are eager to find out and learn it might do so with much labour."

They answered, "We admitted this."

"Listen, therefore," say I, "to what follows; for Moses first exhibited this seeming curse of Christ's by the signs which he made."

"Of what [signs] do you speak?" said he.

"When the people," replied I, "waged war with Amalek, and the son of Nave (Nun), by name Jesus (Joshua), led the fight, Moses himself prayed to God, stretching out both hands, and Hur with Aaron supported them during the whole day, so that they might not hang down when he got wearied. For if he gave up any part of this sign, which was an imitation of the cross, the people were beaten, as is recorded in the writings of Moses; but if he remained in this form, Amalek was proportionally defeated, and he who prevailed prevailed by the cross. For it was not because Moses so prayed that the people were stronger, but because, while one who bore the name of Jesus (Joshua) was in the forefront of the battle, he himself made the sign of the cross. For who of you knows not that the prayer of one who accompanies it with lamentation and tears, with the body prostrate, or with bended knees, propitiates God most of all? But in such a manner neither he nor any other one, while sitting on a stone, prayed. Now even the stone symbolized Christ, as I have shown.

CHAP. XCI.—*The cross was foretold in the blessings of Joseph, and in the serpent that was lifted up.*

"And God by Moses shows in another way the force of the mystery of the cross, when He said in the blessing wherewith Joseph was blessed, 'From the blessing of the Lord is his land; for the seasons of heaven, and for the dews, and for the deep springs from beneath, and for the seasonable fruits of the sun,[1] and for the coming together of the months, and for the heights of the everlasting mountains, and for the heights of the hills, and for the ever-flowing rivers, and for the fruits of the fatness of the earth; and let the things accepted by Him who appeared in the bush come on the head and crown of Joseph. Let him be glorified among his brethren;[2] his beauty is [like] the firstling of a bullock; his horns the horns of an unicorn: with these shall he push the nations from one end of the earth to another.'[3] Now, no one could say or prove that the horns of an unicorn represent any other fact or figure than the type which portrays the cross. For the one beam is placed upright, from which the highest extremity is raised up into a horn, when the other beam is fitted on to it, and the ends appear on both sides as horns joined on to the one horn. And the part which is fixed in the centre, on which are suspended those who are crucified, also stands out like a horn; and it also looks like a horn conjoined and fixed with the other horns. And the ex-

[1] There is a variety of reading here: either *ἀβύσσου πηγῶν κάτωθεν καθαρῶν*; or, *ἀβύσσου πηγῶν κάτωθεν, καὶ καθ' ὥραν γεννημάτων, κ.τ.λ.*, which we prefer.

[2] The translation in the text is a rendering of the Septuagint. The MSS. of Justin read: "Being glorified as the first-born among his brethren."

[3] Deut. xxxiii. 13–17.

pression, 'With these shall he push as with horns the nations from one end of the earth to another,' is indicative of what is now the fact among all the nations. For some out of all the nations, through the power of this mystery, having been so pushed, that is, pricked in their hearts, have turned from vain idols and demons to serve God. But the same figure is revealed for the destruction and condemnation of the unbelievers; even as Amalek was defeated and Israel victorious when the people came out of Egypt, by means of the type of the stretching out of Moses' hands, and the name of Jesus (Joshua), by which the son of Nave (Nun) was called. And it seems that the type and sign, which was erected to counteract the serpents which bit Israel, was intended for the salvation of those who believe that death was declared to come thereafter on the serpent through Him that would be crucified, but salvation to those who had been bitten by him and had betaken themselves to Him that sent His Son into the world to be crucified. For the Spirit of prophecy by Moses did not teach us to believe in the serpent, since it shows us that he was cursed by God from the beginning; and in Isaiah tells us that he shall be put to death as an enemy by the mighty sword, which is Christ.

CHAP. XCII.—*Unless the Scriptures be understood through God's great grace, God will not appear to have taught always the same righteousness.*

"Unless, therefore, a man by God's great grace receives the power to understand what has been said and done by the prophets, the appearance of being able to repeat the words or the deeds will not profit him, if he cannot explain the argument of them. And will they not assuredly appear contemptible to many, since they are related by those who understood them not? For if one should wish to ask you why, since Enoch, Noah with his sons, and all others in similar circumstances, who neither were circumcised nor kept the Sabbath, pleased God, God demanded by other leaders, and by the giving of the law after the lapse of so many generations, that those who lived between the times of Abraham and of Moses be justified by circumcision, and that those who lived after Moses be justified by circumcision and the other ordinances—to wit, the Sabbath, and sacrifices, and libations,[1] and offerings; [God will be slandered] unless you show, as I have already said, that God who foreknew was aware that your nation would deserve expulsion from Jerusalem, and that none would be permitted to enter into it. (For[2] you are not distinguished in any other way than by the fleshly circumcision, as I remarked previously. For Abraham was declared by God to be righteous, not on account of circumcision, but on account of faith. For before he was circumcised the following statement was made regarding him: 'Abraham believed God, and it was accounted unto him for righteousness.'[3] And we, therefore, in the uncircumcision of our flesh, believing God through Christ, and having that circumcision which is of advantage to us who have acquired it—namely, that of the heart—we hope to appear righteous before and well-pleasing to God: since already we have received His testimony through the words of the prophets.) [And, further, God will be slandered unless you show] that you were commanded to observe the Sabbath, and to present offerings, and that the Lord submitted to have a place called by the name of God, in order that, as has been said, you might not become impious and godless by worshipping idols and forgetting God, as indeed you do always appear to have been. (Now, that God enjoined the ordinances of Sabbaths and offerings for these reasons, I have proved in what I previously remarked; but for the sake of those who came to-day, I wish to repeat nearly the whole.) For if this is not the case, God will be slandered,[4] as having no foreknowledge, and as not teaching all men to know and to do the same acts of righteousness (for many generations of men appear to have existed before Moses); and the scripture is not true

[1] Or, "ashes," *σποδῶν* for *σπονδῶν*.

[2] We have adopted the parenthesis inserted by Maranus. Langus would insert before it, *τί ἕξετε ἀποκρίνασθαι;* "What will you have to answer?"

[3] Gen. xv. 6.

[4] We have supplied this phrase twice above.

which affirms that 'God is true and righteous, and all His ways are judgments, and there is no unrighteousness in Him.' But since the scripture is true, God is always willing that such even as you be neither foolish nor lovers of yourselves, in order that you may obtain the salvation of Christ,[1] who pleased God, and received testimony from Him, as I have already said, by alleging proof from the holy words of prophecy.

CHAP. XCIII.—*The same kind of righteousness is bestowed on all. Christ comprehends it in two precepts.*

"For [God] sets before every race of mankind that which is always and universally just, as well as all righteousness; and every race knows that adultery, and fornication, and homicide,[2] and such like, are sinful; and though they all commit such practices, yet they do not escape from the knowledge that they act unrighteously whenever they so do, with the exception of those who are possessed with an unclean spirit, and who have been debased by education, by wicked customs, and by sinful institutions, and who have lost, or rather quenched and put under, their natural ideas. For we may see that such persons are unwilling to submit to the same things which they inflict upon others, and reproach each other with hostile consciences for the acts which they perpetrate. And hence I think that our Lord and Saviour Jesus Christ spoke well when He summed up all righteousness and piety in two commandments. They are these: 'Thou shalt love the Lord thy God with all thy heart, and with all thy strength, and thy neighbour as thyself.'[3] For the man who loves God with all the heart, and with all the strength, being filled with a God-fearing mind, will reverence no other god; and since God wishes it, he would reverence that angel who is beloved by the same Lord and God. And the man who loves his neighbour as himself will wish for him the same good things that he wishes for himself, and no man will wish evil things for himself. Accordingly, he who loves his neighbour would pray and

1 Literally, salvation along with Christ, that is, salvation by the aid of Christ.

2 ἀνδρομανία is read in MSS. for ἀνδροφονία.

3 Matt. xxii. 37.

labour that his neighbour may be possessed of the same benefits as himself. Now nothing else is neighbour to man than that similarly-affectioned and reasonable being—man. Therefore, since all righteousness is divided into two branches, namely, in so far as it regards God and men, whoever, says the Scripture, loves the Lord God with all the heart, and all the strength, and his neighbour as himself, would be truly a righteous man. But you were never shown to be possessed of friendship or love either towards God, or towards the prophets, or towards yourselves, but, as is evident, you are ever found to be idolaters and murderers of righteous men, so that you laid hands even on Christ Himself; and to this very day you abide in your wickedness, execrating those who prove that this man who was crucified by you is the Christ. Nay, more than this, you suppose that He was crucified as hostile to and cursed by God, which supposition is the product of your most irrational mind. For though you have the means of understanding that this man is Christ from the signs given by Moses, yet you will not; but, in addition, fancying that we can have no arguments, you put whatever question comes into your minds, while you yourselves are at a loss for arguments whenever you meet with some firmly established Christian.

CHAP. XCIV.—*In what sense he who hangs on a tree is cursed.*

"For tell me, was it not God who commanded by Moses that no image or likeness of anything which was in heaven above or which was on the earth should be made, and yet who caused the brazen serpent to be made by Moses in the wilderness, and set it up for a sign by which those bitten by serpents were saved? Yet is He free from unrighteousness. For by this, as I previously remarked, He proclaimed the mystery, by which He declared that He would break the power of the serpent which occasioned the transgression of Adam, and [would bring] to them that believe on Him [who was foreshadowed] by this sign, *i.e.* Him who was to be crucified, salvation from the fangs of the serpent, which are wicked deeds, idolatries, and other unrighteous acts. Unless the matter be so understood, give me a reason why Moses set up the brazen serpent for a sign, and bade those that were bitten gaze at it, and the wounded were healed; and this, too, when he had himself commanded that no likeness of anything whatsoever should be made."

On this, another of those who came on the second day said, "You have spoken truly: we cannot give a reason. For I have frequently interrogated the teachers about this matter, and none of them gave me a reason: therefore continue what you are speaking; for we are paying attention while you unfold the mystery, on account of which the doctrines of the prophets are falsely slandered."

Then I replied, "Just as God commanded the sign to be made by the brazen serpent, and yet He is blameless; even so, though a curse lies in the law against persons who are crucified, yet no curse lies on the Christ of God, by whom all that have committed things worthy of a curse are saved.

CHAP. XCV.—*Christ took upon Himself the curse due to us.*

"For the whole human race will be found to be under a curse. For it is written in the law of Moses, 'Cursed is every one that continueth not in all things that are written in the book of the law to do them.'[1] And no one has accurately done all, nor will you venture to deny this; but some more and some less than others have observed the ordinances enjoined. But if those who are under this law appear to be under a curse for not having observed all the requirements, how much more shall all the nations appear to be under a curse who practise idolatry, who seduce youths, and commit other crimes? If, then, the Father of all wished His Christ for the whole human family to take upon Him the curses of all, knowing that, after He had been crucified and was dead, He would raise Him up, why do you argue about Him, who submitted to suffer these things according to the Father's will, as if He were accursed, and do not rather bewail yourselves? For although His Father caused Him to suffer these

[1] Deut. xxvii. 26.

things in behalf of the human family, yet you did not commit the deed as in obedience to the will of God. For you did not practise piety when you slew the prophets. And let none of you say: If His Father wished Him to suffer this, in order that by His stripes the human race might be healed, we have done no wrong. If, indeed, you repent of your sins, and recognise Him to be Christ, and observe His commandments, then you may assert this; for, as I have said before, remission of sins shall be yours. But if you curse Him and them that believe on Him, and, when you have the power, put them to death, how is it possible that requisition shall not be made of you, as of unrighteous and sinful men, altogether hard-hearted and without understanding, because you laid your hands on Him?

CHAP. XCVI.—*That curse was a prediction of the things which the Jews would do.*

"For the statement in the law, 'Cursed is every one that hangeth on a tree,'[1] confirms our hope which depends on the crucified Christ, not because He who has been crucified is cursed by God, but because God foretold that which would be done by you all, and by those like to you, who do not know[2] that this is He who existed before all, who is the eternal Priest of God, and King, and Christ. And you clearly see that this has come to pass. For you curse in your synagogues all those who are called[3] from Him Christians; and other nations effectively carry out the curse, putting to death those who simply confess themselves to be Christians; to all of whom we say, You are our brethren; rather recognise the truth of God. And while neither they nor you are persuaded by us, but strive earnestly to cause us to deny the name of Christ, we choose rather and submit to death, in the full assurance that all the good which God has promised through Christ He will reward us with. And in addition to all this we pray for you, that Christ may have mercy upon you. For He taught

1 Deut. xxi. 23.

2 We read ἐπισταμένων for ἐπιστάμενον. Otherwise to be translated: "God foretold that which you did not know," etc.

3 λεγομένων for γενομένων.

us to pray for our enemies also, saying, 'Love your enemies; be kind and merciful, as your heavenly Father is.'[1] For we see that the Almighty God is kind and merciful, causing His sun to rise on the unthankful and on the righteous, and sending rain on the holy and on the wicked; all of whom He has taught us He will judge.

CHAP. XCVII.—*Other predictions of the cross of Christ.*

"For it was not without design that the prophet Moses, when Hur and Aaron upheld his hands, remained in this form until evening. For indeed the Lord remained upon the tree almost until evening, and they buried Him at eventide; then on the third day He rose again. This was declared by David thus: 'With my voice I cried to the Lord, and He heard me out of His holy hill. I laid me down, and slept; I awaked, for the Lord sustained me.'[2] And Isaiah likewise mentions concerning Him the manner in which He would die, thus: 'I have spread out my hands unto a people disobedient, and gainsaying, that walk in a way which is not good.'[3] And that He would rise again, Isaiah himself said: 'His burial has been taken away from the midst, and I will give the rich for His death.'[4] And again, in other words, David in the twenty-first[5] Psalm thus refers to the suffering and to the cross in a parable of mystery: 'They pierced my hands and my feet; they counted all my bones. They considered and gazed on me; they parted my garments among themselves, and cast lots upon my vesture.' For when they crucified Him, driving in the nails, they pierced His hands and feet; and those who crucified Him parted His garments among themselves, each casting lots for what he chose to have, and receiving according to the decision of the lot. And this very Psalm you maintain does not refer to Christ; for you are in all respects blind, and do not understand that no one in your nation who has been called King or Christ

[1] Luke vi. 35.
[2] Ps. iii. 4, 5.
[3] Isa. lxv. 2; comp. also Rom. x. 21.
[4] Isa. liii. 9.
[5] That is, Ps. xxii. 16–18.

has ever had his hands or feet pierced while alive, or has died in this mysterious fashion—to wit, by the cross—save this Jesus alone.

CHAP. XCVIII.—*Predictions of Christ in Ps.* xxii.

"I shall repeat the whole Psalm, in order that you may hear His reverence to the Father, and how He refers all things to Him, and prays to be delivered by Him from this death; at the same time declaring in the Psalm who they are that rise up against Him, and showing that He has truly become man capable of suffering. It is as follows: 'O God, my God, attend to me: why hast Thou forsaken me? The words of my transgressions are far from my salvation. O my God, I will cry to Thee in the day-time, and Thou wilt not hear; and in the night-season, and it is not for want of understanding in me. But Thou, the Praise of Israel, inhabitest the holy place. Our fathers trusted in Thee; they trusted, and Thou didst deliver them. They cried unto Thee, and were delivered: they trusted in Thee, and were not confounded. But I am a worm, and no man; a reproach of men, and despised of the people. All they that see me laughed me to scorn; they spake with the lips, they shook the head: He trusted on the Lord: let Him deliver him, let Him save him, since he desires Him. For Thou art He that took me out of the womb; my hope from the breasts of my mother: I was cast upon Thee from the womb. Thou art my God from my mother's belly: be not far from me, for trouble is near; for there is none to help. Many calves have compassed me; fat bulls have beset me round. They opened their mouth upon me, as a ravening and roaring lion. All my bones are poured out and dispersed like water. My heart has become like wax melting in the midst of my belly. My strength is dried up like a potsherd; and my tongue has cleaved to my throat; and Thou hast brought me into the dust of death. For many dogs have surrounded me; the assembly of the wicked have beset me round. They pierced my hands and my feet, they did tell all my bones. They did look and stare upon me; they parted my garments among them, and cast lots upon my vesture. But do not Thou remove Thine assistance from me, O Lord: give heed to help me: deliver my soul from the sword, and my[1] only-begotten from the hand of the dog. Save me from the lion's mouth, and my humility from the horns of the unicorns. I will declare Thy name to my brethren; in the midst of the church will I praise Thee. Ye that fear the Lord, praise Him: all ye the seed of Jacob, glorify Him. Let all the seed of Israel fear Him.'"

CHAP. XCIX.—*In the commencement of the Psalm are Christ's dying words.*

And when I had said these words, I continued: "Now I will demonstrate to you that the whole Psalm refers thus to Christ, by the words which I shall again explain. What is said at first—'O God, my God, attend to me: why hast Thou forsaken me?'—announced from the beginning that which was to be said in the time of Christ. For when crucified, He spake: 'O God, my God, why hast Thou forsaken me?' And what follows: 'The words of my transgressions are far from my salvation. O my God, I will cry to Thee in the day-time, and Thou wilt not hear; and in the night-season, and it is not for want of understanding in me.' These, as well as the things which He was to do, were spoken. For on the day on which He was to be crucified, having taken three of His disciples to the hill called Olivet, situated opposite to the temple in Jerusalem, He prayed in these words: 'Father, if it be possible, let this cup pass from me.'[2] And again He prayed: 'Not as I will, but as Thou wilt;'[3] showing by this that He had become truly a suffering man. But lest any one should say, He did not know then that He had to suffer, He adds immediately in the Psalm: 'And it is not for want of understanding in me.' Even as there was no ignorance on God's part when He asked Adam where he was, or asked Cain where Abel was; but [it was done] to convince each what kind of man he was, and in order that through the record [of Scripture] we might have a knowledge of all: so

[1] Probably should be "Thy." [2] Matt. xxvi. 39. [3] *Ibid.*

likewise Christ declared that ignorance was not on His side, but on theirs, who thought that He was not the Christ, but fancied they would put Him to death, and that He, like some common mortal, would remain in Hades.

Chap. c.—*In what sense Christ is [called] Jacob, and Israel, and Son of man.*

"Then what follows—'But Thou, the praise of Israel, inhabitest the holy place'—declared that He is to do something worthy of praise and wonderment, being about to rise again from the dead on the third day after the crucifixion; and this He has obtained from the Father. For I have showed already that Christ is called both Jacob and Israel; and I have proved that it is not in the blessing of Joseph and Judah alone that what relates to Him was proclaimed mysteriously, but also in the Gospel it is written that He said: 'All things are delivered unto me by my Father;' and, 'No man knoweth the Father but the Son; nor the Son but the Father, and they to whom the Son will reveal Him.'[1] Accordingly He revealed to us all that we have perceived by His grace out of the Scriptures, so that we know Him to be the first-begotten of God, and to be before all creatures; likewise to be the Son of the patriarchs, since He assumed flesh by the Virgin of their family, and submitted to become a man without comeliness, dishonoured, and subject to suffering. Hence, also, among His words He said, when He was discoursing about His future sufferings: 'The Son of man must suffer many things, and be rejected by the Pharisees and scribes, and be crucified, and on the third day rise again.'[2] He said then that He was the Son of man, either because of His birth by the Virgin, who was, as I said, of the family of David, and Jacob, and Isaac, and Abraham; or because Adam[3] was the father both of Himself and of those who have been first enumerated from whom Mary derives her descent. For we know that the fathers of women are the fathers

[1] Matt. xi. 27.

[2] Matt. xvi. 21.

[3] The text is, *αὐτὸν τὸν Ἀβραὰμ πατέρα.* Thirlby proposed *αὐτὸν τὸν Ἀδὰμ*; Maranus changed this into *αὐτοῦ τὸν Ἀδὰμ πατέρα.*

likewise of those children whom their daughters bear. For [Christ] called one of His disciples—previously known by the name of Simon—Peter; since he recognised Him to be Christ the Son of God, by the revelation of His Father: and since we find it recorded in the memoirs of His apostles that He is the Son of God, and since we call Him the Son, we have understood that He proceeded before all creatures from the Father by His power and will (for He is addressed in the writings of the prophets in one way or another as Wisdom, and the Day,[1] and the East, and a Sword, and a Stone, and a Rod, and Jacob, and Israel); and that He became man by the Virgin, in order that the disobedience which proceeded from the serpent might receive its destruction in the same manner in which it derived its origin. For Eve, who was a virgin and undefiled, having conceived the word of the serpent, brought forth disobedience and death. But the Virgin Mary received faith and joy, when the angel Gabriel announced the good tidings to her that the Spirit of the Lord would come upon her, and the power of the Highest would overshadow her: wherefore also the Holy Thing begotten of her is the Son of God;[2] and she replied, 'Be it unto me according to thy word."[3] And by her has He been born, to whom we have proved so many scriptures refer, and by whom God destroys both the serpent and those angels and men who are like him; but works deliverance from death to those who repent of their wickedness and believe upon Him.

CHAP. CI.—*Christ refers all things to the Father.*

"Then what follows of the Psalm is this, in which He says: 'Our fathers trusted in Thee; they trusted, and Thou didst deliver them. They cried unto Thee, and were not confounded. But I am a worm, and no man; a reproach

[1] It is not easy, says Maranus, to say in what scripture Christ is so called. Perhaps Justin had in his mind the passage, "This is the *day* which the Lord hath made" (Ps. cxviii. 24). Clem. Alex. teaches that Christ is here referred to.

[2] Luke i. 35. See Meyer *in loc.*

[3] Luke i. 38.

of men, and despised of the people;' which show that He admits them to be His fathers, who trusted in God and were saved by Him, who also were the fathers of the Virgin, by whom He was born and became man; and He foretells that He shall be saved by the same God, but boasts not in accomplishing anything through His own will or might. For when on earth He acted in the very same manner, and answered to one who addressed Him as 'Good Master:' 'Why callest thou me good? One is good, my Father who is in heaven.'[1] But when He says, 'I am a worm, and no man; a reproach of men, and despised of the people,' He prophesied the things which do exist, and which happen to Him. For we who believe on Him are everywhere a reproach, 'despised of the people;' for, rejected and dishonoured by your nation, He suffered those indignities which you planned against Him. And the following: 'All they that see me laughed me to scorn; they spake with the lips, they shook the head: He trusted in the Lord; let Him deliver him, since he desires Him;' this likewise He foretold should happen to Him. For they that saw Him crucified shook their heads each one of them, and distorted their lips, and twisting their noses to each other,[2] they spake in mockery the words which are recorded in the memoirs of His apostles: 'He said he was the Son of God: let him come down; let God save him.'

CHAP. CII.—*The prediction of the events which happened to Christ when He was born. Why God permitted it.*

"And what follows—'My hope from the breasts of my mother. On Thee have I been cast from the womb; from my mother's belly Thou art my God: for there is no helper. Many calves have compassed me; fat bulls have beset me round. They opened their mouth upon me, as a ravening and a roaring lion. All my bones are poured out and dispersed like water. My heart has become like wax melting

[1] Luke xviii. 18 f.

[2] The text is corrupt, and the meaning doubtful. Otto translates: *naribus inter se certantes.*

in the midst of my belly. My strength is become dry like a potsherd; and my tongue has cleaved to my throat'—foretold what would come to pass; for the statement, 'My hope from the breasts of my mother,' [is thus explained]. As soon as He was born in Bethlehem, as I previously remarked, king Herod, having learned from the Arabian Magi about Him, made a plot to put Him to death; and by God's command Joseph took Him with Mary and departed into Egypt. For the Father had decreed that He whom He had begotten should be put to death, but not before He had grown to manhood, and proclaimed the word which proceeded from Him. But if any of you say to us, Could not God rather have put Herod to death? I return answer by anticipation: Could not God have cut off in the beginning the serpent, so that he exist not, rather than have said, 'And I will put enmity between him and the woman, and between his seed and her seed?'[1] Could He not have at once created a multitude of men? But yet, since He knew that it would be good, He created both angels and men free to do that which is righteous, and He appointed periods of time during which He knew it would be good for them to have the exercise of free-will; and because He likewise knew it would be good, He made general and particular judgments; each one's freedom of will, however, being guarded. Hence Scripture says the following, at the destruction of the tower, and division and alteration of tongues: 'And the Lord said, Behold, the people is one, and they have all one language; and this they have begun to do: and now nothing will be restrained from them of all which they have attempted to do.'[2] And the statement, 'My strength is become dry like a potsherd, and my tongue has cleaved to my throat,' was also a prophecy of what would be done by Him according to the Father's will. For the power of His strong word, by which He always confuted the Pharisees and scribes, and, in short, all your nation's teachers that questioned Him, had a cessation like a plentiful and strong spring, the waters of which have been turned off, when He kept silence, and chose to

[1] Gen. iii. 15. [2] Gen. xi. 6.

return no answer to any one in the presence of Pilate; as has been declared in the memoirs of His apostles, in order that what is recorded by Isaiah might have efficacious fruit, where it is written, 'The Lord gives me a tongue, that I may know when I ought to speak.'[1] Again, when He said, 'Thou art my God; be not far from me,' He taught that all men ought to hope in God who created all things, and seek salvation and help from Him alone; and not suppose, as the rest of men do, that salvation can be obtained by birth, or wealth, or strength, or wisdom. And such have ever been your practices: at one time you made a calf, and always you have shown yourselves ungrateful, murderers of the righteous, and proud of your descent. For if the Son of God evidently states that He can be saved, [neither][2] because He is a son, nor because He is strong or wise, but that without God He cannot be saved, even though He be sinless, as Isaiah declares in words to the effect that even in regard to His very language He committed no sin (for He committed no iniquity or guile with His mouth), how do you or others who expect to be saved without this hope, suppose that you are not deceiving yourselves?

CHAP. CIII.—*The Pharisees are the bulls: the roaring lion is Herod or the devil.*

"Then what is next said in the Psalm—'For trouble is near, for there is none to help me. Many calves have compassed me; fat bulls have beset me round. They opened their mouth upon me as a ravening and roaring lion. All my bones are poured out and dispersed like water,'—was likewise a prediction of the events which happened to Him. For on that night when some of your nation, who had been sent by the Pharisees, and scribes, and teachers,[3] came upon Him from the Mount[4] of Olives, those whom Scripture called

[1] Isa. l. 4.

[2] Not found in MSS.

[3] *καὶ τῶν διδασκάλων*, adopted instead of *κατὰ τὴν διδασκαλίαν*, "according to their instructions."

[4] *ἀπὸ τοῦ ὄρους.* Justin seems to have supposed that the Jews came on Christ from some point of the hill while He was in the valley below. *Ἐπὶ τοῦ ὄρους* and *ἐπὶ τὸ ὄρος* have been suggested.

butting and prematurely destructive calves surrounded Him. And the expression, 'Fat bulls have beset me round,' He spoke beforehand of those who acted similarly to the calves, when He was led before your teachers. And the scripture described them as bulls, since we know that bulls are authors of calves' existence. As therefore the bulls are the begetters of the calves, so your teachers were the cause why their children went out to the Mount of Olives to take Him and bring Him to them. And the expression, 'For there is none to help,' is also indicative of what took place. For there was not even a single man to assist Him as an innocent person. And the expression, 'They opened their mouth upon me like a roaring lion,' designates him who was then king of the Jews, and was called Herod, a successor of the Herod who, when Christ was born, slew all the infants in Bethlehem born about the same time, because he imagined that amongst them He would assuredly be of whom the Magi from Arabia had spoken; for he was ignorant of the will of Him that is stronger than all, how He had commanded Joseph and Mary to take the child and depart into Egypt, and there to remain until a revelation should again be made to them to return into their own country. And there they did remain until Herod, who slew the infants in Bethlehem, was dead, and Archelaus had succeeded him. And he died before Christ came to the dispensation on the cross which was given Him by His Father. And when Herod succeeded Archelaus, having received the authority which had been allotted to him, Pilate sent to him by way of compliment Jesus bound; and God foreknowing that this would happen, had thus spoken: 'And they brought Him to the Assyrian, a present to the king.'[1] Or He meant the devil by the lion roaring against Him: whom Moses calls the serpent, but in Job and Zechariah he is called the devil, and by Jesus is addressed as Satan, showing that a compounded name was acquired by him from the deeds which he performed. For 'Sata' in the Jewish and Syrian tongue means apostate; and 'Nas' is the word from which he is called by interpretation the *serpent*, *i.e.* according

[1] Hos. x. 6.

to the interpretation of the Hebrew term, from both of which there arises the single word *Satanas*. For this devil, when [Jesus] went up from the river Jordan, at the time when the voice spake to Him, 'Thou art my Son: this day have I begotten Thee,'[1] is recorded in the memoirs of the apostles to have come to Him and tempted Him, even so far as to say to Him, 'Worship me;' and Christ answered him, 'Get thee behind me, Satan: thou shalt worship the Lord thy God, and Him only shalt thou serve.'[2] For as he had deceived Adam, so he hoped[3] that he might contrive some mischief against Christ also. Moreover, the statement, 'All my bones are poured out[4] and dispersed like water; my heart has become like wax, melting in the midst of my belly,' was a prediction of that which happened to Him on that night when men came out against Him to the Mount of Olives to seize Him. For in the memoirs which I say were drawn up by His apostles and those who followed them, [it is recorded] that His sweat fell down like drops of blood while He was praying, and saying, 'If it be possible, let this cup pass:'[5] His heart and also His bones trembling; His heart being like wax melting in His belly: in order that we may perceive that the Father wished His Son really[6] to undergo such sufferings for our sakes, and may not say that He, being the Son of God, did not feel what was happening to Him and inflicted on Him. Further, the expression, 'My strength is dried up like a potsherd, and my tongue has cleaved to my throat,' was a prediction, as I previously remarked, of that silence, when He who convicted all your teachers of being unwise returned no answer at all.

1 Ps. ii. 7; comp. Matt. iii. 17.

2 Matt. iv. 9, 10.

3 Literally, "said."

4 Maranus says it is hardly to be doubted that Justin read, "I am poured out like water," etc.

5 Luke xxii. 44, 42.

6 Justin refers to the opinion of the Docetes, that Christ suffered in appearance merely, and not in reality.

CHAP. CIV.—*Circumstances of Christ's death are predicted in this Psalm.*

"And the statement, 'Thou hast brought me into the dust of death; for many dogs have surrounded me: the assembly of the wicked have beset me round. They pierced my hands and my feet. They did tell all my bones. They did look and stare upon me. They parted my garments among them, and cast lots upon my vesture,'—was a prediction, as I said before, of the death to which the synagogue of the wicked would condemn Him, whom He calls both dogs and hunters, declaring that those who hunted Him were both gathered together and assiduously striving to condemn Him. And this is recorded to have happened in the memoirs of His apostles. And I have shown that, after His crucifixion, they who crucified Him parted His garments among them.

CHAP. CV.—*The Psalm also predicts the crucifixion and the subject of the last prayers of Christ on earth.*

"And what follows of the Psalm,—'But Thou, Lord, do not remove Thine assistance from me; give heed to help me. Deliver my soul from the sword, and my[1] only-begotten from the hand of the dog; save me from the lion's mouth, and my humility from the horns of the unicorns,'—was also information and prediction of the events which should befall Him. For I have already proved that He was the only-begotten of the Father of all things, being begotten in a peculiar manner Word and Power by Him, and having afterwards become man through the Virgin, as we have learned from the memoirs. Moreover, it was similarly foretold that He would die by crucifixion. For the passage, 'Deliver my soul from the sword, and my[2] only-begotten from the hand of the dog; save me from the lion's mouth, and my humility from the horns of the unicorns,' is indicative of the suffering by which He should die, *i.e.* by crucifixion. For the 'horns of the unicorns,' I have already explained to you, are the figure of the cross only. And the prayer that His soul should be saved

[1] See note on chap. xcviii. [2] *Ibid.*

from the sword, and lion's mouth, and hand of the dog, was a prayer that no one should take possession of His soul: so that, when we arrive at the end of life, we may ask the same petition from God, who is able to turn away every shameless evil angel from taking our souls. And that the souls survive, I have shown[1] to you from the fact that the soul of Samuel was called up by the witch, as Saul demanded. And it appears also, that all the souls of similar righteous men and prophets fell under the dominion of such powers, as is indeed to be inferred from the very facts in the case of that witch. Hence also God by His Son teaches[2] us for whose sake these things seem to have been done, always to strive earnestly, and at death to pray that our souls may not fall into the hands of any such power. For when Christ was giving up His spirit on the cross, He said, 'Father, into Thy hands I commend my spirit,'[3] as I have learned also from the memoirs. For He exhorted His disciples to surpass the pharisaic way of living, with the warning, that if they did not, they might be sure they could not be saved; and these words are recorded in the memoirs: 'Unless your righteousness exceed that of the scribes and Pharisees, ye shall not enter into the kingdom of heaven.'[4]

CHAP. CVI.—*Christ's resurrection is foretold in the conclusion of the Psalm.*

"The remainder of the Psalm makes it manifest that He knew His Father would grant to Him all things which He asked, and would raise Him from the dead; and that He urged all who fear God to praise Him because He had compassion on all races of believing men, through the mystery of Him who was crucified; and that He stood in the midst of His brethren the apostles (who repented of their flight from Him when He was crucified, after He rose from the dead, and after they were persuaded by Himself, that before His

[1] This demonstration is not given.

[2] Sylburg proposed *δικαίους γίνεσθαι* for *δἰ οὗς γίν.*, "to strive earnestly to become righteous, and at death to pray."

[3] Luke xxiii. 46.

[4] Matt. v. 20.

passion He had mentioned to them that He must suffer these things, and that they were announced beforehand by the prophets), and when living with them sang praises to God, as is made evident in the memoirs of the apostles. The words are the following: 'I will declare Thy name to my brethren; in the midst of the church will I praise Thee. Ye that fear the Lord, praise Him; all ye, the seed of Jacob, glorify Him. Let all the seed of Israel fear Him.' And when it is said that He changed the name of one of the apostles to Peter; and when it is written in the memoirs of Him that this so happened, as well as that He changed the names of other two brothers, the sons of Zebedee, to Boanerges, which means sons of thunder; this was an announcement of the fact that it was He by whom Jacob was called Israel, and Oshea called Jesus (Joshua), under whose name the people who survived of those that came from Egypt were conducted into the land promised to the patriarchs. And that He should arise like a star from the seed of Abraham, Moses showed beforehand when he thus said, 'A star shall arise from Jacob, and a leader from Israel;'[1] and another scripture says, 'Behold a Man; the East is His name.'[2] Accordingly, when a star rose in heaven at the time of His birth, as is recorded in the memoirs of His apostles, the Magi from Arabia, recognising the sign by this, came and worshipped Him.

CHAP. CVII.—*The same is taught from the history of Jonah.*

"And that He would rise again on the third day after the crucifixion, it is written[3] in the memoirs that some of your nation, questioning Him, said, 'Show us a sign;' and He replied to them, 'An evil and adulterous generation seeketh after a sign; and no sign shall be given them, save the sign of Jonah.' And since He spoke this obscurely, it was to be understood by the audience that after His crucifixion He should rise again on the third day. And He showed that your generation was more wicked and more adulterous than

[1] Num. xxiv. 17. [2] Zech. vi. 12 (according to LXX.). [3] Matt. xii. 38 f.

the city of Nineveh; for the latter, when Jonah preached to them, after he had been cast up on the third day from the belly of the great fish, that after three (in other versions, forty)[1] days they should all perish, proclaimed a fast of all creatures, men and beasts, with sackcloth, and with earnest lamentation, with true repentance from the heart, and turning away from unrighteousness, in the belief that God is merciful and kind to all who turn from wickedness; so that the king of that city himself, with his nobles also, put on sackcloth and remained fasting and praying, and obtained their request that the city should not be overthrown. But when Jonah was grieved that on the (fortieth) third day, as he proclaimed, the city was not overthrown, by the dispensation of a gourd[2] springing up from the earth for him, under which he sat and was shaded from the heat (now the gourd had sprung up suddenly, and Jonah had neither planted nor watered it, but it had come up all at once to afford him shade), and by the other dispensation of its withering away, for which Jonah grieved, [God] convicted him of being unjustly displeased because the city of Nineveh had not been overthrown, and said, 'Thou hast had pity on the gourd, for the which thou hast not laboured, neither madest it grow; which came up in a night, and perished in a night. And shall not I spare Nineveh, the great city, wherein dwell more than six score thousand persons that cannot discern between their right hand and their left hand; and also much cattle?'[3]

CHAP. CVIII.—*The resurrection of Christ did not convert the Jews. But through the whole world they have sent men to accuse Christ.*

"And though all the men of your nation knew the incidents in the life of Jonah, and though Christ said amongst you that He would give the sign of Jonah, exhorting you to

[1] In the LXX. only *three* days are recorded, though in the Hebrew and other versions *forty*. The parenthetic clause is probably the work of a transcriber.

[2] Read *κικυῶνα* for *σικυῶνα*.

[3] Jonah iv. 10 f.

repent of your wicked deeds at least after He rose again from the dead, and to mourn before God as did the Ninevites, in order that your nation and city might not be taken and destroyed, as they have been destroyed; yet you not only have not repented, after you learned that He rose from the dead, but, as I said before,[1] you have sent chosen and ordained men throughout all the world to proclaim that a godless and lawless heresy had sprung from one Jesus, a Galilæan deceiver, whom we crucified, but his disciples stole him by night from the tomb, where he was laid when unfastened from the cross, and now deceive men by asserting that he has risen from the dead and ascended to heaven. Moreover, you accuse Him of having taught those godless, lawless, and unholy doctrines which you mention to the condemnation of those who confess Him to be Christ, and a Teacher from and Son of God. Besides this, even when your city is captured, and your land ravaged, you do not repent, but dare to utter imprecations on Him and all who believe in Him. Yet we do not hate you or those who, by your means, have conceived such prejudices against us; but we pray that even now all of you may repent and obtain mercy from God, the compassionate and long-suffering Father of all.

CHAP. CIX.—*The conversion of the Gentiles has been predicted by Micah.*

"But that the Gentiles would repent of the evil in which they led erring lives, when they heard the doctrine preached by His apostles from Jerusalem, and which they learned[2] through them, suffer me to show you by quoting a short statement from the prophecy of Micah, one of the twelve [minor prophets]. This is as follows: 'And in the last days the mountain of the Lord shall be manifest, established on the top of the mountains; it shall be exalted above the hills, and people shall flow unto it.[3] And many nations shall go, and say, Come, let us go up to the mountain of the Lord, and to the house of the God of Jacob; and they shall enlighten

1 Chap. xvii. 2 Read μαθόντα for παθόντα.

3 Literally, "people shall place a river in it."

us in His way, and we shall walk in His paths: for out of Zion shall go forth the law, and the word of the Lord from Jerusalem. And He shall judge among many peoples, and shall rebuke strong nations afar off; and they shall beat their swords into ploughshares, and their spears into sickles: nation shall not lift up a sword against nation, neither shall they learn war any more. And each man shall sit under his vine and under his fig tree; and there shall be none to terrify: for the mouth of the Lord of hosts hath spoken it. For all people will walk in the name of their gods; but we will walk in the name of the Lord our God for ever. And it shall come to pass in that day, that I will assemble her that is afflicted, and gather her that is driven out, and whom I had plagued; and I shall make her that is afflicted a remnant, and her that is oppressed a strong nation. And the Lord shall reign over them in Mount Zion from henceforth, and even for ever.' "[1]

CHAP. CX.—*A portion of the prophecy already fulfilled in the Christians: the rest shall be fulfilled at the second advent.*

And when I had finished these words, I continued: "Now I am aware that your teachers, sirs, admit the whole of the words of this passage to refer to Christ; and I am likewise aware that they maintain He has not yet come; or if they say that He has come, they assert that it is not known who He is; but when He shall become manifest and glorious, then it shall be known who He is. And then, they say, the events mentioned in this passage shall happen, just as if there was no fruit as yet from the words of the prophecy. O unreasoning men! understanding not what has been proved by all these passages, that two advents of Christ have been announced: the one, in which He is set forth as suffering, inglorious, dishonoured, and crucified; but the other, in which he shall come from heaven with glory, when the man of apostasy,[2] who speaks strange things against the Most High, shall venture to do unlawful deeds on the earth against

[1] Mic. iv. 1 ff.

[2] 2 Thess. ii. 3; and see chap. xxxii.

us the Christians, who, having learned the true worship of God from the law, and the word which went forth from Jerusalem by means of the apostles of Jesus, have fled for safety to the God of Jacob and God of Israel; and we who were filled with war, and mutual slaughter, and every wickedness, have each through the whole earth changed our warlike weapons,—our swords into ploughshares, and our spears into implements of tillage,—and we cultivate piety, righteousness, philanthropy, faith, and hope, which we have from the Father Himself through Him who was crucified; and sitting each under his vine, *i.e.* each man possessing his own married wife. For you are aware that the prophetic word says, 'And his wife shall be like a fruitful vine.'[1] Now it is evident that no one can terrify or subdue us who have believed in Jesus over all the world. For it is plain that, though beheaded, and crucified, and thrown to wild beasts, and chains, and fire, and all other kinds of torture, we do not give up our confession; but the more such things happen, the more do others and in larger numbers become faithful, and worshippers of God through the name of Jesus. For just as if one should cut away the fruit-bearing parts of a vine, it grows up again, and yields other branches flourishing and fruitful; even so the same thing happens with us. For the vine planted by God and Christ the Saviour is His people. But the rest of the prophecy shall be fulfilled at His second coming. For the expression, 'He that is afflicted [and driven out],' *i.e.* from the world, [implies] that, so far as you and all other men have it in your power, each Christian has been driven out not only from his own property, but even from the whole world; for you permit no Christian to live. But you say that the same fate has befallen your own nation. Now, if you have been cast out after defeat in battle, you have suffered such treatment justly indeed, as all the Scriptures bear witness; but we, though we have done no such [evil acts] after we knew the truth of God, are testified to by God, that, together with the most righteous, and only spotless and sinless Christ, we are taken away out of the earth. For Isaiah cries, 'Behold how

[1] Ps. cxxviii. 3.

the righteous perishes, and no man lays it to heart; and righteous men are taken away, and no man considers it.'[1]

CHAP. CXI.—*The two advents were signified by the two goats. Other figures of the first advent, in which the Gentiles are freed by the blood of Christ.*

"And that it was declared by symbol, even in the time of Moses, that there would be two advents of this Christ, as I have mentioned previously, [is manifest] from the symbol of the goats presented for sacrifice during the fast. And again, by what Moses and Joshua did, the same thing was symbolically announced and told beforehand. For the one of them, stretching out his hands, remained till evening on the hill, his hands being supported; and this reveals a type of no other thing than of the cross: and the other, whose name was altered to Jesus (Joshua), led the fight, and Israel conquered. Now this took place in the case of both those holy men and prophets of God, that you may perceive how one of them could not bear up both the mysteries: I mean, the type of the cross and the type of the name. For this is, was, and shall be the strength of Him alone, whose name every power dreads, being very much tormented because they shall be destroyed by Him. Therefore our suffering and crucified Christ was not cursed by the law, but made it manifest that He alone would save those who do not depart from His faith. And the blood of the passover, sprinkled on each man's door-posts and lintel, delivered those who were saved in Egypt, when the first-born of the Egyptians were destroyed. For the passover was Christ, who was afterwards sacrificed, as also Isaiah said, 'He was led as a sheep to the slaughter.'[2] And it is written, that on the day of the passover you seized Him, and that also during the passover you crucified Him. And as the blood of the passover saved those who were in Egypt, so also the blood of Christ will deliver from death those who have believed. Would God, then, have been deceived if this sign had not been above the doors? I do not say that; but I affirm that He announced beforehand

[1] Isa. lvii. 1. [2] Isa. liii. 7.

the future salvation for the human race through the blood of Christ. For the sign of the scarlet thread, which the spies, sent to Jericho by Joshua, son of Nave (Nun), gave to Rahab the harlot, telling her to bind it to the window through which she let them down to escape from their enemies, also manifested the symbol of the blood of Christ, by which those who were at one time harlots and unrighteous persons out of all nations are saved, receiving remission of sins, and continuing no longer in sin.

CHAP. CXII.—*The Jews expound these signs jejunely and feebly, and take up their attention only with insignificant matters.*

"But you, expounding these things in a low [and earthly] manner, impute much weakness to God, if you thus listen to them merely, and do not investigate the force of the words spoken. Since even Moses would in this way be considered a transgressor: for he enjoined that no likeness of anything in heaven, or on earth, or in the sea, be made; and then he himself made a brazen serpent and set it on a standard, and bade those who were bitten look at it: and they were saved when they looked at it. Will the serpent, then, which (I have already said) God had in the beginning cursed and cut off by the great sword, as Isaiah says,[1] be understood as having preserved at that time the people? and shall we receive these things in the foolish acceptation of your teachers, and [regard] them not as signs? And shall we not rather refer the standard to the resemblance of the crucified Jesus, since also Moses by his outstretched hands, together with him who was named Jesus (Joshua), achieved a victory for your people? For in this way we shall cease to be at a loss about the things which the lawgiver did, when he, without forsaking God, persuaded the people to hope in a beast through which transgression and disobedience had their origin. And this was done and said by the blessed prophet with much intelligence and mystery; and there is nothing said or done by any one of the prophets, without exception, which one can justly reprehend, if he possess the knowledge

[1] Isa. xxvii. 1.

which is in them. But if your teachers only expound to you why female camels are spoken of in this passage, and are not in that; or why so many measures of fine flour and so many measures of oil [are used] in the offerings; and do so in a low and sordid manner, while they never venture either to speak of or to expound the points which are great and worthy of investigation, or command you to give no audience to us while we expound them, and to come not into conversation with us; will they not deserve to hear what our Lord Jesus Christ said to them: 'Whited sepulchres, which appear beautiful outward, and within are full of dead men's bones; which pay tithe of mint, and swallow a camel: ye blind guides!'[1] If, then, you will not despise the doctrines of those who exalt themselves and wish to be called Rabbi, Rabbi, and come with such earnestness and intelligence to the words of prophecy as to suffer the same inflictions from your own people which the prophets themselves did, you cannot receive any advantage whatsoever from the prophetic writings.

CHAP. CXIII.—*Joshua was a figure of Christ.*

"What I mean is this. Jesus (Joshua), as I have now frequently remarked, who was called Oshea, when he was sent to spy out the land of Canaan, was named by Moses Jesus (Joshua). Why he did this you neither ask, nor are at a loss about it, nor make strict inquiries. Therefore Christ has escaped your notice; and though you read, you understand not; and even now, though you hear that Jesus is our Christ, you consider not that the name was bestowed on Him not purposelessly nor by chance. But you make a theological discussion as to why one '*α*' was added to Abraham's first name; and as to why one '*ρ*' was added to Sarah's name, you use similar high-sounding disputations.[2] But why do you not similarly investigate the reason why the name of Oshea the son of Nave (Nun), which his father gave him, was changed to Jesus (Joshua)? But since not only was his name altered, but

[1] Matt. xxiii. 27, 23, 24.

[2] According to the LXX., *Σάρα* was altered to *Σάῤῥα*, and *Ἄβραμ* to *Ἀβραάμ*.

he was also appointed successor to Moses, being the only one of his contemporaries who came out from Egypt, he led the surviving people into the Holy Land; and as he, not Moses, led the people into the Holy Land, and as he distributed it by lot to those who entered along with him, so also Jesus the Christ will turn again the dispersion of the people, and will distribute the good land to each one, though not in the same manner. For the former gave them a temporary inheritance, seeing he was neither Christ who is God, nor the Son of God; but the latter, after the holy resurrection,[1] shall give us the eternal possession. The former, after he had been named Jesus (Joshua), and after he had received strength from His Spirit, caused the sun to stand still. For I have proved that it was Jesus who appeared to and conversed with Moses, and Abraham, and all the other patriarchs without exception, ministering to the will of the Father; who also, I say, came to be born man by the Virgin Mary, and lives for ever. For the latter is He after[2] whom and by whom the Father will renew both the heaven and the earth; this is He who shall shine an eternal light in Jerusalem; this is he who is the king of Salem after the order of Melchizedek, and the eternal Priest of the Most High. The former is said to have circumcised the people a second time with knives of stone (which was a sign of this circumcision with which Jesus Christ Himself has circumcised us from the idols made of stone and of other materials), and to have collected together those who were circumcised from the uncircumcision, *i.e.* from the error of the world, in every place by the knives of stone, to wit, the words of our Lord Jesus. For I have shown that Christ was proclaimed by the prophets in parables a Stone and a Rock. Accordingly, the knives of stone we shall take to mean His words, by means of which so many who were in error have been circumcised from uncircumcision with the circumcision of the heart, with which God by Jesus commanded those from that time to be

[1] Or, "resurrection of the saints."

[2] Justin seems to mean that the renewal of heaven and earth dates from the incarnation of Christ.

circumcised who derived their circumcision from Abraham, saying that Jesus (Joshua) would circumcise a second time with knives of stone those who entered into that holy land.

CHAP. CXIV.—*Some rules for discerning what is said about Christ. The circumcision of the Jews is very different from that which Christians receive.*

"For the Holy Spirit sometimes brought about that something, which was the type of the future, should be done clearly; sometimes He uttered words about what was to take place, as if it was then taking place, or had taken place. And unless those who read perceive this art, they will not be able to follow the words of the prophets as they ought. For example's sake, I shall repeat some prophetic passages, that you may understand what I say. When He speaks by Isaiah, 'He was led as a sheep to the slaughter, and like a lamb before the shearer,'[1] He speaks as if the suffering had already taken place. And when He says again, 'I have stretched out my hands to a disobedient and gainsaying people;'[2] and when He says, 'Lord, who hath believed our report?'[3]—the words are spoken as if announcing events which had already come to pass. For I have shown that Christ is oftentimes called a Stone in parable, and in figurative speech Jacob and Israel. And again, when He says, 'I shall behold the heavens, the works of Thy fingers,'[4] unless I understand His method of using words,[5] I shall not understand intelligently, but just as your teachers suppose, fancying that the Father of all, the unbegotten God, has hands and feet, and fingers, and a soul, like a composite being; and they for this reason teach that it was the Father Himself who appeared to Abraham and to Jacob. Blessed therefore are we who have been circumcised the second time with knives of stone. For your first circumcision was and is performed by iron instruments, for you remain hard-hearted; but our circumcision, which is the second, having been instituted after yours, circumcises us

[1] Isa. liii. 7. [2] Isa. lxv. 2. [3] Isa. liii. 1. [4] Ps. viii. 3.

[5] Literally, "the operation of His words." Editors have changed τῶν λόγων into τὸν λόγον or τοῦ λόγου; but there is no need of change.

from idolatry and from absolutely every kind of wickedness by sharp stones, *i.e.* by the words [preached] by the apostles of the corner-stone cut out without hands. And our hearts are thus circumcised from evil, so that we are happy to die for the name of the good Rock, which causes living water to burst forth for the hearts of those who by Him have loved the Father of all, and which gives those who are willing to drink of the water of life. But you do not comprehend me when I speak these things; for you have not understood what it has been prophesied that Christ would do, and you do not believe us who draw your attention to what has been written. For Jeremiah thus cries: 'Woe unto you! because you have forsaken the living fountain, and have digged for yourselves broken cisterns that can hold no water. Shall there be a wilderness where Mount Zion is, because I gave Jerusalem a bill of divorce in your sight?'[1]

CHAP. CXV.—*Prediction about the Christians in Zechariah. The malignant way which the Jews have in disputations.*

"But you ought to believe Zechariah when he shows in parable the mystery of Christ, and announces it obscurely. The following are his words: 'Rejoice, and be glad, O daughter of Zion: for, lo, I come, and I shall dwell in the midst of thee, saith the Lord. And many nations shall be added to the Lord in that day. And they shall be my people, and I will dwell in the midst of thee; and they shall know that the Lord of hosts hath sent me unto thee. And the Lord shall inherit Judah his portion in the holy land, and He shall choose Jerusalem again. Let all flesh fear before the Lord, for He is raised up out of His holy clouds. And He showed me Jesus (Joshua) the high priest standing before the angel [of the Lord[2]]; and the devil stood at his right hand to resist him. And the Lord said to the devil, The Lord who hath chosen Jerusalem rebuke thee. Behold, is not this a brand plucked out of the fire?'"[3]

1 Jer. ii. 13.
2 Omitted by Justin in this place.
3 Zech. ii. 10–13, iii. 1, 2.

As Trypho was about to reply and contradict me, I said, "Wait and hear what I say first: for I am not to give the explanation which you suppose, as if there had been no priest of the name of Joshua (Jesus) in the land of Babylon, where your nation were prisoners. But even if I did, I have shown that if there[1] was a priest named Joshua (Jesus) in your nation, yet the prophet had not seen him in his revelation, just as he had not seen either the devil or the angel of the Lord by eyesight, and in his waking condition, but in a trance, at the time when the revelation was made to him. But I now say, that as [Scripture] said that the Son of Nave (Nun) by the name Jesus (Joshua) wrought powerful works and exploits which proclaimed beforehand what would be performed by our Lord; so I proceed now to show that the revelation made among your people in Babylon in the days of Jesus (Joshua) the priest, was an announcement of the things to be accomplished by our Priest, who is God, and Christ the Son of God the Father of all.

"Indeed, I wondered," continued I, "why a little ago you kept silence while I was speaking, and why you did not interrupt me when I said that the son of Nave (Nun) was the only one of his contemporaries who came out of Egypt that entered the Holy Land along with the men described as younger than that generation. For you swarm and light on sores like flies. For though one should speak ten thousand words well, if there happen to be one little word displeasing to you, because not sufficiently intelligible or accurate, you make no account of the many good words, but lay hold of the little word, and are very zealous in setting it up as something impious and guilty; in order that, when you are judged with the very same judgment by God, you may have a much heavier account to render for your great audacities, whether evil actions, or bad interpretations which you obtain by falsifying the true. For with what judgment you judge, it is righteous that you be judged withal.

[1] The reading suggested by Maranus, *εἰ μὲν ἦν*.

CHAP. CXVI.—*It is shown how this prophecy suits the Christians.*

"But to give you the account of the revelation of the holy Jesus Christ, I take up again my discourse, and I assert that even that revelation was made for us who believe on Christ the High Priest, namely this crucified One; and though we lived in fornication and all kinds of filthy conversation, we have by the grace of our Jesus, according to His Father's will, stripped ourselves of all those filthy wickednesses with which we were imbued. And though the devil is ever at hand to resist us, and anxious to seduce all to himself, yet the Angel of God, *i.e.* the Power of God sent to us through Jesus Christ, rebukes him, and he departs from us. And we are just as if drawn out from the fire, when purified from our former sins, and [rescued] from the affliction and the fiery trial by which the devil and all his coadjutors try us; out of which Jesus the Son of God has promised again to deliver us,[1] and invest us with prepared garments, if we do His commandments; and has undertaken to provide an eternal kingdom [for us]. For just as that Jesus (Joshua), called by the prophet a priest, evidently had on filthy garments because he is said to have taken a harlot for a wife,[2] and is called a brand plucked out of the fire, because he had received remission of sins when the devil that resisted him was rebuked; even so we, who through the name of Jesus have believed as one man in God the Maker of all, have been stripped, through the name of His first-begotten Son, of the filthy garments, *i.e.* of our sins; and being vehemently inflamed by the word of His calling, we are the true high-priestly race of God, as even God Himself bears witness,

[1] Maranus changed ἀποσπᾷ into ἀποσπᾶν, an emendation adopted in our translation. Otto retains the reading of the MSS., "out of which Jesus the Son of God again snatches us. He promised that He would clothe us with," etc.

[2] Justin either confuses Joshua son of Josedech with Hosea the prophet, or he refers to the Jewish tradition that "filthy garments" signified either an illicit marriage, or sins of the people, or the squalor of captivity.

saying that in every place among the Gentiles sacrifices are presented to Him well-pleasing and pure. Now God receives sacrifices from no one, except through His priests.

CHAP. CXVII.—*Malachi's prophecy concerning the sacrifices of the Christians. It cannot be taken as referring to the prayers of Jews of the dispersion.*

"Accordingly, God, anticipating all the sacrifices which we offer through this name, and which Jesus the Christ enjoined us to offer, *i.e.* in the Eucharist of the bread and the cup, and which are presented by Christians in all places throughout the world, bears witness that they are well-pleasing to Him. But He utterly rejects those presented by you and by those priests of yours, saying, 'And I will not accept your sacrifices at your hands; for from the rising of the sun to its setting my name is glorified among the Gentiles (He says); but ye profane it.'[1] Yet even now, in your love of contention, you assert that God does not accept the sacrifices of those who dwelt then in Jerusalem, and were called Israelites; but says that He is pleased with the prayers of the individuals of that nation then dispersed, and calls their prayers sacrifices. Now, that prayers and giving of thanks, when offered by worthy men, are the only perfect and well-pleasing sacrifices to God, I also admit. For such alone Christians have undertaken to offer, and in the remembrance effected by their solid and liquid food, whereby the suffering of the Son of God[2] which He endured is brought to mind, whose name the high priests of your nation and your teachers have caused to be profaned and blasphemed over all the earth. But these filthy garments, which have been put by you on all who have become Christians by the name of Jesus, God shows shall be taken away from us, when He shall raise all men from the dead, and appoint some to be incorruptible, immortal, and free from sorrow in the everlasting and imperishable kingdom; but shall send others away to the everlasting punishment of fire. But as to you and your teachers deceiving yourselves when you interpret

[1] Mal. i. 10–12.

[2] Or, "God of God."

what the Scripture says as referring to those of your nation then in dispersion, and maintain that their prayers and sacrifices offered in every place are pure and well-pleasing, learn that you are speaking falsely, and trying by all means to cheat yourselves: for, first of all, not even now does your nation extend from the rising to the setting of the sun, but there are nations among which none of your race ever dwelt. For there is not one single race of men, whether barbarians, or Greeks, or whatever they may be called, nomads, or vagrants, or herdsmen living in tents, among whom prayers and giving of thanks are not offered through the name of the crucified Jesus. And then,[1] as the Scriptures show, at the time when Malachi wrote this, your dispersion over all the earth, which now exists, had not taken place.

CHAP. CXVIII.—*He exhorts to repentance before Christ comes; in whom Christians, since they believe, are far more religious than Jews.*

"So that you ought rather to desist from the love of strife, and repent before the great day of judgment come, wherein all those of your tribes who have pierced this Christ shall mourn, as I have shown has been declared by the Scriptures. And I have explained that the Lord swore, 'after the order of Melchizedek,'[2] and what this prediction means; and the prophecy of Isaiah which says, 'His burial is taken away from the midst,'[3] I have already said, referred to the future burying and rising again of Christ; and I have frequently remarked that this very Christ is the Judge of all the living and the dead. And Nathan likewise, speaking to David about Him, thus continued: 'I will be His Father, and He shall be my Son; and my mercy shall I not take away from Him, as I did from them that went before Him; and I will establish Him in my house, and in His kingdom for ever.'[4] And Ezekiel says, 'There shall be no other prince in the house but He.'[5] For He is the chosen Priest and eternal King, the Christ, inasmuch as He is the Son of God; and do

1 εἶτα δὲ for εἰδότες.
2 Ps. cx. 4.
3 Isa. liii. 8.
4 2 Sam. vii. 14 f.
5 Ezek. xliv. 3.

not suppose that Isaiah or the other prophets speak of sacrifices of blood or libations being presented at the altar on His second advent, but of true and spiritual praises and giving of thanks. And we have not in vain believed in Him, and have not been led astray by those who taught us such doctrines; but this has come to pass through the wonderful foreknowledge of God, in order that we, through the calling of the new and eternal covenant, that is, of Christ, might be found more intelligent and God-fearing than yourselves, who are considered to be lovers of God and men of understanding, but are not. Isaiah, filled with admiration of this, said: 'And kings shall shut their mouths: for those to whom no announcement has been made in regard to Him[1] shall see; and those who heard not shall understand. Lord, who hath believed our report? and to whom is the arm of the Lord revealed?'[2]

"And in repeating this, Trypho," I continued, "as far as is allowable, I endeavour to do so for the sake of those who came with you to-day, yet briefly and concisely."

Then he replied, "You do well; and though you repeat the same things at considerable length, be assured that I and my companions listen with pleasure."

CHAP. CXIX.—*Christians are the holy people promised to Abraham. They have been called like Abraham.*

Then I said again, "Would you suppose, sirs, that we could ever have understood these matters in the Scriptures, if we had not received grace to discern by the will of Him whose pleasure it was? in order that the saying of Moses[3] might come to pass, 'They provoked me with strange [gods], they provoked me to anger with their abominations. They sacrificed to demons whom they knew not; new gods that came newly up, whom their fathers knew not. Thou hast forsaken God that begat thee, and forgotten God that brought thee up. And the Lord saw, and was jealous, and was provoked to anger by reason of the rage of His sons and daughters:

[1] The MSS. read "them." Otto has changed it to "Him."

[2] Isa. lii. 15, liii. 1.

[3] Literally, "in the time of Moses."

and He said, I will turn my face away from them, and I will show what shall come on them at the last; for it is a very froward generation, children in whom is no faith. They have moved me to jealousy with that which is not God, they have provoked me to anger with their idols; and I will move them to jealousy with that which is not a nation, I will provoke them to anger with a foolish people. For a fire is kindled from mine anger, and it shall burn to Hades. It shall consume the earth and her increase, and set on fire the foundations of the mountains; I will heap mischief on them.'[1] And after that Righteous One was put to death, we flourished as another people, and shot forth as new and prosperous corn; as the prophets said, 'And many nations shall betake themselves to the Lord in that day for a people: and they shall dwell in the midst of all the earth.'[2] But we are not only a people, but also a holy people, as we have shown already.[3] 'And they shall call them the holy people, redeemed by the Lord.'[4] Therefore we are not a people to be despised, nor a barbarous race, nor such as the Carian and Phrygian nations; but God has even chosen us, and He has become manifest to those who asked not after Him. 'Behold, I am God,' He says, 'to the nation which called not on my name.'[5] For this is that nation which God of old promised to Abraham, when He declared that He would make him a father of many nations; not meaning, however, the Arabians, or Egyptians, or Idumæans, since Ishmael became the father of a mighty nation, and so did Esau; and there is now a great multitude of Ammonites. Noah, moreover, was the father of Abraham, and in fact of all men; and others were the progenitors of others. What larger measure of grace, then, did Christ bestow on Abraham? This, namely, that He called him with His voice by the like calling, telling him to quit the land wherein he dwelt. And He has called all of us by that voice, and we have left already the way of living in which we used to spend our days, passing our time in evil after the fashions of the other inhabitants of the earth; and

[1] Deut. xxxii. 16-23.
[2] Zech. ii. 11.
[3] See chap. cx.
[4] Isa. lxii. 12.
[5] Isa. lxv. 1.

along with Abraham we shall inherit the holy land, when we shall receive the inheritance for an endless eternity, being children of Abraham through the like faith. For as he believed the voice of God, and it was imputed to him for righteousness, in like manner we, having believed God's voice spoken by the apostles of Christ, and promulgated to us by the prophets, have renounced even to death all the things of the world. Accordingly, He promises to him a nation of similar faith, God-fearing, righteous, and delighting the Father; but it is not you, 'in whom is no faith.'

CHAP. CXX.—*Christians were promised to Isaac, Jacob, and Judah.*

"Observe, too, how the same promises are made to Isaac and to Jacob. For thus He speaks to Isaac: 'And in thy seed shall all the nations of the earth be blessed.'[1] And to Jacob: 'And in thee and in thy seed shall all families of the earth be blessed.'[2] He says that neither to Esau nor to Reuben, nor to any other; only to those of whom the Christ should arise, according to the dispensation, through the Virgin Mary. But if you would consider the blessing of Judah, you would perceive what I say. For the seed is divided from Jacob, and comes down through Judah, and Phares, and Jesse, and David. And this was a symbol of the fact that some of your nation would be found children of Abraham, and found, too, in the lot of Christ; but that others, who are indeed children of Abraham, would be like the sand on the sea-shore, barren and fruitless, much in quantity, and without number indeed, but bearing no fruit whatever, and only drinking the water of the sea. And a vast multitude in your nation are convicted of being of this kind, imbibing doctrines of bitterness and godlessness, but spurning the word of God. He speaks therefore in the passage relating to Judah: 'A prince shall not fail from Judah, nor a ruler from his thighs, till that which is laid up for him come; and He shall be the expectation of the nations.'[3] And it is plain that this was spoken not of Judah, but of Christ. For all we out of

[1] Gen. xxvi. 4. [2] Gen. xxviii. 14. [3] Gen. xlix. 10.

all nations do expect not Judah, but Jesus, who led your fathers out of Egypt. For the prophecy referred even to the advent of Christ: 'Till He come for whom this is laid up, and He shall be the expectation of nations.' Jesus came, therefore, as we have shown at length, and is expected again to appear above the clouds; whose name you profane, and labour hard to get it profaned over all the earth. It were possible for me, sirs," I continued, "to contend against you about the reading which you so interpret, saying it is written, 'Till the things laid up for Him come;' though the Seventy have not so explained it, but thus, 'Till He comes for whom this is laid up.' But since what follows indicates that the reference is to Christ (for it is, 'and He shall be the expectation of nations'), I do not proceed to have a mere verbal controversy with you, as I have not attempted to establish proof about Christ from the passages of Scripture which are not admitted by you, which I quoted from the words of Jeremiah the prophet, and Esdras, and David; but from those which are even now admitted by you, which had your teachers comprehended, be well assured they would have deleted them, as they did those about the death of Isaiah, whom you sawed asunder with a wooden saw. And this was a mysterious type of Christ being about to cut your nation in two, and to raise those worthy of the honour to the everlasting kingdom along with the holy patriarchs and prophets; but He has said that He will send others to the condemnation of the unquenchable fire along with similar disobedient and impenitent men from all the nations. 'For they shall come,' He said, 'from the west and from the east, and shall sit down with Abraham, and Isaac, and Jacob in the kingdom of heaven; but the children of the kingdom shall be cast out into outer darkness.'[1] And I have mentioned these things, taking nothing whatever into consideration, except the speaking of the truth, and refusing to be coerced by any one, even though I should be forthwith torn in pieces by you. For I gave no thought to any of my people, that is, the Samaritans, when I had a communication in writing with Cæsar,[2]

[1] Matt. viii. 11 f.

[2] The *Apology*, i. chap. xxvi.; ii. chap. xv.

but stated that they were wrong in trusting to the magician Simon of their own nation, who, they say, is God above all power, and authority, and might."

CHAP. CXXI.—*From the fact that the Gentiles believe in Jesus, it is evident that He is Christ.*

And as they kept silence, I went on: "[The scripture], speaking by David about this Christ, my friends, said no longer that 'in His seed' the nations should be blessed, but 'in Him.' So it is here: 'His name shall rise up for ever above the sun; and in Him shall all nations be blessed.'[1] But if all nations are blessed in Christ, and we of all nations believe in Him, then He is indeed the Christ, and we are those blessed by Him. God formerly gave the sun as an object of worship,[2] as it is written, but no one ever was seen to endure death on account of his faith in the sun; but for the name of Jesus you may see men of every nation who have endured and do endure all sufferings, rather than deny Him. For the word of His truth and wisdom is more ardent and more light-giving than the rays of the sun, and sinks down into the depths of heart and mind. Hence also the scripture said, 'His name shall rise up above the sun.' And again, Zechariah says, 'His name is the East.'[3] And speaking of the same, he says that 'each tribe shall mourn.'[4] But if He so shone forth and was so mighty in His first advent (which was without honour and comeliness, and very contemptible), that in no nation He is unknown, and everywhere men have repented of the old wickedness in each nation's way of living, so that even demons were subject to His name, and all powers and kingdoms feared His name more than they feared all the dead, shall He not on His glorious advent destroy by all means all those who hated Him, and who unrighteously departed from Him, but give rest to His own, rewarding them with all they have looked for? To us, therefore, it has been granted to hear, and to understand, and

[1] Ps. lxxii. 17.
[2] So Justin concludes from Deut. iv. 19; comp. chap. lv.
[3] Zech. vi. 12.
[4] Zech. xii. 12.

to be saved by this Christ, and to recognise all the [truths revealed] by the Father. Wherefore He said to Him: 'It is a great thing for Thee to be called my servant, to raise up the tribes of Jacob, and turn again the dispersed of Israel. I have appointed Thee for a light to the Gentiles, that Thou mayest be their salvation unto the end of the earth.'[1]

CHAP. CXXII.—*The Jews understand this of the proselytes without reason.*

"You think that these words refer to the stranger[2] and the proselytes, but in fact they refer to us who have been illumined by Jesus. For Christ would have borne witness even to them; but now you are become twofold more the children of hell, as He said Himself.[3] Therefore what was written by the prophets was spoken not of those persons, but of us, concerning whom the scripture speaks: 'I will lead the blind by a way which they knew not; and they shall walk in paths which they have not known. And I am witness, saith the Lord God, and my servant whom I have chosen.'[4] To whom, then, does Christ bear witness? Manifestly to those who have believed. But the proselytes not only do not believe, but twofold more than yourselves blaspheme His name, and wish to torture and put to death us who believe in Him; for in all points they strive to be like you. And again in other words He cries: 'I the Lord have called Thee in righteousness, and will hold Thine hand, and will strengthen Thee, and will give Thee for a covenant of the people, for a light of the Gentiles, to open the eyes of the blind, to bring out the prisoners from their bonds.'[5] These words, indeed, sirs, refer also to Christ, and concern the enlightened nations; or will you say again, He speaks to them of the law and the proselytes?"

Then some of those who had come on the second day cried out as if they had been in a theatre, "But what? does He

[1] Isa. xlix. 6.
[2] Γηόρα or Γειόρα. Found in LXX., Ex. xii. 19 and Isa. xiv. 1.
[3] Matt. xxiii. 15. [4] Isa. xlii. 16, xliii. 10. [5] Isa. xlii. 6.

not refer to the law, and to those illumined by it? Now these are proselytes."

"No," I said, looking towards Trypho, "since, if the law were able to enlighten the nations and those who possess it, what need is there of a new covenant? But since God announced beforehand that He would send a new covenant, and an everlasting law and commandment, we will not understand this of the old law and its proselytes, but of Christ and His proselytes, namely us Gentiles, whom He has illumined, as He says somewhere: 'Thus saith the Lord, In an acceptable time have I heard Thee, and in a day of salvation have I helped Thee, and I have given Thee for a covenant of the people, to establish the earth, and to inherit the deserted.'[1] What, then, is Christ's inheritance? Is it not the nations? What is the covenant of God? Is it not Christ? As He says in another place: 'Thou art my Son; this day have I begotten Thee. Ask of me, and I shall give Thee the nations for Thine inheritance, and the uttermost parts of the earth for Thy possession.'[2]

Chap. CXXIII.—*Ridiculous interpretations of the Jews. Christians are the true Israel.*

"As, therefore, all these latter prophecies refer to Christ and the nations, you should believe that the former refer to Him and them in like manner. For the proselytes have no need of a covenant, if, since there is one and the same law imposed on all that are circumcised, the scripture speaks about them thus: 'And the stranger shall also be joined with them, and shall be joined to the house of Jacob;'[3] and because the proselyte, who is circumcised that he may have access to the people, becomes like one of themselves,[4] while we who have been deemed worthy to be called a people are yet Gentiles, because we have not been circumcised. Besides, it is ridiculous for you to imagine that the eyes of the proselytes are to be opened while your own are not, and that you be understood as blind and deaf while they are enlightened.

1 Isa. xlix. 8.
2 Ps. ii. 7 f.
3 Isa. xiv. 1.
4 Literally, "a native of the land."

And it will be still more ridiculous for you, if you say that the law has been given to the nations, but you have not known it. For you would have stood in awe of God's wrath, and would not have been lawless, wandering sons; being much afraid of hearing God always say, 'Children in whom is no faith. And who are blind, but my servants? and deaf, but they that rule over them? And the servants of God have been made blind. You see often, but have not observed; your ears have been opened, and you have not heard.'[1] Is God's commendation of you honourable? and is God's testimony seemly for His servants? You are not ashamed though you often hear these words. You do not tremble at God's threats, for you are a people foolish and hard-hearted. 'Therefore, behold, I will proceed to remove this people,' saith the Lord; 'and I will remove them, and destroy the wisdom of the wise, and hide the understanding of the prudent.'[2] Deservedly too: for you are neither wise nor prudent, but crafty and unscrupulous; wise only to do evil, but utterly incompetent to know the hidden counsel of God, or the faithful covenant of the Lord, or to find out the everlasting paths. Therefore, saith the Lord, I will raise up to Israel and to Judah the seed of men and the seed of beasts.'[3] And by Isaiah He speaks thus concerning another Israel: 'In that day shall there be a third Israel among the Assyrians and the Egyptians, blessed in the land which the Lord of Sabaoth hath blessed, saying, Blessed shall my people in Egypt and in Assyria be, and Israel mine inheritance.'[4] Since then God blesses this people, and calls them Israel, and declares them to be His inheritance, how is it that you repent not of the deception you practise on yourselves, as if you alone were the Israel, and of execrating the people whom God has blessed? For when He speaks to Jerusalem and its environs, He thus added: 'And I will beget men upon you, even my people Israel; and they shall inherit you, and you shall be a possession for them; and you shall be no longer bereaved of them.'"[5]

[1] Deut. xxxii. 20; Isa. xlii. 19 f. [2] Isa. xxix. 14.
[3] Jer. xxxi. 27. [4] Isa. xix. 24 f. [5] Ezek. xxxvi. 12.

"What, then?" says Trypho; "are you Israel? and speaks He such things of you?"

"If, indeed," I replied to him, "we had not entered into a lengthy discussion on these topics, I might have doubted whether you ask this question in ignorance; but since we have brought the matter to a conclusion by demonstration and with your assent, I do not believe that you are ignorant of what I have just said, or desire again mere contention, but that you are urging me to exhibit the same proof to these men." And in compliance with the assent expressed in his eyes, I continued: "Again in Isaiah, if you have ears to hear it, God, speaking of Christ in parable, calls Him Jacob and Israel. He speaks thus: 'Jacob is my servant, I will uphold Him; Israel is mine elect, I will put my Spirit upon Him, and He shall bring forth judgment to the Gentiles. He shall not strive, nor cry, neither shall any one hear His voice in the street: a bruised reed He shall not break, and smoking flax He shall not quench; but He shall bring forth judgment to truth: He shall shine,[1] and shall not be broken till He have set judgment on the earth. And in His name shall the Gentiles trust.'[2] As therefore from the one man Jacob, who was surnamed Israel, all your nation has been called Jacob and Israel; so we from Christ, who begat us unto God, like Jacob, and Israel, and Judah, and Joseph, and David, are called and are the true sons of God, and keep the commandments of Christ."

CHAP. CXXIV.—*Christians are the sons of God.*

And when I saw that they were perturbed because I said that we are the sons of God, I anticipated their questioning, and said, "Listen, sirs, how the Holy Ghost speaks of this people, saying that they are all sons of the Highest; and how this very Christ will be present in their assembly, rendering judgment to all men. The words are spoken by David, and are, according to your version of them, thus: 'God standeth in the congregation of gods; He judgeth

[1] LXX. *ἀναλάμψει*, as above. The reading of the text is *ἀναλήψει*.
[2] Isa. xlii. 1–4.

among the gods. How long do ye judge unjustly, and accept the persons of the wicked? Judge for the orphan and the poor, and do justice to the humble and needy. Deliver the needy, and save the poor out of the hand of the wicked. They know not, neither have they understood; they walk on in darkness: all the foundations of the earth shall be shaken. I said, Ye are gods, and are all children of the Most High. But ye die like men, and fall like one of the princes. Arise, O God! judge the earth, for Thou shalt inherit all nations.'[1] But in the version of the Seventy it is written, 'Behold, ye die like men, and fall like one of the princes,'[2] in order to manifest the disobedience of men,—I mean of Adam and Eve,—and the fall of one of the princes, *i.e.* of him who was called the serpent, who fell with a great overthrow, because he deceived Eve. But as my discourse is not intended to touch on this point, but to prove to you that the Holy Ghost reproaches men because they were made like God, free from suffering and death, provided that they kept His commandments, and were deemed deserving of the name of His sons, and yet they, becoming like Adam and Eve, work out death for themselves; let the interpretation of the Psalm be held just as you wish, yet thereby it is demonstrated that all men are deemed worthy of becoming gods, and of having power to become sons of the Highest; and shall be each by himself judged and condemned like Adam and Eve. Now I have proved at length that Christ is called God.

CHAP. CXXV.—*He explains what force the word Israel has, and how it suits Christ.*

"I wish, sirs," I said, "to learn from you what is the force of the name Israel." And as they were silent, I continued: "I shall tell you what I know: for I do not think it right, when I know, not to speak; or, suspecting that you do know,

[1] Ps. lxxxii.

[2] In the text there is certainly no distinction given. But if we read *ὡς ἄνθρωπος* (כְּאָדָם), "as a man," in the first quotation we shall be able to follow Justin's argument.

and yet from envy or from voluntary ignorance deceive yourselves,[1] to be continually solicitous; but I speak all things simply and candidly, as my Lord said: 'A sower went forth to sow the seed; and some fell by the wayside, and some among thorns, and some on stony ground, and some on good ground.'[2] I must speak, then, in the hope of finding good ground somewhere; since that Lord of mine, as One strong and powerful, comes to demand back His own from all, and will not condemn His steward if He recognises that he, by the knowledge that the Lord is powerful and has come to demand His own, has given it to every bank, and has not digged for any cause whatsoever. Accordingly the name Israel signifies this, A man who overcomes power; for *Isra* is a man overcoming, and *El* is power. And that Christ would act so when He became man was foretold by the mystery of Jacob's wrestling with Him who appeared to him, in that He ministered to the will of the Father, yet nevertheless is God, in that He is the first-begotten of all creatures. For when He became man, as I previously remarked, the devil came to Him—*i.e.* that power which is called the serpent and Satan—tempting Him, and striving to effect His downfall by asking Him to worship him. But He destroyed and overthrew the devil, having proved him to be wicked, in that he asked to be worshipped as God, contrary to the scripture; who is an apostate from the will of God. For He answers him, 'It is written, Thou shalt worship the Lord thy God, and Him only shalt thou serve.'[3] Then, overcome and convicted, the devil departed at that time. But since our Christ was to be numbed, *i.e.* by pain and experience of suffering, He made a previous intimation of this by touching Jacob's thigh, and causing it to shrink. But Israel was His name from the beginning, to which He altered the name of the blessed Jacob when He blessed him with His own name, proclaiming thereby that all who through Him have fled for refuge to the Father, constitute the blessed Israel. But you, having understood none of this, and not being prepared to understand, since you are the children of

[1] The reading here is *ἐπίσταμαι αὐτός*, which is generally abandoned for *ἀπατᾶν ἑαυτούς*.
[2] Matt. xiii. 3.
[3] Matt. iv. 10.

Jacob after the fleshly seed, expect that you shall be assuredly saved. But that you deceive yourselves in such matters, I have proved by many words.

CHAP. CXXVI.—*The various names of Christ according to both natures. It is shown that He is God, and appeared to the patriarchs.*

"But if you knew, Trypho," continued I, "who He is that is called at one time the Angel of great counsel, and a Man by Ezekiel, and like the Son of man by Daniel, and a Child by Isaiah, and Christ and God to be worshipped by David, and Christ and a Stone by many, and Wisdom by Solomon, and Joseph and Judah and a Star by Moses, and the East by Zechariah, and the Suffering One and Jacob and Israel by Isaiah again, and a Rod, and Flower, and Corner-stone, and Son of God, you would not have blasphemed Him who has now come, and been born, and suffered, and ascended to heaven; who shall also come again, and then your twelve tribes shall mourn. For if you had understood what has been written by the prophets, you would not have denied that He was God, Son of the only, unbegotten, unutterable God. For Moses says somewhere in Exodus the following: 'The Lord spake to Moses, and said to him, I am the Lord, and I appeared to Abraham, to Isaac, and to Jacob, being their God; and my name I revealed not to them, and I established my covenant with them.'[1] And thus again he says, 'A man wrestled with Jacob,'[2] and asserts it was God; narrating that Jacob said, 'I have seen God face to face, and my life is preserved.' And it is recorded that he called the place where He wrestled with him, appeared to and blessed him, the Face of God (Peniel). And Moses says that God appeared also to Abraham near the oak in Mamre, when he was sitting at the door of his tent at mid-day. Then he goes on to say: 'And he lifted up his eyes and looked, and, behold, three men stood before him; and when he saw them, he ran to meet them.'[3] After a little, one of them promises a son to Abraham: 'Wherefore did Sarah laugh, saying, Shall I of a surety bear a

[1] Ex. vi. 2 ff. [2] Gen. xxxii. 24, 30. [3] Gen. xviii. 2.

child, and I am old? Is anything impossible with God? At the time appointed I will return, according to the time of life, and Sarah shall have a son. And they went away from Abraham.'[1] Again he speaks of them thus: 'And the men rose up from thence, and looked toward Sodom.'[2] Then to Abraham He who was and is again speaks: 'I will not hide from Abraham, my servant, what I intend to do.'"[3] And what follows in the writings of Moses I quoted and explained; "from which I have demonstrated," I said, "that He who is described as God appeared to Abraham, to Isaac, and to Jacob, and the other patriarchs, was appointed under the authority of the Father and Lord, and ministers to His will." Then I went on to say what I had not said before: "And so, when the people desired to eat flesh, and Moses had lost faith in Him, who also there is called the Angel, and who promised that God would give them to satiety, He who is both God and the Angel, sent by the Father, is described as saying and doing these things. For thus the scripture says: 'And the Lord said to Moses, Will the Lord's hand not be sufficient? thou shalt know now whether my word shall conceal thee or not.'[4] And again, in other words, it thus says: 'But the Lord spake unto me, Thou shalt not go over this Jordan: the Lord thy God, who goeth before thy face, He shall cut off the nations.'[5]

CHAP. CXXVII.—*These passages of Scripture do not apply to the Father, but to the Word.*

"These and other such sayings are recorded by the lawgiver and by the prophets; and I suppose that I have stated sufficiently, that wherever[6] God says, 'God went up from Abraham,'[7] or, 'The Lord spake to Moses,'[8] and, 'The Lord came down to behold the tower which the sons of men had built,'[9] or when 'God shut Noah into the ark,'[10] you must not imagine that the unbegotten God Himself came down or went up from any place. For the ineffable Father and Lord of all

[1] Gen. xviii. 13 f. [2] Gen. xviii. 16. [3] Gen. xviii. 17.
[4] Num. xi. 23. [5] Deut. xxxi. 2 f.
[6] ὅταν που instead of ὅταν μου. [7] Gen. xviii. 22.
[8] Ex. vi. 29. [9] Gen. xi. 5. [10] Gen. vii. 16.

neither has come to any place, nor walks, nor sleeps, nor rises up, but remains in His own place, wherever that is, quick to behold and quick to hear, having neither eyes nor ears, but being of indescribable might; and He sees all things, and knows all things, and none of us escapes His observation; and He is not moved or confined to a spot in the whole world, for He existed before the world was made. How, then, could He talk with any one, or be seen by any one, or appear on the smallest portion of the earth, when the people at Sinai were not able to look even on the glory of Him who was sent from Him; and Moses himself could not enter into the tabernacle which he had erected, when it was filled with the glory of God; and the priest could not endure to stand before the temple when Solomon conveyed the ark into the house in Jerusalem which he had built for it? Therefore neither Abraham, nor Isaac, nor Jacob, nor any other man, saw the Father and ineffable Lord of all, and also of Christ, but [saw] Him who was according to His will His Son, being God, and the Angel because He ministered to His will; whom also it pleased Him to be born man by the Virgin; who also was fire when He conversed with Moses from the bush. Since, unless we thus comprehend the Scriptures, it must follow that the Father and Lord of all had not been in heaven when what Moses wrote took place: 'And the Lord rained upon Sodom fire and brimstone from the Lord out of heaven;[1] and again, when it is thus said by David: 'Lift up your gates, ye rulers; and be ye lift up, ye everlasting gates; and the King of glory shall enter;'[2] and again, when He says: 'The Lord says to my Lord, Sit at my right hand, till I make Thine enemies Thy footstool.'[3]

CHAP. CXXVIII.—*The Word is sent not as an inanimate power, but as a Person begotten of the Father's substance.*

"And that Christ being Lord, and God the Son of God, and appearing formerly in power as Man, and Angel, and in the glory of fire as at the bush, so also was manifested at the judgment executed on Sodom, has been demonstrated

[1] Gen. xix. 24. [2] Ps. xxiv. 7. [3] Ps. cx. 1.

fully by what has been said." Then I repeated once more all that I had previously quoted from Exodus, about the vision in the bush, and the naming of Joshua (Jesus), and continued: "And do not suppose, sirs, that I am speaking superfluously when I repeat these words frequently: but it is because I know that some wish to anticipate these remarks, and to say that the power sent from the Father of all which appeared to Moses, or to Abraham, or to Jacob, is called an Angel because He came to men (for by Him the commands of the Father have been proclaimed to men); is called Glory, because He appears in a vision sometimes that cannot be borne; is called a man, and a human being, because He appears arrayed in such forms as the Father pleases; and they call Him the Word, because He carries tidings from the Father to men: but maintain that this power is indivisible and inseparable from the Father, just as they say that the light of the sun on earth is indivisible and inseparable from the sun in the heavens; as when it sinks, the light sinks along with it; so the Father, when He chooses, say they, causes His power to spring forth, and when He chooses, He makes it return to Himself. In this way, they teach, He made the angels. But it is proved that there are angels who always exist, and are never reduced to that form out of which they sprang. And that this power which the prophetic word calls God, as has been also amply demonstrated, and Angel, is not numbered [as different] in name only like the light of the sun, but is indeed something numerically distinct, I have discussed briefly in what has gone before; when I asserted that this power was begotten from the Father, by His power and will, but not by abscission, as if the essence of the Father were divided; as all other things partitioned and divided are not the same after as before they were divided: and, for the sake of example, I took the case of fires kindled from a fire, which we see to be distinct from it, and yet that from which many can be kindled is by no means made less, but remains the same.

CHAP. CXXIX.—*That is confirmed from other passages of Scripture.*

"And now I shall again recite the words which I have spoken in proof of this point. When Scripture says, 'The Lord rained fire from the Lord out of heaven,' the prophetic word indicates that there were two in number: One upon the earth, who, it says, descended to behold the cry of Sodom; Another in heaven, who also is Lord of the Lord on earth, as He is Father and God; the cause of His power and of His being Lord and God. Again, when the Scripture records that God said in the beginning, 'Behold, Adam has become like one of us,'[1] this phrase, 'like one of us,' is also indicative of number; and the words do not admit of a figurative meaning, as the sophists endeavour to affix on them, who are able neither to tell nor to understand the truth. And it is written in the book of Wisdom: 'If I should tell you daily events, I would be mindful to enumerate them from the beginning. The Lord created me the beginning of His ways for His works. From everlasting He established me in the beginning, before He formed the earth, and before He made the depths, and before the springs of waters came forth, before the mountains were settled; He begets me before all the hills.'"[2] When I repeated these words, I added: "You perceive, my hearers, if you bestow attention, that the Scripture has declared that this Offspring was begotten by the Father before all things created; and that that which is begotten is numerically distinct from that which begets, any one will admit."

CHAP. CXXX.—*He returns to the conversion of the Gentiles, and shows that it was foretold.*

And when all had given assent, I said: "I would now adduce some passages which I had not recounted before. They are recorded by the faithful servant Moses in parable, and are as follows: 'Rejoice, O ye heavens, with Him, and let all the angels of God worship Him;'"[3] and I added what

[1] Gen. iii. 22. [2] Prov. viii. 22 ff. [3] Deut. xxxii. 43.

follows of the passage: "'Rejoice, O ye nations, with His people, and let all the angels of God be strengthened in Him: for the blood of His sons He avenges, and will avenge, and will recompense His enemies with vengeance, and will recompense those that hate Him; and the Lord will purify the land of His people.' And by these words He declares that we, the nations, rejoice with His people,—to wit, Abraham, and Isaac, and Jacob, and the prophets, and, in short, all of that people who are well-pleasing to God, according to what has been already agreed on between us. But we will not receive it of all your nation; since we know from Isaiah[1] that the members of those who have transgressed shall be consumed by the worm and unquenchable fire, remaining immortal; so that they become a spectacle to all flesh. But in addition to these, I wish, sirs," said I, "to add some other passages from the very words of Moses, from which you may understand that God has from of old dispersed all men according to their kindreds and tongues; and out of all kindreds has taken to Himself your kindred, a useless, disobedient, and faithless generation; and has shown that those who were selected out of every nation have obeyed His will through Christ,—whom He calls also Jacob, and names Israel,—and these, then, as I mentioned fully previously, must be Jacob and Israel. For when He says, 'Rejoice, O ye nations, with His people,' He allots the same inheritance to them, and does not call them by the same name;[2] but when He says that they as Gentiles rejoice with His people, He calls them Gentiles to reproach you. For even as you provoked Him to anger by your idolatry, so also He has deemed those who were idolaters worthy of knowing His will, and of inheriting His inheritance.

CHAP. CXXXI.—*How much more faithful to God the Gentiles are who are converted to Christ than the Jews.*

"But I shall quote the passage by which it is made known that God divided all the nations. It is as follows: 'Ask

[1] Isa. lxvi. 24.

[2] The reading is, "and calls them by the same name." But the whole argument shows that the Jews and Gentiles are distinguished by name.

thy father, and he will show thee; thine elders, and they will tell thee; when the Most High divided the nations, as He dispersed the sons of Adam. He set the bounds of the nations according to the numbers of the children of Israel; and the Lord's portion became His people Jacob, and Israel was the lot of His inheritance.'"[1] And having said this, I added: "The Seventy have translated it, 'He set the bounds of the nations according to the number of the angels of God.' But because my argument is again in nowise weakened by this, I have adopted your exposition. And you yourselves, if you will confess the truth, must acknowledge that we, who have been called by God through the despised and shameful mystery of the cross (for the confession of which, and obedience to which, and for our piety, punishments even to death have been inflicted on us by demons, and by the host of the devil, through the aid ministered to them by you), and endure all torments rather than deny Christ even by word, through whom we are called to the salvation prepared beforehand by the Father, are more faithful to God than you, who were redeemed from Egypt with a high hand and a visitation of great glory, when the sea was parted for you, and a passage left dry, in which [God] slew those who pursued you with a very great equipment, and splendid chariots, bringing back upon them the sea which had been made a way for your sakes; on whom also a pillar of light shone, in order that you, more than any other nation in the world, might possess a peculiar light, never-failing and never-setting; for whom He rained manna as nourishment, fit for the heavenly angels, in order that you might have no need to prepare your food; and the water at Marah was made sweet; and a sign of Him that was to be crucified was made, both in the matter of the serpents which bit you, as I already mentioned (God anticipating before the proper times these mysteries, in order to confer grace upon you, to whom you are always convicted of being thankless), as well as in the type of the extending of the hands of Moses, and of Oshea being named Jesus (Joshua); when you fought against Amalek: con-

[1] Deut. xxxii. 7 ff.

cerning which God enjoined that the incident be recorded, and the name of Jesus laid up in your understandings; saying that this is He who would blot out the memorial of Amalek from under heaven. Now it is clear that the memorial of Amalek remained after the son of Nave (Nun): but He makes it manifest that through Jesus, who was crucified, of whom also those symbols were fore-announcements of all that would happen to Him, the demons would be destroyed, and would dread His name, and that all principalities and kingdoms would fear Him; and that they who believe in Him out of all nations would be shown as God-fearing and peaceful men; and the facts already quoted by me, Trypho, indicate this. Again, when you desired flesh, so vast a quantity of quails was given you, that they could not be told; for whom also water gushed from the rock; and a cloud followed you for a shade from heat, and covering from cold, declaring the manner and signification of another and new heaven; the latchets of your shoes did not break, and your shoes waxed not old, and your garments wore not away, but even those of the children grew along with them.

CHAP. CXXXII.—*How great the power was of the name of Jesus in the Old Testament.*

"Yet after this you made a calf, and were very zealous in committing fornication with the daughters of strangers, and in serving idols. And again, when the land was given up to you with so great a display of power, that you witnessed the sun stand still in the heavens by the order of that man whose name was Jesus (Joshua), and not go down for thirty-six hours, as well as all the other miracles which were wrought for you as time served;[1] and of these it seems good to me now to speak of another, for it conduces to your hereby knowing Jesus, whom we also know to have been Christ the Son of God, who was crucified, and rose again, and ascended to heaven, and will come again to judge all men, even up to Adam himself. You are aware, then," I continued, "that when the ark of the testimony was seized by the enemies of

[1] The anacolouthon is in the original.

Ashdod,[1] and a terrible and incurable malady had broken out among them, they resolved to place it on a cart to which they yoked cows that had recently calved, for the purpose of ascertaining by trial whether or not they had been plagued by God's power on account of the ark, and if God wished it to be taken back to the place from which it had been carried away. And when they had done this, the cows, led by no man, went not to the place whence the ark had been taken, but to the fields of a certain man whose name was Oshea, the same as his whose name was altered to Jesus (Joshua), as has been previously mentioned, who also led the people into the land and meted it out to them: and when the cows had come into these fields they remained there, showing to you thereby that they were guided by the name of power;[2] just as formerly the people who survived of those that came out of Egypt, were guided into the land by him who had received the name Jesus (Joshua), who before was called Oshea.

CHAP. CXXXIII.—*The hard-heartedness of the Jews, for whom the Christians pray.*

"Now, although these and all other such unexpected and marvellous works were wrought amongst and seen by you at different times, yet you are convicted by the prophets of having gone to such a length as offering your own children to demons; and besides all this, of having dared to do such things against Christ; and you still dare to do them: for all which may it be granted to you to obtain mercy and salvation from God and His Christ. For God, knowing before that you would do such things, pronounced this curse upon you by the prophet Isaiah: 'Woe unto their soul! they have devised evil counsel against themselves, saying, Let us bind the righteous man, for he is distasteful to us. Therefore they shall eat the fruit of their own doings. Woe to the wicked! evil, according to the works of his hands, shall befall him. O my people, your exactors glean you, and those who extort from you shall rule over you. O my people, they who call you blessed cause you to err, and disorder the way of your paths. But now the

[1] See 1 Sam. v.

[2] Or, "by the power of the name."

Lord shall sist His people to judgment, and He shall enter into judgment with the elders of the people and the princes thereof. But why have you burnt up my vineyard? and why is the spoil of the poor found in your houses? Why do you wrong my people, and put to shame the countenance of the humble?'[1] Again, in other words, the same prophet spake to the same effect: 'Woe unto them that draw their iniquity as with a long cord, and their transgressions as with the harness of an heifer's yoke: who say, Let His speed come near, and let the counsel of the Holy One of Israel come, that we may know it. Woe unto them that call evil good, and good evil! that put light for darkness, and darkness for light! that put bitter for sweet, and sweet for bitter! Woe unto them that are wise in their own eyes, and prudent in their own sight! Woe unto those that are mighty among you, who drink wine, who are men of strength, who mingle strong drink! who justify the wicked for a reward, and take away justice from the righteous! Therefore, as the stubble shall be burnt by the coal of fire, and utterly consumed by the burning flame, their root shall be as wool, and their flower shall go up like dust. For they would not have the law of the Lord of Sabaoth, but despised[2] the word of the Lord, the Holy One of Israel. And the Lord of Sabaoth was very angry, and laid His hands upon them, and smote them; and He was provoked against the mountains, and their carcases were in the midst like dung on the road. And for all this they have not repented,[3] but their hand is still high.'[4] For verily your hand is high to commit evil, because ye slew the Christ, and do not repent of it; but so far from that, ye hate and murder us who have believed through Him in the God and Father of all, as often as ye can; and ye curse Him without ceasing, as well as those who side with Him; while all of us pray for you, and for all men, as our Christ and Lord taught us to do, when He enjoined us to pray even for our enemies, and to love them that hate us, and to bless them that curse us.

[1] Isa. iii. 9–15.
[2] Literally, "provoked."
[3] Literally, "turned away."
[4] Isa. v. 18–25.

CHAP. CXXXIV.—*The marriages of Jacob are a figure of the church.*

"If, then, the teaching of the prophets and of Himself moves you, it is better for you to follow God than your imprudent and blind masters, who even till this time permit each man to have four or five wives; and if any one see a beautiful woman and desire to have her, they quote the doings of Jacob [called] Israel, and of the other patriarchs, and maintain that it is not wrong to do such things: for they are miserably ignorant in this matter. For, as I before said, certain dispensations of weighty mysteries were accomplished in each act of this sort. For in the marriages of Jacob I shall mention what dispensation and prophecy were accomplished, in order that you may thereby know that your teachers never looked at the divine motive which prompted each act, but only at the grovelling and corrupting passions. Attend therefore to what I say. The marriages of Jacob were types of that which Christ was about to accomplish. For it was not lawful for Jacob to marry two sisters at once. And he serves Laban for [one of] the daughters; and being deceived in [the obtaining of] the younger, he again served seven years. Now Leah is your people and synagogue; but Rachel is our church. And for these, and for the servants in both, Christ even now serves. For while Noah gave to the two sons the seed of the third as servants, now on the other hand Christ has come to restore both the free sons and the servants amongst them, conferring the same honour on all of them who keep His commandments; even as the children of the free women and the children of the bond women born to Jacob were all sons, and equal in dignity. And it was foretold what each should be according to rank and according to fore-knowledge. Jacob served Laban for speckled and many-spotted sheep; and Christ served, even to the slavery of the cross, for the various and many-formed races of mankind, acquiring them by the blood and mystery of the cross. Leah was weak-eyed; for the eyes of your souls are excessively weak. Rachel stole the gods of Laban, and has hid them to this day; and we have lost our paternal and material gods. Jacob was hated for all time by his brother; and we now, and our Lord Himself, are hated by you and by all men, though we are brothers by nature. Jacob was called Israel; and Israel has been demonstrated to be the Christ, who is, and is called, Jesus.

CHAP. CXXXV.—*Christ is King of Israel, and Christians are the Israelitic race.*

"And when Scripture says, 'I am the Lord God, the Holy One of Israel, who have made known Israel your King,'[1] will you not understand that truly Christ is the everlasting King? For you are aware that Jacob the son of Isaac was never a king. And therefore Scripture again, explaining to us, says what king is meant by Jacob and Israel: 'Jacob is my servant, I will uphold Him; and Israel is mine Elect, my soul shall receive Him. I have given Him my Spirit; and He shall bring forth judgment to the Gentiles. He shall not cry, and His voice shall not be heard without. The bruised reed He shall not break, and the smoking flax He shall not quench, until He shall bring forth judgment to victory. He shall shine, and shall not be broken, until He set judgment on the earth. And in His name shall the Gentiles trust.'[2] Then is it Jacob the patriarch in whom the Gentiles and yourselves shall trust? or is it not Christ? As, therefore, Christ is the Israel and the Jacob, even so we, who have been quarried out from the belly of Christ, are the true Israelitic race. But let us attend rather to the very word: 'And I will bring forth,' He says, 'the seed out of Jacob, and out of Judah: and it shall inherit my holy mountain; and mine Elect and my servants shall possess the inheritance, and shall dwell there; and there shall be folds of flocks in the thicket, and the valley of Achor shall be a resting-place of cattle for the people who have sought me. But as for you, who forsake me, and forget my holy mountain, and prepare a table for demons, and fill out drink for the demon, I shall give you to the sword. You shall all fall with a slaughter; for I called you, and you hearkened

[1] Isa. xliii. 15. [2] Isa. xlii. 1–4.

not, and did evil before me, and did choose that wherein I delighted not.'[1] Such are the words of Scripture; understand, therefore, that the seed of Jacob now referred to is something else, and not, as may be supposed, spoken of your people. For it is not possible for the seed of Jacob to leave an entrance for the descendants of Jacob, or for [God] to have accepted the very same persons whom He had reproached with unfitness for the inheritance, and promise it to them again; but as there the prophet says, 'And now, O house of Jacob, come and let us walk in the light of the Lord; for He has sent away His people, the house of Jacob, because their land was full, as at the first, of soothsayers and divinations;'[2] even so it is necessary for us here to observe that there are two seeds of Judah, and two races, as there are two houses of Jacob: the one begotten by blood and flesh, the other by faith and the Spirit.

CHAP. CXXXVI.—*The Jews, in rejecting Christ, rejected God who sent Him.*

"For you see how He now addresses the people, saying a little before: 'As the grape shall be found in the cluster, and they will say, Destroy it not, for a blessing is in it; so will I do for my servant's sake: for His sake I will not destroy them all.'[3] And thereafter He adds: 'And I shall bring forth the seed out of Jacob, and out of Judah.' It is plain, then, that if He thus be angry with them, and threaten to leave very few of them, He promises to bring forth certain others, who shall dwell in His mountain. But these are the persons whom He said He would sow and beget. For you neither suffer Him when He calls you, nor hear Him when He speaks to you, but have done evil in the presence of the Lord. But the highest pitch of your wickedness lies in this, that you hate the Righteous One, and slew Him; and so treat those who have received from Him all that they are and have, and who are pious, righteous, and humane. Therefore 'woe unto their soul,' says the Lord,[4] 'for they have devised an evil counsel against themselves, saying, Let us take away the

[1] Isa. lxv. 9–12. [2] Isa. ii. 5 f. [3] Isa. lxv. 8 f. [4] Isa. iii. 9.

righteous, for he is distasteful to us.' For indeed you are not in the habit of sacrificing to Baal, as were your fathers, or of placing cakes in groves and on high places for the host of heaven: but you have not accepted God's Christ. For he who knows not Him, knows not the will of God; and he who insults and hates Him, insults and hates Him that sent Him. And whoever believes not in Him, believes not the declarations of the prophets, who preached and proclaimed Him to all.

CHAP. CXXXVII.—*He exhorts the Jews to be converted.*

"Say no evil thing, my brothers, against Him that was crucified, and treat not scornfully the stripes wherewith all may be healed, even as we are healed. For it will be well if, persuaded by the Scriptures, you are circumcised from hard-heartedness: not that circumcision which you have from the tenets that are put into you; for that was given for a sign, and not for a work of righteousness, as the Scriptures compel you [to admit]. Assent, therefore, and pour no ridicule on the Son of God; obey not the pharisaic teachers, and scoff not at the King of Israel, as the rulers of your synagogues teach you to do after your prayers: for if he that touches those who are not pleasing[1] to God, is as one that touches the apple of God's eye, how much more so is he that touches His beloved! And that this is He, has been sufficiently demonstrated."

And as they kept silence, I continued: "My friends, I now refer to the Scriptures as the Seventy have interpreted them; for when I quoted them formerly as you possess them, I made proof of you [to ascertain] how you were disposed. For, mentioning the scripture which says, 'Woe unto them! for they have devised evil counsel against themselves, saying'[2] (as the Seventy have translated, I continued): 'Let us take away the righteous, for he is distasteful to us;' whereas at the commencement of the discussion I added what your version has: 'Let us bind the righteous, for he is distasteful to us.' But you had been busy about some other matter, and

[1] Zech. ii. 8. [2] Isa. iii. 9.

seem to have listened to the words without attending to them. But now, since the day is drawing to a close, for the sun is about to set, I shall add one remark to what I have said, and conclude. I have indeed made the very same remark already, but I think it would be right to bestow some consideration on it again.

CHAP. CXXXVIII.—*Noah is a figure of Christ, who has regenerated us by water, and faith, and wood.*

"You know, then, sirs," I said, "that God has said in Isaiah to Jerusalem: 'I saved thee in the deluge of Noah.'[1] By this which God said was meant that the mystery of saved men appeared in the deluge. For righteous Noah, along with the other mortals at the deluge, *i.e.* with his own wife, his three sons and their wives, being eight in number, were a symbol of the eighth day, wherein Christ appeared when He rose from the dead, for ever the first in power. For Christ, being the first-born of every creature, became again the chief of another race regenerated by Himself through water, and faith, and wood, containing the mystery of the cross; even as Noah was saved by wood when he rode over the waters with his household. Accordingly, when the prophet says, 'I saved thee in the times of Noah,' as I have already remarked, he addresses the people who are equally faithful to God, and possess the same signs. For when Moses had the rod in his hands, he led your nation through the sea. And you believe that this was spoken to your nation only, or to the land. But the whole earth, as the Scripture says, was inundated, and the water rose in height fifteen cubits above all the mountains: so that it is evident this was not spoken to the land, but to the people who obeyed Him: for whom also He had before prepared a resting-place in Jerusalem, as was previously demonstrated by all the symbols of the deluge; I mean, that by water, faith, and wood, those who are afore-prepared, and who repent of the sins which they have committed, shall escape from the impending judgment of God.

[1] Isa. liv. 9 comes nearer to these words than any other passage; but still the exact quotation is not in Isaiah, or in any other part of Scripture.

CHAP. CXXXIX.—*The blessings, and also the curse, pronounced by Noah were prophecies of the future.*

"For another mystery was accomplished and predicted in the days of Noah, of which you are not aware. It is this: in the blessings wherewith Noah blessed his two sons, and in the curse pronounced on his son's son. For the Spirit of prophecy would not curse the son that had been by God blessed along with [his brothers]. But since the punishment of the sin would cleave to the whole descent of the son that mocked at his father's nakedness, he made the curse originate with *his* son. Now, in what he said, he foretold that the descendants of Shem would keep in retention the property and dwellings of Canaan: and again, that the descendants of Japheth would take possession of the property of which Shem's descendants had dispossessed Canaan's descendants; and spoil the descendants of Shem, even as they plundered the sons of Canaan. And listen to the way in which it has so come to pass. For you, who have derived your lineage from Shem, invaded the territory of the sons of Canaan by the will of God; and you possessed it. And it is manifest that the sons of Japheth, having invaded you in turn by the judgment of God, have taken your land from you, and have possessed it. Thus it is written: 'And Noah awoke from the wine, and knew what his younger son had done unto him; and he said, Cursed be Canaan, the servant; a servant shall he be unto his brethren. And he said, Blessed be the Lord God of Shem; and Canaan shall be his servant. May the Lord enlarge Japheth, and let him dwell in the houses of Shem; and let Canaan be his servant.'[1] Accordingly, as two peoples were blessed,—those from Shem, and those from Japheth,—and as the offspring of Shem were decreed first to possess the dwellings of Canaan, and the offspring of Japheth were predicted as in turn receiving the same possessions, and to the two peoples there was the one people of Canaan handed over for servants; so Christ has come according to the power given Him from the Almighty Father, and summoning men

[1] Gen. ix. 24-27.

to friendship, and blessing, and repentance, and dwelling together, has promised, as has already been proved, that there shall be a future possession for all the saints in this same land. And hence all men everywhere, whether bond or free, who believe in Christ, and recognise the truth in His own words and those of His prophets, know that they shall be with Him in that land, and inherit everlasting and incorruptible good.

CHAP. CXL.—*In Christ all are free. The Jews hope for salvation in vain because they are sons of Abraham.*

"Hence also Jacob, as I remarked before, being himself a type of Christ, had married the two handmaids of his two free wives, and of them begat sons, for the purpose of indicating beforehand that Christ would receive even all those who amongst Japheth's race are descendants of Canaan, equally with the free, and would have the children fellow-heirs. And we are such; but you cannot comprehend this, because you cannot drink of the living fountain of God, but of broken cisterns which can hold no water, as the Scripture says.[1] But they are cisterns broken, and holding no water, which your own teachers have digged, as the Scripture also expressly asserts, 'teaching for doctrines the commandments of men.'[2] And besides, they beguile themselves and you, supposing that the everlasting kingdom will be assuredly given to those of the dispersion who are of Abraham after the flesh, although they be sinners, and faithless, and disobedient towards God, which the Scriptures have proved is not the case. For if so, Isaiah would never have said this: 'And unless the Lord of Sabaoth had left us a seed, we would have been like Sodom and Gomorrah.'[3] And Ezekiel: 'Even if Noah, and Jacob, and Daniel were to pray for sons or daughters, their request should not be granted.'[4] But neither shall the father perish for the son, nor the son for the father; but every one for his own sin, and each shall be saved for his own righteousness.[5] And again Isaiah says: 'They shall look on the car-

[1] Jer. ii. 13. [2] Isa. xxix. 13. [3] Isa. i. 9.
[4] Ezek. xiv. 18, 20. [5] Ezek. xviii. 20.

cases[1] of them that have transgressed: their worm shall not cease, and their fire shall not be quenched; and they shall be a spectacle to all flesh.'[2] And our Lord, according to the will of Him that sent Him, who is the Father and Lord of all, would not have said, 'They shall come from the east, and from the west, and shall sit down with Abraham, and Isaac, and Jacob in the kingdom of heaven. But the children of the kingdom shall be cast out into outer darkness.'[3] Furthermore, I have proved in what has preceded,[4] that those who were foreknown to be unrighteous, whether men or angels, are not made wicked by God's fault, but each man by his own fault is what he will appear to be.

CHAP. CXLI.—*Free-will in men and angels.*

"But that you may not have a pretext for saying that Christ must have been crucified, and that those who transgressed must have been among your nation, and that the matter could not have been otherwise, I said briefly by anticipation, that God, wishing men and angels to follow His will, resolved to create them free to do righteousness; possessing reason, that they may know by whom they are created, and through whom they, not existing formerly, do now exist; and with a law that they should be judged by Him, if they do anything contrary to right reason: and of ourselves we, men and angels, shall be convicted of having acted sinfully, unless we repent beforehand. But if the word of God foretells that some angels and men shall be certainly punished, it did so because it foreknew that they would be unchangeably [wicked], but not because God had created them so. So that if they repent, all who wish for it can obtain mercy from God: and the Scripture foretells that they shall be blessed, saying, 'Blessed is the man to whom the Lord imputeth not sin;'[5] that is, having repented of his sins, that he may receive remission of them from God; and not as you deceive yourselves, and some others who resemble you in this, who say,

[1] Literally, "limbs."
[2] Isa. lxvi. 24.
[3] Matt. viii. 11 f.
[4] Chap. lxxxviii. cii.
[5] Ps. xxxii. 2.

that even though they be sinners, but know God, the Lord will not impute sin to them. We have as proof of this the one fall of David, which happened through his boasting, which was forgiven then when he so mourned and wept, as it is written. But if even to such a man no remission was granted before repentance, and only when this great king, and anointed one, and prophet, mourned and conducted himself so, how can the impure and utterly abandoned, if they weep not, and mourn not, and repent not, entertain the hope that the Lord will not impute to them sin? And this one fall of David, in the matter of Uriah's wife, proves, sirs," I said, "that the patriarchs had many wives, not to commit fornication, but that a certain dispensation and all mysteries might be accomplished by them; since, if it were allowable to take any wife, or as many wives as one chooses, and how he chooses, which the men of your nation do over all the earth, wherever they sojourn, or wherever they have been sent, taking women under the name of marriage, much more would David have been permitted to do this."

When I had said this, dearest Marcus Pompeius, I came to an end.

Chap. cxlii.—*The Jews return thanks, and leave Justin.*

Then Trypho, after a little delay, said, "You see that it was not intentionally that we came to discuss these points. And I confess that I have been particularly pleased with the conference; and I think that these are of quite the same opinion as myself. For we have found more than we expected, and more than it was possible to have expected. And if we could do this more frequently, we should be much helped in the searching of the Scriptures themselves. But since," he said, "you are on the eve of departure, and expect daily to set sail, do not hesitate to remember us as friends when you are gone."

"For my part," I replied, "if I had remained, I would have wished to do the same thing daily. But now, since I expect, with God's will and aid, to set sail, I exhort you to give all diligence in this very great struggle for your own salvation, and to be earnest in setting a higher value on the Christ of the Almighty God than on your own teachers."

After this they left me, wishing me safety in my voyage, and from every misfortune. And I, praying for them, said, "I can wish no better thing for you, sirs, than this, that, recognising in this way that intelligence is given to every man, you may be of the same opinion as ourselves, and believe that Jesus is the Christ of God."[1]

[1] The last sentence is very dubious. For παντὶ ἀνθρώπινον νοῦν read παντὶ ἀνθρώπῳ τὸν νοῦν. For ποιήσητε read πιστεύσητε. And lastly, for τὸ ἡμῶν read τὸν Ἰησοῦν.

THE DISCOURSE TO THE GREEKS.

CHAP. I.—*Justin justifies his departure from Greek customs.*

O not suppose, ye Greeks, that my separation from your customs is unreasonable and unthinking; for I found in them nothing that is holy or acceptable to God. For the very compositions of your poets are monuments of madness and intemperance. For any one who becomes the scholar of your most eminent instructor, is more beset by difficulties than all men besides. For first they say that Agamemnon, abetting the extravagant lust of his brother, and his madness and unrestrained desire, readily gave even his daughter to be sacrificed, and troubled all Greece that he might rescue Helen, who had been ravished by the leprous[1] shepherd. But when in the course of the war they took captives, Agamemnon was himself taken captive by Chryseis, and for Briseis' sake kindled a feud with the son of Thetis. And Pelides himself, who crossed the river,[2] overthrew Troy, and subdued Hector, this your hero became the slave of Polyxena, and was conquered by a dead Amazon; and putting off the god-fabricated armour, and donning the hymeneal robe, he became a sacrifice of love in the temple of Apollo. And the Ithacan Ulysses made a virtue of a vice.[3] And indeed his sailing past the Sirens[4] gave evidence that

[1] Potter would here read λιπαροῦ, "elegant;" but the above reading is defended by Sylburg, on the ground that shepherds were so greatly despised, that this is not too hard an epithet to apply to Paris.

[2] Of the many attempts to amend this clause, there seems to be none satisfactory.

[3] Or, won the reputation of the virtue of wisdom by the vice of deceit.

[4] That is, the manner in which he did it, stopping his companions' ears with wax, and having himself bound to the mast of his ship.

he was destitute of worthy prudence, because he could not depend on his prudence for stopping his ears. Ajax, son of Telamon, who bore the shield of sevenfold ox-hide, went mad when he was defeated in the contest with Ulysses for the armour. Such things I have no desire to be instructed in. Of such virtue I am not covetous, that I should believe the myths of Homer. For the whole rhapsody, the beginning and end both of the Iliad and the Odyssey is—a woman.

Chap. ii.—*The Greek theogony exposed.*

But since, next to Homer, Hesiod wrote his *Works and Days*, who will believe his drivelling theogony? For they say that Chronos, the son of Ouranos,[1] in the beginning slew his father, and possessed himself of his rule; and that, being seized with a panic lest he should himself suffer in the same way, he preferred devouring his children; but that, by the craft of the Curetes, Jupiter was conveyed away and kept in secret, and afterwards bound his father with chains, and divided the empire; Jupiter receiving, as the story goes, the air, and Neptune the deep, and Pluto the portion of Hades. But Pluto ravished Proserpine; and Ceres sought her child wandering through the deserts. And this myth was celebrated in the Eleusinian fire.[2] Again, Neptune ravished Melanippe when she was drawing water, besides abusing a host of Nereids not a few, whose names, were we to recount them, would cost us a multitude of words. And as for Jupiter, he was a various adulterer, with Antiope as a satyr, with Danaë as gold, and with Europa as a bull; with Leda, moreover, he assumed wings. For the love of Semele proved both his unchastity and the jealousy of Semele. And they say that he carried off the Phrygian Ganymede to be his cup-bearer. These, then, are the exploits of the sons of Saturn. And your illustrious son of Latona [Apollo], who professed soothsaying, convicted himself of lying. He pursued Daphne,

[1] Or, Saturn son of Heaven.

[2] In the mysteries of Eleusis, the return of Proserpine from the lower world was celebrated.

but did not gain possession of her; and to Hyacinthus,[1] who loved him, he did not foretell his death. And I say nothing of the masculine character of Minerva, nor of the feminine nature of Bacchus, nor of the fornicating disposition of Venus. Read to Jupiter, ye Greeks, the law against parricides, and the penalty of adultery, and the ignominy of pæderasty. Teach Minerva and Diana the works of women, and Bacchus the works of men. What seemliness is there in a woman's girding herself with armour, or in a man's decorating himself with cymbals, and garlands, and female attire, and accompanied by a herd of bacchanalian women?

CHAP. III.—*Follies of the Greek mythology.*

For Hercules, celebrated by his three nights,[2] sung by the poets for his successful labours, the son of Jupiter, who slew the lion and destroyed the many-headed hydra; who put to death the fierce and mighty boar, and was able to kill the fleet man-eating birds, and brought up from Hades the three-headed dog; who effectually cleansed the huge Augean building from its dung, and killed the bulls and the stag whose nostrils breathed fire, and plucked the golden fruit from the tree, and slew the poisonous serpent (and for some reason, which it is not lawful to utter, killed Achelous, and the guest-slaying Busiris), and crossed the mountains that he might get water which gave forth an articulate speech, as the story goes: he who was able to do so many and such like and so great deeds as these, how childishly he was delighted to be stunned by the cymbals of the satyrs, and to be conquered by the love of woman, and to be struck on the buttocks by the laughing Lyda! And at last, not being able to put off the tunic of Nessus, himself kindling his own funeral pile, he so died. Let Vulcan lay aside his envy, and not be jealous if he is hated because he is old and

[1] Apollo accidentally killed Hyacinthus by striking him on the head with a quoit.

[2] Τριέσπερον, so called, as Potter thinks, from his being three nights in the belly of a whale, which swallowed him when shipwrecked, and vomited him safely on shore.

club-footed, and Mars loved, because young and beautiful. Since, therefore, ye Greeks, your gods are convicted of intemperance, and your heroes are effeminate, as the histories on which your dramas are founded have declared, such as the curse of Atreus, the bed of Thyestes,[1] and the taint in the house of Pelops, and Danaus murdering through hatred and making Ægyptus childless in the intoxication of his rage, and the Thyestean banquet spread by the Furies.[2] And Procne is to this day flitting about, lamenting; and her sister of Athens shrills with her tongue cut out. For what need is there of speaking of the goad[3] of Œdipus, and the murder of Laius, and the marrying his mother, and the mutual slaughter of those who were at once his brothers and his sons?

CHAP. IV.—*Shameless practices of the Greeks.*

And your public assemblies I have come to hate. For there are excessive banquetings, and subtle flutes which provoke to lustful movements, and useless and luxurious anointings, and crowning with garlands. With such a mass of evils do you banish shame; and ye fill your minds with them, and are carried away by intemperance, and indulge as a common practice in wicked and insane fornication. And this further I would say to you, why are you, being a Greek, indignant at your son when he imitates Jupiter, and rises against you and defrauds you of your own wife? Why do you count him your enemy, and yet worship one that is like him? And why do you blame your wife for living in unchastity, and yet honour Venus with shrines? If indeed these things had been related by others, they would have seemed to be mere slanderous accusations, and not truth. But now your own poets sing these things, and your histories noisily publish them.

[1] Thyestes seduced the wife of his brother Atreus, whence the tragic career of the family.

[2] There is no apodosis in the Greek.

[3] Not, as the editors dispute, either the tongue of the buckle with which he put out his eyes, nor the awl with which his heels were bored through, but the goad with which he killed his father.

CHAP. V.—*Closing appeal.*

Henceforth, ye Greeks, come and partake of incomparable wisdom, and be instructed by the Divine Word, and acquaint yourselves with the King immortal; and do not recognise those men as heroes who slaughter whole nations. For our own Ruler,[1] the Divine Word, who even now constantly aids us, does not desire strength of body and beauty of feature, nor yet the high spirit of earth's nobility, but a pure soul, fortified by holiness, and the watchwords of our King, holy actions, for through the Word power passes into the soul. O trumpet of peace to the soul that is at war! O weapon that puttest to flight terrible passions! O instruction that quenches the innate fire of the soul! The Word exercises an influence which does not make poets: it does not equip philosophers nor skilled orators, but by its instruction it makes mortals immortal, mortals gods; and from the earth transports them to the realms above Olympus. Come, be taught; become as I am, for I, too, was as ye are. These have conquered me—the divinity of the instruction, and the power of the Word: for as a skilled serpent-charmer lures the terrible reptile from his den and causes it to flee, so the Word drives the fearful passions of our sensual nature from the very recesses of the soul; first driving forth lust, through which every ill is begotten—hatreds, strife, envy, emulations, anger, and such like. Lust being once banished, the soul becomes calm and serene. And being set free from the ills in which it was sunk up to the neck, it returns to Him who made it. For it is fit that it be restored to that state whence it departed, whence every soul was or is.

[1] Αὐτὸς γὰρ ἡμῶν.

JUSTIN'S HORTATORY ADDRESS TO THE GREEKS.

CHAP. I.—*Reasons for addressing the Greeks.*

AS I begin this hortatory address to you, ye men of Greece, I pray God that I may know what I ought to say to you, and that you, shaking off your habitual[1] love of disputing, and being delivered from the error of your fathers, may now choose what is profitable; not fancying that you commit any offence against your forefathers, though the things which you formerly considered by no means salutary should now seem useful to you. For accurate investigation of matters, putting truth to the question with a more searching scrutiny, often reveals that things which have passed for excellent are of quite another sort. Since, then, we propose to discourse of the true religion (than which, I think, there is nothing which is counted more valuable by those who desire to pass through life without danger, on account of the judgment which is to be after the termination of this life, and which is announced not only by our forefathers according to God, to wit the prophets and lawgivers, but also by those among yourselves who have been esteemed wise, not poets alone, but also philosophers, who professed among you that they had attained the true and divine knowledge), I think it well first of all to examine the teachers of religion, both our own and yours, who they were, and how great, and in what times they lived; in order that those who have formerly received from their fathers the false religion, may now, when they perceive this, be extricated from that

[1] Literally, "former."

inveterate error; and that we may clearly and manifestly show that we ourselves follow the religion of our forefathers according to God.

CHAP. II.—*The poets are unfit to be religious teachers.*

Whom, then, ye men of Greece, do ye call your teachers of religion? The poets? It will do your cause no good to say so to men who know the poets; for they know how very ridiculous a theogony they have composed,—as we can learn from Homer, your most distinguished and prince of poets. For he says, first, that the gods were in the beginning generated from water; for he has written thus:[1]

"Both ocean, the origin of the gods, and their mother Tethys."

And then we must also remind you of what he further says of him whom ye consider the first of the gods, and whom he often calls "the father of gods and men;" for he said:[2]

"Zeus, who is the dispenser of war to men."

Indeed, he says that he was not only the dispenser of war to the army, but also the cause of perjury to the Trojans, by means of his daughter;[3] and Homer introduces him in love, and bitterly complaining, and bewailing himself, and plotted against by the other gods, and at one time exclaiming concerning his own son:[4]

"Alas! he falls, my most beloved of men!
Sarpedon, vanquished by Patroclus, falls!
So will the fates."

And at another time concerning Hector:[5]

"Ah! I behold a warrior dear to me
Around the walls of Ilium driven, and grieve
For Hector."

---

1 *Iliad*, xiv. 302. 2 *Iliad*, xix. 224.

3 That is, Venus, who, after Paris had sworn that the war should be decided by single combat between himself and Menelaus, carried him off, and induced him, though defeated, to refuse performance of the articles agreed upon.

4 *Iliad*, xvi. 433. Sarpedon was a son of Zeus. 5 *Iliad*, xxii. 168.

And what he says of the conspiracy of the other gods against Zeus, they know who read these words:[1] "When the other Olympians—Juno, and Neptune, and Minerva—wished to bind him." And unless the blessed gods had feared him whom gods call Briareus, Zeus would have been bound by them. And what Homer says of his intemperate loves, we must remind you in the very words he used. For he said that Zeus spake thus to Juno:[2]

"For never goddess pour'd, nor woman yet,
So full a tide of love into my breast;
I never loved Ixion's consort thus,
Nor sweet Acrisian Danaë, from whom
Sprang Perseus, noblest of the race of man;
Nor Phœnix' daughter fair, of whom were born
Minos, unmatch'd but by the powers above,
And Rhadamanthus; nor yet Semele,
Nor yet Alcmene, who in Thebes produced
The valiant Hercules; and though my son
By Semele were Bacchus, joy of man;
Nor Ceres golden-hair'd, nor high-enthron'd
Latona in the skies; no—nor thyself
As now I love thee, and my soul perceive
O'erwhelm'd with sweetness of intense desire."

It is fit that we now mention what one can learn from the work of Homer of the other gods, and what they suffered at the hands of men. For he says that Mars and Venus were wounded by Diomed, and of many others of the gods he relates the sufferings. For thus we can gather from the case of Dione consoling her daughter; for she said to her:[3]

"Have patience, dearest child; though much enforc'd,
Restrain thine anger: we, in heav'n who dwell,
Have much to bear from mortals; and ourselves
Too oft upon each other suff'rings lay:
Mars had his suff'rings; by Alöeus' sons,
Otus and Ephialtes, strongly bound,
He thirteen months in brazen fetters lay:

---

[1] *Iliad*, i. 399, etc.

[2] *Iliad*, xiv. 315. (The passage is here given in full from Cowper's translation. In Justin's quotation one or two lines are omitted.)

[3] *Iliad*, v. 382 (from Lord Derby's translation).

Juno, too, suffer'd, when Amphitryon's son
Thro' her right breast a three-barb'd arrow sent:
Dire, and unheard of, were the pangs she bore,
Great Pluto's self the stinging arrow felt,
When that same son of Ægis-bearing Jove
Assail'd him in the very gates of hell,
And wrought him keenest anguish; pierced with pain,
To high Olympus, to the courts of Jove,
Groaning, he came; the bitter shaft remain'd
Deep in his shoulder fix'd, and griev'd his soul."

But if it is right to remind you of the battle of the gods, opposed to one another, your own poet himself will recount it, saying:[1]

" Such was the shock when gods in battle met;
For there to royal Neptune stood oppos'd
Phœbus Apollo with his arrows keen;
The blue-eyed Pallas to the god of war;
To Juno, Dian, heav'nly archeress,
Sister of Phœbus, golden-shafted queen.
Stout Hermes, helpful god, Latona fac'd."

These and such like things did Homer teach you; and not Homer only, but also Hesiod. So that if you believe your most distinguished poets, who have given the genealogies of your gods, you must of necessity either suppose that the gods are such beings as these, or believe that there are no gods at all.

Chap. III.—*Opinions of the school of Thales.*

And if you decline citing the poets, because you say it is allowable for them to frame myths, and to relate in a mythical way many things about the gods which are far from true, do you suppose you have some others for your religious teachers, or how do you say that they themselves[2] have learned this religion of yours? For it is impossible that any should know matters so great and divine, who have not themselves learned them first from the initiated.[3] You will no doubt say, "The sages and philosophers." For to them, as to a fortified wall, you are wont to flee, when any one quotes the

[1] *Iliad*, xx. 66 (from Lord Derby's translation).
[2] *i.e.* these teachers. [3] Literally, "those who knew."

opinions of your poets about the gods. Therefore, since it is fit that we commence with the ancients and the earliest, beginning thence I will produce the opinion of each, much more ridiculous as it is than the theology of the poets. For Thales of Miletus, who took the lead in the study of natural philosophy, declared that water was the first principle of all things; for from water he says that all things are, and that into water all are resolved. And after him Anaximander, who came from the same Miletus, said that the infinite was the first principle of all things; for that from this indeed all things are produced, and into this do all decay. Thirdly, Anaximenes—and he too was from Miletus—says that air is the first principle of all things; for he says that from this all things are produced, and into this all are resolved. Heraclitus and Hippasus, from Metapontus, say that fire is the first principle of all things; for from fire all things proceed, and in fire do all things terminate. Anaxagoras of Clazomenæ said that the homogeneous parts are the first principles of all things. Archelaus, the son of Apollodorus, an Athenian, says that the infinite air and its density and rarity are the first principle of all things. All these, forming a succession from Thales, followed the philosophy called by themselves physical.

CHAP. IV.—*Opinions of Pythagoras and Epicurus.*

Then, in regular succession from another starting-point, Pythagoras the Samian, son of Mnesarchus, calls numbers, with their proportions and harmonies, and the elements composed of both, the first principles; and he includes also unity and the indefinite binary.[1] Epicurus, an Athenian, the son of Neocles, says that the first principles of the things that exist are bodies perceptible by reason, admitting no vacuity,[2]

[1] *μονάδα καὶ τὴν ἀόριστον δυάδα.* One, or unity, was considered by Pythagoras as the essence of number, and also as God. Two, or the indefinite binary, was the equivalent of evil. So Plutarch, *De placit. philosoph.* c. 7; from which treatise the above opinions of the various sects are quoted, generally verbatim.

[2] *ἀμέτοχα κενοῦ*; the void being that in which these bodies move, while they themselves are of a different nature from it.

unbegotten, indestructible, which can neither be broken, nor admit of any formation of their parts, nor alteration, and are therefore perceptible by reason. Empedocles of Agrigentum, son of Meton, maintained that there were four elements—fire, air, water, earth; and two elementary powers—love and hate,[1] of which the former is a power of union, the latter of separation. You see, then, the confusion of those who are considered by you to have been wise men, whom you assert to be your teachers of religion: some of them declaring that water is the first principle of all things; others, air; others, fire; and others, some other of these fore-mentioned elements; and all of them employing persuasive arguments for the establishment of their own errors, and attempting to prove their own peculiar dogma to be the most valuable. These things were said by them. How then, ye men of Greece, can it be safe for those who desire to be saved, to fancy that they can learn the true religion from these philosophers, who were neither able so to convince themselves as to prevent sectarian wrangling with one another, and not to appear definitely opposed to one another's opinions?

CHAP. V.—*Opinions of Plato and Aristotle.*

But possibly those who are unwilling to give up the ancient and inveterate error, maintain that they have received the doctrine of their religion not from those who have now been mentioned, but from those who are esteemed among them as the most renowned and finished philosophers, Plato and Aristotle. For these, they say, have learned the perfect and true religion. But I would be glad to ask, first of all, from those who say so, from whom they say that these men have learned this knowledge; for it is impossible that men who have not learned these so great and divine matters from some who knew them, should either themselves know them, or be able correctly to teach others; and, in the second place, I think we ought to examine the opinions even of these sages. For we shall see whether each of these does not manifestly contradict the other. But if we find that even they do not

[1] Or, accord and discord, attraction and repulsion.

agree with each other, I think it is easy to see clearly that they too are ignorant. For Plato, with the air of one that has descended from above, and has accurately ascertained and seen all that is in heaven, says that the most high God exists in a fiery substance.[1] But Aristotle, in a book addressed to Alexander of Macedon, giving a compendious explanation of his own philosophy, clearly and manifestly overthrows the opinion of Plato, saying that God does not exist in a fiery substance: but inventing, as a fifth substance, some kind of ætherial and unchangeable body, says that God exists in it. Thus, at least, he wrote: "Not, as some of those who have erred regarding the Deity say, that God exists in a fiery substance." Then, as if he were not satisfied with this blasphemy against Plato, he further, for the sake of proving what he says about the ætherial body, cites as a witness him whom Plato had banished from his republic as a liar, and as being an imitator of the images of truth at three removes,[2] for so Plato calls Homer; for he wrote: "Thus at least did Homer speak,[3] 'And Zeus obtained the wide heaven in the air and the clouds,'" wishing to make his own opinion appear more worthy of credit by the testimony of Homer; not being aware that if he used Homer as a witness to prove that he spoke truth, many of his tenets would be proved untrue. For Thales of Miletus, who was the founder of philosophy among them, taking occasion from him,[4] will contradict his first opinions about first principles. For Aristotle himself, having said that God and matter are the first principles of all things, Thales, the eldest of all their sages, says that water is the first principle of the things that exist; for he

[1] Or, "is of a fiery nature."

[2] See the *Republic*, x. 2. By the Platonic doctrine, the ideas of things in the mind of God were the realities; the things themselves, as seen by us, were the images of these realities; and poetry, therefore, describing the images of realities, was only at the third remove from nature. As Plato puts it briefly in this same passage, "the painter, the bed-maker, God—these three are the masters of three species of beds."

[3] *Iliad*, xv. 192.

[4] *i.e.* from Homer; using Homer's words as suggestive and confirmatory of his doctrine.

says that all things are from water, and that all things are resolved into water. And he conjectures this, first, from the fact that the seed of all living creatures, which is their first principle, is moist; and secondly, because all plants grow and bear fruit in moisture, but when deprived of moisture, wither. Then, as if not satisfied with his conjectures, he cites Homer as a most trustworthy testimony, who speaks thus:

"Ocean, who is the origin of all."[1]

May not Thales, then, very fairly say to him, "What is the reason, Aristotle, why you give heed to Homer, as if he spoke truth, when you wish to demolish the opinions of Plato; but when you promulgate an opinion contrary to ours, you think Homer untruthful?"

CHAP. VI.—*Further disagreements between Plato and Aristotle.*

And that these very wonderful sages of yours do not even agree in other respects, can be easily learned from this. For while Plato says that there are three first principles of all things, God, and matter, and form,—God, the maker of all; and matter, which is the subject of the first production of all that is produced, and affords to God opportunity for His workmanship; and form, which is the type of each of the things produced,—Aristotle makes no mention at all of form as a first principle, but says that there are two, God and matter. And again, while Plato says that the highest God and the ideas exist in the first place of the highest heavens, and in fixed sphere, Aristotle says that, next to the most high God, there are, not ideas, but certain gods, who can be perceived by the mind. Thus, then, do they differ concerning things heavenly. So that one can see that they not only are unable to understand our earthly matters, but also, being at variance among themselves regarding these things, they will appear unworthy of credit when they treat of things heavenly. And that even their doctrine regarding the human soul as it now is does not harmonize, is manifest from what has been said by each of

[1] *Iliad*, xiv. 246.

them concerning it. For Plato says that it is of three parts, having the faculty of reason, of affection, and of appetite.[1] But Aristotle says that the soul is not so comprehensive as to include also corruptible parts, but only reason. And Plato loudly maintains that "the whole soul is immortal." But Aristotle, naming it "the actuality,"[2] would have it to be mortal, not immortal. And the former says it is always in motion; but Aristotle says that it is immoveable, since it must itself precede all motion.

CHAP. VII.—*Inconsistencies of Plato's doctrine.*

But in these things they are convicted of thinking in contradiction to each other. And if any one will accurately criticise their writings, they have chosen to abide in harmony not even with their own opinions. Plato, at any rate, at one time says that there are three first principles of the universe—God, and matter, and form; but at another time four, for he adds the universal soul. And again, when he has already said that matter is eternal,[3] he afterwards says that it is produced; and when he has first given to form its peculiar rank as a first principle, and has asserted for it self-subsistence, he afterwards says that this same thing is among the things perceived by the understanding. Moreover, having first declared that everything that is made is mortal,[4] he afterwards states that some of the things that are made are indestructible and immortal. What, then, is the cause why those who have been esteemed wise among you disagree not only with one another, but also with themselves? Manifestly, their unwillingness to learn from those who know, and their desire to attain accurate knowledge of things heavenly by their own human excess of wisdom; though they were able to understand not even earthly matters. Certainly some of your philosophers

[1] τὸ λογικὸν, τὸ θυμικὸν, τὸ ἐπιθυμητικὸν,—corresponding to what we roughly speak of as reason, the heart, and the appetites.

[2] ἐντελέχεια,—the completion or actuality to which each thing, by virtue of its peculiar nature (or potentiality, δύναμις), can arrive.

[3] Literally, "unbegotten."

[4] Or, "liable to destruction."

say that the human soul is in us; others, that it is around us. For not even in this did they choose to agree with one another, but, distributing, as it were, ignorance in various ways among themselves, they thought fit to wrangle and dispute with one another even about the soul. For some of them say that the soul is fire, and some that it is the air; and others, the mind; and others, motion; and others, an exhalation; and certain others say that it is a power flowing from the stars; and others, number capable of motion; and others, a generating water. And a wholly confused and inharmonious opinion has prevailed among them, which only in this one respect appears praiseworthy to those who can form a right judgment, that they have been anxious to convict one another of error and falsehood.

Chap. viii.—*Antiquity, inspiration, and harmony of Christian teachers.*

Since therefore it is impossible to learn anything true concerning religion from your teachers, who by their mutual disagreement have furnished you with sufficient proof of their own ignorance, I consider it reasonable to recur to our progenitors, who both in point of time have by a great way the precedence of your teachers, and who have taught us nothing from their own private fancy, nor differed with one another, nor attempted to overturn one another's positions, but without wrangling and contention received from God the knowledge which also they taught to us. For neither by nature nor by human conception is it possible for men to know things so great and divine, but by the gift which then descended from above upon the holy men, who had no need of rhetorical art,[1] nor of uttering anything in a contentious or quarrelsome manner, but to present themselves pure[2] to the energy of the Divine Spirit, in order that the divine plectrum itself, descending from heaven, and using righteous men as an instrument like a harp or lyre, might reveal to us the knowledge of things divine and heavenly. Wherefore, as if with one mouth and one tongue, they have in succession,

[1] Literally, "the art of words."
[2] Literally, "clean," free from other influences.

and in harmony with one another, taught us both concerning God, and the creation of the world, and the formation of man, and concerning the immortality of the human soul, and the judgment which is to be after this life, and concerning all things which it is needful for us to know, and thus in divers times and places have afforded us the divine instruction.

CHAP. IX.—*The antiquity of Moses proved by Greek writers.*

I will begin, then, with our first prophet and lawgiver, Moses; first explaining the times in which he lived, on authorities which among you are worthy of all credit. For I do not propose to prove these things only from our own divine histories, which as yet you are unwilling to credit on account of the inveterate error of your forefathers, but also from your own histories, and such, too, as have no reference to our worship, that you may know that, of all your teachers, whether sages, poets, historians, philosophers, or lawgivers, by far the oldest, as the Greek histories show us, was Moses, who was our first religious teacher.[1] For in the times of Ogyges and Inachus, whom some of your poets supposed to have been earth-born,[2] Moses is mentioned as the leader and ruler of the Jewish nation. For in this way he is mentioned both by Polemon in the first book of his *Hellenics*, and by Appion son of Posidonius in his book against the Jews, and in the fourth book of his history, where he says that during the reign of Inachus over Argos the Jews revolted from Amasis king of the Egyptians, and that Moses led them. And Ptolemæus the Mendesian, in relating the history of Egypt, concurs in all this. And those who write the Athenian history, Hellanicus and Philochorus (the author of *The Attic History*), Castor and Thallus, and Alexander Polyhistor, and also the very well informed writers on Jewish affairs, Philo and Josephus, have mentioned Moses as a very ancient and time-honoured prince of the Jews. Josephus certainly, desiring to signify even by the title of his work

1 The incongruity in this sentence is Justin's.

2 That is, sprung from the soil; and hence the oldest inhabitants, the aborigines.

the antiquity and age of the history, wrote thus at the commencement of the history: "The Jewish antiquities[1] of Flavius Josephus,"—signifying the oldness of the history by the word "antiquities." And your most renowned historian Diodorus, who employed thirty whole years in epitomizing the libraries, and who, as he himself wrote, travelled over both Asia and Europe for the sake of great accuracy, and thus became an eye-witness of very many things, wrote forty entire books of his own history. And he in the first book, having said that he had learned from the Egyptian priests that Moses was an ancient lawgiver, and even the first, wrote of him in these very words: "For subsequent to the ancient manner of living in Egypt which gods and heroes are fabled to have regulated, they say that Moses[2] first persuaded the people to use written laws, and to live by them; and he is recorded to have been a man both great of soul and of great faculty in social matters." Then, having proceeded a little further, and wishing to mention the ancient lawgivers, he mentions Moses first. For he spoke in these words: "Among the Jews they say that Moses ascribed his laws[3] to that God who is called Jehovah, whether because they judged it a marvellous and quite divine conception which promised to benefit a multitude of men, or because they were of opinion that the people would be the more obedient when they contemplated the majesty and power of those who were said to have invented the laws. And they say that Sasunchis was the second Egyptian legislator, a man of excellent understanding. And the third, they say, was Sesonchosis the king, who not only performed the most brilliant military exploits of any in Egypt, but also consolidated that warlike race by legislation. And the fourth lawgiver, they say, was Bocchoris the king, a wise and surpassingly skilful man. And after him it is said that Amasis the king acceded to the government, whom they relate to have regulated all that

[1] Literally, archæology.

[2] Unfortunately, Justin here mistook Menes for Moses.

[3] This sentence must be so completed from the context in Diodorus. See the note of Maranus.

pertains to the rulers of provinces, and to the general administration of the government of Egypt. And they say that Darius, the father of Xerxes, was the sixth who legislated for the Egyptians."

CHAP. X.—*Training and inspiration of Moses.*

These things, ye men of Greece, have been recorded in writing concerning the antiquity of Moses by those who were not of our religion; and they said that they learned all these things from the Egyptian priests, among whom Moses was not only born, but also was thought worthy of partaking of all the education of the Egyptians, on account of his being adopted by the king's daughter as her son; and for the same reason was thought worthy of great attention, as the wisest of the historians relate, who have chosen to record his life and actions, and the rank of his descent,—I speak of Philo and Josephus. For these, in their narration of the history of the Jews, say that Moses was sprung from the race of the Chaldæans, and that he was born in Egypt when his forefathers had migrated on account of famine from Phœnicia to that country; and him God chose to honour on account of his exceeding virtue, and judged him worthy to become the leader and lawgiver of his own race, when He thought it right that the people of the Hebrews should return out of Egypt into their own land. To him first did God communicate that divine and prophetic gift which in those days descended upon the holy men, and him also did He first furnish that he might be our teacher in religion, and then after him the rest of the prophets, who both obtained the same gift as he, and taught us the same doctrines concerning the same subjects. These we assert to have been our teachers, who taught us nothing from their own human conception, but from the gift vouchsafed to them by God from above.

CHAP. XI.—*Heathen oracles testify of Moses.*

But as you do not see the necessity of giving up the ancient error of your forefathers in obedience to these teachers [of ours], what teachers of your own do you maintain to have lived worthy of credit in the matter of religion? For, as I have frequently said, it is impossible that those who have not themselves learned these so great and divine things from such persons as are acquainted with them, should either themselves know them, or be able rightly to teach others. Since, therefore, it has been sufficiently proved that the opinions of your philosophers are obviously full of all ignorance and deceit, having now perhaps wholly abandoned the philosophers as formerly you abandoned the poets, you will turn to the deceit of the oracles; for in this style I have heard some speaking. Therefore I think it fit to tell you at this step in our discourse what I formerly heard among you concerning their utterances. For when one inquired at your oracle—it is your own story—what religious men had at any time happened to live, you say that the oracle answered thus: "Only the Chaldæans have obtained wisdom, and the Hebrews, who worship God Himself, the self-begotten King."

Since, therefore, you think that the truth can be learned from your oracles, when you read the histories and what has been written regarding the life of Moses by those who do not belong to our religion, and when you know that Moses and the rest of the prophets were descended from the race of the Chaldæans and Hebrews, do not think that anything incredible has taken place if a man sprung from a godly line, and who lived worthily of the godliness of his fathers, was chosen by God to be honoured with this great gift, and to be set forth as the first of all the prophets.

CHAP. XII.—*Antiquity of Moses proved.*

And I think it necessary also to consider the times in which your philosophers lived, that you may see that the time which produced them for you is very recent, and also short. For thus you will be able easily to recognise also the antiquity of Moses. But lest, by a complete survey of the periods, and by the use of a greater number of proofs, I should seem to be prolix, I think it may be sufficiently demonstrated from the following. For Socrates was the teacher of Plato, and Plato of Aristotle. Now these men flourished in the time of

Philip and Alexander of Macedon, in which time also the Athenian orators flourished, as the Philippics of Demosthenes plainly show us. And those who have narrated the deeds of Alexander sufficiently prove that during his reign Aristotle associated with him. From all manner of proofs, then, it is easy to see that the history of Moses is by far more ancient than all profane[1] histories. And, besides, it is fit that you recognise this fact also, that nothing has been accurately recorded by Greeks before the era of the Olympiads, and that there is no ancient work which makes known any action of the Greeks or Barbarians. But before that period existed only the history of the prophet Moses, which he wrote in the Hebrew character by the divine inspiration. For the Greek character was not yet in use, as the teachers of language themselves prove, telling us that Cadmus first brought the letters from Phœnicia, and communicated them to the Greeks. And your first of philosophers, Plato, testifies that they were a recent discovery. For in the *Timæus*[2] he wrote that Solon, the wisest of the wise men, on his return from Egypt, said to Critias that he had heard this from a very aged Egyptian priest, who said to him, "O Solon, Solon, you Greeks are ever children, and aged Greek there is none." Then again he said, "You are all youths in soul, for you hold no ancient opinion derived through remote tradition, nor any system of instruction hoary with time; but all these things escape your knowledge, because for many generations the posterity of these ancient ages died mute, not having the use of letters." It is fit, therefore, that you understand that it is the fact that every history has been written in these recently-discovered Greek letters; and if any one would make mention of old poets, or legislators, or historians, or philosophers, or orators, he will find that they wrote their own works in the Greek character.

CHAP. XIII.—*History of the Septuagint.*

But if any one says that the writings of Moses and of the rest of the prophets were also written in the Greek character,

[1] Literally, "without," not belonging to the true faith. [2] C. 5.

let him read profane histories, and know that Ptolemy, king of Egypt, when he had built the library in Alexandria, and by gathering books from every quarter had filled it, then learnt that very ancient histories written in Hebrew happened to be carefully preserved; and wishing to know their contents, he sent for seventy wise men from Jerusalem, who were acquainted with both the Greek and Hebrew language, and appointed them to translate the books; and that in freedom from all disturbance they might the more speedily complete the translation, he ordered that there should be constructed, not in the city itself, but seven stadia off (where the Pharos was built), as many little cots as there were translators, so that each by himself might complete his own translation; and enjoined upon those officers who were appointed to this duty, to afford them all attendance, but to prevent communication with one another, in order that the accuracy of the translation might be discernible even by their agreement. And when he ascertained that the seventy men had not only given the same meaning, but had employed the same words, and had failed in agreement with one another not even to the extent of one word, but had written the same things, and concerning the same things, he was struck with amazement, and believed that the translation had been written by divine power, and perceived that the men were worthy of all honour, as beloved of God; and with many gifts ordered them to return to their own country. And having, as was natural, marvelled at the books, and concluded them to be divine, he consecrated them in that library. These things, ye men of Greece, are no fable, nor do we narrate fictions; but we ourselves having been in Alexandria, saw the remains of the little cots at the Pharos still preserved, and having heard these things from the inhabitants, who had received them as part of their country's tradition, we now tell to you what you can also learn from others, and specially from those wise and esteemed men who have written of these things, Philo and Josephus, and many others. But if any of those who are wont to be forward in contradiction should say that these books do not belong to us, but to the Jews, and should assert that we in vain profess to have learnt our religion from them, let him know, as he may from those very things which are written in these books, that not to them, but to us, does the doctrine of them refer. That the books relating to our religion are to this day preserved among the Jews, has been a work of Divine Providence on our behalf; for lest, by producing them out of the church, we should give occasion to those who wish to slander us to charge us with fraud, we demand that they be produced from the synagogue of the Jews, that from the very books still preserved among them it might clearly and evidently appear, that the laws which were written by holy men for instruction pertain to us.

CHAP. XIV.—*A warning appeal to the Greeks.*

It is therefore necessary, ye Greeks, that you contemplate the things that are to be, and consider the judgment which is predicted by all, not only by the godly, but also by those who are irreligious, that ye do not without investigation commit yourselves to the error of your fathers, nor suppose that if they themselves have been in error, and have transmitted it to you, that this which they have taught you is true; but looking to the danger of so terrible a mistake, inquire and investigate carefully into those things which are, as you say, spoken of even by your own teachers. For even unwillingly they were on your account forced to say many things by the Divine regard for mankind, especially those of them who were in Egypt, and profited by the godliness of Moses and his ancestry. For I think that some of you, when you read even carelessly the history of Diodorus, and of those others who wrote of these things, cannot fail to see that both Orpheus, and Homer, and Solon, who wrote the laws of the Athenians, and Pythagoras, and Plato, and some others, when they had been in Egypt, and had taken advantage of the history of Moses, afterwards published doctrines concerning the gods quite contrary to those which they had formerly erroneously promulgated.

CHAP. XV.—*Testimony of Orpheus to Monotheism.*

At all events, we must remind you what Orpheus, who was, as one might say, your first teacher of polytheism, latterly addressed to his son Musæus, and to the other legitimate auditors, concerning the one and only God. And he spoke thus:

"I speak to those who lawfully may hear:
All others, ye profane, now close the doors,
And, O Musæus! hearken thou to me,
Who offspring art of the light-bringing moon:
The words I utter now are true indeed;
And if thou former thoughts of mine hast seen,
Let them not rob thee of the blessed life,
But rather turn the depths of thine own heart
Unto the place where light and knowledge dwell.
Take thou the word divine to guide thy steps,
And walking well in the straight certain path,
Look to the one and universal King—
One, self-begotten, and the only One,
Of whom all things and we ourselves are sprung.
All things are open to His piercing gaze,
While He Himself is still invisible.
Present in all His works, though still unseen,
He gives to mortals evil out of good,
Sending both chilling wars and tearful griefs;
And other than the great King there is none.
The clouds for ever settle round His throne,
And mortal eyeballs in mere mortal eyes
Are weak, to see Jove reigning over all.
He sits established in the brazen heavens
Upon His golden throne; under His feet
He treads the earth, and stretches His right hand
To all the ends of ocean, and around
Tremble the mountain ranges and the streams,
The depths, too, of the blue and hoary sea."

And again in some other place he says:

"There is one Zeus alone, one sun, one hell,
One Bacchus; and in all things but one God;
Nor of all these as diverse let me speak."

And when he swears he says:

"Now I adjure thee by the highest heaven,
The work of the great God, the only wise;
And I adjure thee by the Father's voice,
Which first He uttered when He stablished
The whole world by His counsel."

What does he mean by "I adjure thee by the Father's voice, which first He uttered?" It is the Word of God which he here names "the voice," by whom heaven and earth and the whole creation were made, as the divine prophecies of the holy men teach us; and these he himself also paid some attention to in Egypt, and understood that all creation was made by the Word of God; and therefore, after he says, "I adjure thee by the Father's voice, which first He uttered," he adds this besides, "when by His counsel He established the whole world." Here he calls the Word "voice," for the sake of the poetical metre. And that this is so, is manifest from the fact, that a little further on, where the metre permits him, he names it "Word." For he said:

"Take thou the *Word* divine to guide thy steps."

CHAP. XVI.—*Testimony of the Sibyl.*

We must also mention what the ancient and exceedingly remote Sibyl, whom Plato and Aristophanes, and others besides, mention as a prophetess, taught you in her oracular verses concerning one only God. And she speaks thus:

"There is one only unbegotten God,
Omnipotent, invisible, most high,
All-seeing, but Himself seen by no flesh."

Then elsewhere thus:

"But we have strayed from the Immortal's ways,
And worship with a dull and senseless mind
Idols, the workmanship of our own hands,
And images and figures of dead men."

And again somewhere else:

"Blessed shall be those men upon the earth
Who shall love the great God before all else,
Blessing Him when they eat and when they drink;

Trusting in this their piety alone.
Who shall abjure all shrines which they may see,
All altars and vain figures of dumb stones,
Worthless and stained with blood of animals,
And sacrifice of the four-footed tribes,
Beholding the great glory of One God."

These are the Sibyl's words.

CHAP. XVII.—*Testimony of Homer.*

And the poet Homer, using the licence of poetry, and rivalling the original opinion of Orpheus regarding the plurality of the gods, mentions, indeed, several gods in a mythical style, lest he should seem to sing in a different strain from the poem of Orpheus, which he so distinctly proposed to rival, that even in the first line of his poem he indicated the relation he held to him. For as Orpheus in the beginning of his poem had said, "O goddess, sing the wrath of Demeter, who brings the goodly fruit," Homer began thus, "O goddess, sing the wrath of Achilles, son of Peleus," preferring, as it seems to me, even to violate the poetical metre in his first line, than that he should seem not to have remembered before all else the names of the gods. But shortly after he also clearly and explicitly presents his own opinion regarding one God only, somewhere[1] saying to Achilles by the mouth of Phœnix, "Not though God Himself were to promise that He would peel off my old age, and give me the vigour of my youth," where he indicates by the pronoun the real and true God. And somewhere[2] he makes Ulysses address the host of the Greeks thus: "The rule of many is not a good thing; let there be one ruler." And that the rule of many is not a good thing, but on the contrary an evil, he proposed to evince by fact, recounting the wars which took place on account of the multitude of rulers, and the fights and factions, and their mutual counterplots. For monarchy *is* free from contention. So far the poet Homer.

[1] *Iliad*, ix. 445. [2] *Iliad*, ii. 204.

CHAP. XVIII.—*Testimony of Sophocles.*

And if it is needful that we add testimonies concerning one God, even from the dramatists, hear even Sophocles speaking thus:

> "There is one God, in truth there is but one,
> Who made the heavens and the broad earth beneath,
> The glancing waves of ocean and the winds.
> But many of us mortals err in heart,
> And set up for a solace in our woes
> Images of the gods in stone and wood,
> Or figures carved in brass or ivory,
> And, furnishing for these our handiworks,
> Both sacrifice and rite magnificent,
> We think that thus we do a pious work."

Thus, then, Sophocles.

CHAP. XIX.—*Testimony of Pythagoras.*

And Pythagoras, son of Mnesarchus, who expounded the doctrines of his own philosophy mystically by means of symbols, as those who have written his life show, himself seems to have entertained thoughts about the unity of God not unworthy of his foreign residence in Egypt. For when he says that unity is the first principle of all things, and that it is the cause of all good, he teaches by an allegory that God is one, and alone.[1] And that this is so, is evident from his saying that unity and one differ widely from one another. For he says that unity belongs to the class of things perceived by the mind, but that one belongs to numbers. And if you desire to see a clearer proof of the opinion of Pythagoras concerning one God, hear his own opinion, for he spoke as follows: "God is one; and He Himself does not, as some suppose, exist outside the world, but in it, He being wholly present in the whole circle, and beholding all generations; being the regulating ingredient of all the ages, and the administrator of His own powers and works, the first principle of all things, the light of heaven, and Father of all, the intelligence and animating soul of the universe, the movement of all orbits." Thus, then, Pythagoras.

[1] Has no fellow.

CHAP. XX.—*Testimony of Plato.*

But Plato, though he accepted, as is likely, the doctrine of Moses and the other prophets regarding one only God, which he learned while in Egypt, yet fearing, on account of what had befallen Socrates, lest he also should raise up some Anytus or Meletus against himself, who should accuse him before the Athenians, and say, "Plato is doing harm, and making himself mischievously busy, not acknowledging the gods recognised by the state;" in fear of the hemlock-juice, contrives an elaborate and ambiguous discourse concerning the gods, furnishing by his treatise gods to those who wish them, and none for those who are differently disposed, as may readily be seen from his own statements. For when he has laid down that everything that is made is mortal, he afterwards says that the gods were made. If, then, he would have God and matter to be the origin of all things, manifestly it is inevitably necessary to say that the gods were made of matter; but if of matter, out of which he said that evil also had its origin, he leaves right-thinking persons to consider what kind of beings the gods should be thought who are produced out of matter. For, for this very reason did he say that matter was eternal,[1] that he might not seem to say that God is the creator of evil. And regarding the gods who were made by God, there is no doubt he said this: "Gods of gods, of whom I am the creator." And he manifestly held the correct opinion concerning the really existing God. For having heard in Egypt that God had said to Moses, when He was about to send him to the Hebrews, "I am that I am,"[2] he understood that God had not mentioned to him His own proper name.

CHAP. XXI.—*The namelessness of God.*

For God cannot be called by any proper name, for names are given to mark out and distinguish their subject-matters, because these are many and diverse; but neither did any one exist before God who could give Him a name, nor did He Himself think it right to name Himself, seeing that He is one

[1] Or, "uncreated."

[2] ὁ ὤν, "He who is; the Being."

and unique, as He Himself also by His own prophets testifies, when He says, "I God am the first," and after this, "And beside me there is no other God."[1] On this account, then, as I before said, God did not, when He sent Moses to the Hebrews, mention any name, but by a participle He mystically teaches them that He is the one and only God. "For," says He, "I am the *Being;*" manifestly contrasting Himself, "the Being," with those who are not,[2] that those who had hitherto been deceived might see that they were attaching themselves, not to beings, but to those who had no being. Since, therefore, God knew that the first men remembered the old delusion of their forefathers, whereby the misanthropic demon contrived to deceive them when he said to them, "If ye obey me in transgressing the commandment of God, ye shall be as gods," calling those gods which had no being, in order that men, supposing that there were other gods in existence, might believe that they themselves could become gods. On this account He said to Moses, "I am the Being," that by the participle "being" He might teach the difference between God who is and those who are not.[3] Men, therefore, having been duped by the deceiving demon, and having dared to disobey God, were cast out of Paradise, remembering the name of gods, but no longer being taught by God that there are no other gods. For it was not just that they who did not keep the first commandment, which it was easy to keep, should any longer be taught, but should rather be driven to just punishment. Being therefore banished from Paradise, and thinking that they were expelled on account of their disobedience only, not knowing that it was also because they had believed in the existence of gods which did not exist, they gave the name of gods even to the men who were afterwards born of themselves. This first false fancy, therefore, concerning gods, had its origin with the father of lies. God, therefore, knowing that the false opinion about the plurality of gods was burdening the soul of man like some disease, and wishing to remove and eradicate it, appeared first to Moses,

[1] Isa. xliv. 6. [2] Literally, "with the not-beings."
[3] Literally, "between the God being and not-beings."

and said to him, "I am He who is." For it was necessary, I think, that he who was to be the ruler and leader of the Hebrew people should first of all know the living God. Wherefore, having appeared to him first, as it was possible for God to appear to a man, He said to him, "I am He who is;" then, being about to send him to the Hebrews, He further orders him to say, "He who is hath sent me to you."

Chap. xxii.—*Studied ambiguity of Plato.*

Plato accordingly having learned this in Egypt, and being greatly taken with what was said about one God, did indeed consider it unsafe to mention the name of Moses, on account of his teaching the doctrine of one only God, for he dreaded the Areopagus; but what is very well expressed by him in his elaborate treatise, the *Timæus*, he has written in exact correspondence with what Moses said regarding God, though he has done so, not as if he had learned it from him, but as if he were expressing his own opinion. For he said, "In my opinion, then, we must first define what that is which exists eternally, and has no generation,[1] and what that is which is always being generated, but never really is." Does not this, ye men of Greece, seem to those who are able to understand the matter to be one and the same thing, saving only the difference of the article? For Moses said, "*He* who is," and Plato, "That which is." But either of the expressions seems to apply to the ever-existent God. For He is the only one who eternally exists, and has no generation. What, then, that other thing is which is contrasted with the ever-existent, and of which he said, "And what that is which is always being generated, but never really is," we must attentively consider. For we shall find him clearly and evidently saying that He who is unbegotten is eternal, but that those that are begotten and made are generated and perish[2]—as he said of the same class, "gods of gods, of whom I am maker"—for he speaks in the following words: "In my opinion, then, we must first define what that is which is always existent and has

[1] That is, "is not produced or created; has no birth."
[2] Or, "are born and die."

no birth, and what that is which is always being generated but never really is. The former, indeed, which is apprehended by reflection combined with reason, always exists in the same way;[1] while the latter, on the other hand, is conjectured by opinion formed by the perception of the senses unaided by reason, since it never really is, but is coming into being and perishing." These expressions declare to those who can rightly understand them the death and destruction of the gods that have been brought into being. And I think it necessary to attend to this also, that Plato never names him the creator, but the fashioner[2] of the gods, although, in the opinion of Plato, there is considerable difference between these two. For the creator creates the creature by his own capability and power, being in need of nothing else; but the fashioner frames his production when he has received from matter the capability for his work.

CHAP. XXIII.—*Plato's self-contradiction.*

But, perhaps, some who are unwilling to abandon the doctrines of polytheism, will say that to these fashioned gods the maker said, "Since ye have been produced, ye are not immortal, nor at all imperishable; yet shall ye not perish nor succumb to the fatality of death, because you have obtained my will,[3] which is a still greater and mightier bond." Here Plato, through fear of the adherents of polytheism, introduces his "maker" uttering words which contradict himself. For having formerly stated that he said that everything which is produced is perishable, he now introduces him saying the very opposite; and he does not see that it is thus absolutely impossible for him to escape the charge of falsehood. For he either at first uttered what is false when he said that everything which is produced is perishable, or now, when he propounds the very opposite to what he had formerly said. For if, according to his former definition, it is absolutely necessary that every created thing be perishable, how can he

[1] κατὰ ταὐτά, "according to the same things," *i.e.* in eternal immutability.
[2] Or, "demiurge or maker."
[3] That is, "my will to the contrary." See Plato, *Tim.* p. 41.

consistently make that possible which is absolutely impossible? So that Plato seems to grant an empty and impossible prerogative to his "maker," when he propounds that those who were once perishable because made from matter should again, by his intervention, become imperishable and enduring. For it is quite natural that the power of matter, which, according to Plato's opinion, is uncreated, and contemporary and coæval with the maker, should resist his will. For he who has not created has no power, in respect of that which is uncreated, so that it is not possible that it (matter), being free, can be controlled by any external necessity. Wherefore Plato himself, in consideration of this, has written thus: "It is necessary to affirm that God cannot suffer violence."

CHAP. XXIV.—*Agreement of Plato and Homer.*

How, then, does Plato banish Homer from his republic, since, in the embassy to Achilles, he represents Phœnix as saying to Achilles, "Even the gods themselves are not inflexible,"[1] though Homer said this not of the king and Platonic maker of the gods, but of some of the multitude whom the Greeks esteem as gods, as one can gather from Plato's saying, "gods of gods?" For Homer, by that golden chain,[2] refers all power and might to the one highest God. And the rest of the gods, he said, were so far distant from his divinity, that he thought fit to name them even along with men. At least he introduces Ulysses saying of Hector to Achilles, "He is raging terribly, trusting in Zeus, and values neither men nor gods."[3] In this passage Homer seems to me without doubt to have learnt in Egypt, like Plato, concerning the one God, and plainly and openly to declare this, that he who trusts in the really existent God makes no account of those that do not exist. For thus the poet, in another passage, and employing another but equivalent word, to wit, a pronoun, made use of the same participle employed by Plato to designate the really existent God, concerning whom Plato

[1] *Iliad*, ix. 493.
[2] That is, by the challenge of the chain introduced—*Iliad*, viii. 18.
[3] *Iliad*, ix. 238.

said, "What that is which always exists, and has no birth." For not without a double sense does this expression of Phœnix seem to have been used: "Not even if God Himself were to promise me, that, having burnished off my old age, He should set me forth in the flower of youth." For the pronoun "Himself" signifies the really existing God. For thus, too, the oracle which was given to you concerning the Chaldæans and Hebrews signifies. For when some one inquired what men had ever lived godly, you say the answer was:

> "Only the Chaldæans and the Hebrews found wisdom,
> Worshipping God *Himself*, the unbegotten King."

CHAP. XXV.—*Plato's knowledge of God's eternity.*

How, then, does Plato blame Homer for saying that the gods are not inflexible, although, as is obvious from the expressions used, Homer said this for a useful purpose? For it is the property of those who expect to obtain mercy by prayer and sacrifices, to cease from and repent of their sins. For those who think that the Deity is inflexible, are by no means moved to abandon their sins, since they suppose that they will derive no benefit from repentance. How, then, does Plato the philosopher condemn the poet Homer for saying, "Even the gods themselves are not inflexible," and yet himself represent the maker of the gods as so easily turned, that he sometimes declares the gods to be mortal, and at other times declares the same to be immortal? And not only concerning them, but also concerning matter, from which, as he says, it is necessary that the created gods have been produced, he sometimes says that it is uncreated, and at other times that it is created; and yet he does not see that he himself, when he says that the maker of the gods is so easily turned, is convicted of having fallen into the very errors for which he blames Homer, though Homer said the very opposite concerning the maker of the gods. For he said that he spoke thus of himself:

> "For ne'er my promise shall deceive, or fail,
> Or be recall'd, if with a nod confirm'd."[1]

[1] *Iliad*, i. 526.

But Plato, as it seems, unwillingly entered into these strange dissertations concerning the gods, for he feared those who were attached to polytheism. And whatever he thinks fit to tell of all that he had learned from Moses and the prophets concerning one God, he preferred delivering in a mystical style, so that those who desired to be worshippers of God might have an inkling of his own opinion. For being charmed with that saying of God to Moses, "I am the really existing," and accepting with a great deal of thought the brief participial expression, he understood that God desired to signify to Moses His eternity, and therefore said, "I am the really existing;" for this word "existing" expresses not one time only, but the three—the past, the present, and the future. For when Plato says, "and which never really is," he uses the verb "is" of time indefinite. For the word "never" is not spoken, as some suppose, of the past, but of the future time. And this has been accurately understood even by profane writers. And therefore, when Plato wished, as it were, to interpret to the uninitiated what had been mystically expressed by the participle concerning the eternity of God, he employed the following language: "God indeed, as the old tradition runs, includes the beginning, and end, and middle of all things." In this sentence he plainly and obviously names the law of Moses "the old tradition," fearing, through dread of the hemlock-cup, to mention the name of Moses; for he understood that the teaching of the man was hateful to the Greeks; and he clearly enough indicates Moses by the antiquity of the tradition. And we have sufficiently proved from Diodorus and the rest of the historians, in the foregoing chapters, that the law of Moses is not only old, but even the first. For Diodorus says that he was the first of all lawgivers; the letters which belong to the Greeks, and which they employed in the writing of their histories, having not yet been discovered.

CHAP. XXVI.—*Plato indebted to the prophets.*

And let no one wonder that Plato should believe Moses regarding the eternity of God. For you will find him mystically referring the true knowledge of realities to the prophets, next in order after the really existent God. For, discoursing in the *Timæus* about certain first principles, he wrote thus: "This we lay down as the first principle of fire and the other bodies, proceeding according to probability and necessity. But the first principles of these again God above knows, and whosoever among men is beloved of Him."[1] And what men does he think beloved of God, but Moses and the rest of the prophets? For their prophecies he read, and, having learned from them the doctrine of the judgment, he thus proclaims it in the first book of the *Republic*: "When a man begins to think he is soon to die, fear invades him, and concern about things which had never before entered his head. And those stories about what goes on in Hades, which tell us that the man who has here been unjust must there be punished, though formerly ridiculed, now torment his soul with apprehensions that they may be true. And he, either through the feebleness of age, or even because he is now nearer to the things of the other world, views them more attentively. He becomes, therefore, full of apprehension and dread, and begins to call himself to account, and to consider whether he has done any one an injury. And that man who finds in his life many iniquities, and who continually starts from his sleep as children do, lives in terror, and with a forlorn prospect. But to him who is conscious of no wrong-doing, sweet hope is the constant companion and good nurse of old age, as Pindar says.[2] For this, Socrates, he has elegantly expressed, that 'whoever leads a life of holiness and justice, him sweet hope, the nurse of age, accompanies, cheering his heart, for she powerfully sways the changeful mind of mortals.'"[3] This Plato wrote in the first book of the *Republic*.

[1] Plato, *Tim.* p. 53 D.

[2] Pind. *Fr.* 233, a fragment preserved in this place.

[3] Plato, *Rep.* p. 330 D.

CHAP. XXVII.—*Plato's knowledge of the judgment.*

And in the tenth book he plainly and manifestly wrote what he had learned from the prophets about the judgment, not as if he had learned it from them, but, on account of his fear of the Greeks, as if he had heard it from a man who had been slain in battle—for this story he thought fit to invent—and who, when he was about to be buried on the twelfth day, and was lying on the funeral pile, came to life again, and described the other world. The following are his very words:[1] "For he said that he was present when one was asked by another person where the great Aridæus was. This Aridæus had been prince in a certain city of Pamphylia, and had killed his aged father and his elder brother, and done many other unhallowed deeds, as was reported. He said, then, that the person who was asked said: He neither comes nor ever will come hither. For we saw, among other terrible sights, this also. When we were close to the mouth [of the pit], and were about to return to the upper air, and had suffered everything else, we suddenly beheld both him and others likewise, most of whom were tyrants. But there were also some private sinners who had committed great crimes. And these, when they thought they were to ascend, the mouth would not permit, but bellowed when any of those who were so incurably wicked attempted to ascend, unless they had paid the full penalty. Then fierce men, fiery to look at, stood close by, and hearing the din,[2] took some and led them away; but Aridæus and the rest, having bound hand and foot, and striking their heads down, and flaying, they dragged to the road outside, tearing them with thorns, and signifying to those who were present the cause of their suffering these things, and that they were leading them away to cast them into Tartarus. Hence, he said, that amidst all their various fears, this one was the greatest, lest the mouth should bellow when they ascended, since if it were silent each one would most gladly ascend; and that the punishments and torments were

[1] Plato, *Rep.* p. 615.

[2] The bellowing of the mouth of the pit.

such as these, and that, on the other hand, the rewards were the reverse of these." Here Plato seems to me to have learnt from the prophets not only the doctrine of the judgment, but also of the resurrection, which the Greeks refuse to believe. For his saying that the soul is judged along with the body, proves nothing more clearly than that he believed the doctrine of the resurrection. Since how could Aridæus and the rest have undergone such punishment in Hades, had they left on earth the body, with its head, hands, feet, and skin? For certainly they will never say that the soul has a head and hands, and feet and skin. But Plato, having fallen in with the testimonies of the prophets in Egypt, and having accepted what they teach concerning the resurrection of the body, teaches that the soul is judged in company with the body.

CHAP. XXVIII.—*Homer's obligations to the sacred writers.*

And not only Plato, but Homer also, having received similar enlightenment in Egypt, said that Tityus was in like manner punished. For Ulysses speaks thus to Alcinous when he is recounting his divination by the shades of the dead:[1]

> "There Tityus, large and long, in fetters bound,
> O'erspread nine acres of infernal ground;
> Two ravenous vultures, furious for their food,
> Scream o'er the fiend, and riot in his blood,
> Incessant gore the liver in his breast,
> Th' immortal liver grows, and gives th' immortal feast."

For it is plain that it is not the soul, but the body, which has a liver. And in the same manner he has described both Sisyphus and Tantalus as enduring punishment with the body. And that Homer had been in Egypt, and introduced into his own poem much of what he there learnt, Diodorus, the most esteemed of historians, plainly enough teaches us. For he said that when he was in Egypt he had learnt that Helen, having received from Theon's wife, Polydamna, a drug, "lulling all sorrow and melancholy, and causing forgetfulness of all ills,"[2] brought it to Sparta. And Homer said

[1] *Odyssey*, xi. 576 (Pope's translation, line 709).
[2] *Odyssey*, iv. 221.

that by making use of that drug Helen put an end to the lamentation of Menelaus, caused by the presence of Telemachus. And he also called Venus "golden," from what he had seen in Egypt. For he had seen the temple which in Egypt is called "the temple of golden Venus," and the plain which is named "the plain of golden Venus." And why do I now make mention of this? To show that the poet transferred to his own poem much of what is contained in the divine writings of the prophets. And first he transferred what Moses had related as the beginning of the creation of the world. For Moses wrote thus: "In the beginning God created the heaven and the earth,"[1] then the sun, and the moon, and the stars. For having learned this in Egypt, and having been much taken with what Moses had written in the Genesis of the world, he fabled that Vulcan had made in the shield of Achilles a kind of representation of the creation of the world. For he wrote thus:[2]

> "There he described the earth, the heaven, the sea,
> The sun that rests not, and the moon full-orb'd;
> There also, all the stars which round about,
> As with a radiant frontlet, bind the skies."

And he contrived also that the garden of Alcinous should preserve the likeness of Paradise, and through this likeness he represented it as ever-blooming and full of all fruits. For thus he wrote:[3]

> "Tall thriving trees confess'd the fruitful mould;
> The reddening apple ripens here to gold.
> Here the blue fig with luscious juice o'erflows,
> With deeper red the full pomegranate glows;
> The branch here bends beneath the weighty pear,
> And verdant olives flourish round the year.
> The balmy spirit of the western gale
> Eternal breathes on fruits, untaught to fail;
> Each dropping pear a following pear supplies,
> On apples apples, figs on figs arise.
> The same mild season gives the blooms to blow,
> The buds to harden, and the fruits to grow.

---

[1] Gen. i. 1. [2] *Iliad*, xviii. 483.
[3] *Odyssey*, vii. 114 (Pope's translation, line 146).

Here order'd vines in equal ranks appear,
With all th' united labours of the year.
Some to unload the fertile branches run,
Some dry the blackening clusters in the sun,
Others to tread the liquid harvest join.
The groaning presses foam with floods of wine.
Here are the vines in early flower descry'd,
Here grapes discoloured on the sunny side,
And there in autumn's richest purple dy'd."

Do not these words present a manifest and clear imitation of what the first prophet Moses said about Paradise? And if any one wish to know something of the building of the tower by which the men of that day fancied they would obtain access to heaven, he will find a sufficiently exact allegorical imitation of this in what the poet has ascribed to Otus and Ephialtes. For of them he wrote thus:[1]

"Proud of their strength, and more than mortal size,
The gods they challenge, and affect the skies.
Heav'd on Olympus tottering Ossa stood;
On Ossa, Pelion nods with all his wood."

And the same holds good regarding the enemy of mankind who was cast out of heaven, whom the sacred Scriptures call the Devil,[2] a name which he obtained from his first devilry against man; and if any one would attentively consider the matter, he would find that the poet, though he certainly never mentions the name of "the devil," yet gives him a name from his wickedest action. For the poet, calling him Ate,[3] says that he was hurled from heaven by their god, just as if he had a distinct remembrance of the expressions which Isaiah the prophet had uttered regarding him. He wrote thus in his own poem:[4]

"And, seizing by her glossy locks
The goddess Ate, in his wrath he swore
That never to the starry skies again,

---

1 *Odyssey*, xi. 312 (Pope's translation, line 385).

2 The false accuser; one who does injury by slanderous accusations.

3 Ἄτη, the goddess of mischief, from whom spring all rash, blind deeds and their results.

4 *Iliad*, xix. 126.

And the Olympian heights, he would permit
The universal mischief to return.
Then, whirling her around, he cast her down
To earth. She, mingling with all works of men,
Caused many a pang to Jove."

CHAP. XXIX.—*Origin of Plato's doctrine of form.*

And Plato, too, when he says that form is the third original principle next to God and matter, has manifestly received this suggestion from no other source than from Moses, having learned, indeed, from the words of Moses the name of form, but not having at the same time been instructed by the initiated, that without mystic insight it is impossible to have any distinct knowledge of the writings of Moses. For Moses wrote that God had spoken to him regarding the tabernacle in the following words: "And thou shalt make for me according to all that I show thee in the mount, the pattern of the tabernacle."[1] And again: "And thou shalt erect the tabernacle according to the pattern of all the instruments thereof, even so shalt thou make it."[1] And again, a little afterwards: "Thus then thou shalt make it according to the pattern which was showed to thee in the mount."[2] Plato, then, reading these passages, and not receiving what was written with the suitable insight, thought that form had some kind of separate existence before that which the senses perceive, and he often calls it the pattern of the things which are made, since the writing of Moses spoke thus of the tabernacle: "According to the form showed to thee in the mount, so shalt thou make it."

CHAP. XXX.—*Homer's knowledge of man's origin.*

And he was obviously deceived in the same way regarding the earth and heaven and man; for he supposes that there are "ideas" of these. For as Moses wrote thus, "In the beginning God created the heaven and the earth," and then subjoins this sentence, "And the earth was invisible and unfashioned," he thought that it was the pre-existent earth which was spoken of in the words, "The earth was," because

[1] Ex. xxv. 9. Ex. xxv. 40.

Moses said, "And the earth was invisible and unfashioned;" and he thought that the earth, concerning which he says, "God created the heaven and the earth," was that earth which we perceive by the senses, and which God made according to the pre-existent form. And so also, of the heaven which was created, he thought that the heaven which was created—and which he also called the firmament—was that creation which the senses perceive; and that the heaven which the intellect perceives is that other of which the prophet said, "The heaven of heavens is the Lord's, but the earth hath He given to the children of men."[1] And so also concerning man: Moses first mentions the name of man, and then after many other creations he makes mention of the formation of man, saying, "And God made man, taking dust from the earth."[2] He thought, accordingly, that the man first so named existed before the man who was made, and that he who was formed of the earth was afterwards made according to the pre-existent form. And that man was formed of earth, Homer, too, having discovered from the ancient and divine history which says, "Dust thou art, and unto dust shalt thou return,"[3] calls the lifeless body of Hector dumb clay. For in condemnation of Achilles dragging the corpse of Hector after death, he says somewhere:[4]

> "On the dumb clay he cast indignity,
> Blinded with rage."

And again, somewhere else,[5] he introduces Menelaus, thus addressing those who were not accepting Hector's challenge to single combat with becoming alacrity:

> "To earth and water may you all return,"

resolving them in his violent rage into their original and pristine formation from earth. These things Homer and Plato, having learned in Egypt from the ancient histories, wrote in their own words.

1 Ps. cxv. 16. 2 Gen. ii. 7. 3 Gen. iii. 19.
4 *Iliad*, xxi. 5 *Iliad*, vii. 99.

CHAP. XXXI.—*Further proof of Plato's acquaintance with Scripture.*

For from what other source, if not from his reading the writings of the prophets, could Plato have derived the information he gives us, that Jupiter drives a winged chariot in heaven? For he knew this from the following expressions of the prophet about the cherubim: "And the glory of the Lord went out from the house and rested on the cherubim; and the cherubim lift up their wings, and the wheels beside them; and the glory of the Lord God of Israel was over them above."[1] And borrowing this idea, the magniloquent Plato shouts aloud with vast assurance, "The great Jove, indeed, driving his winged chariot in heaven." For from what other source, if not from Moses and the prophets, did he learn this and so write? And whence did he receive the suggestion of his saying that God exists in a fiery substance? Was it not from the third book of the history of the Kings, where it is written, "The Lord was not in the wind; and after the wind an earthquake, but the Lord was not in the earthquake; and after the earthquake a fire, but the Lord was not in the fire; and after the fire a still small voice?"[2] But these things pious men must understand in a higher sense with profound and meditative insight. But Plato, not attending to the words with the suitable insight, said that God exists in a fiery substance.

CHAP. XXXII.—*Plato's doctrine of the heavenly gift.*

And if any one will attentively consider the gift that descends from God on the holy men,—which gift the sacred prophets call the Holy Ghost,—he shall find that this was announced under another name by Plato in the dialogue with Meno. For, fearing to name the gift of God "the Holy Ghost," lest he should seem, by following the teaching of the prophets, to be an enemy to the Greeks, he acknowledges, indeed, that it comes down from God, yet does not think fit to name it the Holy Ghost, but virtue. For so in

[1] Ezek. xi. 22. [2] 1 Kings xix. 11, 12.

the dialogue with Meno, concerning reminiscence, after he had put many questions regarding virtue, whether it could be taught or whether it could not be taught, but must be gained by practice, or whether it could be attained neither by practice nor by learning, but was a natural gift in men, or whether it comes in some other way, he makes this declaration in these very words: "But if now through this whole dialogue we have conducted our inquiry and discussion aright, virtue must be neither a natural gift, nor what one can receive by teaching, but comes to those to whom it does come by divine destiny." These things, I think, Plato having learned from the prophets regarding the Holy Ghost, he has manifestly transferred to what he calls virtue. For as the sacred prophets say that one and the same spirit is divided into seven spirits, so he also, naming it one and the same virtue, says this is divided into four virtues; wishing by all means to avoid mention of the Holy Spirit, but clearly declaring in a kind of allegory what the prophets said of the Holy Spirit. For to this effect he spoke in the dialogue with Meno towards the close: "From this reasoning, Meno, it appears that virtue comes to those to whom it does come by a divine destiny. But we shall know clearly about this, in what kind of way virtue comes to men, when, as a first step, we shall have set ourselves to investigate, as an independent inquiry, what virtue itself is." You see how he calls only by the name of virtue, the gift that descends from above; and yet he counts it worthy of inquiry, whether it is right that this [gift] be called virtue or some other thing, fearing to name it openly the Holy Spirit, lest he should seem to be following the teaching of the prophets.

CHAP. XXXIII.—*Plato's idea of the beginning of time drawn from Moses.*

And from what source did Plato draw the information that time was created along with the heavens? For he wrote thus: "Time, accordingly, was created along with the heavens; in order that, coming into being together, they might also be together dissolved, if ever their dissolution should take place." Had he not learned this from the divine history of Moses? For he knew that the creation of time had received its original constitution from days and months and years. Since, then, the first day which was created along with the heavens constituted the beginning of all time (for thus Moses wrote, "In the beginning God created the heavens and the earth," and then immediately subjoins, "And one day was made," as if he would designate the whole of time by one part of it), Plato names the day "time," lest, if he mentioned the "day," he should seem to lay himself open to the accusation of the Athenians, that he was completely adopting the expressions of Moses. And from what source did he derive what he has written regarding the dissolution of the heavens? Had he not learned this, too, from the sacred prophets, and did he not think that this was their doctrine?

CHAP. XXXIV.—*Whence men attributed to God human form.*

And if any person investigates the subject of images, and inquires on what ground those who first fashioned your gods conceived that they had the forms of men, he will find that this also was derived from the divine history. For seeing that Moses' history, speaking in the person of God, says, "Let us make man in our image and likeness," these persons, under the impression that this meant that men were like God in form, began thus to fashion their gods, supposing they would make a likeness from the likeness. But why, ye men of Greece, am I now induced to recount these things? That ye may know that it is not possible to learn the true religion from those who were unable, even on those subjects by which they won the admiration of the heathen,[1] to write anything original, but merely propounded by some allegorical device in their own writings what they had learned from Moses and the other prophets.

[1] Literally, "those without."

CHAP. XXXV.—*Appeal to the Greeks.*

The time, then, ye men of Greece, is now come, that ye, having been persuaded by the secular histories that Moses and the rest of the prophets were far more ancient than any of those who have been esteemed sages among you, abandon the ancient delusion of your forefathers, and read the divine histories of the prophets, and ascertain from them the true religion; for they do not present to you artful discourses, nor speak speciously and plausibly—for this is the property of those who wish to rob you of the truth—but use with simplicity the words and expressions which offer themselves, and declare to you whatever the Holy Ghost, who descended upon them, chose to teach through them to those who are desirous to learn the true religion. Having then laid aside all false shame, and the inveterate error of mankind, with all its bombastic parade and empty noise, though by means of it you fancy you are possessed of all advantages, do you give yourselves to the things that profit you. For neither will you commit any offence against your fathers, if you now show a desire to betake yourselves to that which is quite opposed to their error, since it is likely enough that they themselves are now lamenting in Hades, and repenting with a too late repentance; and if it were possible for them to show you thence what had befallen them after the termination of this life, ye would know from what fearful ills they desired to deliver you. But now, since it is not possible in this present life that ye either learn from them, or from those who here profess to teach that philosophy which is falsely so called, it follows as the one thing that remains for you to do, that, renouncing the error of your fathers, ye read the prophecies of the sacred writers,[1] not requiring from them unexceptionable diction (for the matters of our religion lie in works, not in words), and learn from them what will give you life everlasting. For those who bootlessly disgrace the name of philosophy are convicted of knowing nothing at all, as they are themselves forced, though unwillingly, to confess, since

[1] Literally, "sacred men."

not only do they disagree with each other, but also expressed their own opinions sometimes in one way, sometimes in another.

CHAP. XXXVI.—*True knowledge not held by the philosophers.*

And if "the discovery of the truth" be given among them as one definition of philosophy, how are they who are not in possession of the true knowledge worthy of the name of philosophy? For if Socrates, the wisest of your wise men, to whom even your oracle, as you yourselves say, bears witness, saying, "Of all men, Socrates is the wisest"—if he confesses that he knows nothing, how did those who came after him profess to know even things heavenly? For Socrates said that he was on this account called wise, because, while other men pretended to know what they were ignorant of, he himself did not shrink from confessing that he knew nothing. For he said, "I seem to myself to be wisest by this little particular, that what I do not know, I do not suppose I know." Let no one fancy that Socrates ironically feigned ignorance, because he often used to do so in his dialogues. For the last expression of his apology which he uttered as he was being led away to the prison, proves that in seriousness and truth he was confessing his ignorance: "But now it is time to go away, I indeed to die, but you to live. And which of us goes to the better state, is hidden to all but God." Socrates, indeed, having uttered this last sentence in the Areopagus, departed to the prison, ascribing to God alone the knowledge of those things which are hidden from us; but those who came after him, though they are unable to comprehend even earthly things, profess to understand things heavenly as if they had seen them. Aristotle at least—as if he had seen things heavenly with greater accuracy than Plato—declared that God did not exist, as Plato said, in the fiery substance (for this was Plato's doctrine), but in the fifth element, air. And while he demanded that concerning these matters he should be believed on account of the excellence of his language, he yet departed this life because he was overwhelmed with the infamy and disgrace of being unable to discover even the nature of the Euripus in Chalcis.[1] Let not any one, therefore, of sound judgment prefer the elegant diction of these men to his own salvation, but let him, according to that old story, stop his ears with wax, and flee the sweet hurt which these sirens would inflict upon him. For the above-mentioned men, presenting their elegant language as a kind of bait, have sought to seduce many from the right religion, in imitation of him who dared to teach the first men polytheism. Be not persuaded by these persons, I entreat you, but read the prophecies of the sacred writers.[2] And if any slothfulness or old hereditary superstition prevents you from reading the prophecies of the holy men through which you can be instructed regarding the one only God, which is the first article of the true religion, yet believe him who, though at first he taught you polytheism, yet afterwards preferred to sing a useful and necessary recantation—I mean Orpheus, who said what I quoted a little before; and believe the others who wrote the same things concerning one God. For it was the work of Divine Providence on your behalf, that they, though unwillingly, bore testimony that what the prophets said regarding one God was true, in order that, the doctrine of a plurality of gods being rejected by all, occasion might be afforded you of knowing the truth.

CHAP. XXXVII.—*Of the Sibyl.*

And you may in part easily learn the right religion from the ancient Sibyl, who by some kind of potent inspiration teaches you, through her oracular predictions, truths which seem to be much akin to the teaching of the prophets. She, they say, was of Babylonian extraction, being the daughter of Berosus, who wrote the Chaldæan History; and when she had crossed over (how, I know not) into the region of Campania, she there uttered her oracular sayings in a city called Cumæ, six miles from Baiæ, where the hot springs of Campania are found. And being in that city, we saw also a certain place, in which we were shown a very large basilica

[1] This is now supposed to be fable.

[2] Literally, "sacred men."

cut out of one stone; a vast affair, and worthy of all admiration. And they who had heard it from their fathers as part of their country's tradition, told us that it was here she used to publish her oracles. And in the middle of the basilica they showed us three receptacles cut out of one stone, in which, when filled with water, they said that she washed, and having put on her robe again, retires into the inmost chamber of the basilica, which is still a part of the one stone; and sitting in the middle of the chamber on a high rostrum and throne, thus proclaims her oracles. And both by many other writers has the Sibyl been mentioned as a prophetess, and also by Plato in his *Phædrus*. And Plato seems to me to have counted prophets divinely inspired when he read her prophecies. For he saw that what she had long ago predicted was accomplished; and on this account he expresses in the Dialogue with Meno his wonder at and admiration of prophets in the following terms: "Those whom we now call prophetic persons we should rightly name divine. And not least would we say that they are divine, and are raised to the prophetic ecstasy by the inspiration and possession of God, when they correctly speak of many and important matters, and yet know nothing of what they are saying,"—plainly and manifestly referring to the prophecies of the Sibyl. For, unlike the poets who, after their poems are penned, have power to correct and polish, specially in the way of increasing the accuracy of their verse, she was filled indeed with prophecy at the time of the inspiration, but as soon as the inspiration ceased, there ceased also the remembrance of all she had said. And this indeed was the cause why some only, and not all, the metres of the verses of the Sibyl were preserved. For we ourselves, when in that city, ascertained from our cicerone, who showed us the places in which she used to prophesy, that there was a certain coffer made of brass in which they said that her remains were preserved. And besides all else which they told us as they had heard it from their fathers, they said also that they who then took down her prophecies, being illiterate persons, often went quite astray from the accuracy of the metres; and this, they said, was the cause of the want of metre in some of the verses, the prophetess having no remembrance of what she had said, after the possession and inspiration ceased, and the reporters having, through their lack of education, failed to record the metres with accuracy. And on this account, it is manifest that Plato had an eye to the prophecies of the Sibyl when he said this about prophets, for he said, "When they correctly speak of many and important matters, and yet know nothing of what they are saying."

CHAP. XXXVIII.—*Concluding appeal.*

But since, ye men of Greece, the matters of the true religion lie not in the metrical numbers of poetry, nor yet in that culture which is highly esteemed among you, do ye henceforward pay less devotion to accuracy of metres and of language; and giving heed without contentiousness to the words of the Sibyl, recognise how great are the benefits which she will confer upon you by predicting, as she does in a clear and patent manner, the advent of our Saviour Jesus Christ; who, being the Word of God, inseparable from Him in power, having assumed man, who had been made in the image and likeness of God, restored to us the knowledge of the religion of our ancient forefathers, which the men who lived after them abandoned through the bewitching counsel of the envious devil, and turned to the worship of those who were no gods. And if you still hesitate and are hindered from belief regarding the formation of man, believe those whom you have hitherto thought it right to give heed to, and know that your own oracle, when asked by some one to utter a hymn of praise to the Almighty God, in the middle of the hymn spoke thus, "Who formed the first of men, and called him Adam." And this hymn is preserved by many whom we know, for the conviction of those who are unwilling to believe the truth which all bear witness to. If therefore, ye men of Greece, ye do not esteem the false fancy concerning those that are no gods at a higher rate than your own salvation, believe, as I said, the most ancient and time-honoured Sibyl, whose books are preserved in all the world, and who by some kind of potent inspiration both teaches us in her oracular utterances concerning those that are called gods, that they have no existence; and also clearly and manifestly prophesies concerning the predicted advent of our Saviour Jesus Christ, and concerning all those things which were to be done by Him. For the knowledge of these things will constitute your necessary preparatory training for the study of the prophecies of the sacred writers. And if any one supposes that he has learned the doctrine concerning God from the most ancient of those whom you name philosophers, let him listen to Ammon and Mercury: to Ammon, who in his discourse concerning God calls Him wholly hidden; and to Mercury, who says plainly and distinctly, "that it is difficult to comprehend God, and that it is impossible even for the man who can comprehend Him to declare Him to others." From every point of view, therefore, it must be seen that in no other way than only from the prophets who teach us by divine inspiration, is it at all possible to learn anything concerning God and the true religion.

JUSTIN ON THE SOLE GOVERNMENT OF GOD.[1]

CHAP. I.—*Object of the author.*

ALTHOUGH human nature at first received a union of intelligence and safety to discern the truth, and the worship due to the one Lord of all, yet envy, insinuating the excellence of human greatness, turned men away to the making of idols; and this superstitious custom, after continuing for a long period, is handed down to the majority as if it were natural and true. It is the part of a lover of man, or rather of a lover of God, to remind men who have neglected it of that which they ought to know. For the truth is of itself sufficient to show forth, by means of those things which are contained under the pole of heaven, the order [instituted by] Him who has created them. But forgetfulness having taken possession of the minds of men, through the long-suffering of God, has acted recklessly in transferring to mortals the name which is applicable to the only true God; and from the few the infection of sin spread to the many, who were blinded by popular usage to the knowledge of that which was lasting and unchangeable. For the men of former generations, who instituted private and public rites in honour of such as were more powerful, caused forgetfulness of the catholic[2] faith to take possession of their posterity; but I, as I have just stated, along with a God-loving mind, shall employ the speech of

[1] Θεοῦ is omitted in MSS., but μοναρχία of itself implies it.

[2] *i.e.* the doctrine that God only is to be worshipped.

one who loves man, and set it before those who have intelligence, which all ought to have who are privileged to witness the administration of the universe, so that they should worship unchangeably Him who knows all things. This I shall do, not by mere display of words, but by altogether using demonstration drawn from the old poetry in Greek literature,[1] and from writings very common amongst all. For from these the famous men who have handed down as law idol-worship to the multitudes, shall be taught and convicted by their own poets and literature of great ignorance.

CHAP. II.—*Testimonies to the unity of God.*

First, then, Æschylus,[2] in expounding the arrangement of his work,[3] expressed himself also as follows respecting the only God:

"Afar from mortals place the holy God,
Nor ever think that He, like to thyself,
In fleshly robes is clad; for all unknown
Is the great God to such a worm as thou.
Divers similitudes He bears; at times
He seems as a consuming fire that burns
Unsated; now like water, then again
In sable folds of darkness shrouds Himself.
Nay, even the very beasts of earth reflect
His sacred image; whilst the wind, clouds, rain,
The roll of thunder and the lightning flash,
Reveal to men their great and sovereign Lord.
Before Him sea and rocks, with every fount,
And all the water floods, in reverence bend;
And as they gaze upon His awful face,
Mountains and earth, with the profoundest depths
Of ocean, and the highest peaks of hills,
Tremble: for He is Lord Omnipotent;
And this the glory is of God Most High."

1 Literally, "history."

2 Grotius supposes this to be Æschylus the younger in some prologue.

3 This may also be translated: "expounding the set of opinions prevalent in his day."

But he was not the only man initiated in the knowledge of God; for Sophocles also thus describes the nature of the only Creator of all things, the One God:

"There is one God, in truth there is but one,
Who made the heavens and the broad earth beneath,
The glancing waves of ocean, and the winds;
But many of us mortals err in heart,
And set up, for a solace in our woes,
Images of the gods in stone and brass,
Or figures carved in gold or ivory;
And, furnishing for these, our handiworks,
Both sacrifice and rite magnificent,
We think that thus we do a pious work."

And Philemon also, who published many explanations of ancient customs, shares in the knowledge of the truth; and thus he writes:

"Tell me what thoughts of God we should conceive?
One, all things seeing, yet Himself unseen."

Even Orpheus, too, who introduces three hundred and sixty gods, will bear testimony in my favour from the tract called *Diathecæ*, in which he appears to repent of his error by writing the following:

"I'll speak to those who lawfully may hear;
All others, ye profane, now close the doors!
And, O Musæus, hearken thou to me,
Who offspring art of the light-bringing moon.
The words I tell thee now are true indeed,
And if thou former thoughts of mine hast seen,
Let them not rob thee of the blessed life;
But rather turn the depths of thine own heart
Unto that place where light and knowledge dwell.
Take thou the word divine to guide thy steps;
And walking well in the straight certain path,
Look to the one and universal King,
One, self-begotten, and the only One

Of whom all things, and we ourselves, are sprung.
All things are open to His piercing gaze,
While He Himself is still invisible;
Present in all His works, though still unseen,
He gives to mortals evil out of good,
Sending both chilling wars and tearful griefs;
And other than the Great King there is none.
The clouds for ever settle round His throne;
And mortal eyeballs in mere mortal eyes
Are weak to see Jove, who reigns over all.
He sits established in the brazen heavens
Upon His throne; and underneath His feet
He treads the earth, and stretches His right hand
To all the ends of ocean, and around
Tremble the mountain ranges, and the streams,
The depths, too, of the blue and hoary sea."

He speaks indeed as if he had been an eye-witness of God's greatness. And Pythagoras[1] agrees with him when he writes:

"Should one in boldness say, Lo, I am God!
Besides the One—Eternal—Infinite,
Then let him from the throne he has usurped
Put forth his power and form another globe,
Such as we dwell in, saying, This is mine.
Nor only so, but in this new domain
For ever let him dwell. If this he can,
Then verily he is a god proclaimed."

CHAP. III.—*Testimonies to a future judgment.*

Then further concerning Him, that He alone is powerful, both to institute judgment on the deeds performed in life, and on the ignorance of the Deity [displayed by men], I can adduce witnesses from your own ranks; and first Sophocles, who speaks as follows:—

"That time of times shall come, shall surely come,
When from the golden ether down shall fall

[1] "Pythagorei cujusdam fetus."—*Otto*, after Goezius.

Fire's teeming treasure, and in burning flames
All things of earth and heaven shall be consumed;
And then, when all creation is dissolved,
The sea's last wave shall die upon the shore,
The bald earth stript of trees, the burning air
No winged thing upon its breast shall bear.
There are two roads to Hades, well we know;[1]
By this the righteous, and by that the bad,
On to their separate fates shall tend; and He,
Who all things had destroyed, shall all things save."

And Philemon[2] again:

"Think'st thou, Nicostratus, the dead, who here
Enjoyed whate'er of good life offers man,
Escape the notice of Divinity,
As if they might forgotten be of Him?
Nay, there's an eye of Justice watching all;
For if the good and bad find the same end,
Then go thou, rob, steal, plunder, at thy will,
Do all the evil that to thee seems good.
Yet be not thou deceived; for underneath
There is a throne and place of judgment set,
Which God the Lord of all shall occupy;
Whose name is terrible, nor shall I dare
To breathe it forth in feeble human speech."

And Euripides:[3]

"Not grudgingly he gives a lease of life,
That we the holders may be fairly judged;
And if a mortal man doth think to hide
His daily guilt from the keen eye of God,
It is an evil thought; so if perchance

1 Some propose to insert these three lines in the centre of the next quotation from Philemon, after the line, "Nay, there's an eye," etc.

2 Some say *Diphilus*.

3 Grotius joins these lines to the preceding. Clement of Alexandria assigns them, and the others, which are under the name of Euripides, to Diphilus.

He meets with leisure-taking Justice, she
Demands him as her lawful prisoner:
But many of you hastily commit
A twofold sin, and say there is no God.
But, ah! there is; there is. Then see that he
Who, being wicked, prospers, may redeem
The time so precious, else hereafter waits
For him the due reward of punishment."

CHAP. IV.—*God desires not sacrifices, but righteousness.*

And that God is not appeased by the libations and incense of evil-doers, but awards vengeance in righteousness to each one, Philemon[1] again shall bear testimony to me:

"If any one should dream, O Pamphilus,
By sacrifice of bulls or goats—nay, then,
By Jupiter—of any such like things;
Or by presenting gold or purple robes,
Or images of ivory and gems;
If thus he thinks he may propitiate God,
He errs, and shows himself a silly one.
But let him rather useful be, and good,
Committing neither theft nor lustful deeds,
Nor murder foul, for earthly riches' sake.
Let him of no man covet wife or child,
His splendid house, his wide-spread property,
His maiden, or his slave born in his house,
His horses, or his cattle, or his beeves.
Nay, covet not a pin, O Pamphilus,
For God, close by you, sees whate'er you do.
He ever with the wicked man is wroth,
But in the righteous takes a pleasure still,
Permitting him to reap fruit of his toil,
And to enjoy the bread his sweat has won.
But being righteous, see thou pay thy vows,
And unto God the giver offer gifts.
Place thy adorning not in outward shows,

[1] Some attribute these lines to Menander, others regard them as spurious.

But in an inward purity of heart;
Hearing the thunder then, thou shalt not fear,
Nor shalt thou flee, O master, at its voice,
For thou art conscious of no evil deed,
And God, close by you, sees whate'er you do."

Again, Plato, in *Timæus*,[1] says: "But if any one on consideration should actually institute a rigid inquiry, he would be ignorant of the distinction between the human and the divine nature; because God mingles many[2] things up into one, [and again is able to dissolve one into many things,] seeing that He is endued with knowledge and power; but no man either is, or ever shall be, able to perform any of these."

CHAP. V.—*The vain pretensions of false gods.*

But concerning those who think that they shall share the holy and perfect name, which some have received by a vain tradition as if they were gods, Menander in the *Auriga* says:

"If there exists a god who walketh out
With an old woman, or who enters in
By stealth to houses through the folding-doors,
He ne'er can please me; nay, but only he
Who stays at home, a just and righteous God,
To give salvation to His worshippers."

The same Menander, in the *Sacerdos*, says:

"There is no God, O woman, that can save
One man by another; if indeed a man,
With sound of tinkling cymbals, charm a god
Where'er he listeth, then assuredly
He who doth so is much the greater god.
But these, O Rhode, are but the cunning schemes
Which daring men of intrigue, unabashed,

[1] P. 68, D.

[2] The MSS. are corrupt here. They seem to read, and one actually does read, "all" for "many." "Many" is in Plato, and the clause in brackets is taken from Plato to fill up the sense.

Invent to earn themselves a livelihood,
And yield a laughing-stock unto the age."

Again, the same Menander, stating his opinion about those who are received as gods, proving rather that they are not so, says:

"Yea, if I this beheld, I then should wish
That back to me again my soul returned.
For tell me where, O Getas, in the world
'Tis possible to find out righteous gods?"

And in the *Depositum*:

"There's an unrighteous judgment, as it seems,
Even with the gods."

And Euripides the tragedian, in *Orestes*, says:

"Apollo having caused by his command
The murder of the mother, knoweth not
What honesty and justice signify.
We serve the gods, whoever they may be;
But from the central regions of the earth
You see Apollo plainly gives response
To mortals, and whate'er he says we do.
I him obeyed, when she that bore me fell
Slain by my hand: *he* is the wicked man.
Then slay him, for 'twas he that sinned, not I.
What could I do? Think you not that the god
Should free me from the blame which I do bear?"

The same also in *Hippolytus*:

"But on these points the gods do not judge right."

And in *Ion*:

"But in the daughter of Erechtheus
What interest have I? for that pertains
Not unto such as me. But when I come
With golden vessels for libations, I
The dew shall sprinkle, and yet needs must warn

Apollo of his deeds; for when he weds
Maidens by force, the children secretly
Begotten he betrays, and them neglects
When dying. Thus not you; but while you may
Always pursue the virtues, for the gods
Will surely punish men of wickedness.
How is it right that you, who have prescribed
Laws for men's guidance, live unrighteously?
But ye being absent, I shall freely speak,
And ye to men shall satisfaction give
For marriage forced, thou Neptune, Jupiter,
Who over heaven presides. The temples ye
Have emptied, while injustice ye repay.
And though ye laud the prudent to the skies,
Yet have ye filled your hands with wickedness.
No longer is it right to call men ill
If they do imitate the sins[1] of gods;
Nay, evil let their teachers rather be."

And in *Archelaus:*

"Full oft, my son, do gods mankind perplex."

And in *Bellerophon:*

"They are no gods, who do not what is right."

And again in the same:

"Gods reign in heaven most certainly, says one;
But it is false,—yea, false: and let not him
Who speaks thus, be so foolish as to use
Ancient tradition, or to pay regard
Unto my words: but with unclouded eye
Behold the matter in its clearest light.
Power absolute, I say, robs men of life
And property; transgresses plighted faith;
Nor spares even cities, but with cruel hand
Despoils and devastates them ruthlessly.
But they that do these things have more success

[1] κακά in Euripides, καλά in text.

Than those who live a gentle pious life;
And cities small, I know, which reverence gods,
Submissive bend before the many spears
Of larger impious ones; yea, and methinks
If any man lounge idly, and abstain
From working with his hands for sustenance,
Yet pray the gods; he very soon will know
If they from him misfortunes will avert."

And Menander in *Diphilus*:[1]

"Therefore ascribe we praise and honour great
To Him who Father is, and Lord of all;
Sole maker and preserver of mankind,
And who with all good things our earth has stored."

The same also in the *Piscatores*:

"For I deem that which nourishes my life
Is God; but he whose custom 'tis to meet
The wants of men,—He needs not at our hands
Renewed supplies, Himself being all in all."[2]

The same in the *Fratres*:

"God ever is intelligence to those
Who righteous are: so wisest men have thought."

And in the *Tibicinæ*:

"Good reason finds a temple in all things
Wherein to worship; for what is the mind,
But just the voice of God within us placed?"

And the tragedian in *Phrixus*:

"But if the pious and the impious
Share the same lot, how could we think it just,
If Jove, the best, judges not uprightly?"

[1] These lines are assigned to Diphilus.

[2] The words from "but" to "all" are assigned by Otto to Justin, not to Menander.

In *Philoctetes:*

> "You see how honourable gain is deemed
> Even to the gods; and how he is admired
> Whose shrine is laden most with yellow gold.
> What, then, doth hinder thee, since it is good
> To be like gods, from thus accepting gain?"

In *Hecuba:*

> "O Jupiter! whoever thou mayest be,
> Of whom except in word all knowledge fails;"

And, "Jupiter, whether thou art indeed
> A great necessity, or the mind of man,
> I worship thee!"

CHAP. VI.—*We should acknowledge one only God.*

Here, then, is a proof of virtue, and of a mind loving prudence, to recur to the communion of the unity,[1] and to attach one's self to prudence for salvation, and make choice of the better things according to the free-will placed in man; and not to think that those who are possessed of human passions are lords of all, when they shall not appear to have even equal power with men. For in Homer,[2] Demodocus says he is self-taught—

> "God inspired me with strains"—

though he is a mortal. Æsculapius and Apollo are taught to heal by Chiron the Centaur,—a very novel thing indeed, for gods to be taught by a man. What need I speak of Bacchus, who the poet says is mad? or of Hercules, who he says is unhappy? What need to speak of Mars and Venus, the leaders of adultery; and by means of all these to establish the proof which has been undertaken? For if some one, in ignorance, should imitate the deeds which are said to be divine, he would be reckoned among impure men, and a stranger to life and humanity; and if any one does so

[1] See chap. i., the opening sentence.

[2] *Odyss.* xv. 347.

knowingly, he will have a plausible excuse for escaping vengeance, by showing that imitation of godlike deeds of audacity is no sin. But if any one should blame these deeds, he will take away their well-known names, and not cover them up with specious and plausible words. It is necessary, then, to accept the true and invariable Name, not proclaimed by my words only, but by the words of those who have introduced us to the elements of learning, in order that we may not, by living idly in this present state of existence, not only as those who are ignorant of the heavenly glory, but also as having proved ourselves ungrateful, render our account to the Judge.

EXTANT FRAGMENTS OF THE LOST WORK OF JUSTIN ON THE RESURRECTION.

CHAP. I.—*The self-evidencing power of truth.*

THE word of truth is free, and carries its own authority, disdaining to fall under any skilful argument, or to endure the logical scrutiny of its hearers. But it would be believed for its own nobility, and for the confidence due to Him who sends it. Now the word of truth is sent from God; wherefore the freedom claimed by the truth is not arrogant. For being sent with authority, it were not fit that it should be required to produce proof of what is said; since neither is there any proof beyond itself, which is God. For every proof is more powerful and trustworthy than that which it proves; since what is disbelieved, until proof is produced, gets credit when such proof is produced, and is recognised as being what it was stated to be. But nothing is either more powerful or more trustworthy than the truth; so that he who requires proof of this, is like one who wishes it demonstrated why the things that appear to the senses do appear. For the test of those things which are received through the reason, is sense; but of sense itself there is no test beyond itself. As then we bring those things which reason hunts after, to sense, and by it judge what kind of things they are, whether the things spoken be true or false, and then sit in judgment no longer, giving full credit to its decision; so also we refer all that is said regarding men and the world to the truth, and by it judge whether it be worthless or no. But the utterances of truth we judge by no separate test, giving full credit to itself.

And God, the Father of the universe, who is the perfect intelligence, is the truth. And the Word, being His Son, came to us, having put on flesh, revealing both Himself and the Father, giving to us in Himself resurrection from the dead, and eternal life afterwards. And this is Jesus Christ, our Saviour and Lord. He, therefore, is Himself both the faith and the proof of Himself and of all things. Wherefore those who follow Him, and know Him, having faith in Him as their proof, shall rest in Him. But since the adversary does not cease to resist many, and uses many and divers arts to ensnare them, that he may seduce the faithful from their faith, and that he may prevent the faithless from believing, it seems to me necessary that we also, being armed with the invulnerable doctrines of the faith, do battle against him in behalf of the weak.

CHAP. II.—*Objections to the resurrection of the flesh.*

They who maintain the wrong opinion say that there is no resurrection of the flesh; giving as their reason that it is impossible that what is corrupted and dissolved should be restored to the same as it had been. And besides the impossibility, they say that the salvation of the flesh is disadvantageous; and they abuse the flesh, adducing its infirmities, and declare that it only is the cause of our sins, so that if the flesh, say they, rise again, our infirmities also rise with it. And such sophistical reasons as the following they elaborate: If the flesh rise again, it must rise either entire and possessed of all its parts, or imperfect. But its rising imperfect argues a want of power on God's part, if some parts could be saved, and others not; but if all the parts are saved, then the body will manifestly have all its members. But is it not absurd to say that these members will exist after the resurrection from the dead, since the Saviour said, "They neither marry, nor are given in marriage, but shall be as the angels in heaven?"[1] And the angels, say they, have neither flesh, nor do they eat, nor have sexual intercourse; therefore there shall be no resurrection of the flesh. By these and such like

[1] Mark xii. 25.

arguments, they attempt to distract men from the faith. And there are some who maintain that even Jesus Himself appeared only as spiritual, and not in flesh, but presented merely the appearance of flesh: these persons seek to rob the flesh of the promise. First, then, let us solve those things which seem to them to be insoluble; then we will introduce in an orderly manner the demonstration concerning the flesh, proving that it partakes of salvation.

Chap. III.—*If the members rise, must they discharge the same functions as now?*

They say, then, if the body shall rise entire, and in possession of all its members, it necessarily follows that the functions of the members shall also be in existence; that the womb shall become pregnant, and the male also discharge his function of generation, and the rest of the members in like manner. Now let this argument stand or fall by this one assertion. For this being proved false, their whole objection will be removed. Now it is indeed evident that the members which discharge functions discharge those functions which in the present life we see; but it does not follow that they necessarily discharge the same functions from the beginning. And that this may be more clearly seen, let us consider it thus. The function of the womb is to become pregnant; and of the member of the male to impregnate. But as, though these members are destined to discharge such functions, it is not therefore necessary that they from the beginning discharge them (since we see many women who do not become pregnant, as those that are barren, even though they have wombs), so pregnancy is not the immediate and necessary consequence of having a womb; but those even who are not barren abstain from sexual intercourse, some being virgins from the first, and others from a certain time. And we see men also keeping themselves virgins, some from the first, and some from a certain time; so that by their means, marriage, made lawless through lust, is destroyed.[1] And we find that

[1] That is to say, their lives are a protest against entering into marriage for any other purpose than that of begetting children.

some even of the lower animals, though possessed of wombs, do not bear, such as the mule; and the male mules do not beget their kind. So that both in the case of men and the irrational animals we can see sexual intercourse abolished; and this, too, before the future world. And our Lord Jesus Christ was born of a virgin, for no other reason than that He might destroy the begetting by lawless desire, and might show to the ruler[1] that the formation of man was possible to God without human intervention. And when He had been born, and had submitted to the other conditions of the flesh,—I mean food, drink, and clothing,—this one condition only of discharging the sexual function He did not submit to; for, regarding the desires of the flesh, He accepted some as necessary, while others, which were unnecessary, He did not submit to. For if the flesh were deprived of food, drink, and clothing, it would be destroyed; but being deprived of lawless desire, it suffers no harm. And at the same time He foretold that, in the future world, sexual intercourse should be done away with; as He says, "The children of this world marry, and are given in marriage; but the children of the world to come neither marry nor are given in marriage, but shall be like the angels in heaven."[2] Let not, then, those that are unbelieving marvel, if in the world to come He do away with those acts of our fleshly members which even in this present life are abolished.

CHAP. IV.—*Must the deformed rise deformed?*

Well, they say, if then the flesh rise, it must rise the same as it falls; so that if it die with one eye, it must rise one-eyed; if lame, lame; if defective in any part of the body, in this part the man must rise deficient. How truly blinded are they in the eyes of their hearts! For they have not seen on the earth blind men seeing again, and the lame walking by His word. All things which the Saviour did, He did in the first place in order that what was spoken concerning Him in the prophets might be fulfilled, "that the blind should receive sight, and the deaf hear,"[3] and so on; but also to

[1] *i.e.* to the devil. [2] Luke xx. 34, 35. [3] Isa. xxxv. 5.

induce the belief that in the resurrection the flesh shall rise entire. For if on earth He healed the sicknesses of the flesh, and made the body whole, much more will He do this in the resurrection, so that the flesh shall rise perfect and entire. In this manner, then, shall those dreaded difficulties of theirs be healed.

CHAP. V.—*The resurrection of the flesh is not impossible.*

But again, of those who maintain that the flesh has no resurrection, some assert that it is impossible; others that, considering how vile and despicable the flesh is, it is not fit that God should raise it; and others, that it did not at the first receive the promise. First, then, in respect of those who say that it is impossible for God to raise it, it seems to me that I should show that they are ignorant, professing as they do in word that they are believers, yet by their works proving themselves to be unbelieving, even more unbelieving than the unbelievers. For, seeing that all the heathen believe in their idols, and are persuaded that to them all things are possible (as even their poet Homer says,[1] "The gods can do all things, and that easily;" and he added the word "easily" that he might bring out the greatness of the power of the gods), many do seem to be more unbelieving than they. For if the heathen believe in their gods, which are idols ("which have ears, and they hear not; they have eyes, and they see not"[2]), that they can do all things, though they be but devils, as saith the scripture, "The gods of the nations are devils,"[3] much more ought we, who hold the right, excellent, and true faith, to believe in our God, since also we have proofs [of His power], first in the creation of the first man, for he was made from the earth by God; and this is sufficient evidence of God's power; and then they who observe things can see how men are generated one by another, and can marvel in a still greater degree that from a little drop of moisture so grand a living creature is formed. And certainly if this were only recorded in a promise, and not seen accomplished, this too would be much more incredible than the other; but

[1] *Odyss.* ii. 304. [2] Ps. cxv. 5. [3] Ps. xcvi. 5.

it is rendered more credible by accomplishment.[1] But even in the case of the resurrection the Saviour has shown us accomplishments, of which we will in a little speak. But now we are demonstrating that the resurrection of the flesh is possible, asking pardon of the children of the church if we adduce arguments which seem to be secular[2] and physical:[3] first, because to God nothing is secular,[2] not even the world itself, for it is His workmanship; and secondly, because we are conducting our argument so as to meet unbelievers. For if we argued with believers, it were enough to say that we believe; but now we must proceed by demonstrations. The foregoing proofs are indeed quite sufficient to evince the possibility of the resurrection of the flesh; but since these men are exceedingly unbelieving, we will further adduce a more convincing argument still,—an argument drawn not from faith, for they are not within its scope, but from their own mother unbelief,—I mean, of course, from physical reasons. For if by such arguments we prove to them that the resurrection of the flesh is possible, they are certainly worthy of great contempt if they can be persuaded neither by the deliverances of faith nor by the arguments of the world.

CHAP. VI.—*The resurrection consistent with the opinions of the philosophers.*

Those, then, who are called natural philosophers, say, some of them, as Plato, that the universe is matter and God; others, as Epicurus, that it is atoms and the void;[4] others, like the Stoics, that it is these four—fire, water, air, earth. For it is sufficient to mention the most prevalent opinions. And Plato says that all things are made from matter by God,

[1] *i.e.* by actually happening under our observation.

[2] ἔξωθεν, "without" or "outside," to which reference is made in the next clause, which may be translated, "because nothing is outside God," or, "because to God nothing is 'without.'"

[3] κοσμικῶν, arguments drawn from the laws by which the world is governed.

[4] τὸ κενόν, the void of space in which the infinity of atoms moved.

and according to His design; but Epicurus and his followers say that all things are made from the atom and the void by some kind of self-regulating action of the natural movement of the bodies; and the Stoics, that all are made of the four elements, God pervading them. But while there is such discrepancy among them, there are some doctrines acknowledged by them all in common, one of which is that neither can anything be produced from what is not in being, nor anything be destroyed or dissolved into what has not any being, and that the elements exist indestructible out of which all things are generated. And this being so, the regeneration of the flesh will, according to all these philosophers, appear to be possible. For if, according to Plato, it is matter and God, both these are indestructible and God; and God indeed occupies the position of an artificer, to wit, a potter; and matter occupies the place of clay or wax, or some such thing. That, then, which is formed of matter, be it an image or a statue, is destructible; but the matter itself is indestructible, such as clay or wax, or any other such kind of matter. Thus the artist designs in the clay or wax, and makes the form of a living animal; and again, if his handiwork be destroyed, it is not impossible for him to make the same form, by working up the same material, and fashioning it anew. So that, according to Plato, neither will it be impossible for God, who is Himself indestructible, and has also indestructible material, even after that which has been first formed of it has been destroyed, to make it anew again, and to make the same form just as it was before. But according to the Stoics even, the body being produced by the mixture of the four elementary substances, when this body has been dissolved into the four elements, these remaining indestructible, it is possible that they receive a second time the same fusion and composition, from God pervading them, and so re-make the body which they formerly made. Like as if a man shall make a composition of gold and silver, and brass and tin, and then shall wish to dissolve it again, so that each element exist separately, having again mixed them, he may, if he pleases, make the very same composition as he had formerly made. Again, according to Epicurus, the atoms and the void being indestructible, it is by a definite arrangement and adjustment of the atoms as they come together, that both all other formations are produced, and the body itself; and it being in course of time dissolved, is dissolved again into those atoms from which it was also produced. And as these remain indestructible, it is not at all impossible, that by coming together again, and receiving the same arrangement and position, they should make a body of like nature to what was formerly produced by them; as if a jeweller should make in mosaic the form of an animal, and the stones should be scattered by time or by the man himself who made them, he having still in his possession the scattered stones, may gather them together again, and having gathered, may dispose them in the same way, and make the same form of an animal. And shall not God be able to collect again the decomposed members of the flesh, and make the same body as was formerly produced by Him?

Chap. VII.—*The body valuable in God's sight.*

But the proof of the possibility of the resurrection of the flesh I have sufficiently demonstrated, in answer to men of the world. And if the resurrection of the flesh is not found impossible on the principles even of unbelievers, how much more will it be found in accordance with the mind of believers! But following our order, we must now speak with respect to those who think meanly of the flesh, and say that it is not worthy of the resurrection nor of the heavenly economy;[1] because, first, its substance is earth; and besides, because it is full of all wickedness, so that it forces the soul to sin along with it. But these persons seem to be ignorant of the whole work of God, both of the genesis and formation of man at the first, and why the things in the world were made.[2] For does not the word say, "Let us make man in our image,

[1] Or, "citizenship."

[2] This might also be rendered, "and the things in the world, on account of which he was made;" but the subsequent argument shows the propriety of the above rendering.

and after our likeness?[1]" What kind of man? Manifestly He means fleshly man. For the word says, "And God took dust of the earth, and made man."[2] It is evident, therefore, that man made in the image of God was of flesh. Is it not, then, absurd to say, that the flesh made by God in His own image is contemptible, and worth nothing? But that the flesh is with God a precious possession is manifest, first from its being formed by Him, if at least the image is valuable to the former and artist; and besides, its value can be gathered from the creation of the rest of the world. For that on account of which the rest is made, is the most precious of all to the maker.

CHAP. VIII.—*Does the body cause the soul to sin?*

Quite true, say they; yet the flesh is a sinner, so much so, that it forces the soul to sin along with it. And thus they vainly accuse it, and lay to its charge alone the sins of both. But in what instance can the flesh possibly sin by itself, if it have not the soul going before it and inciting it? For as in the case of a yoke of oxen, if one or other is loosed from the yoke, neither of them can plough alone; so neither can soul or body alone effect anything, if they be unyoked from their communion. And if it is the flesh that is the sinner, then on its account alone did the Saviour come, as He says, "I am not come to call the righteous, but sinners to repentance."[3] Since, then, the flesh has been proved to be valuable in the sight of God, and glorious above all His works, it would very justly be saved by Him.

We must meet, therefore, those who say, that even though it be the special handiwork of God, and beyond all else valued by Him, it would not immediately follow that it has the promise of the resurrection. Yet is it not absurd, that that which has been produced with such circumstance, and which is beyond all else valuable, should be so neglected by its Maker, as to pass to nonentity? Then the sculptor and painter, if they wish the works they have made to endure, that they may win glory by them, renew

[1] Gen. i. 26. [2] Gen. ii. 7. [3] Mark ii. 17.

them when they begin to decay; but God would so neglect His own possession and work, that it becomes annihilated, and no longer exists. Should we not call this labour in vain? As if a man who has built a house should forthwith destroy it, or should neglect it, though he sees it falling into decay, and is able to repair it: we would blame him for labouring in vain; and should we not so blame God? But not such an one is the Incorruptible,—not senseless is the Intelligence of the universe. Let the unbelieving be silent, even though they themselves do not believe.

But, in truth, He has even called the flesh to the resurrection, and promises to it everlasting life. For where He promises to save man, there He gives the promise to the flesh. For what is man but the reasonable animal composed of body and soul? Is the soul by itself man? No; but the soul of man. Would the body be called man? No, but it is called the body of man. If, then, neither of these is by itself man, but that which is made up of the two together is called man, and God has called *man* to life and resurrection, He has called not a part, but the whole, which is the soul and the body. Since would it not be unquestionably absurd, if, while these two are in the same being and according to the same law, the one were saved and the other not? And if it be not impossible, as has already been proved, that the flesh be regenerated, what is the distinction on the ground of which the soul is saved and the body not? Do they make God a grudging God? But He is good, and will have all to be saved. And by God and His proclamation, not only has your soul heard and believed on Jesus Christ, and with it the flesh,[1] but both were washed, and both wrought righteousness. They make God, then, ungrateful and unjust, if, while both believe on Him, He desires to save one and not the other. Well, they say, but the soul is incorruptible, being a part of God and inspired by Him, and therefore He desires to save

[1] Migne proposes to read here *καὶ οὐ σὺν αὐτῇ*, "without the flesh," which gives a more obvious meaning. The above reading is, however, defensible. Justin means that the flesh was not merely partaking of the soul's faith and promise, but had rights of its own.

what is peculiarly His own and akin to Himself; but the flesh is corruptible, and not from Him, as the soul is. Then what thanks are due to Him, and what manifestation of His power and goodness is it, if He purposed to save what is by nature saved and exists as a part of Himself? For it had its salvation from itself; so that in saving the soul, God does no great thing. For to be saved is its natural destiny, because it is a part of Himself, being His inspiration. But no thanks are due to one who saves what is his own; for this is to save himself. For he who saves a part of himself, saves himself by his own means, lest he become defective in that part; and this is not the act of a good man. For not even when a man does good to his children and offspring, does one call him a good man; for even the most savage of the wild beasts do so, and indeed willingly endure death, if need be, for the sake of their cubs. But if a man were to perform the same acts in behalf of his slaves, that man would justly be called good. Wherefore the Saviour also taught us to love our enemies, since, says He, what thank have ye? So that He has shown us that it is a good work not only to love those that are begotten of Him, but also those that are without. And what He enjoins upon us, He Himself first of all does.[1]

. . . .

Chap. IX.—*The resurrection of Christ proves that the body rises.*

If He had no need of the flesh, why did He heal it? And what is most forcible of all, He raised the dead. Why? Was it not to show what the resurrection should be? How then did He raise the dead? Their souls or their bodies? Manifestly both. If the resurrection were only spiritual, it was requisite that He, in raising the dead, should show the body lying apart by itself, and the soul living apart by itself. But now He did not do so, but raised the body, confirming in it the promise of life. Why did He rise in the flesh in which He suffered, unless to show the resurrection of the flesh? And wishing to confirm this, when His disciples did

1 It is supposed that a part of the treatise has been here dropped out.

not know whether to believe He had truly risen in the body, and were looking upon Him and doubting, He said to them, "Ye have not yet faith, see that it is I;"[1] and He let them handle Him, and showed them the prints of the nails in His hands. And when they were by every kind of proof persuaded that it was Himself, and in the body, they asked Him to eat with them, that they might thus still more accurately ascertain that He had in verity risen bodily; and He did eat honey-comb and fish. And when He had thus shown them that there is truly a resurrection of the flesh, wishing to show them this also, that it is not impossible for flesh to ascend into heaven (as He had said that our dwelling-place is in heaven), "He was taken up into heaven while they beheld,"[2] as He was in the flesh. If, therefore, after all that has been said, any one demand demonstration of the resurrection, he is in no respect different from the Sadducees, since the resurrection of the flesh is the power of God, and, being above all reasoning, is established by faith, and seen in works.

. . . .

Chap. x.—*The body saved, and will therefore rise.*

The resurrection is a resurrection of the flesh which died. For the spirit dies not; the soul is in the body, and without a soul it cannot live. The body, when the soul forsakes it, is not. For the body is the house of the soul; and the soul the house of the spirit. These three, in all those who cherish a sincere hope and unquestioning faith in God, will be saved. Considering, therefore, even such arguments as are suited to this world, and finding that, even according to them, it is not impossible that the flesh be regenerated; and seeing that, besides all these proofs, the Saviour in the whole gospel shows that there is salvation for the flesh, why do we any longer endure those unbelieving and dangerous arguments, and fail to see that we are retrograding when we listen to such an argument as this: that the soul is immortal, but the body mortal, and incapable of being revived? For this we

[1] Comp. Luke xxiv. 32, etc.

[2] Acts i. 9.

used to hear from Pythagoras and Plato, even before we learned the truth. If then the Saviour said this, and proclaimed salvation to the soul alone, what new thing, beyond what we heard from Pythagoras and Plato and all their band, did He bring us? But now He has come proclaiming the glad tidings of a new and strange hope to men. For indeed it was a strange and new thing for God to promise that He would not keep incorruption in incorruption, but would make corruption incorruption. But because the prince of wickedness could in no other way corrupt the truth, he sent forth his apostles (evil men who introduced pestilent doctrines), choosing them from among those who crucified our Saviour; and these men bore the name of the Saviour, but did the works of him that sent them, through whom the name itself has been evilly spoken against. But if the flesh do not rise, why is it also guarded, and why do we not rather suffer it to indulge its desires? Why do we not imitate physicians, who, it is said, when they get a patient that is despaired of and incurable, allow him to indulge his desires? For they know that he is dying; and this indeed those who hate the flesh surely do, casting it out of its inheritance, so far as they can; for on this account they also despise it, because it is shortly to become a corpse. But if our physician Christ, God, having rescued us from our desires, regulates our flesh with His own wise and temperate rule, it is evident that He guards it from sins because it possesses a hope of salvation, as physicians do not suffer men whom they hope to save to indulge in what pleasures they please.

OTHER FRAGMENTS FROM THE LOST WRITINGS OF JUSTIN.

I.

HE most admirable Justin rightly declared that the aforesaid demons resembled robbers.

(Tatian's *Address to the Greeks*, chap. xviii.)

II.

And Justin well said in his book against Marcion, that he would not have believed the Lord Himself, if He had announced any other God than the Fashioner and Maker [of the world], and our Nourisher. But since, from the one God, who both made this world and formed us, and contains as well as administers all things, there came to us the only-begotten Son, summing up His own workmanship in Himself, my faith in Him is stedfast, and my love towards the Father is immoveable, God bestowing both upon us.

(Irenæus, *Heresies*, iv. 6.)

III.

Justin well said: Before the advent of the Lord, Satan never ventured to blaspheme God, inasmuch as he was not yet sure of his own damnation, since that was announced concerning him by the prophets only in parables and allegories. But after the advent of the Lord, learning plainly from the discourses of Christ and His apostles that eternal fire was prepared for him who voluntarily departed from God, and for all who, without repentance, persevere in apostasy, then, by means of a man of this sort, he, as if already condemned, blasphemes that God who inflicts judgment upon him, and imputes the sin of his apostasy to his Maker, instead of to his own will and predilection.

(Irenæus, *Heresies*, v. 26.)

IV.

Expounding the reason of the incessant plotting of the devil against us, he declares: Before the advent of the Lord, the devil did not so plainly know the measure of his own punishment, inasmuch as the divine prophets had but enigmatically announced it; as, for instance, Isaiah, who in the person of the Assyrian tragically revealed the course to be followed against the devil. But when the Lord appeared, and the devil clearly understood that eternal fire was laid up and prepared for him and his angels, he then began to plot without ceasing against the faithful, being desirous to have many companions in his apostasy, that he might not by himself endure the shame of condemnation, comforting himself by this cold and malicious consolation.

(*From the writings of John of Antioch.*)

V.

And Justin of Neapolis, a man who was not far separated from the apostles either in age or excellence, says that that which is mortal is inherited, but that which is immortal inherits; and that the flesh indeed dies, but the kingdom of heaven lives.

(From Methodius *On the Resurrection*, in Photius.)

VI.

Neither is there straitness with God, nor anything that is not absolutely perfect.

(*From* MS. *of the writings of Justin.*)

VII.

We shall not injure God by remaining ignorant of Him, but shall deprive ourselves of His friendship.

VIII.

The unskilfulness of the teacher proves destructive to his disciples, and the carelessness of the disciples entails danger on the teacher, and especially should they owe their negligence to his want of knowledge.

IX.

The soul can with difficulty be recalled to those good things from which it has fallen, and is with difficulty dragged away from those evils to which it has become accustomed. If at any time thou showest a disposition to blame thyself, then perhaps, through the medicine of repentance, I should cherish good hopes regarding thee. But when thou altogether despisest fear, and rejectest with scorn the very faith of Christ, it were better for thee that thou hadst never been born from the womb.

(*From the writings of John of Damascus.*)

X.

By the two birds[1] Christ is denoted, both dead as man, and living as God. He is likened to a bird, because He is understood and declared to be from above, and from heaven. And the living bird, having been dipped in the blood of the dead one, was afterwards let go. For the living and divine Word was in the crucified and dead temple [of the body], as being a partaker of the passion, and yet impassible as God.

By that which took place in the running[2] water, in which the wood and the hyssop and the scarlet were dipped, is set forth the bloody passion of Christ on the cross for the salvation of those who are sprinkled with the Spirit, and the water, and the blood: Wherefore the material for purification was not provided chiefly with reference to leprosy, but with regard to the forgiveness of sins, that both leprosy might be understood to be an emblem of sin, and the things which were sacrificed an emblem of Him who was to be sacrificed for sins.

For this reason, consequently, he ordered that the scarlet

[1] See Lev. xiv. 49–53.

[2] Literally, "living."

should be dipped at the same time in the water, thus predicting that the flesh should no longer possess its natural [evil] properties. For this reason, also, were there the two birds, the one being sacrificed in the water, and the other dipped both in the blood and in the water, and then sent away, just as is narrated also respecting the goats.

The goat that was sent away presented a type of Him who taketh away the sins of men. But the two contained a representation of the one economy of God incarnate. For He was wounded for our transgressions, and He bare the sins of many, and He was delivered for our iniquities.

(*From* MS. *of writings of Justin.*)

XI.

When God formed man at the beginning, He suspended the things of nature on his will, and made an experiment by means of one commandment. For He ordained that, if he kept this, he should partake of immortal existence; but if he transgressed it, the contrary should be his lot. Man having been thus made, and immediately looking towards transgression, naturally became subject to corruption. Corruption then becoming inherent in nature, it was necessary that He who wished to save should be one who destroyed the efficient cause of corruption. And this could not otherwise be done than by the life which is according to nature being united to that which had received the corruption, and so destroying the corruption, while preserving as immortal for the future that which had received it. It was therefore necessary that the Word should become possessed of a body, that He might deliver us from the death of natural corruption. For if, as ye[1] say, He had simply by a nod warded off death from us, death indeed would not have approached us on account of the expression of His will; but none the less would we again have become corruptible, inasmuch as we carried about in ourselves that natural corruption.

(Leontius *against Eutychians*, etc., Book II.)

[1] The Gentiles are here referred to, who saw no necessity for the incarnation.

XII.

As it is inherent in all bodies formed by God to have a shadow, so it is fitting that God, who is just, should render to those who choose what is good, and to those who prefer what is evil, to every one according to his deserts.

(*From the writings of John of Damascus.*)

XIII.

He speaks not of the Gentiles in foreign lands, but concerning [the people] who agree with the Gentiles, according to that which is spoken by Jeremiah: "It is a bitter thing for thee, that thou hast forsaken me, saith the Lord thy God, that of old thou hast broken thy yoke, and torn asunder thy bands, and said, I will not serve Thee, but will go to every high hill, and underneath every tree, and there shall I become dissolute in my fornication."[1]

(*From* MS. *of the writings of Justin.*)

XIV.

Neither shall light ever be darkness as long as light exists, nor shall the truth of the things pertaining to us be controverted. For truth is that than which nothing is more powerful. Every one who might speak the truth, and speaks it not, shall be judged by God.

(MS. *and works of John of Damascus.*)

XV.

And the fact that it was not said of the seventh day equally with the other days, "And there was evening, and there was morning," is a distinct indication of the consummation which is to take place in it before it is finished, as the fathers declare, especially St Clement, and Irenæus, and Justin the martyr and philosopher, who, commenting with exceeding wisdom on the number six of the sixth day, affirms that the intelligent soul of man and his five susceptible senses were the six works of the sixth day. Whence also, having dis-

[1] Jer. ii. 19, etc. (LXX.)

coursed at length on the number six, he declares that all things which have been framed by God are divided into six classes,—viz. into things intelligent and immortal, such as are the angels; into things reasonable and mortal, such as mankind; into things sensitive and irrational, such as cattle, and birds, and fishes; into things that can advance, and move, and are insensible, such as the winds, and the clouds, and the waters, and the stars; into things which increase and are immoveable, such as the trees; and into things which are insensible and immoveable, such as the mountains, the earth, and such like. For all the creatures of God, in heaven and on earth, fall under one or other of these divisions, and are circumscribed by them.

(*From the writings of Anastasius.*)

XVI.

Sound doctrine does not enter into the hard and disobedient heart; but, as if beaten back, enters anew into itself.

XVII.

As the good of the body is health, so the good of the soul is knowledge, which is indeed a kind of health of soul, by which a likeness to God is attained.

(*From the writings of John of Damascus.*)

XVIII.

To yield and give way to our passions is the lowest slavery, even as to rule over them is the only liberty.

The greatest of all good is to be free from sin, the next is to be justified; but he must be reckoned the most unfortunate of men, who, while living unrighteously, remains for a long time unpunished.

Animals in harness cannot but be carried over a precipice by the inexperience and badness of their driver, even as by his skilfulness and excellence they will be saved.

The end contemplated by a philosopher is likeness to God, so far as that is possible.

(*From the writings of A. Melissa.*)

XIX.

[The words] of St Justin, philosopher and martyr, from the fifth part of his *Apology:*[1]—I reckon prosperity, O men, to consist in nothing else than in living according to truth. But we do not live properly, or according to truth, unless we understand the nature of things.

It escapes them apparently, that he who has by a true faith come forth from error to the truth, has truly known himself, not, as they say, as being in a state of frenzy, but as free from the unstable and (as to every variety of error) changeable corruption, by the simple and ever identical truth.

(From the writings of John of Damascus.)

[1] It is doubtful if these words are really Justin's, or, if so, from which, or what part, of his *Apologies* they are derived.

THE MARTYRDOM OF JUSTIN AND OTHERS.

INTRODUCTORY NOTICE.

THOUGH nothing is known as to the date or authorship of the following narrative, it is generally reckoned among the most trustworthy of the Martyria. An absurd addition was in some copies made to it, to the effect that Justin died by means of hemlock. Some have thought it necessary, on account of this story, to conceive of two Justins, one of whom, the celebrated defender of the Christian faith whose writings are given in this volume, died through poison, while the other suffered in the way here described, along with several of his friends. But the description of Justin given in the following account, is evidently such as compels us to refer it to the famous apologist and martyr of the second century.

THE MARTYRDOM OF THE HOLY MARTYRS,

JUSTIN, CHARITON, CHARITES, PÆON, AND LIBERIANUS, WHO SUFFERED AT ROME.

Chap. I.—*Examination of Justin by the prefect.*

N the time of the lawless partisans of idolatry, wicked decrees were passed against the godly Christians in town and country, to force them to offer libations to vain idols; and accordingly the holy men, having been apprehended, were brought before the prefect of Rome, Rusticus by name. And when they had been brought before his judgment-seat, Rusticus the prefect said to Justin, "Obey the gods at once, and submit to the kings."[1] Justin said, "To obey the commandments of our Saviour Jesus Christ is worthy neither of blame nor of condemnation." Rusticus the prefect said, "What kind of doctrines do you profess?" Justin said, "I have endeavoured to learn all doctrines; but I have acquiesced at last in the true doctrines, those namely of the Christians, even though they do not please those who hold false opinions." Rusticus the prefect said, "Are those the doctrines that please you, you utterly wretched man?" Justin said, "Yes, since I adhere to them with right dogma."[2] Rusticus the prefect said, "What is the dogma?" Justin said, "That according to which we worship the God of the Christians, whom we reckon to be one from the beginning, the maker and fashioner

[1] *i.e.* the emperors.

[2] Μετὰ δόγματος ὀρθοῦ, orthodoxy.

of the whole creation, visible and invisible; and the Lord Jesus Christ, the Son of God, who had also been preached beforehand by the prophets as about to be present with the race of men, the herald of salvation and teacher of good disciples. And I, being a man, think that what I can say is insignificant in comparison with His boundless divinity, acknowledging a certain prophetic power,[1] since it was prophesied concerning Him of whom now I say that He is the Son of God. For I know that of old the prophets foretold His appearance among men."

CHAP. II.—*Examination of Justin continued.*

Rusticus the prefect said, "Where do you assemble?" Justin said, "Where each one chooses and can: for do you fancy that we all meet in the very same place? Not so; because the God of the Christians is not circumscribed by place; but being invisible, fills heaven and earth, and everywhere is worshipped and glorified by the faithful." Rusticus the prefect said, "Tell me where you assemble, or into what place do you collect your followers?" Justin said, "I live above one Martinus, at the Timiotinian Bath; and during the whole time (and I am now living in Rome for the second time) I am unaware of any other meeting than his. And if any one wished to come to me, I communicated to him the doctrines of truth." Rusticus said, "Are you not, then, a Christian?" Justin said, "Yes, I am a Christian."

CHAP. III.—*Examination of Chariton and others.*

Then said the prefect Rusticus to Chariton, "Tell me further, Chariton, are you also a Christian?" Chariton said, "I am a Christian by the command of God." Rusticus the prefect asked the woman Charito, "What say you, Charito?" Charito said, "I am a Christian by the grace of God." Rusticus said to Euelpistus, "And what are you?" Euelpistus, a servant of Cæsar, answered, "I too am a Christian, having been freed by Christ; and by the grace of Christ I

[1] That is, that a prophetic inspiration is required to speak worthily of Christ.

partake of the same hope." Rusticus the prefect said to Hierax, "And you, are you a Christian?" Hierax said, "Yes, I am a Christian, for I revere and worship the same God." Rusticus the prefect said, "Did Justin make you Christians?" Hierax said, "I was a Christian, and will be a Christian." And Pæon stood up and said, "I too am a Christian." Rusticus the prefect said, "Who taught you?" Pæon said, "From our parents we received this good confession." Euelpistus said, "I willingly heard the words of Justin. But from my parents also I learned to be a Christian." Rusticus the prefect said, "Where are your parents?" Euelpistus said, "In Cappadocia." Rusticus says to Hierax, "Where are your parents?" And he answered, and said, "Christ is our true father, and faith in Him is our mother; and my earthly parents died; and I, when I was driven from Iconium in Phrygia, came here." Rusticus the prefect said to Liberianus, "And what say you? Are you a Christian, and unwilling to worship [the gods]?" Liberianus said, "I too am a Christian, for I worship and reverence the only true God."

CHAP. IV.—*Rusticus threatens the Christians with death.*

The prefect says to Justin, "Hearken, you who are called learned, and think that you know true doctrines; if you are scourged and beheaded, do you believe you will ascend into heaven?" Justin said, "I hope that, if I endure these things, I shall have His gifts.[1] For I know that, to all who have thus lived, there abides the divine favour until the completion of the whole world." Rusticus the prefect said, "Do you suppose, then, that you will ascend into heaven to receive some recompense?" Justin said, "I do not suppose it, but I know and am fully persuaded of it." Rusticus the prefect said, "Let us, then, now come to the matter in hand, and which presses. Having come together, offer sacrifice with one accord to the gods." Justin said, "No right-thinking person falls away from piety to impiety." Rusticus the

[1] Another reading is δόγματα, which may be translated, "I shall have what He teaches [us to expect]."

prefect said, "Unless ye obey, ye shall be mercilessly punished." Justin said, "Through prayer we can be saved on account of our Lord Jesus Christ, even when we have been punished,[1] because this shall become to us salvation and confidence at the more fearful and universal judgment-seat of our Lord and Saviour." Thus also said the other martyrs: "Do what you will, for we are Christians, and do not sacrifice to idols."

CHAP. V.—*Sentence pronounced and executed.*

Rusticus the prefect pronounced sentence, saying, "Let those who have refused to sacrifice to the gods and to yield to the command of the emperor be scourged, and led away to suffer the punishment of decapitation, according to the laws." The holy martyrs having glorified God, and having gone forth to the accustomed place, were beheaded, and perfected their testimony in the confession of the Saviour. And some of the faithful having secretly removed their bodies, laid them in a suitable place, the grace of our Lord Jesus Christ having wrought along with them, to whom be glory for ever and ever. Amen.

[1] This passage admits of another rendering. Lord Hailes, following the common Latin version, thus translates: "It was our chief wish to endure tortures for the sake of our Lord Jesus Christ, and so to be saved."

WRITINGS OF ATHENAGORAS.

INTRODUCTORY NOTICE.

T is one of the most singular facts in early ecclesiastical history, that the name of Athenagoras is scarcely ever mentioned. Only two references to him and his writings have been discovered. One of these occurs in the work of Methodius, *On the Resurrection of the Body*, as preserved by Epiphanius (*Hær.* lxiv.), and Photius (*Biblioth.* ccxxxiv.). The other notice of him is found in the writings[1] of Philip of Side, in Pamphylia, who flourished in the early part of the fifth century. It is very remarkable that Eusebius should have been altogether silent regarding him; and that writings, so elegant and powerful as are those which still exist under his name, should have been allowed in early times to sink into almost entire oblivion.

We know with certainty regarding Athenagoras, that he was an Athenian philosopher who had embraced Christianity, and that his *Apology*, or, as he styles it, "Embassy" (πρεσβεία), was presented to the Emperors Aurelius and Commodus about A.D. 177. He is supposed to have written a considerable number of works, but the only other production of his extant is his treatise on the Resurrection. It is probable that this work was composed somewhat later than the *Apology* (see chap. xxxvi.), though its exact date cannot be determined. Philip of Side also states that he preceded Pantænus as head of the catechetical school at Alexandria; but this is probably incorrect, and is contradicted by Eusebius. A more interesting and perhaps well-founded statement is made by the same writer respecting Athenagoras, to the effect that he was won

[1] The fragment in which the notice occurs was extracted from the works of Philip by some unknown writer. It is published as an appendix to Dodwell's *Dissertationes in Irenæum*

over to Christianity while reading the Scriptures in order to controvert them. Both his *Apology* and his treatise on the Resurrection display a practised pen and a richly cultured mind. He is by far the most elegant, and certainly at the same time one of the ablest, of the early Christian Apologists.

A PLEA[1] FOR THE CHRISTIANS,

BY ATHENAGORAS THE ATHENIAN: PHILOSOPHER AND CHRISTIAN.

O the Emperors Marcus Aurelius Antoninus and Lucius Aurelius Commodus, conquerors of Armenia and Sarmatia, and more than all, philosophers.

Chap. i.—*Injustice shown towards the Christians.*

In your empire, greatest of sovereigns, different nations have different customs and laws; and no one is hindered by law or fear of punishment from following his ancestral usages, however ridiculous these may be. A citizen of Ilium calls Hector a god, and pays divine honours to Helen, taking her for Adrasteia. The Lacedæmonian venerates Agamemnon as Zeus, and Phylonoë the daughter of Tyndarus; and the man of Tenedos worships Tennes.[2] The Athenian sacrifices to Erechtheus as Poseidon. The Athenians also perform religious rites and celebrate mysteries in honour of Agraulus and Pandrosus, women who were deemed guilty of impiety for opening the box. In short, among every nation and people, men offer whatever sacrifices and celebrate whatever mysteries they please. The Egyptians reckon among their gods even cats, and crocodiles, and serpents, and asps, and dogs. And to all these both you and the laws give permission so to act, deeming, on the one hand, that to believe in no god at all is impious and wicked, and on the other, that it

[1] Literally, "embassy."

[2] There are here many varieties of reading: we have followed the text suggested by Gesner.

is necessary for each man to worship the gods he prefers, in order that, through fear of the deity, men may be kept from wrong-doing. But why—for do not, like the multitude, be led astray by hearsay—why is a mere name odious to you?[1] Names are not deserving of hatred: it is the unjust act that calls for penalty and punishment. And accordingly, with admiration of your mildness and gentleness, and your peaceful and benevolent disposition towards every man, individuals live in the possession of equal rights; and the cities, according to their rank, share in equal honour; and the whole empire, under your intelligent sway, enjoys profound peace. But for us who are called Christians you have not in like manner cared; but although we commit no wrong—nay, as will appear in the sequel of this discourse, are of all men most piously and righteously disposed towards the Deity and towards your government—you allow us to be harassed, plundered, and persecuted, the multitude making war upon us for our name alone. We venture, therefore, to lay a statement of our case before you—and you will learn from this discourse that we suffer unjustly, and contrary to all law and reason—and we beseech you to bestow some consideration upon us also, that we may cease at length to be slaughtered at the instigation of false accusers. For the fine imposed by our persecutors does not aim merely at our property, nor their insults at our reputation, nor the damage they do us at any other of our greater interests. These we hold in contempt, though to the generality they appear matters of great importance; for we have learned, not only not to return blow for blow, nor to go to law with those who plunder and rob us, but to those who smite us on one side of the face to offer the other side also, and to those who take away our coat to give likewise our cloak. But, when we have surrendered our property, they plot against our very bodies and souls, pouring upon us wholesale charges of crimes of which we are guiltless even in thought, but which belong to these idle praters themselves, and to the whole tribe of those who are like them.

[1] We here follow the text of Otto: others read ἡμῖν.

CHAP. II.—*Claim to be treated as others are when accused.*

If, indeed, any one can convict us of a crime, be it small or great, we do not ask to be excused from punishment, but are prepared to undergo the sharpest and most merciless inflictions. But if the accusation relates merely to our name—and it is undeniable, that up to the present time the stories told about us rest on nothing better than the common undiscriminating popular talk, nor has any Christian been convicted of crime—it will devolve on you, illustrious and benevolent and most learned sovereigns, to remove by law this despiteful treatment, so that, as throughout the world both individuals and cities partake of your beneficence, we also may feel grateful to you, exulting that we are no longer the victims of false accusation. For it does not comport with your justice, that others when charged with crimes should not be punished till they are convicted, but that in our case the name we bear should have more force than the evidence adduced on the trial, when the judges, instead of inquiring whether the person arraigned have committed any crime, vent their insults on the name, as if that were itself a crime. But no name in and by itself is reckoned either good or bad; names appear bad or good according as the actions underlying them are bad or good. You, however, have yourselves a clear knowledge of this, since you are well instructed in philosophy and all learning. For this reason, too, those who are brought before you for trial, though they may be arraigned on the gravest charges, have no fear, because they know that you will inquire respecting their previous life, and not be influenced by names if they mean nothing, nor by the charges contained in the indictments if they should be false: they accept with equal satisfaction, as regards its fairness, the sentence whether of condemnation or acquittal. What, therefore, is conceded as the common right of all, we claim for ourselves, that we shall not be hated and punished because we are called Christians (for what has the name to do with our being bad men?), but be tried on any charges which may be brought against us, and either be released on our disproving them, or punished if convicted of crime—not for the name (for no Christian is a bad man unless he falsely profess our doctrines), but for the wrong which has been done. It is thus that we see the philosophers judged. None of them before trial is deemed by the judge either good or bad on account of his science or art, but if found guilty of wickedness he is punished, without thereby affixing any stigma on philosophy (for he is a bad man for not cultivating philosophy in a lawful manner, but science is blameless), while if he refutes the false charges he is acquitted. Let this equal justice, then, be done to us. Let the life of the accused persons be investigated, but let the name stand free from all imputation. I must at the outset of my defence entreat you, illustrious emperors, to listen to me impartially: not to be carried away by the common irrational talk and prejudge the case, but to apply your desire of knowledge and love of truth to the examination of our doctrine also. Thus, while you on your part will not err through ignorance, we also, by disproving the charges arising out of the undiscerning rumour of the multitude, shall cease to be assailed.

CHAP. III.—*Charges brought against the Christians.*

Three things are alleged against us: atheism, Thyestean feasts, Œdipodean intercourse. But if these charges are true, spare no class: proceed at once against our crimes; destroy us root and branch, with our wives and children, if any Christian[1] is found to live like the brutes. And yet even the brutes do not touch the flesh of their own kind; and they pair by a law of nature, and only at the regular season, not from simple wantonness; they also recognise those from whom they receive benefits. If any one, therefore, is more savage than the brutes, what punishment that he can endure shall be deemed adequate to such offences? But, if these things are only idle tales and empty slanders, originating in the fact that virtue is opposed by its very nature to vice, and that contraries war against one another by a divine law (and you are yourselves witnesses that no such iniquities are committed by us, for you forbid informations to be laid against us), it remains

[1] Thus Otto; others read, "if any one of men."

for you to make inquiry concerning our life, our opinions, our loyalty and obedience to you and your house and government, and thus at length to grant to us the same rights (we ask nothing more) as to those who persecute us. For we shall then conquer them, unhesitatingly surrendering, as we now do, our very lives for the truth's sake.

CHAP. IV.—*The Christians are not atheists, but acknowledge one only God.*

As regards, first of all, the allegation that we are atheists—for I will meet the charges one by one, that we may not be ridiculed for having no answer to give to those who make them—with reason did the Athenians adjudge Diagoras guilty of atheism, in that he not only divulged the Orphic doctrine, and published the mysteries of Eleusis and of the Cabiri, and chopped up the wooden statue of Hercules to boil his turnips, but openly declared that there was no God at all. But to us, who distinguish God from matter, and teach that matter is one thing and God another, and that they are separated by a wide interval (for that the Deity is uncreated and eternal, to be beheld by the understanding and reason alone, while matter is created and perishable), is it not absurd to apply the name of atheism? If our sentiments were like those of Diagoras, while we have such incentives to piety—in the established order, the universal harmony, the magnitude, the colour, the form, the arrangement of the world—with reason might our reputation for impiety, as well as the cause of our being thus harassed, be charged on ourselves. But, since our doctrine acknowledges one God, the Maker of this universe, who is Himself uncreated (for that which is does not come to be, but that which is not) but has made all things by the Logos which is from Him, we are treated unreasonably in both respects, in that we are both defamed and persecuted.

CHAP. V.—*Testimony of the poets to the unity of God.*

Poets and philosphers have not been voted atheists for inquiring concerning God. Euripides, speaking of those who, according to popular preconception, are ignorantly called gods, says doubtingly:

> "If Zeus indeed does reign in heaven above,
> He ought not on the righteous ills to send."[1]

But speaking of Him who is apprehended by the understanding as matter of certain knowledge, he gives his opinion decidedly, and with intelligence; thus:

> "Seest thou on high him who, with humid arms,
> Clasps both the boundless ether and the earth?
> Him reckon Zeus, and him regard as God."[2]

For, as to these so-called gods, he neither saw any real existences, to which a name is usually assigned, underlying them ("Zeus," for instance: "who Zeus is I know not, but by report"), nor that any names were given to realities which actually do exist (for of what use are names to those who have no real existences underlying them?); but Him he did see by means of His works, considering with an eye to things unseen the things which are manifest in air, in ether, on earth. Him therefore, from whom proceed all created things, and by whose Spirit they are governed, he concluded to be God; and Sophocles agrees with him, when he says:

> "There is one God, in truth there is but one,
> Who made the heavens, and the broad earth beneath."[3]

[Euripides is speaking] of the nature of God, which fills His works with beauty, and teaching both where God must be, and that He must be One.

CHAP. VI.—*Opinions of the philosophers as to the one God.*

Philolaus, too, when he says that all things are included in God as in a stronghold, teaches that He is one, and that He is superior to matter. Lysis and Opsimus[4] thus define God:

[1] From an unknown play.

[2] From an unknown play; the original is ambiguous; comp. Cic. *De nat. Deorum*, ii. c. 25, where the words are translated—"Seest thou this boundless ether on high which embraces the earth in its moist arms? Reckon this Zeus." Athenagoras cannot so have understood Euripides.

[3] Not found in his extant works. [4] Thus Otto; common text has ὄψει.

the one says that He is an ineffable number, the other that He is the excess of the greatest number beyond that which comes nearest to it. So that since ten is the greatest number according to the Pythagoreans, being the Tetractys,[1] and containing all the arithmetic and harmonic principles, and the Nine stands next to it, God is a unit—that is, one. For the greatest number exceeds the next least by one. Then there are Plato and Aristotle—not that I am about to go through all that the philosophers have said about God, as if I wished to exhibit a complete summary of their opinions; for I know that, as you excel all men in intelligence and in the power of your rule, in the same proportion do you surpass them all in an accurate acquaintance with all learning, cultivating as you do each several branch with more success than even those who have devoted themselves exclusively to any one. But, inasmuch as it is impossible to demonstrate without the citation of names that we are not alone in confining the notion of God to unity, I have ventured on an enumeration of opinions. Plato, then, says, "To find out the Maker and Father of this universe is difficult; and, when found, it is impossible to declare Him to all,"[2] conceiving of one uncreated and eternal God. And if he recognises others as well, such as the sun, moon, and stars, yet he recognises them as created: "gods, offspring of gods, of whom I am the Maker, and the Father of works which are indissoluble apart from my will; but whatever is compounded can be dissolved."[3] If, therefore, Plato is not an atheist for conceiving of one uncreated God, the Framer of the universe, neither are we atheists who acknowledge and firmly hold that He is God who has framed all things by the Logos, and holds them in being by His Spirit. Aristotle, again, and his followers, recognising the existence of one whom they regard as a sort of compound living creature (ζῶον), speak of God as consisting of soul and body, thinking His body to be the etherial space and the planetary stars and the sphere of the fixed stars, moving in circles; but His soul, the reason which presides over the

[1] One, two, three, and four together forming *ten*.

[2] *Timæus*, p. 28, C. [3] *Timæus*, p. 41, A.

motion of the body, itself not subject to motion, but becoming the cause of motion to the other. The Stoics also, although by the appellations they employ to suit the changes of matter, which they say is permeated by the Spirit of God, they multiply the Deity in name, yet in reality they consider God to be one. For, if God is an artistic fire advancing methodically to the production of the several things in the world, embracing in Himself all the seminal principles by which each thing is produced in accordance with fate, and if His Spirit pervades the whole world, then God is one according to them, being named Zeus in respect of the fervid part (τὸ ζέον) of matter, and Hera in respect of the air (ὁ ἀήρ), and called by other names in respect of that particular part of matter which He pervades.

CHAP. VII.—*Superiority of the Christian doctrine respecting God.*

Since, therefore, the unity of the Deity is confessed by almost all, even against their will, when they come to treat of the first principles of the universe, and we in our turn likewise assert that He who arranged this universe is God,—why is it that they can say and write with impunity what they please concerning the Deity, but that against us a law lies in force, though we are able to demonstrate what we apprehend and justly believe, namely that there is one God, with proofs and reasons accordant with truth? For poets and philosophers, as to other subjects so also to this, have applied themselves in the way of conjecture, moved, by reason of their affinity with the afflatus from God, each one by his own soul, to try whether he could find out and apprehend the truth; but they have not been found competent fully to apprehend it, because they thought fit to learn, not from God concerning God, but each one from himself; hence they came each to his own conclusion respecting God, and matter, and forms, and the world. But we have for witnesses of the things we apprehend and believe, prophets, men who have pronounced concerning God and the things of God, guided by the Spirit of God. And you too will admit, excelling all others as you do in intelligence and in piety towards the true God (*τὸ ὄντως θεῖον*), that it would be irrational for us to cease to believe in the Spirit from God, who moved the mouths of the prophets like musical instruments, and to give heed to mere human opinions.

CHAP. VIII.—*Absurdities of polytheism.*

As regards, then, the doctrine that there was from the beginning one God, the Maker of this universe, consider it in this wise, that you may be acquainted with the argumentative grounds also of our faith. If there were from the beginning two or more gods, they were either in one and the same place, or each of them separately in his own. In one and the same place they could not be. For, if they are gods, they are not alike; but because they are uncreated they are unlike: for created things are like their patterns; but the uncreated are unlike, being neither produced from any one, nor formed after the pattern of any one. Hand and eye and foot are parts of one body, making up together one man: is God in this sense one?[1] And indeed Socrates was compounded and divided into parts, just because he was created and perishable; but God is uncreated, and impassible, and indivisible—does not, therefore, consist of parts. But if, on the contrary, each of them exists separately, since He that made the world is above the things created, and about the things He has made and set in order, where can the other or the rest be? For if the world, being made spherical, is confined within the circles of heaven, and the Creator of the world is above the things created, managing that[2] by His providential care of these, what place is there for the second god, or for the other gods? For he is not in the world, because it belongs to the other; nor about the world, for God the Maker of the world is above it. But if he is neither in the world nor about the world (for all that surrounds it is occupied by this one[3]), where is he? Is he

[1] *i.e.* Do several gods make up one God?—*Otto.* Others read affirmatively, "God is one."

[2] *i.e.* the world.

[3] *i.e.* the Creator, or first God.

above the world and [the first] God? In another world, or about another? But if he is in another or about another, then he is not about us, for he does not govern the world; nor is his power great, for he exists in a circumscribed space. But if he is neither in another world (for all things are filled by the other), nor about another (for all things are occupied by the other), he clearly does not exist at all, for there is no place in which he can be. Or what does he do, seeing that there is another to whom the world belongs, and he is above the Maker of the world, and yet is neither in the world nor about the world? Is there, then, some other place where he can stand? But God, and what belongs to God, are above him. And what, too, shall be the place, seeing that the other fills the regions which are above the world? Perhaps he exerts a providential care? [By no means.] And yet, unless he does so, he has done nothing. If, then, he neither does anything nor exercises providential care, and if there is not another place in which he is, then this Being of whom we speak is the one God from the beginning, and the sole Maker of the world.

CHAP. IX.—*The testimonies of the prophets.*

If we satisfied ourselves with advancing such considerations as these, our doctrines might by some be looked upon as human. But, since the voices of the prophets confirm our arguments—for I think that you also, with your great zeal for knowledge, and your great attainments in learning, cannot be ignorant of the writings either of Moses or of Isaiah and Jeremiah, and the other prophets, who, lifted in ecstasy above the natural operations of their minds by the impulses of the Divine Spirit, uttered the things with which they were inspired, the Spirit making use of them as a flute-player breathes into a flute;—what, then, do these men say? "The Lord is our God; no other can be compared with Him."[1] And again: "I am God, the first and the last, and besides me there is no God."[2] In like manner: "Before me there was no other God, and after me there shall be none; I

[1] Isa. xli. 4; Ex. xx. 2, 3 (as to sense). [2] Isa. xliv. 6.

am God, and there is none besides me."[1] And as to His greatness: "Heaven is my throne, and the earth is the footstool of my feet: what house will ye build for me, or what is the place of my rest?"[2] But I leave it to you, when you meet with the books themselves, to examine carefully the prophecies contained in them, that you may on fitting grounds defend us from the abuse cast upon us.

CHAP. X.—*The Christians worship the Father, Son, and Holy Ghost.*

That we are not atheists, therefore, seeing that we acknowledge one God, uncreated, eternal, invisible, impassible, incomprehensible, illimitable, who is apprehended by the understanding only and the reason, who is encompassed by light, and beauty, and spirit, and power ineffable, by whom the universe has been created through His Logos, and set in order, and is kept in being—I have sufficiently demonstrated. [I say "His Logos"], for we acknowledge also a Son of God. Nor let any one think it ridiculous that God should have a Son. For though the poets, in their fictions, represent the gods as no better than men, our mode of thinking is not the same as theirs, concerning either God the Father or the Son. But the Son of God is the Logos of the Father, in idea and in operation; for after the pattern of Him and by Him[3] were all things made, the Father and the Son being one. And, the Son being in the Father and the Father in the Son, in oneness and power of spirit, the understanding and reason (νοῦς καὶ λόγος) of the Father is the Son of God. But if, in your surpassing intelligence, it occurs to you to inquire what is meant by the Son, I will state briefly that He is the first product of the Father, not as having been brought into existence (for from the beginning, God, who is the eternal mind [νοῦς], had the Logos in Himself, being from eternity instinct with Logos [λογικός]); but inasmuch as He came forth to be the idea and energizing power of all material things, which lay like a nature without attributes, and an

[1] Isa. xliii. 10, 11. [2] Isa. lxvi. 1.

[3] Or, "by Him and through Him."

inactive earth, the grosser particles being mixed up with the lighter. The prophetic Spirit also agrees with our statements. "The Lord," it says, "made me, the beginning of His ways to His works."[1] The Holy Spirit Himself also, which operates in the prophets, we assert to be an effluence of God, flowing from Him, and returning back again like a beam of the sun. Who, then, would not be astonished to hear men who speak of God the Father, and of God the Son, and of the Holy Spirit, and who declare both their power in union and their distinction in order, called atheists? Nor is our teaching in what relates to the divine nature confined to these points; but we recognise also a multitude of angels and ministers, whom God the Maker and Framer of the world distributed and appointed to their several posts by His Logos, to occupy themselves about the elements, and the heavens, and the world, and the things in it, and the goodly ordering of them all.

CHAP. XI.—*The moral teaching of the Christians repels the charge brought against them.*

If I go minutely into the particulars of our doctrine, let it not surprise you. It is that you may not be carried away by the popular and irrational opinion, but may have the truth clearly before you. For presenting the opinions themselves to which we adhere, as being not human, but uttered and taught by God, we shall be able to persuade you not to think of us as atheists. What, then, are those teachings in which we are brought up? "I say unto you, Love your enemies; bless them that curse you; pray for them that persecute you; that ye may be the sons of your Father who is in heaven, who causes His sun to rise on the evil and the good, and sends rain on the just and the unjust."[2] Allow me here to lift up my voice boldly in loud and audible outcry, pleading as I do before philosophic princes. For who of those that reduce syllogisms, and clear up ambiguities, and explain etymologies, or of those who teach homonyms and synonyms, and predicaments and axioms, and what is the subject and what the predicate, and who promise their disciples by these and such like

[1] Prov. viii. 22. [2] Luke vi. 27, 28; Matt. v. 44, 45.

instructions to make them happy: who of them have so purged their souls as, instead of hating their enemies, to love them; and, instead of speaking ill of those who have reviled them (to abstain from which is of itself an evidence of no mean forbearance), to bless them; and to pray for those who plot against their lives? On the contrary, they never cease with evil intent to search out skilfully the secrets of their art,[1] and are ever bent on working some ill, making the art of words and not the exhibition of deeds their business and profession. But among us you will find uneducated persons, and artisans, and old women, who, if they are unable in words to prove the benefit of our doctrine, yet by their deeds exhibit the benefit arising from their persuasion of its truth: they do not rehearse speeches, but exhibit good works; when struck, they do not strike again; when robbed, they do not go to law; they give to those that ask of them, and love their neighbours as themselves.

CHAP. XII.—*Consequent absurdity of the charge of atheism.*

Should we, then, unless we believed that a God presides over the human race, thus purge ourselves from evil? Most certainly not. But, because we are persuaded that we shall give an account of everything in the present life to God, who made us and the world, we adopt a temperate and benevolent and generally despised method of life, believing that we shall suffer no such great evil here, even should our lives be taken from us, compared with what we shall there receive for our meek and benevolent and moderate life from the great Judge. Plato indeed has said that Minos and Rhadamanthus will judge and punish the wicked; but we say that, even if a man be Minos or Rhadamanthus himself, or their father, even he will not escape the judgment of God. Are, then, those who consider life to be comprised in this, "Let us eat and drink, for to-morrow we die," and who regard death as a deep sleep and forgetfulness ("sleep and death, twin-brothers" [2]), to be

[1] The meaning is here doubtful; but the probable reference is to the practices of the Sophists.

[2] Hom. *Il.* xvi. 672.

accounted pious; while men who reckon the present life of very small worth indeed, and who are conducted to the future life by this one thing alone, that they know God and His Logos, what is the oneness of the Son with the Father, what the communion of the Father with the Son, what is the Spirit, what is the unity of these three, the Spirit, the Son, the Father, and their distinction in unity; and who know that the life for which we look is far better than can be described in words, provided we arrive at it pure from all wrong-doing; who, moreover, carry our benevolence to such an extent, that we not only love our friends ("for if ye love them," He says, "that love you, and lend to them that lend to you, what reward will ye have?"[1]),—shall we, I say, when such is our character, and when we live such a life as this, that we may escape condemnation at last, not be accounted pious? These, however, are only small matters taken from great, and a few things from many, that we may not further trespass on your patience; for those who test honey and whey, judge by a small quantity whether the whole is good.

CHAP. XIII.—*Why the Christians do not offer sacrifices.*

But, as most of those who charge us with atheism, and that because they have not even the dreamiest conception of what God is, and are doltish and utterly unacquainted with natural and divine things, and such as measure piety by the rule of sacrifices, charge us with not acknowledging the same gods as the cities, be pleased to attend to the following considerations, O emperors, on both points. And first, as to our not sacrificing: the Framer and Father of this universe does not need blood, nor the odour of burnt-offerings, nor the fragrance of flowers and incense, forasmuch as He is Himself perfect fragrance, needing nothing either within or without; but the noblest sacrifice to Him is for us to know who stretched out and vaulted the heavens, and fixed the earth in its place like a centre, who gathered the water into seas and divided the light from the darkness, who adorned the sky

[1] Luke vi. 32, 34; Matt. v. 46.

with stars and made the earth to bring forth seed of every kind, who made animals and fashioned man. When, holding God to be this Framer of all things, who preserves them in being and superintends them all by knowledge and administrative skill, we "lift up holy hands" to Him, what need has He further of a hecatomb?

> "For they, when mortals have transgress'd or fail'd
> To do aright, by sacrifice and pray'r,
> Libations and burnt-offerings, may be soothed."[1]

And what have I to do with holocausts, which God does not stand in need of?—though indeed it does behove us to offer a bloodless sacrifice and "the service of our reason."[2]

Chap. xiv.—*Inconsistency of those who accuse the Christians.*

Then, as to the other complaint, that we do not pray to and believe in the same gods as the cities, it is an exceedingly silly one. Why, the very men who charge us with atheism for not admitting the same gods as they acknowledge, are not agreed among themselves concerning the gods. The Athenians have set up as gods Celeus and Metanira: the Lacedæmonians Menelaus; and they offer sacrifices and hold festivals to him, while the men of Ilium cannot endure the very sound of his name, and pay their adoration to Hector. The Ceans worship Aristæus, considering him to be the same as Zeus and Apollo; the Thasians Theagenes, a man who committed murder at the Olympic games; the Samians Lysander, notwithstanding all the slaughters and all the crimes perpetrated by him; Alcman and Hesiod Medea, and the Cilicians Niobe; the Sicilians Philip the son of Butacides; the Amathusians Onesilus; the Carthaginians Hamilcar. Time would fail me to enumerate the whole. When, therefore, they differ among themselves concerning their gods, why do they bring the charge against us of not agreeing with them? Then look at the practices prevailing among the Egyptians: are they not perfectly ridiculous? For in the

[1] Hom. *Il.* ix. 499 sq., Lord Derby's translation, which version the translator has for the most part used.

[2] Comp. Rom. xii. 1.

temples at their solemn festivals they beat their breasts as for the dead, and sacrifice to the same beings as gods; and no wonder, when they look upon the brutes as gods, and shave themselves when they die, and bury them in temples, and make public lamentation. If, then, we are guilty of impiety because we do not practise a piety corresponding with theirs, then all cities and all nations are guilty of impiety, for they do not all acknowledge the same gods.

CHAP. XV.—*The Christians distinguish God from matter.*

But grant that they acknowledge the same. What then? Because the multitude, who cannot distinguish between matter and God, or see how great is the interval which lies between them, pray to idols made of matter, are we therefore, who do distinguish and separate the uncreated and the created, that which is and that which is not, that which is apprehended by the understanding and that which is perceived by the senses, and who give the fitting name to each of them,—are we to come and worship images? If, indeed, matter and God are the same, two names for one thing, then certainly, in not regarding stocks and stones, gold and silver, as gods, we are guilty of impiety. But if they are at the greatest possible remove from one another—as far asunder as the artist and the materials of his art—why are we called to account? For as is the potter and the clay (matter being the clay, and the artist the potter), so is God, the Framer of the world, and matter, which is subservient to Him for the purposes of His art. But as the clay cannot become vessels of itself without art, so neither did matter, which is capable of taking all forms, receive, apart from God the Framer, distinction and shape and order. And as we do not hold the pottery of more worth than him who made it, nor the vessels of glass and gold than him who wrought them; but if there is anything about them elegant in art we praise the artificer, and it is he who reaps the glory of the vessels: even so with matter and God—the glory and honour of the orderly arrangement of the world belongs of right not to matter, but to God, the Framer of matter. So that, if we were to regard the various forms of matter as gods, we should seem to be without any sense of the true God, because we should be putting the things which are dissoluble and perishable on a level with that which is eternal.

CHAP. XVI.—*The Christians do not worship the universe.*

Beautiful without doubt is the world, excelling,[1] as well in its magnitude as in the arrangement of its parts, both those in the oblique circle and those about the north, and also in its spherical form. Yet it is not this, but its Artificer, that we must worship. For when any of your subjects come to you, they do not neglect to pay their homage to you, their rulers and lords, from whom they will obtain whatever they need, and address themselves to the magnificence of your palace; but, if they chance to come upon the royal residence, they bestow a passing glance of admiration on its beautiful structure: but it is to you yourselves that they show honour, as being "all in all." You sovereigns, indeed, rear and adorn your palaces for yourselves; but the world was not created because God needed it; for God is Himself everything to Himself,—light unapproachable, a perfect world, spirit, power, reason. If, therefore, the world is an instrument in tune, and moving in well-measured time, I adore the Being who gave its harmony, and strikes its notes, and sings the accordant strain, and not the instrument. For at the musical contests the adjudicators do not pass by the lute-players and crown the lutes. Whether, then, as Plato says, the world be a product of divine art, I admire its beauty, and adore the Artificer; or whether it be His essence and body, as the Peripatetics affirm, we do not neglect to adore God, who is the cause of the motion of the body, and descend "to the poor and weak elements," adoring in the impassible[2] air (as they term it), passible matter; or, if any one apprehends the several parts of the world to be powers of God, we do not approach and do homage to the powers, but their Maker and Lord. I do not ask of matter what it has not to give,

1 Thus Otto; others render "comprising."

2 Some refer this to the human spirit.

nor passing God by do I pay homage to the elements, which can do nothing more than what they were bidden; for, although they are beautiful to look upon, by reason of the art of their Framer, yet they still have the nature of matter. And to this view Plato also bears testimony; "for," says he, "that which is called heaven and earth has received many blessings from the Father, but yet partakes of body; hence it cannot possibly be free from change."[1] If, therefore, while I admire the heavens and the elements in respect of their art, I do not worship them as gods, knowing that the law of dissolution is upon them, how can I call those objects gods of which I know the makers to be men? Attend, I beg, to a few words on this subject.

CHAP. XVII.—*The names of the gods and their images are but of recent date.*

An apologist must adduce more precise arguments than I have yet given, both concerning the names of the gods, to show that they are of recent origin, and concerning their images, to show that they are, so to say, but of yesterday. You yourselves, however, are thoroughly acquainted with these matters, since you are versed in all departments of knowledge, and are beyond all other men familiar with the ancients. I assert, then, that it was Orpheus, and Homer, and Hesiod who[2] gave both genealogies and names to those whom they call gods. Such, too, is the testimony of Herodotus.[3] "My opinion," he says, "is that Hesiod and Homer preceded me by four hundred years, and no more; and it was they who framed a theogony for the Greeks, and gave the gods their names, and assigned them their several honours and functions, and described their forms." Representations of the gods, again, were not in use at all, so long as statuary, and painting, and sculpture were unknown; nor did they become common until Saurias the Samian, and Crato the

[1] *Polit.* p. 269, D.

[2] We here follow the text of Otto; others place the clause in the following sentence.

[3] ii. 53.

Sicyonian, and Cleanthes the Corinthian, and the Corinthian damsel[1] appeared, when drawing in outline was invented by Saurias, who sketched a horse in the sun, and painting by Crato, who painted in oil on a whitened tablet the outlines of a man and woman; and the art of making figures in relief (*κοροπλαθική*) was invented by the damsel,[1] who, being in love with a person, traced his shadow on a wall as he lay asleep, and her father, being delighted with the exactness of the resemblance (he was a potter), carved out the sketch and filled it up with clay: this figure is still preserved at Corinth. After these, Dædalus and Theodorus the Milesian further invented sculpture and statuary. You perceive, then, that the time since representations of form and the making of images began is so short, that we can name the artist of each particular god. The image of Artemis at Ephesus, for example, and that of Athenâ (or rather of Athelâ, for so is she named by those who speak more in the style of the mysteries; for thus was the ancient image made of the olive-tree called), and the sitting figure of the same goddess, were made by Endœus, a pupil of Dædalus; the Pythian god was the work of Theodorus and Telecles; and the Delian god and Artemis are due to the art of Tectæus and Angelio; Hera in Samos and in Argos came from the hands of Smilis, and the other statues[2] were by Phidias; Aphrodité the courtezan in Cnidus is the production of Praxiteles; Asclepius in Epidaurus is the work of Phidias. In a word, of not one of these statues can it be said that it was not made by man. If, then, these are gods, why did they not exist from the beginning? Why, in sooth, are they younger than those who made them? Why, in sooth, in order to their coming into existence, did they need the aid of men and art? They are nothing but earth, and stones, and matter, and curious art.

1 Or, Koré. It is doubtful whether or not this should be regarded as a proper name.

2 The reading is here doubtful.

CHAP. XVIII.—*The gods themselves have been created, as the poets confess.*

But, since it is affirmed by some that, although these are only images, yet there exist gods in honour of whom they are made; and that the supplications and sacrifices presented to the images are to be referred to the gods, and are in fact made to the gods; and that there is not any other way of coming to them, for

"'Tis hard for man
To meet in presence visible a God;"[1]

and whereas, in proof that such is the fact, they adduce the energies possessed by certain images, let us examine into the power attached to their names. And I would beseech you, greatest of emperors, before I enter on this discussion, to be indulgent to me while I bring forward true considerations; for it is not my design to show the fallacy of idols, but, by disproving the calumnies vented against us, to offer a reason for the course of life we follow. May you, by considering yourselves, be able to discover the heavenly kingdom also! For as all things are subservient to you, father and son, who have received the kingdom from above (for "the king's soul is in the hand of God,"[2] saith the prophetic Spirit), so to the one God and the Logos proceeding from Him, the Son, apprehended by us as inseparable from Him, all things are in like manner subjected. This then especially I beg you carefully to consider. The gods, as they affirm, were not from the beginning, but every one of them has come into existence just like ourselves. And in this opinion they all agree. Homer speaks of

"Old Oceanus,
The sire of gods, and Tethys;"[3]

and Orpheus (who, moreover, was the first to invent their names, and recounted their births, and narrated the exploits of each, and is believed by them to treat with greater truth than others of divine things, whom Homer himself follows in

[1] Hom. *Il.* xx. 131.
[2] Prov. xxi. 1.
[3] Hom. *Il.* xiv. 301, 302.

most matters, especially in reference to the gods)—he, too, has fixed their first origin to be from water:

"Oceanus, the origin of all."

For, according to him, water was the beginning of all things, and from water mud was formed, and from both was produced an animal, a dragon with the head of a lion growing to it, and between the two heads there was the face of a god, named Heracles and Kronos. This Heracles generated an egg of enormous size, which, on becoming full, was, by the powerful friction of its generator, burst into two, the part at the top receiving the form of heaven (*οὐρανός*), and the lower part that of earth (*γῆ*). The goddess Gê, moreover, came forth with a body; and Ouranos, by his union with Gê, begat females, Clotho, Lachesis, and Atropos; and males, the hundred-handed Cottys, Gyges, Briareus, and the Cyclopes Brontes, and Steropes, and Argos, whom also he bound and hurled down to Tartarus, having learnt that he was to be ejected from his government by his children; whereupon Gê, being enraged, brought forth the Titans.[1]

"The godlike Gaia bore to Ouranos
Sons who are by the name of Titans known,
Because they vengeance[2] took on Ouranos,
Majestic, glitt'ring with his starry crown."[3]

CHAP. XIX.—*The philosophers agree with the poets respecting the gods.*

Such was the beginning of the existence both of their gods and of the universe. Now what are we to make of this? For each of those things to which divinity is ascribed is conceived of as having existed from the first. For, if they have come into being, having previously had no existence, as those say who treat of the gods, they do not exist. For, a thing is either uncreated and eternal, or created and perishable. Nor do I think one thing and the philosophers another. "What is that which always is, and has no origin; or what is that which has been originated, yet never is?"[4] Discoursing of

[1] Hom. *Il.* xiv. 246.
[2] *τισάσθην.*
[3] Orpheus, *Fragments.*
[4] Plat. *Tim.* p. 27, D.

the intelligible and the sensible, Plato teaches that that which always is, the intelligible, is unoriginated, but that that which is not, the sensible, is originated, beginning to be and ceasing to exist. In like manner, the Stoics also say that all things will be burnt up and will again exist, the world receiving another beginning. But if, although there is, according to them, a twofold cause, one active and governing, namely providence, the other passive and changeable, namely matter, it is nevertheless impossible for the world, even though under the care of Providence, to remain in the same state, because it is created—how can the constitution of these gods remain, who are not self-existent,[1] but have been originated? And in what are the gods superior to matter, since they derive their constitution from water? But not even water, according to them, is the beginning of all things. From simple and homogeneous elements what could be constituted? Moreover, matter requires an artificer, and the artificer requires matter. For how could figures be made without matter or an artificer? Neither, again, is it reasonable that matter should be older than God; for the efficient cause must of necessity exist before the things that are made.

CHAP. XX.—*Absurd representations of the gods.*

If the absurdity of their theology were confined to saying that the gods were created, and owed their constitution to water, since I have demonstrated that nothing is made which is not also liable to dissolution, I might proceed to the remaining charges. But, on the one hand, they have described their bodily forms: speaking of Hercules, for instance, as a god in the shape of a dragon coiled up; of others as hundred-handed; of the daughter of Zeus, whom he begat of his mother Rhea; or of Demeter, as having two eyes in the natural order, and two in her forehead, and the face of an animal on the back part of her neck, and as having also horns, so that Rhea, frightened at her monster of a child, fled from her, and did not give her the breast (θηλή), whence mystically she is called Athêlâ, but commonly Phersephoné

1 Literally, "by nature."

and Koré, though she is not the same as Athênâ,[1] who is called Koré from the pupil of the eye;—and, on the other hand, they have described their admirable[2] achievements, as they deem them: how Kronos, for instance, castrated his father, and hurled him down from his chariot, and how he murdered his children, and swallowed the males of them; and how Zeus bound his father, and cast him down to Tartarus, as did Ouranos also to his sons, and fought with the Titans for the government; and how he persecuted his mother Rhea when she refused to wed him, and, she becoming a she-dragon, and he himself being changed into a dragon, bound her with what is called the Herculean knot, and accomplished his purpose, of which fact the rod of Hermes is a symbol; and again, how he violated his daughter Phersephoné, in this case also assuming the form of a dragon, and became the father of Dionysus. In face of narrations like these, I must say at least this much, What that is becoming or useful is there in such a history, that we must believe Kronos, Zeus, Koré, and the rest, to be gods? Is it the descriptions of their bodies? Why, what man of judgment and reflection will believe that a viper was begotten by a god (thus Orpheus:

> "But from the sacred womb Phanes begat
> Another offspring, horrible and fierce,
> In sight a frightful viper, on whose head
> Were hairs: its face was comely; but the rest,
> From the neck downwards, bore the aspect dire
> Of a dread dragon"[3]);

or who will admit that Phanes himself, being a first-born god (for he it was that was produced from the egg), has the body or shape of a dragon, or was swallowed by Zeus, that Zeus might be too large to be contained? For if they differ in no respect from the lowest brutes (since it is evident that the Deity must differ from the things of earth and those that are derived from matter), they are not gods. How, then, I ask, can we approach them as suppliants, when their origin

[1] *i.e.* Minerva.
[2] Or, "have accurately described."
[3] *Fragments.*

resembles that of cattle, and they themselves have the form of brutes, and are ugly to behold?

Chap. xxi.—*Impure loves ascribed to the gods.*

But should it be said that they only had fleshly forms, and possess blood and seed, and the affections of anger and sexual desire, even then we must regard such assertions as nonsensical and ridiculous; for there is neither anger, nor desire and appetite, nor procreative seed, in gods. Let them, then, have fleshly forms, but let them be superior to wrath and anger, that Athênâ may not be seen

"Burning with rage and inly wroth with Jove;"[1]

nor Hera appear thus:

"Juno's breast
Could not contain her rage."[2]

And let them be superior to grief:

"A woful sight mine eyes behold: a man
I love in flight around the walls! My heart
For Hector grieves."[3]

For I call even men rude and stupid who give way to anger and grief. But when the "father of men and gods" mourns for his son,

"Woe, woe! that fate decrees my best belov'd
Sarpedon, by Patroclus' hand to fall;"[4]

and is not able while he mourns to rescue him from his peril:

"The son of Jove, yet Jove preserv'd him not;"[5]

who would not blame the folly of those who, with tales like these, are lovers of the gods, or rather, live without any god? Let them have fleshly forms, but let not Aphrodité be wounded by Diomedes in her body:

"The haughty son of Tydeus, Diomed,
Hath wounded me;"[6]

---

[1] Hom. *Il.* iv. 23.
[2] *Ibid.* iv. 24.
[3] *Ibid.* xxii. 168 sq.
[4] *Ibid.* xvi. 433 sq.
[5] *Ibid.* xvi. 522.
[6] *Ibid.* v. 376.

or by Arês in her soul:

> "Me, awkward me, she scorns; and yields her charms
> To that fair lecher, the strong god of arms."[1]
> "The weapon pierced the flesh."[2]

He who was terrible in battle, the ally of Zeus against the Titans, is shown to be weaker than Diomedes:

> "He raged, as Mars, when brandishing his spear."[3]

Hush! Homer, a god never rages. But you describe the god to me as blood-stained, and the bane of mortals:

> "Mars, Mars, the bane of mortals, stained with blood;"[4]

and you tell of his adultery and his bonds:

> "Then, nothing loth, th' enamour'd fair he led,
> And sunk transported on the conscious bed.
> Down rushed the toils."[5]

Do they not pour forth impious stuff of this sort in abundance concerning the gods? Ouranos is castrated; Kronos is bound, and thrust down to Tartarus; the Titans revolt; Styx dies in battle: yea, they even represent them as mortal; they are in love with one another; they are in love with human beings:

> "Æneas, amid Ida's jutting peaks,
> Immortal Venus to Anchises bore."[6]

Are they not in love? Do they not suffer? Nay, verily, they are gods, and desire cannot touch them! Even though a god assume flesh in pursuance of a divine purpose, is he therefore the slave of desire?

> "For never yet did such a flood of love,
> For goddess or for mortal, fill my soul;
> Not for Ixion's beauteous wife, who bore
> Pïrithöus, sage in council as the gods;
> Nor the neat-footed maiden Danäe,
> Acrisius' daughter, her who Perséus bore,
> Th' observ'd of all; nor noble Phœnix' child;
> . . . . . nor for Semele;

---

[1] Hom. *Od.* viii. 308 sq., Pope's transl.
[2] Hom. *Il.* v. 858.
[3] *Ibid.* 605.
[4] *Ibid.* 531.
[5] Hom. *Od.* viii. 296–298, Pope's transl.
[6] Hom. *Il.* ii. 820.

Nor for Alcmena fair; . . .
No, nor for Ceres, golden-tressèd queen;
Nor for Latona bright; nor for thyself."[1]

He is created, he is perishable, with no trace of a god in him. Nay, they are even the hired servants of men:

"Admetus' halls, in which I have endured
To praise the menial table, though a god."[2]

And they tend cattle:

"And coming to this land, I cattle fed,
For him that was my host, and kept this house."[3]

Admetus, therefore, was superior to the god. O prophet and wise one, and who canst foresee for others the things that shall be, thou didst not divine the slaughter of thy beloved, but didst even kill him with thine own hand, dear as he was:

"And I believed Apollo's mouth divine
Was full of truth, as well as prophet's art.

(Æschylus is reproaching Apollo for being a false prophet:)

The very one who sings while at the feast,
The one who said these things, alas! is he
Who slew my son."[4]

CHAP. XXII.—*Pretended symbolical explanations.*

But perhaps these things are poetic vagary, and there is some natural explanation of them, such as this by Empedocles:

"Let Jove be fire, and Juno source of life,
With Pluto and Nêstis, who bathes with tears
The human founts."

If, then, Zeus is fire, and Hera the earth, and Aïdoneus the air, and Nêstis water, and these are elements—fire, water, air—none of them is a god, neither Zeus, nor Hera, nor

[1] Hom. *Il.* xiv. 315 sqq.
[2] Eurip. *Alcest.* 1 sq. [3] *Ibid.* 8 sq.
[4] From an unknown play of Æschylus.

Aïdoneus; for from matter separated into parts by God is their constitution and origin:

> "Fire, water, earth, and the air's gentle height,
> And harmony with these."

Here are things which without harmony cannot abide; which would be brought to ruin by strife: how then can any one say that they are gods? Friendship, according to Empedocles, has an aptitude to govern, things that are compounded are governed, and that which is apt to govern has the dominion; so that if we make the power of the governed and the governing one and the same, we shall be, unawares to ourselves, putting perishable and fluctuating and changeable matter on an equality with the uncreated, and eternal, and ever self-accordant God. Zeus is, according to the Stoics, the fervid part of nature; Hera is the air (ἀήρ)—the very name, if it be joined to itself, signifying this;[1] Poseidon is what is drunk (water, πόσις). But these things are by different persons explained of natural objects in different ways. Some call Zeus twofold masculine-feminine air; others the season which brings about mild weather, on which account it was that he alone escaped from Kronos. But to the Stoics it may be said, If you acknowledge one God, the supreme and uncreated and eternal One, and as many compound bodies as there are changes of matter, and say that the Spirit of God, which pervades matter, obtains according to its variations a diversity of names, the forms of matter will become the body of God; but when the elements are destroyed in the conflagration, the names will necessarily perish along with the forms, the Spirit of God alone remaining. Who, then, can believe that those bodies, of which the variation according to matter is allied to corruption, are gods? But to those who say that Kronos is time, and Rhea the earth, and that she becomes pregnant by Kronos, and brings forth, whence she is regarded as the mother of all; and that he begets and devours his offspring; and that the castration is the intercourse of the male with the female, which cuts off

[1] Perhaps ἥρ(αηρ)α.

the seed and casts it into the womb, and generates a human being, who has in himself the sexual desire, which is Aphrodité; and that the madness of Kronos is the turn of season, which destroys animate and inanimate things; and that the bonds and Tartarus are time, which is changed by seasons and disappears;—to such persons we say, If Kronos is time, he changes; if a season, he turns about; if darkness, or frost, or the moist part of nature, none of these is abiding; but the Deity is immortal, and immoveable, and unalterable: so that neither is Kronos nor his image God. As regards Zeus again: If he is air, born of Kronos, of which the male part is called Zeus and the female Hera (whence both sister and wife), he is subject to change; if a season, he turns about: but the Deity neither changes nor shifts about. But why should I trespass on your patience by saying more, when you know so well what has been said by each of those who have resolved these things into nature, or what various writers have thought concerning nature, or what they say concerning Athênâ, whom they affirm to be the wisdom (φρόνησις) pervading all things; and concerning Isis, whom they call the birth of all time (φύσις αἰῶνος), from whom all have sprung, and by whom all exist; or concerning Osiris, on whose murder by Typhon his brother Isis with her son Orus sought after his limbs, and finding them honoured them with a sepulchre, which sepulchre is to this day called the tomb of Osiris? For whilst they wander up and down about the forms of matter, they miss to find the God who can only be beheld by the reason, while they deify the elements and their several parts, applying different names to them at different times: calling the sowing of the corn, for instance, Osiris (hence they say, that in the mysteries, on the finding of the members of his body, or the fruits, Isis is thus addressed: We have found, we wish thee joy), the fruit of the vine Dionysus, the vine itself Semelé, the heat of the sun the thunderbolt. And yet, in fact, they who refer the fables to actual gods, do anything rather than add to their divine character; for they do not perceive, that by the very defence they make for the gods, they confirm the things which are alleged concerning them.

What have Europa, and the bull, and the swan, and Leda, to do with the earth and air, that the abominable intercourse of Zeus with them should be taken for the intercourse of the earth and air? But missing to discover the greatness of God, and not being able to rise on high with their reason (for they have no affinity for the heavenly place), they pine away among the forms of matter, and rooted to the earth, deify the changes of the elements: just as if any one should put the ship he sailed in in the place of the steersman. But as the ship, although equipped with everything, is of no use if it have not a steersman, so neither are the elements, though arranged in perfect order, of any service apart from the providence of God. For the ship will not sail of itself; and the elements without their Framer will not move.

CHAP. XXIII.—*Opinions of Thales and Plato.*

You may say, however, since you excel all men in understanding, How comes it to pass, then, that some of the idols manifest power, if those to whom we erect the statues are not gods? For it is not likely that images destitute of life and motion can of themselves do anything without a mover. That in various places, cities, and nations, certain effects are brought about in the name of idols, we are far from denying. None the more, however, if some have received benefit, and others, on the contrary, suffered harm, shall we deem those to be gods who have produced the effects in either case. But I have made careful inquiry, both why it is that you think the idols to have this power, and who they are that, usurping their names, produce the effects. It is necessary for me, however, in attempting to show who they are that produce the effects ascribed to the idols, and that they are not gods, to have recourse to some witnesses from among the philosophers. First Thales, as those who have accurately examined his opinions report, divides [superior beings] into God, demons, and heroes. God he recognises as the Intelligence (*νοῦς*) of the world; by demons he understands beings possessed of soul (*ψυχικαί*); and by heroes the separated souls of men, the good being the good souls, and the bad the worthless. Plato again, while withholding his assent on other points, also divides [superior beings] into the uncreated God and those produced by the uncreated One for the adornment of heaven, the planets, and the fixed stars, and into demons; concerning which demons, while he does not think fit to speak himself, he thinks that those ought to be listened to who have spoken about them. "To speak concerning the other demons, and to know their origin, is beyond our powers; but we ought to believe those who have before spoken, the descendants of gods, as they say—and surely they must be well acquainted with their own ancestors: it is impossible, therefore, to disbelieve the sons of gods, even though they speak without probable or convincing proofs; but as they profess to tell of their own family affairs, we are bound, in pursuance of custom, to believe them. In this way, then, let us hold and speak as they do concerning the origin of the gods themselves. Of Gê and Ouranos were born Oceanus and Tethys; and of these Phorcus, Kronos, and Rhea, and the rest; and of Kronos and Rhea, Zeus, Hera, and all the others, who, we know, are all called their brothers; besides other descendants again of these."[1] Did, then, he who had contemplated the eternal Intelligence and God who is apprehended by reason, and declared His attributes—His real existence, the simplicity of His nature, the good that flows forth from Him that is truth, and discoursed of primal power, and how "all things are about the King of all, and all things exist for His sake, and He is the cause of all;" and about two and three, that He is "the second moving about the seconds, and the third about the thirds;"[2]—did this man think, that to learn the truth concerning those who are said to have been produced from sensible things, namely earth and heaven, was a task transcending his powers? It is not to be believed for a moment. But because he thought it impossible to believe that gods beget and are brought forth, since everything that begins to be is followed by an end, and (for this is much more difficult) to change the views of the multitude, who receive the fables

[1] *Tim.* p. 40, D. E.

[2] Pseudo-Plat. *Epist.* ii. p. 312, D. E. The meaning is very obscure.

without examination, on this account it was that he declared it to be beyond his powers to know and to speak concerning the origin of the other demons, since he was unable either to admit or teach that gods were begotten. And as regards that saying of his, "The great sovereign in heaven, Zeus, driving a winged car, advances first, ordering and managing all things, and there follow him a host of gods and demons,"[1] this does not refer to the Zeus who is said to have sprung from Kronos; for here the name is given to the Maker of the universe. This is shown by Plato himself: not being able to designate Him by another title that should be suitable, he availed himself of the popular name, not as peculiar to God, but for distinctness, because it is not possible to discourse of God to all men as fully as one might; and he adds at the same time the epithet "Great," so as to distinguish the heavenly from the earthly, the uncreated from the created, who is younger than heaven and earth, and younger than the Cretans, who stole him away, that he might not be killed by his father.

CHAP. XXIV.—*Concerning the angels and giants.*

What need is there, in speaking to you who have searched into every department of knowledge, to mention the poets, or to examine opinions of another kind? Let it suffice to say thus much. If the poets and philosophers did not acknowledge that there is one God, and concerning these gods were not of opinion, some that they are demons, others that they are matter, and others that they once were men,—there might be some show of reason for our being harassed as we are, since we employ language which makes a distinction between God and matter, and the natures of the two. For, as we acknowledge a God, and a Son his Logos, and a Holy Spirit, united in essence,—the Father, the Son, the Spirit, because the Son is the Intelligence, Reason, Wisdom of the Father, and the Spirit an effluence, as light from fire; so also do we apprehend the existence of other powers, which exercise dominion about matter, and by means of it, and one in par-

[1] Plat. *Phædr.* p. 246, E.

ticular, which is hostile to God: not that anything is really opposed to God, like strife to friendship, according to Empedocles, and night to day, according to the appearing and disappearing of the stars (for even if anything *had* placed itself in opposition to God, it would have ceased to exist, its structure being destroyed by the power and might of God), but that to the good that is in God, which belongs of necessity to Him, and co-exists with Him, as colour with body, without which it has no existence (not as being part of it, but as an attendant property co-existing with it, united and blended, just as it is natural for fire to be yellow and the ether dark blue),—to the good that is in God, I say, the spirit which is about matter, who was created by God, just as the other angels were created by Him, and entrusted with the control of matter and the forms of matter, is opposed. For this is the office of the angels,—to exercise providence for God over the things created and ordered by Him; so that God may have the universal and general providence of the whole, while the particular parts are provided for by the angels appointed over them. Just as with men, who have freedom of choice as to both virtue and vice (for you would not either honour the good or punish the bad, unless vice and virtue were in their own power; and some are diligent in the matters entrusted to them by you, and others faithless), so is it among the angels. Some, free agents, you will observe, such as they were created by God, continued in those things for which God had made and over which He had ordained them; but some outraged both the constitution of their nature and the government entrusted to them: namely, this ruler of matter and its various forms, and others of those who were placed about this first firmament (you know that we say nothing without witnesses, but state the things which have been declared by the prophets); these fell into impure love of virgins, and were subjugated by the flesh, and he became negligent and wicked in the management of the things entrusted to him. Of these lovers of virgins, therefore, were begotten those who are called giants. And if something has been said by the poets, too, about the giants, be not surprised at this: worldly wisdom and divine differ as much from each other as truth and plausibility: the one is of heaven and the other of earth; and, indeed, according to the prince of matter,

> "We know we oft speak lies that look like truths."[1]

CHAP. XXV.—*The poets and philosophers have denied a divine Providence.*

These angels, then, who have fallen from heaven, and haunt the air and the earth, and are no longer able to rise to heavenly things, and the souls of the giants, which are the demons who wander about the world, perform actions similar, the one (that is, the demons) to the natures they have received, the other (that is, the angels) to the appetites they have indulged. But the prince of matter, as may be seen merely from what transpires, exercises a control and management contrary to the good that is in God:

> "Ofttimes this anxious thought has crossed my mind,
> Whether 'tis chance or deity that rules
> The small affairs of men; and, spite of hope
> As well as justice, drives to exile some
> Stripped of all means of life, while others still
> Continue to enjoy prosperity."[2]

Prosperity and adversity, contrary to hope and justice, made it impossible for Euripides to say to whom belongs the administration of earthly affairs, which is of such a kind that one might say of it:

> "How then, while seeing these things, can we say
> There is a race of gods, or yield to laws?"[3]

The same thing led Aristotle to say that the things below the heaven are not under the care of Providence, although the eternal providence of God concerns itself equally with us below—

> "The earth, let willingness move her or not,
> Must herbs produce, and thus sustain my flocks"[4]—

---

[1] Hesiod, *Theog.* 27.
[2] Eurip.: from an unknown play.
[3] *Ibid.* [4] Eurip. *Cycl.* 332 sq.

and addresses itself to the deserving individually, according to truth and not according to opinion; and all other things, according to the general constitution of nature, are provided for by the law of reason. But because the demoniac movements and operations proceeding from the adverse spirit produce these disorderly sallies, and moreover move men, some in one way and some in another, as individuals and as nations, separately and in common, in accordance with the tendency of matter on the one hand, and of the affinity for divine things on the other, from within and from without,—some who are of no mean reputation have therefore thought that this universe is constituted without any definite order, and is driven hither and thither by an irrational chance. But they do not understand, that of those things which belong to the constitution of the whole world there is nothing out of order or neglected, but that each one of them has been produced by reason, and that, therefore, they do not transgress the order prescribed to them; and that man himself, too, so far as He that made him is concerned, is well ordered, both by his original nature, which has one common character for all, and by the constitution of his body, which does not transgress the law imposed upon it, and by the termination of his life, which remains equal and common to all alike; but that, according to the character peculiar to himself and the operation of the ruling prince and of the demons his followers, he is impelled and moved in this direction or in that, notwithstanding that all possess in common the same original constitution of mind.[1]

CHAP. XXVI.—*The demons allure men to the worship of images.*

They who draw men to idols, then, are the aforesaid demons, who are eager for the blood of the sacrifices, and lick them; but the gods that please the multitude, and whose names are given to the images, were men, as may be learned from their history. And that it is the demons who act under their names, is proved by the nature of their operations. For some castrate, as Rhea; others wound and slaughter, as

[1] Or, "powers of reasoning" (λογισμός).

Artemis; the Tauric goddess puts all strangers to death. I pass over those who lacerate with knives and scourges of bones, and shall not attempt to describe all the kinds of demons; for it is not the part of a god to incite to things against nature.

> "But when the demon plots against a man,
> He first inflicts some hurt upon his mind."[1]

But God, being perfectly good, is eternally doing good. That, moreover, those who exert the power are not the same as those to whom the statues are erected, very strong evidence is afford by Troas and Parium. The one has statues of Neryllinus, a man of our own times; and Parium of Alexander and Proteus: both the sepulchre and the statue of Alexander are still in the forum. The other statues of Neryllinus, then, are a public ornament, if indeed a city can be adorned by such objects as these; but one of them is supposed to utter oracles and to heal the sick, and on this account the people of the Troad offer sacrifices to this statue, and overlay it with gold, and hang chaplets upon it. But of the statues of Alexander and Proteus (the latter, you are aware, threw himself into the fire near Olympia), that of Proteus is likewise said to utter oracles; and to that of Alexander—

> "Wretched Paris, though in form so fair,
> Thou slave of woman"[2]—

sacrifices are offered and festivals are held at the public cost, as to a god who can hear. Is it, then, Neryllinus, and Proteus, and Alexander who exert these energies in connection with the statues, or is it the nature of the matter itself? But the matter is brass. And what can brass do of itself, which may be made again into a different form, as Amasis treated the footpan, as told by Herodotus? And Neryllinus, and Proteus, and Alexander, what good are they to the sick? For what the image is said now to effect, it effected when Neryllinus was alive and sick.

[1] From an unknown tragedian. [2] Hom. *Il.* iii. 39.

Chap. xxvii.—*Artifices of the demons.*

What then? In the first place, the irrational and fantastic movements of the soul about opinions produce a diversity of images (εἴδωλα) from time to time: some they derive from matter, and some they fashion and bring forth for themselves; and this happens to a soul especially when it partakes of the material spirit and becomes mingled with it, looking not at heavenly things and their Maker, but downwards to earthly things, wholly at the earth, as being now mere flesh and blood, and no longer pure spirit. These irrational and fantastic movements of the soul, then, give birth to empty visions in the mind, by which it becomes madly set on idols. When, too, a tender and susceptible soul, which has no knowledge or experience of sounder doctrines, and is unaccustomed to contemplate truth, and to consider thoughtfully the Father and Maker of all things, gets impressed with false opinions respecting itself, then the demons who hover about matter, greedy of sacrificial odours and the blood of victims, and ever ready to lead men into error, avail themselves of these delusive movements of the souls of the multitude; and, taking possession of their thoughts, cause to flow into the mind empty visions as if coming from the idols and the statues; and when, too, a soul of itself, as being immortal, moves conformably to reason, either predicting the future or healing the present, the demons claim the glory for themselves.

Chap. xxviii.—*The heathen gods were simply men.*

But it is perhaps necessary, in accordance with what has already been adduced, to say a little about their names. Herodotus, then, and Alexander the son of Philip, in his letter to his mother (and each of them is said to have conversed with the priests at Heliopolis, and Memphis, and Thebes), affirm that they learnt from them that the gods had been men. Herodotus speaks thus: "Of such a nature were, they said, the beings represented by these images, they were very far indeed from being gods. However, in the times anterior to them it was otherwise; then Egypt had gods for its rulers, who dwelt upon the earth with men, one being always supreme above the rest. The last of these was Horus the son of Osiris, called by the Greeks Apollo. He deposed Typhon, and ruled over Egypt as its last god-king. Osiris is named Dionysus (Bacchus) by the Greeks."[1] "Almost all the names of the gods came into Greece from Egypt."[2] Apollo was the son of Dionysus and Isis, as Herodotus likewise affirms: "According to the Egyptians, Apollo and Diana are the children of Bacchus and Isis; while Latona is their nurse and their preserver."[3] These beings of heavenly origin they had for their first kings: partly from ignorance of the true worship of the Deity, partly from gratitude for their government, they esteemed them as gods together with their wives. "The male kine, if clean, and the male calves, are used for sacrifice by the Egyptians universally; but the females, they are not allowed to sacrifice, since they are sacred to Isis. The statue of this goddess has the form of a woman, but with horns like a cow, resembling those of the Greek representations of Io."[4] And who can be more deserving of credit in making these statements, than those who in family succession, son from father, received not only the priesthood, but also the history? For it is not likely that the priests, who make it their business to commend the idols to men's reverence, would assert falsely that they were men. If Herodotus alone had said that the Egyptians spoke in their histories of the gods as of men, when he says, "What they told me concerning their religion it is not my intention to repeat, except only the names of their deities, things of very trifling importance,"[5] it would behove us not to credit even Herodotus as being a fabulist. But as Alexander and Hermes surnamed Trismegistus, who shares with them in the attribute of eternity, and innumerable others, not to name them indi-

[1] ii. 144. Mr Rawlinson's translation is used in the extracts from Herodotus.

[2] ii. 50. [3] ii. 156. [4] ii. 41.

[5] ii. 3. The text is here uncertain, and differs from that of Herodotus.

vidually, [declare the same], no room is left even for doubt that they, being kings, were esteemed gods. That they were men, the most learned of the Egyptians also testify, who, while saying that ether, earth, sun, moon, are gods, regard the rest as mortal men, and the temples as their sepulchres. Apollodorus, too, asserts the same thing in his treatise concerning the gods. But Herodotus calls even their sufferings mysteries. "The ceremonies at the feast of Isis in the city of Busiris have been already spoken of. It is there that the whole multitude, both of men and women, many thousands in number, beat themselves at the close of the sacrifice in honour of a god whose name a religious scruple forbids me to mention."[1] If they are gods, they are also immortal; but if people are beaten for them, and their sufferings are mysteries, they are men, as Herodotus himself says: "Here, too, in this same precinct of Minerva at Saïs, is the burial-place of one whom I think it not right to mention in such a connection. It stands behind the temple against the back wall, which it entirely covers. There are also some large stone obelisks in the enclosure, and there is a lake near them, adorned with an edging of stone. In form it is circular, and in size, as it seemed to me, about equal to the lake at Delos called the Hoop. On this lake it is that the Egyptians represent by night his sufferings whose name I refrain from mentioning, and this representation they call their mysteries."[2] And not only is the sepulchre of Osiris shown, but also his embalming: "When a body is brought to them, they show the bearer various models of corpses made in wood, and painted so as to resemble nature. The most perfect is said to be after the manner of him whom I do not think it religious to name in connection with such a matter."[3]

CHAP. XXIX.—*Proof of the same from the poets.*

But among the Greeks, also, those who are eminent in poetry and history say the same thing. Thus of Heracles:

> "That lawless wretch, that man of brutal strength,
> Deaf to Heaven's voice, the social rite transgressed."[4]

[1] ii. 61. [2] ii. 170. [3] ii. 86. [4] Hom. *Od.* xxi. 28 sq.

Such being his nature, deservedly did he go mad, and deservedly did he light the funeral pile and burn himself to death. Of Asklepius, Hesiod says:

> "The mighty father both of gods and men
> Was filled with wrath, and from Olympus' top
> With flaming thunderbolt cast down and slew
> Latona's well-lov'd son—such was his ire."[1]

And Pindar:

> "But even wisdom is ensnared by gain.
> The brilliant bribe of gold seen in the hand
> Ev'n him[2] perverted: therefore Kronos' son
> With both hands quickly stopp'd his vital breath,
> And by a bolt of fire ensured his doom."[3]

Either, therefore, they were gods and did not hanker after gold—

> "O gold, the fairest prize to mortal men,
> Which neither mother equals in delight,
> Nor children dear"[4]—

for the Deity is in want of nought, and is superior to carnal desire, nor did they die; or, having been born men, they were wicked by reason of ignorance, and overcome by love of money. What more need I say, or refer to Castor, or Pollux, or Amphiarus, who, having been born, so to speak, only the other day, men of men, are looked upon as gods, when they imagine even Ino after her madness and its consequent sufferings to have become a goddess?

> "Sea-rovers will her name Leucothea,"[5]

And her son:

> "August Palæmon, sailors will invoke."

CHAP. XXX.—*Reasons why divinity has been ascribed to men.*

For if detestable and god-hated men had the reputation of being gods, and the daughter of Derceto, Semiramis, a lascivious and blood-stained woman, was esteemed a Syrian

---

1 Hesiod, *Frag.* 2 *i.e.* Æsculapius. 3 *Pyth.* iii. 96 sq.
4 Ascribed by Seneca to the *Bellerophon* of Eurip.
5 From the *Ino* of Eurip.

goddess; and if, on account of Derceto, the Syrians worship doves and Semiramis (for, a thing impossible, a woman was changed into a dove: the story is in Ctesias), what wonder if some should be called gods by their people on the ground of their rule and sovereignty (the Sibyl, of whom Plato also makes mention, says:

> "It was the generation then the tenth,
> Of men endow'd with speech, since forth the flood
> Had burst upon the men of former times,
> And Kronos, Japetus, and Titan reigned,
> Whom men, of Ouranos and Gaïa
> Proclaimed the noblest sons, and named them so,[1]
> Because of men endowed with gift of speech
> They were the first"); [2]

and others for their strength, as Heracles and Perseus; and others for their art, as Asclepius? Those, therefore, to whom either the subjects gave honour or the rulers themselves [assumed it], obtained the name, some from fear, others from reverence. Thus Antinous, through the benevolence of your ancestors towards their subjects, came to be regarded as a god. But those who came after adopted the worship without examination.

> "The Cretans always lie; for they, O king,
> Have built a tomb to thee who art not dead."[3]

Though you believe, O Callimachus, in the nativity of Zeus, you do not believe in his sepulchre; and whilst you think to obscure the truth, you in fact proclaim him dead, even to those who are ignorant; and if you see the cave, you call to mind the childbirth of Rhea; but when you see the coffin, you throw a shadow over his death, not considering that the unbegotten God alone is eternal. For either the tales told by the multitude and the poets about the gods are unworthy of credit, and the reverence shown them is superfluous (for those do not exist, the tales concerning whom are untrue);

[1] *i.e.* after Gaia and Ouranos, *Earth* and *Heaven*.
[2] Oracc. *Sibyll.* iii. 108–113.
[3] Callim. *Hym. Jov.* 8 sq.

or if the births, the amours, the murders, the thefts, the castrations, the thunderbolts, are true, they no longer exist, having ceased to be since they were born, having previously had no being. And on what principle must we believe some things and disbelieve others, when the poets have written their stories in order to gain greater veneration for them? For surely those through whom they have got to be considered gods, and who have striven to represent their deeds as worthy of reverence, cannot have invented their sufferings. That, therefore, we are not atheists, acknowledging as we do God the Maker of this universe and His Logos, has been proved according to my ability, if not according to the importance of the subject.

Chap. xxxi.—*Confutation of the other charges brought against the Christians.*

But they have further also made up stories against us of impious feasts and forbidden intercourse between the sexes, both that they may appear to themselves to have rational grounds of hatred, and because they think either by fear to lead us away from our way of life, or to render the rulers harsh and inexorable by the magnitude of the charges they bring. But they lose their labour with those who know that from of old it has been the custom, and not in our time only, for vice to make war on virtue. Thus Pythagoras, with three hundred others, was burnt to death; Heraclitus and Democritus were banished, the one from the city of the Ephesians, the other from Abdera, because he was charged with being mad; and the Athenians condemned Socrates to death. But as they were none the worse in respect of virtue because of the opinion of the multitude, so neither does the undiscriminating calumny of some persons cast any shade upon us as regards rectitude of life, for with God we stand in good repute. Nevertheless, I will meet these charges also, although I am well assured that by what has been already said I have cleared myself to you. For as you excel all men in intelligence, you know that those whose life is directed towards God as its rule, so that each one among us may be blameless and irreproachable before Him, will not entertain even the thought of the slightest sin. For if we believed that we should live only the present life, then we might be suspected of sinning, through being enslaved to flesh and blood, or overmastered by gain or carnal desire; but since we know that God is witness to what we think and what we say both by night and by day, and that He, being Himself light, sees all things in our heart, we are persuaded that when we are removed from the present life we shall live another life, better than the present one, and heavenly, not earthly (since we shall abide near God, and with God, free from all change or suffering in the soul, not as flesh, even though we shall have flesh, but as heavenly spirit), or, falling with the rest, a worse one and in fire; for God has not made us as sheep or beasts of burden, a mere by-work, and that we should perish and be annihilated. On these grounds it is not likely that we should wish to do evil, or deliver ourselves over to the great Judge to be punished.

CHAP. XXXII.—*Elevated morality of the Christians.*

It is, however, nothing wonderful that they should get up tales about us such as they tell of their own gods, of the incidents of whose lives they make mysteries. But it behoved them, if they meant to condemn shameless and promiscuous intercourse, to hate either Zeus, who begat children of his mother Rhea and his daughter Koré, and took his own sister to wife, or Orpheus, the inventor of these tales, which made Zeus more unholy and detestable than Thyestes himself; for the latter defiled his daughter in pursuance of an oracle, and when he wanted to obtain the kingdom and avenge himself. But we are so far from practising promiscuous intercourse, that it is not lawful among us to indulge even a lustful look. "For," saith He, "he that looketh on a woman to lust after her, hath committed adultery already in his heart."[1] Those, then, who are forbidden to look at anything more than that for which God formed the eyes, which were intended to be a light to us, and to whom a wanton look is adultery, the

[1] Matt. v. 28.

eyes being made for other purposes, and who are to be called to account for their very thoughts, how can any one doubt that such persons practise self-control? For our account lies not with human laws, which a bad man can evade (at the outset I proved to you, sovereign lords, that our doctrine is from the teaching of God), but we have a law which makes the measure of rectitude to consist in dealing with our neighbour as ourselves.[1] On this account, too, according to age, we recognise some as sons and daughters, others we regard as brothers and sisters, and to the more advanced in life we give the honour due to fathers and mothers. On behalf of those, then, to whom we apply the names of brothers and sisters, and other designations of relationship, we exercise the greatest care that their bodies should remain undefiled and uncorrupted; for the Logos again says to us, "If any one kiss a second time because it has given him pleasure, [he sins];" adding, "Therefore the kiss, or rather the salutation, should be given with the greatest care, since, if there be mixed with it the least defilement of thought, it excludes us from eternal life."[2]

CHAP. XXXIII.—*Chastity of the Christians with respect to marriage.*

Therefore, having the hope of eternal life, we despise the things of this life, even to the pleasures of the soul, each of us reckoning her his wife whom he has married according to the laws laid down by us, and that only for the purpose of having children. For as the husbandman throwing the seed into the ground awaits the harvest, not sowing more upon it, so to us the procreation of children is the measure of our indulgence in appetite. Nay, you would find many among us, both men and women, growing old unmarried, in the hope of living in closer communion with God. But if the remaining in virginity and in the state of an eunuch brings nearer

[1] Otto translates: "which has made us and our neighbours attain the highest degree of rectitude." The text is obscure, but the above seems the probable meaning: comp. Matt. xxii. 39, etc.

[2] Probably from some apocryphal writing.

to God, while the indulgence of carnal thought and desire leads away from Him, in those cases in which we shun the thoughts, much more do we reject the deeds. For we bestow our attention, not on the study of words, but on the exhibition and teaching of actions,—that a person should either remain as he was born, or be content with one marriage; for a second marriage is only a specious adultery. "For whosoever puts away his wife," says He, "and marries another, commits adultery;"[1] not permitting a man to send her away whose virginity he has brought to an end, nor to marry again. For he who deprives himself of his first wife, even though she be dead, is a cloaked adulterer, resisting the hand of God, because in the beginning God made one man and one woman, and dissolving the strictest union of flesh with flesh, formed for the intercourse of the race.

CHAP. XXXIV.—*The vast difference in morals between the Christians and their accusers.*

But though such is our character (Oh! why should I speak of things unfit to be uttered?), the things said of us are an example of the proverb, "The harlot reproves the chaste." For those who have set up a market for fornication, and established infamous resorts for the young for every kind of vile pleasure,—who do not abstain even from males, males with males committing shocking abominations, outraging all the noblest and comeliest bodies in all sorts of ways, so dishonouring the fair workmanship of God (for beauty on earth is not self-made, but sent hither by the hand and will of God),—these men, I say, revile us for the very things which they are conscious of themselves, and ascribe to their own gods, boasting of them as noble deeds, and worthy of the gods. These adulterers and pæderasts defame the eunuchs and the once-married (while they themselves live like fishes; for these gulp down whatever falls in their way, and the stronger chases the weaker: and, in fact, this is to feed upon human flesh, to do violence in contravention of the very laws which you and your ancestors, with due care for all that is fair and right,

[1] Matt. xix. 9.

have enacted), so that not even the governors of the provinces sent by you suffice for the hearing of the complaints against those, to whom it even is not lawful, when they are struck, not to offer themselves for more blows, nor when defamed not to bless: for it is not enough to be just (and justice is to return like for like), but it is incumbent on us to be good and patient of evil.

Chap. xxxv.—*The Christians condemn and detest all cruelty.*

What man of sound mind, therefore, will affirm, while such is our character, that we are murderers? For we cannot eat human flesh till we have killed some one. The former charge, therefore, being false, if any one should ask them in regard to the second, whether they have seen what they assert, not one of them would be so barefaced as to say that he had. And yet we have slaves, some more and some fewer, by whom we could not help being seen; but even of these, not one has been found to invent even such things against us. For when they know that we cannot endure even to see a man put to death, though justly, who of them can accuse us of murder or cannibalism? Who does not reckon among the things of greatest interest the contests of gladiators and wild beasts, especially those which are given by you? But we, deeming that to see a man put to death is much the same as killing him, have abjured such spectacles. How, then, when we do not even look on, lest we should contract guilt and pollution, can we put people to death? And when we say that those women who use drugs to bring on abortion commit murder, and will have to give an account to God for the abortion, on what principle should we commit murder? For it does not belong to the same person to regard the very fœtus in the womb as a created being, and therefore an object of God's care, and when it has passed into life, to kill it; and not to expose an infant, because those who expose them are chargeable with child-murder, and on the other hand, when it has been reared to destroy it. But we are in all things always alike and the same, submitting ourselves to reason, and not ruling over it.

CHAP. XXXVI.—*Bearing of the doctrine of the resurrection on the practices of the Christians.*

Who, then, that believes in a resurrection, would make himself into a tomb for bodies that will rise again? For it is not the part of the same persons to believe that our bodies will rise again, and to eat them as if they would not; and to think that the earth will give back the bodies held by it, but that those which a man has entombed in himself will not be demanded back. On the contrary, it is reasonable to suppose, that those who think they shall have no account to give of the present life, ill or well spent, and that there is no resurrection, but calculate on the soul perishing with the body, and being as it were quenched in it, will refrain from no deed of daring; but as for those who are persuaded that nothing will escape the scrutiny of God, but that even the body which has ministered to the irrational impulses of the soul, and to its desires, will be punished along with it, it is not likely that they will commit even the smallest sin. But if to any one it appears sheer nonsense that the body which has mouldered away, and been dissolved, and reduced to nothing, should be reconstructed, we certainly cannot with any reason be accused of wickedness with reference to those that believe not, but only of folly; for with the opinions by which we deceive ourselves we injure no one else. But that it is not our belief alone that bodies will rise again, but that many philosophers also hold the same view, it is out of place to show just now, lest we should be thought to introduce topics irrelevant to the matter in hand, either by speaking of the intelligible and the sensible, and the nature of these respectively, or by contending that the incorporeal is older than the corporeal, and that the intelligible precedes the sensible, although we become acquainted with the latter earliest, since the corporeal is formed from the incorporeal, by the combination with it of the intelligible, and that the sensible is formed from the intelligible; for nothing hinders, according to Pythagoras and Plato, that when the dissolution of bodies takes place, they should, from the very same elements of which they were constructed at first, be constructed again. But let us defer the discourse concerning the resurrection.

Chap. xxxvii.—*Entreaty to be fairly judged.*

And now do you, who are entirely in everything, by nature and by education, upright, and moderate, and benevolent, and worthy of your rule, now that I have disposed of the several accusations, and proved that we are pious, and gentle, and temperate in spirit, bend your royal head in approval. For who are more deserving to obtain the things they ask, than those who, like us, pray for your government, that you may, as is most equitable, receive the kingdom, son from father, and that your empire may receive increase and addition, all men becoming subject to your sway? And this is also for our advantage, that we may lead a peaceable and quiet life, and may ourselves readily perform all that is commanded us.

THE TREATISE OF ATHENAGORAS

THE ATHENIAN, PHILOSOPHER AND CHRISTIAN, ON THE RESURRECTION OF THE DEAD.

CHAP. I.—*Defence of the truth should precede discussions regarding it.*

BY the side of every opinion and doctrine which agrees with the truth of things, there springs up some falsehood; and it does so, not because it takes its rise naturally from some fundamental principle, or from some cause peculiar to the matter in hand, but because it is invented on purpose by men who set a value on the spurious seed, for its tendency to corrupt the truth. This is apparent, in the first place, from those who in former times addicted themselves to such inquiries, and their want of agreement with their predecessors and contemporaries, and then, not least, from the very confusion which marks the discussions that are now going on. For such men have left no truth free from their calumnious attacks—not the being of God, not His knowledge, not His operations, not those books which follow by a regular and strict sequence from these, and delineate for us the doctrines of piety. On the contrary, some of them utterly, and once for all, give up in despair the truth concerning these things, and some distort it to suit their own views, and some of set purpose doubt even of things which are palpably evident. Hence I think that those who bestow attention on such subjects should adopt two lines of argument, one in defence of the truth, another concerning the truth: that in defence of the truth, for disbelievers and doubters; that concerning the truth, for such as are candid and receive the truth with readiness. Accordingly it behoves those who wish to investigate these matters, to keep in view that which the necessity of the case in each instance requires, and to regulate their discussion by this; to accommodate the order of their treatment of these subjects to what is suitable to the occasion, and not for the sake of appearing always to preserve the same method, to disregard fitness and the place which properly belongs to each topic. For, so far as proof and the natural order are concerned, dissertations concerning the truth always take precedence of those in defence of it; but, for the purpose of greater utility, the order must be reversed, and arguments in defence of it precede those concerning it. For the farmer could not properly cast the seed into the ground, unless he first extirpated the wild wood, and whatever would be hurtful to the good seed; nor the physician introduce any wholesome medicines into the body that needed his care, if he did not previously remove the disease within, or stay that which was approaching. Neither surely can he who wishes to teach the truth persuade any one by speaking about it, so long as there is a false opinion lurking in the mind of his hearers, and barring the entrance of his arguments. And, therefore, from regard to greater utility, I myself sometimes place arguments in defence of the truth before those concerning the truth; and on the present occasion it appears to me, looking at the requirements of the case, not without advantage to follow the same method in treating of the resurrection. For in regard to this subject also we find some utterly disbelieving, and some others doubting, and even among those who have accepted the first principles some who are as much at a loss what to believe as those who doubt; the most unaccountable thing of all being, that they are in this state of mind without having any ground whatsoever in the matters themselves for their disbelief, or finding it possible to assign any reasonable cause why they disbelieve or experience any perplexity.

Chap. II.—*A resurrection is not impossible.*

Let us, then, consider the subject in the way I have indicated. If all disbelief does not arise from levity and inconsideration, but if it springs up in some minds on strong grounds and accompanied by the certainty which belongs to truth, [well and good]; for it then maintains the appearance of being just, when the thing itself to which their disbelief relates appears to them unworthy of belief; but to disbelieve things which are not deserving of disbelief, is the act of men who do not employ a sound judgment about the truth. It behoves, therefore, those who disbelieve or doubt concerning the resurrection, to form their opinion on the subject, not from any view they have hastily adopted, and from what is acceptable to profligate men, but either to assign the origin of men to no cause (a notion which is very easily refuted), or, ascribing the cause of all things to God, to keep steadily in view the principle involved in this article of belief, and from this to demonstrate that the resurrection is utterly unworthy of credit. This they will succeed in, if they are able to show that it is either impossible for God, or contrary to His will, to unite and gather together again bodies that are dead, or even entirely dissolved into their elements, so as to constitute the same persons. If they cannot do this, let them cease from this godless disbelief, and from this blasphemy against sacred things: for, that they do not speak the truth when they say that it is impossible, or not in accordance with the divine will, will clearly appear from what I am about to say. A thing is in strictness of language considered impossible to a person, when it is of such a kind that he either does not know what is to be done, or has not sufficient power for the proper doing of the thing known. For he who is ignorant of anything that requires to be done, is utterly unable either to attempt or to do what he is ignorant of; and he, too, who knows ever so well what has to be done, and by what means, and how, but either has no power at all to do the thing known, or not power sufficient, will not even make the attempt, if he be wise and consider his powers; and if he did attempt it without due consideration, he would not accomplish his purpose. But it is not possible for God to be ignorant, either of the nature of the bodies that are to be raised, as regards both the members entire and the particles of which they consist, or whither each of the dissolved particles passes, and what part of the elements has received that which is dissolved and has passed into that with which it has affinity, although to men it may appear quite impossible that what has again combined according to its nature with the universe should be separable from it again. For He from whom, antecedently to the peculiar formation of each, was not concealed either the nature of the elements of which the bodies of men were to consist, or the parts of these from which He was about to take what seemed to Him suitable for the formation of the human body, will manifestly, after the dissolution of the whole, not be ignorant whither each of the particles has passed which He took for the construction of each. For, viewed relatively to the order of things now obtaining among us, and the judgment we form concerning other matters, it is a greater thing to know beforehand that which has not yet come to pass; but, viewed relatively to the majesty and wisdom of God, both are according to nature, and it is equally easy to know beforehand things that have not yet come into existence, and to know things which have been dissolved.

CHAP. III.—*He who could create, can also raise up the dead.*

Moreover also, that His power is sufficient for the raising of dead bodies, is shown by the creation of these same bodies. For if, when they did not exist, He made at their first formation the bodies of men, and their original elements, He will, when they are dissolved, in whatever manner that may take place, raise them again with equal ease: for this, too, is equally possible to Him. And it is no damage to the argument, if some suppose the first beginnings to be from matter, or the bodies of men at least to be derived from the elements as the first materials, or from seed. For that power which could give shape to what is regarded by them as shapeless matter, and adorn it, when destitute of form and order, with many and diverse forms, and gather into one the several portions of the elements, and divide the seed which was one and simple into many, and organize that which was unorganized, and give life to that which had no life,—that same power can reunite what is dissolved, and raise up what is prostrate, and restore the dead to life again, and put the corruptible into a state of incorruption. And to the same Being it will belong, and to the same power and skill, to separate that which has been broken up and distributed among a multitude of animals of all kinds which are wont to have recourse to such bodies, and glut their appetite upon them,—to separate this, I say, and unite it again with the proper members and parts of members, whether it has passed into some one of those animals, or into many, or thence into others, or, after being dissolved along with these, has been carried back again to the original elements, resolved into these according to a natural law—a matter this which seems to have exceedingly confounded some, even of those admired for wisdom, who, I cannot tell why, think those doubts worthy of serious attention which are brought forward by the many.

CHAP. IV.—*Objection from the fact that some human bodies have become part of others.*

These persons, to wit, say that many bodies of those who have come to an unhappy death in shipwrecks and rivers have become food for fishes, and many of those who perish in war, or who from some other sad cause or state of things are deprived of burial, lie exposed to become the food of any animals which may chance to light upon them. Since, then, bodies are thus consumed, and the members and parts composing them are broken up and distributed among a great multitude of animals, and by means of nutrition become incorporated with the bodies of those that are nourished by them,—in the first place, they say, their separation from these is impossible; and besides this, in the second place, they adduce another circumstance more difficult still. When animals of the kind suitable for human food, which have fed on the bodies of men, pass through their stomach, and become incorporated with the bodies of those who have partaken of them, it is an absolute necessity, they say, that the parts of the bodies of men which have served as nourishment to the animals which have partaken of them should pass into other bodies of men, since the animals which meanwhile have been nourished by them convey the nutriment derived from those by whom they were nourished into those men of whom they become the nutriment. Then to this they tragically add the devouring of offspring perpetrated by people in famine and madness, and the children eaten by their own parents through the contrivance of enemies, and the celebrated Median feast, and the tragic banquet of Thyestes; and they add, moreover, other such like unheard-of occurrences which have taken place among Greeks and barbarians: and from these things they establish, as they suppose, the impossibility of the resurrection, on the ground that the same parts cannot rise again with one set of bodies, and with another as well; for that either the bodies of the former possessors cannot be reconstituted, the parts which composed them having passed into others, or that, these having been restored to the former, the bodies of the last possessors will come short.

CHAP. V.—*Reference to the processes of digestion and nutrition.*

But it appears to me that such persons, in the first place, are ignorant of the power and skill of Him that fashioned and regulates this universe, who has adapted to the nature and kind of each animal the nourishment suitable and correspondent to it, and has neither ordained that everything in nature shall enter into union and combination with every kind of body, nor is at any loss to separate what has been so united, but grants to the nature of each several created being or thing to do or to suffer what is naturally suited to it, and sometimes also hinders and allows or forbids whatever He wishes, and for the purpose He wishes; and, moreover, that they have not considered the power and nature of each of the creatures that nourish or are nourished. Otherwise they would have known that not everything which is taken for food under the pressure of outward necessity turns out to be suitable nourishment for the animal, but that some things no sooner come into contact with the plicatures of the stomach than they are wont to be corrupted, and are vomited or voided, or disposed of in some other way, so that not even for a little time do they undergo the first and natural digestion, much less become incorporated with that which is to be nourished; as also, that not even everything which has been digested in the stomach and received the first change actually arrives at the parts to be nourished, since some of it loses its nutritive power even in the stomach, and some during the second change, and the digestion that takes place in the liver is separated and passes into something else which is destitute of the power to nourish; nay, that the change which takes place in the liver does not all issue in nourishment to men, but the matter changed is separated as refuse according to its natural purpose; and that the nourishment which is left in the members and parts themselves that have to be nourished sometimes changes to something else, according as that predominates which is present in greater or less[1] abundance, and is apt to corrupt or to turn into itself that which comes near it.

CHAP. VI.—*Everything that is useless or hurtful is rejected.*

Since, therefore, great difference of nature obtains in all animals, and the very nourishment which is accordant with nature is varied to suit each kind of animal, and the body which is nourished; and as in the nourishment of every animal there is a threefold cleansing and separation, it follows that whatever is alien from the nourishment of the animal must be wholly destroyed and carried off to its natural place, or change into something else, since it cannot coalesce with it; that the power of the nourishing body must be suitable to the nature of the animal to be nourished, and accordant with its powers; and that this, when it has passed through the strainers appointed for the purpose, and been

[1] The common reading is "excessive."

thoroughly purified by the natural means of purification, must become a most genuine addition to the substance,—the only thing, in fact, which any one calling things by their right names would call nourishment at all; because it rejects everything that is foreign and hurtful to the constitution of the animal nourished, and that mass of superfluous food introduced merely for filling the stomach and gratifying the appetite. This nourishment, no one can doubt, becomes incorporated with the body that is nourished, interwoven and blended with all the members and parts of members; but that which is different and contrary to nature is speedily corrupted if brought into contact with a stronger power, but easily destroys that which is overcome by it, and is converted into hurtful humours and poisonous qualities, because producing nothing akin or friendly to the body which is to be nourished. And it is a very clear proof of this, that in many of the animals nourished, pain, or disease, or death follows from these things, if, owing to a too keen appetite, they take in mingled with their food something poisonous and contrary to nature; which, of course, would tend to the utter destruction of the body to be nourished, since that which is nourished is nourished by substances akin to it and which accord with its nature, but is destroyed by those of a contrary kind. If, therefore, according to the different nature of animals, different kinds of food have been provided suitable to their nature, and none of that which the animal may have taken, not even an accidental part of it, admits of being blended with the body which is nourished, but only that part which has been purified by an entire digestion, and undergone a complete change for union with a particular body, and adapted to the parts which are to receive nourishment,—it is very plain that none of the things contrary to nature can be united with those bodies for which it is not a suitable and correspondent nourishment, but either passes off by the bowels before it produces some other humour, crude and corrupted; or, if it continue for a longer time, produces suffering or disease hard to cure, destroying at the same time the natural nourishment, or even the flesh itself which needs nourishment. But even though it be expelled at length, overcome by certain medicines, or by better food, or by the natural forces, it is not got rid of without doing much harm, since it bears no peaceful aspect towards what is natural, because it cannot coalesce with nature.

CHAP. VII.—*The resurrection-body different from the present.*

Nay, suppose we were to grant that the nourishment coming from these things (let it be so called, as more accordant with the common way of speaking), although against nature, is yet separated and changed into some one of the moist or dry, or warm or cold, matters which the body contains, our opponents would gain nothing by the concession: for the bodies that rise again are reconstituted from the parts which properly belong to them, whereas no one of the things mentioned is such a part, nor has it the form or place of a part; nay, it does not remain always with the parts of the body which are nourished, or rise again with the parts that rise, since no longer does blood, or phlegm, or bile, or breath, contribute anything to the life. Neither, again, will the bodies nourished then require the things they once required, seeing that, along with the want and corruption of the bodies nourished, the need also of those things by which they were nourished is taken away. To this must be added, that if we were to suppose the change arising from such nourishment to reach as far as flesh, in that case too there would be no necessity that the flesh recently changed by food of that kind, if it became united to the body of some other man, should again as a part contribute to the formation of that body, since neither the flesh which takes it up always retains what it takes, nor does the flesh so incorporated abide and remain with that to which it was added, but is subject to a great variety of changes,—at one time being dispersed by toil or care, at another time being wasted by grief or trouble or disease, and by the distempers arising from being heated or chilled, the humours which are changed with the flesh and fat not receiving the nourishment so as to remain what they are. But while such are the changes to which the flesh is subject, we should find that flesh, nourished by food unsuited to it, suffers them in a much greater degree; now swelling out and growing fat by what it has received, and then again rejecting it in some way or other, and decreasing in bulk, from one or more of the causes already mentioned; and that that alone remains in the parts which is adapted to bind together, or cover, or warm the flesh that has been chosen by nature, and adheres to those parts by which it sustains the life which is according to nature, and fulfils the labours of that life. So that whether the investigation in which we have just been engaged be fairly judged of, or the objections urged against our position be conceded, in neither case can it be shown that what is said by our opponents is true, nor can the bodies of men ever combine with those of the same nature, whether at any time, through ignorance and being cheated of their perception by some one else, men have partaken of such a body, or of their own accord, impelled by want or madness, they have defiled themselves with the body of one of like form; for we are very well aware that some brutes have human forms, or have a nature compounded of men and brutes, such as the more daring of the poets are accustomed to represent.

CHAP. VIII.—*Human flesh not the proper or natural food of men.*

But what need is there to speak of bodies not allotted to be the food of any animal, and destined only for a burial in the earth in honour of nature, since the Maker of the world has not allotted any animal whatsoever as food to those of the same kind, although some others of a different kind serve for food according to nature? If, indeed, they are able to show that the flesh of men was allotted to men for food, there will be nothing to hinder its being according to nature that they should eat one another, just like anything else that is allowed by nature, and nothing to prohibit those who dare to say such things from regaling themselves with the bodies of their dearest friends as delicacies, as being specially suited to them, and to entertain their living friends with the same fare. But if it be unlawful even to speak of this, and if for men to partake of the flesh of men is a thing most hateful and abominable, and more detestable than any other unlawful and unnatural food or act; and if what is against nature can never pass into nourishment for the limbs and parts requiring it, and what does not pass into nourishment can never become united with that which it is not adapted to nourish,—then can the bodies of men never combine with bodies like themselves, to which this nourishment would be against nature, even though it were to pass many times through their stomach, owing to some most bitter mischance; but, removed from the influence of the nourishing power, and scattered to those parts of the universe again from which they obtained their first origin, they are united with these for as long a period of time as may be the lot of each; and, separated thence again by the skill and power of Him who has fixed the nature of every animal, and furnished it with its peculiar powers, they are united suitably, each to each, whether they have been burnt up by fire, or rotted by water, or consumed by wild beasts, or by any other animals, or separated from the entire body and dissolved before the other parts; and, being again united with one another, they occupy the same place for the exact construction and formation of the same body, and for the resurrection and life of that which was dead, or even entirely dissolved. To expatiate further, however, on these topics, is not suitable; for all men are agreed in their decision respecting them,—those at least who are not half brutes.

CHAP. IX.—*Absurdity of arguing from man's impotency.*

As there are many things of more importance to the inquiry before us, I beg to be excused from replying for the present to those who take refuge in the works of men, and even the constructors of them, who are unable to make anew such of their works as are broken in pieces, or worn out by time, or otherwise destroyed, and then from the analogy of potters and carpenters attempt to show that God neither can will, nor if He willed would be able, to raise again a body that is dead, or has been dissolved,—not considering that by such reasoning they offer the grossest insult to God, putting, as they do, on the same level the capabilities of things which are altogether different, or rather the natures of those who use them, and comparing the works of art with those of nature. To bestow any serious attention on such arguments would be not undeserving of censure, for it is really foolish to reply to superficial and trifling objections. It is surely far more probable, yea, most absolutely true, to say that what is impossible with men is possible with God. And if by this statement of itself as probable, and by the whole investigation in which we have just been engaged reason shows it to be possible, it is quite clear that it is not impossible. No, nor is it such a thing as God could not will.

CHAP. X.—*It cannot be shown that God does not will a resurrection.*

For that which is not accordant with His will is so either as being unjust or as unworthy of Him. And again, the injustice regards either him who is to rise again, or some other than he. But it is evident that no one of the beings exterior to him, and that are reckoned among the things that have existence, is injured. Spiritual natures (νοηταὶ φύσεις) cannot be injured by the resurrection of men, for the resurrection of men is no hindrance to their existing, nor is any loss or violence inflicted on them by it; nor, again, would the nature of irrational or inanimate beings sustain wrong, for they will have no existence after the resurrection, and no wrong can be done to that which is not. But even if any one should suppose them to exist for ever, they would not suffer wrong by the renewal of human bodies: for if now, in being subservient to the nature of men and their necessities while they require them, and subjected to the yoke and every kind of drudgery, they suffer no wrong, much more, when men have become immortal and free from want, and no longer need their service, and when they are themselves liberated from bondage, will they suffer no wrong. For if they had the gift of speech, they would not bring against the Creator the charge of making them, contrary to justice, inferior to men because they did not share in the same resurrection. For to creatures whose nature is not alike the Just Being does not assign a like end. And, besides, with creatures that have no notion of justice there can be no complaint of injustice. Nor can it be said either that there is any injustice done as regards the man to be raised, for he consists of soul and body, and he suffers no wrong as to either soul or body. No person in his senses will affirm that his soul suffers wrong, because, in speaking so, he would at the same time be unawares reflecting on the present life also; for if now, while dwelling in a body subject to corruption and suffering, it has had no wrong done to it, much less will it suffer wrong when living in conjunction with a body which is free from corruption and suffering. The body, again, suffers no wrong; for if no wrong is done to it now while united a corruptible thing with an incorruptible, manifestly will it not be wronged when united an incorruptible with an incorruptible. No; nor can any one say that it is a work unworthy of God to raise up and bring together again a body which has been dissolved: for if the worse was not unworthy of Him, namely, to make the body which is subject to corruption and suffering, much more is the better not unworthy, to make one not liable to corruption or suffering.

CHAP. XI.—*Recapitulation*

If, then, by means of that which is by nature first and that which follows from it, each of the points investigated has been proved, it is very evident that the resurrection of dissolved bodies is a work which the Creator can perform, and can will, and such as is worthy of Him: for by these considerations the falsehood of the contrary opinion has been shown, and the absurdity of the position taken by disbelievers. For why should I speak of their correspondence each with each, and of their connection with one another? If indeed we ought to use the word connection, as though they were separated by some difference of nature; and not rather say, that what God can do He can also will, and that what God can will it is perfectly possible for Him to do, and that it is accordant with the dignity of Him who wills it. That to discourse concerning the truth is one thing, and to discourse in defence of it is another, has been sufficiently explained in the remarks already made, as also in what respects they differ from each other, and when and in dealing with whom they are severally useful; but perhaps there is no reason why, with a view to the general certainty, and because of the connection of what has been said with what remains, we should not make a fresh beginning from these same points and those which are allied to them. To the one kind of argument it naturally pertains to hold the foremost place, to the other to attend upon the first, and clear the way, and to remove whatever is obstructive or hostile. The discourse concerning the truth, as being necessary to all men for certainty and safety, holds the first place, whether in nature, or order, or usefulness: in nature, as furnishing the knowledge of the subject; in order, as being in those things and along with those things which it informs us of; in usefulness, as being a guarantee of certainty and safety to those who become acquainted with it. The discourse in defence of the truth is inferior in nature and force, for the refutation of falsehood is less important than the establishment of truth; and second in order, for it employs its strength against those who hold false opinions, and false opinions are an aftergrowth from another sowing and from degeneration. But, notwithstanding all this, it is often placed first, and sometimes is found more useful, because it removes and clears away beforehand the disbelief which disquiets some minds, and the doubt or false opinion of such as have but recently come over. And yet each of them is referrible to the same end, for the refutation of falsehood and the establishment of truth both have piety for their object: not, indeed, that they are absolutely one and the same, but the one is necessary, as I have said, to all who believe, and to those who are concerned about the truth and their own salvation; but the other proves to be more useful on some occasions, and to some persons, and in dealing with some. Thus much by way of recapitulation, to recall what has been already said. We must now pass on to what we proposed, and show the truth of the doctrine concerning the resurrection, both from the cause itself, according to which, and on account of which, the first man and his posterity were created, although they were not brought into existence in the same manner, and from the common nature of all men as men; and further, from the judgment of their Maker upon them according to the time each has lived, and according to the rules by which each has regulated his behaviour,—a judgment which no one can doubt will be just.

CHAP. XII.—*Argument for the resurrection from the purpose contemplated in man's creation.*

The argument from the cause will appear, if we consider whether man was made at random and in vain, or for some purpose; and if for some purpose, whether simply that he might live and continue in the natural condition in which he was created, or for the use of another; and if with a view to use, whether for that of the Creator Himself, or of some one of the beings who belong to Him, and are by Him deemed worthy of greater care. Now, if we consider this in the most general way, we find that a person of sound mind, and who is moved by a rational judgment to do anything, does nothing in vain which he does intentionally, but either for his own use, or for the use of some other person for whom he cares, or for the sake of the work itself, being moved by some natural inclination and affection towards its production. For instance (to make use of an illustration, that our meaning may be clear), a man makes a house for his own use, but for cattle and camels and other animals of which he has need he makes the shelter suitable for each of them; not for his own use, if we regard the appearance only, though for that, if we look at the end he has in view, but as regards the immediate object, from concern for those for whom he cares. He has children, too, not for his own use, nor for the sake of anything else belonging to him, but that those who spring from him may exist and continue as long as possible, thus by the succession of children and grandchildren comforting himself respecting the close of his own life, and hoping in this way to immortalize the mortal. Such is the procedure of men. But God can neither have made man in vain, for He is wise, and no work of wisdom is in vain; nor for His own use, for He is in want of nothing. But to a Being absolutely in need of nothing, no one of His works can contribute anything to His own use. Neither, again, did He make man for the sake of any of the other works which He has made. For nothing that is endowed with reason and judgment has been created, or is created, for the use of another, whether greater or less than itself, but for the sake of the life and continuance of the being itself so created. For reason cannot discover any use which might be deemed a cause for the creation of men, since immortals are free from want, and in need of no help from men in order to their existence; and irrational beings are by nature in a state of subjection, and perform those services for men for which each of them was intended, but are not intended in their turn to make use of men: for it neither was nor is right to lower that which rules and takes the lead to the use of the inferior, or to subject the rational to the irrational, which is not suited to rule. Therefore, if man has been created neither without cause and in vain (for none of God's works is in vain, so far at least as the purpose of their Maker is concerned), nor for the use of the Maker Himself, or of any of the works which have proceeded from Him, it is quite clear that although, according to the first and more general view of the subject, God made man for Himself, and in pursuance of the goodness and wisdom which are conspicuous throughout the creation, yet, according to the view which more nearly touches the beings created, He made him for the sake of the life of those created, which is not kindled for a little while and then extinguished. For to creeping things, I suppose, and birds, and fishes, or, to speak more generally, all irrational creatures, God has assigned such a life as that; but to those who bear upon them the image of the Creator Himself, and are endowed with understanding, and blessed with a rational judgment, the Creator has assigned perpetual duration, in order that, recognising their own Maker, and His power and skill, and obeying law and justice, they may pass their whole existence free from suffering, in the possession of those qualities with which they have bravely borne their preceding life, although they lived in corruptible and earthly bodies. For whatever has been created for the sake of something else, when that has ceased to be for the sake of which it was created, will itself also fitly cease to be, and will not continue to exist in vain, since, among the works of God, that which is useless can have no place; but that which was created for the very purpose of existing and living a life naturally suited to it, since the cause itself is bound up with its nature, and is recognised only in connection with existence itself, can never admit of any cause which shall utterly annihilate its existence. But since this cause is seen to lie in perpetual existence, the being so created must be preserved for ever, doing and experiencing what is suitable to its nature, each of the two parts of which it consists contributing what belongs to it, so that the soul may exist and remain without change in the nature in which it was made, and discharge its appropriate functions (such as presiding over the impulses of the body, and judging of and measuring that which occurs from time to time by the proper standards and measures), and the body be moved according to its nature towards its appropriate objects, and undergo the changes allotted to it, and, among the rest (relating to age, or appearance, or size), the resurrection. For the resurrection is a species of change, and the last of all, and a change for the better of what still remains in existence at that time.

CHAP. XIII.—*Continuation of the argument.*

Confident of these things, no less than of those which have already come to pass, and reflecting on our own nature, we are content with a life associated with neediness and corruption, as suited to our present state of existence, and we stedfastly hope for a continuance of being in immortality; and this we do not take without foundation from the inventions of men, feeding ourselves on false hopes, but our belief rests on a most infallible guarantee—the purpose of Him who fashioned us, according to which He made man of an immortal soul and a body, and furnished him with understanding and an innate law for the preservation and safeguard of the things given by Him as suitable to an intelligent existence and a rational life: for we know well that He would not have fashioned such a being, and furnished him with everything belonging to perpetuity, had He not intended that what was so created should continue in perpetuity. If, therefore, the Maker of this universe made man with a view to his partaking of an intelligent life, and that, having become a spectator of His grandeur, and of the wisdom which is manifest in all things, he might continue always in the contemplation of these; then, according to the purpose of his Author, and the nature which he has received, the cause of his creation is a pledge of his continuance for ever, and this continuance is a pledge of the resurrection, without which man could not continue. So that, from what has been said, it is quite clear that the resurrection is plainly proved by the cause of man's creation, and the purpose of Him who made him. Such being the nature of the cause for which man has been brought into this world, the next thing will be to consider that which immediately follows, naturally or in the order proposed; and in our investigation the cause of their creation is followed by the nature of the men so created, and the nature of those created by the just judgment of their Maker upon them, and all these by the end of their existence. Having investigated therefore the point placed first in order, we must now go on to consider the nature of men.

Chap. xiv.—*The resurrection does not rest solely on the fact of a future judgment.*

The proof of the several doctrines of which the truth consists, or of any matters whatsoever proposed for examination, if it is to produce an unwavering confidence in what is said, must begin, not from anything without, nor from what certain persons think or have thought, but from the common and natural notion of the matter, or from the connection of secondary truths with primary ones. For the question relates either to primary beliefs, and then all that is necessary is reminiscence, so as to stir up the natural notion; or to things which naturally follow from the first and to their natural sequence. And in these things we must observe order, showing what strictly follows from the first truths, or from those which are placed first, so as neither to be unmindful of the truth, or of our certainty respecting it, nor to confound the things arranged by nature and distinguished from each other, or break up the natural order. Hence I think it behoves those who desire to handle the subject with fairness, and who wish to form an intelligent judgment whether there is a resurrection or not, first to consider attentively the force of the arguments contributing to the proof of this, and what place each of them holds—which is first, which second, which third, and which last. And in the arrangement of these they should place first the cause of the creation of men,—namely, the purpose of the Creator in making man; and then connect with this, as is suitable, the nature of the men so created; not as being second in order, but because we are unable to pass our judgment on both at the same time, although they have the closest natural connection with each other, and are of equal force in reference to the subject before us. But while from these proofs as the primary ones, and as being derived from the work of creation, the resurrection is clearly demonstrated, none the less can we gain conviction respecting it from the arguments taken from providence,—I mean from the reward or punishment due to each man in accordance with just judgment, and from the end of human existence. For many, in discussing the subject of the resurrection, have rested the whole cause on the third argument alone, deeming that the cause of the resurrection is the judgment. But the fallacy of this is very clearly shown, from the fact that, although all human beings who die rise again, yet not all who rise again are to be judged: for if only a just judgment were the cause of the resurrection, it would of course follow that those who had done neither evil nor good—namely, very young children—would not rise again; but seeing that all are to rise again, those who have died in infancy as well as others, they too justify our conclusion that the resurrection takes place not for the sake of the judgment as the primary reason, but in consequence of the purpose of God in forming men, and the nature of the beings so formed.

CHAP. XV.—*Argument for the resurrection from the nature of man.*

But while the cause discoverable in the creation of men is of itself sufficient to prove that the resurrection follows by natural sequence on the dissolution of bodies, yet it is perhaps right not to shrink from adducing either of the proposed arguments, but, agreeably to what has been said, to point out to those who are not able of themselves to discern them, the arguments from each of the truths evolved from the primary; and first and foremost, the nature of the men created, which conducts us to the same notion, and has the same force as evidence of the resurrection. For if the whole nature of men in general is composed of an immortal soul and a body which was fitted to it in the creation, and if neither to the nature of the soul by itself, nor to the nature of the body separately, has God assigned such a creation or such a life and entire course of existence as this, but to men compounded of the two, in order that they may, when they have passed through their present existence, arrive at one common end, with the same elements of which they are composed at their birth and during life, it unavoidably follows, since one living-being is formed from the two, experiencing whatever the soul experiences and whatever the body experiences, doing and performing whatever requires the judgment of the senses or of the reason, that the whole series of these things must be referred to some one end, in order that they all, and by means of all,—namely, man's creation, man's nature, man's life, man's doings and sufferings, his course of existence, and the end suitable to his nature,—may concur in one harmony and the same common experience. But if there is some one harmony and community of experience belonging to the whole being, whether of the things which spring from the soul or of those which are accomplished by means of the body, the end for all these must also be one. And the end will be in strictness one, if the being whose end that end is remains the same in its constitution; and the being will be exactly the same, if all those things of which the being consists as parts are the same. And they will be the same in respect of their peculiar union, if the parts dissolved are again united for the constitution of the being. And the constitution of the same men of necessity proves that a resurrection will follow of the dead and dissolved bodies; for without this, neither could the same parts be united according to nature with one another, nor could the nature of the same men be reconstituted. And if both understanding and reason have been given to men for the discernment of things which are perceived by the understanding, and not of existences only, but also of the goodness and wisdom and rectitude of their Giver, it necessarily follows that, since those things continue for the sake of which the rational judgment is given, the judgment given for these things should also continue. But it is impossible for this to continue, unless the nature which has received it, and in which it inheres, continues. But that which has received both understanding and reason is man, not the soul by itself. Man, therefore, who consists of the two parts, must continue for ever. But it is impossible for him to continue unless he rise again. For if no resurrection were to take place, the nature of men as men would not continue. And if the nature of men does not continue, in vain has the soul been fitted to the need of the body and to its experiences; in vain has the body been fettered so that it cannot obtain what it longs for, obedient to the reins of the soul, and guided by it as with a bridle; in vain is the understanding, in vain is wisdom, and the observance of rectitude, or even the practice of every virtue, and the enactment and enforcement of laws, —to say all in a word, whatever is noble in men or for men's sake, or rather the very creation and nature of men. But if vanity is utterly excluded from all the works of God, and from all the gifts bestowed by Him, the conclusion is unavoidable, that, along with the interminable duration of the soul, there will be a perpetual continuance of the body according to its proper nature.

Chap. XVI.—*Analogy of death and sleep, and consequent argument for the resurrection.*

And let no one think it strange that we call by the name of life a continuance of being which is interrupted by death and corruption; but let him consider rather that this word has not one meaning only, nor is there only one measure of continuance, because the nature also of the things that continue is not one. For if each of the things that continue has its continuance according to its peculiar nature, neither in the case of those who are wholly incorruptible and immortal shall we find the continuance like ours, because the natures of superior beings do not take the level of such as are inferior; nor in men is it proper to look for a continuance invariable and unchangeable; inasmuch as the former are from the first created immortal, and continue to exist without end by the simple will of their Maker, and men, in respect of the soul, have from their first origin an unchangeable continuance, but in respect of the body obtain immortality by means of change. This is what is meant by the doctrine of the resurrection; and, looking to this, we both await the dissolution of the body, as the sequel to a life of want and corruption, and after this we hope for a continuance with immortality, not putting either our death on a level with the death of the irrational animals, or the continuance of men with the continuance of immortals, lest we should unawares in this way put human nature and life on a level with things with which it is not proper to compare them. It ought not, therefore, to excite dissatisfaction, if some inequality appears to exist in regard to the duration of men; nor, because the separation of the soul from the members of the body and the dissolution of its parts interrupts the continuity of life, must we therefore despair of the resurrection. For although the relaxation of the senses and of the physical powers, which naturally takes place in sleep, seems to interrupt the sensational life when men sleep at equal intervals of time, and, as it were, come back to life again, yet we do not refuse to call it life; and for this reason, I suppose, some call sleep the brother of death, not as deriving their origin from the same ancestors and fathers, but because those who are dead and those who sleep are subject to similar states, as regards at least the stillness and the absence of all sense of the present or the past, or rather of existence itself and their own life. If, therefore, we do not refuse to call by the name of life the life of men full of such inequality from birth to dissolution, and interrupted by all those things which we have before mentioned, neither ought we to despair of the life succeeding to dissolution, such as involves the resurrection, although for a time it is interrupted by the separation of the soul from the body.

Chap. XVII.—*The series of changes we can now trace in man renders a resurrection probable.*

For this nature of men, which has inequality allotted to it from the first, and according to the purpose of its Maker, has an unequal life and continuance, interrupted sometimes by sleep, at another time by death, and by the changes incident to each period of life, whilst those which follow the first are not clearly seen beforehand. Would any one have believed, unless taught by experience, that in the soft seed alike in all its parts there was deposited such a variety and number of great powers, or of masses, which in this way arise and become consolidated—I mean of bones, and nerves, and cartilages, of muscles too, and flesh, and intestines, and the other parts of the body? For neither in the yet moist seed is anything of this kind to be seen, nor even in infants do any of those things make their appearance which pertain to adults, or in the adult period what belongs to those who are past their prime, or in these what belongs to such as have grown old. But although some of the things I have said exhibit not at all, and others but faintly, the natural sequence and the changes that come upon the nature of men, yet all who are not blinded in their judgment of these matters by vice or sloth, know that there must be first the depositing of the seed, and that when this is completely organized in respect of every member and part and the progeny comes forth to the light, there comes the growth belonging to the first period of life, and the maturity which attends growth, and after the maturity the slackening of the physical powers till old age, and then, when the body is worn out, its dissolution. As, therefore, in this matter, though neither the seed has inscribed upon it the life or form of men, nor the life the dissolution into the primary elements, the succession of natural occurrences makes things credible which have no credibility from the phenomena themselves, much more does reason, tracing out the truth from the natural sequence, afford ground for believing in the resurrection, since it is safer and stronger than experience for establishing the truth.

CHAP. XVIII.—*Judgment must have reference both to soul and body: there will therefore be a resurrection.*

The arguments I just now proposed for examination, as establishing the truth of the resurrection, are all of the same kind, since they all start from the same point; for their starting-point is the origin of the first men by creation. But while some of them derive their strength from the starting-point itself from which they take their rise, others, consequent upon the nature and the life of men, acquire their credibility from the superintendence of God over us; for the cause according to which, and on account of which, men have come into being, being closely connected with the nature of men, derives its force from creation; but the argument from rectitude, which represents God as judging men according as they have lived well or ill, derives its force from the end of their existence: they come into being on the former ground, but their state depends more on God's superintendence. And now that the matters which come first have been demonstrated by me to the best of my ability, it will be well to prove our proposition by those also which come after—I mean by the reward or punishment due to each man in accordance with righteous judgment, and by the final cause of human existence; and of these I put foremost that which takes the lead by nature, and inquire first into the argument relating to the judgment: premising only one thing, from concern for the principle which appertains to the matters before us, and for order—

namely, that it is incumbent on those who admit God to be the Maker of this universe, to ascribe to His wisdom and rectitude the preservation and care of all that has been created, if they wish to keep to their own principles; and with such views to hold that nothing either in earth or in heaven is without guardianship or providence, but that, on the contrary, to everything, invisible and visible alike, small and great, the attention of the Creator reaches; for all created things require the attention of the Creator, and each one in particular, according to its nature and the end for which it was made: though I think it would be a useless expenditure of trouble to go through the list now, or distinguish between the several cases, or mention in detail what is suitable to each nature. Man, at all events, of whom it is now our business to speak, as being in want, requires food; as being mortal, posterity; as being rational, a process of judgment. But if each of these things belongs to man by nature, and he requires food for his life, and requires posterity for the continuance of the race, and requires a judgment in order that food and posterity may be according to law, it of course follows, since food and posterity refer to both together, that the judgment must be referred to them too (by both together I mean man, consisting of soul and body), and that such man becomes accountable for all his actions, and receives for them either reward or punishment. Now, if the righteous judgment awards to both together its retribution for the deeds wrought; and if it is not proper that either the soul alone should receive the wages of the deeds wrought in union with the body (for this of itself has no inclination to the faults which are committed in connection with the pleasure or food and culture of the body), or that the body alone should (for this of itself is incapable of distinguishing law and justice), but man, composed of these, is subjected to trial for each of the deeds wrought by him; and if reason does not find this happening either in this life (for the award according to merit finds no place in the present existence, since many atheists and persons who practise every iniquity and wickedness live on to the last, unvisited by calamity, whilst, on the contrary, those who have manifestly lived an exemplary life in respect of every virtue, live in pain, in insult, in calumny and outrage, and suffering of all kinds) or after death (for both together no longer exist, the soul being separated from the body, and the body itself being resolved again into the materials out of which it was composed, and no longer retaining anything of its former structure or form, much less the remembrance of its actions): the result of all this is very plain to every one,—namely, that, in the language of the apostle, "this corruptible (and dissoluble) must put on incorruption,"[1] in order that those who were dead, having been made alive by the resurrection, and the parts that were separated and entirely dissolved having been again united, each one may, in accordance with justice, receive what he has done by the body, whether it be good or bad.

Chap. xix.—*Man would be more unfavourably situated than the beasts if there were no resurrection.*

In replying, then, to those who acknowledge a divine superintendence, and admit the same principles as we do, yet somehow depart from their own admissions, one may use such arguments as those which have been adduced, and many more than these, should he be disposed to amplify what has been said only concisely and in a cursory manner. But in dealing with those who differ from us concerning primary truths, it will perhaps be well to lay down another principle antecedent to these, joining with them in doubting of the things to which their opinions relate, and examining the matter along with them in this manner—whether the life of men, and their entire course of existence, is overlooked, and a sort of dense darkness is poured down upon the earth, hiding in ignorance and silence both the men themselves and their actions; or whether it is much safer to be of opinion that the Maker presides over the things which He Himself has made, inspecting all things whatsoever which exist, or come into existence, Judge of both deeds and purposes. For if no judgment whatever were to be passed on the actions of men, men would have no advantage over the irrational creatures, but rather

[1] 1 Cor. xv. 55.

would fare worse than these do, inasmuch as they keep in subjection their passions, and concern themselves about piety, and righteousness, and the other virtues; and a life after the manner of brutes would be the best, virtue would be absurd, the threat of judgment a matter for broad laughter, indulgence in every kind of pleasure the highest good, and the common resolve of all these and their one law would be that maxim, so dear to the intemperate and lewd, "Let us eat and drink, for to-morrow we die." For the termination of such a life is not even pleasure, as some suppose, but utter insensibility. But if the Maker of men takes any concern about His own works, and the distinction is anywhere to be found between those who have lived well and ill, it must be either in the present life, while men are still living who have conducted themselves virtuously or viciously, or after death, when men are in a state of separation and dissolution. But according to neither of these suppositions can we find a just judgment taking place; for neither do the good in the present life obtain the rewards of virtue, nor yet do the bad receive the wages of vice. I pass over the fact, that so long as the nature we at present possess is preserved, the mortal nature is not able to bear a punishment commensurate with the more numerous or more serious faults. For the robber, or ruler, or tyrant, who has unjustly put to death myriads on myriads, could not by one death make restitution for these deeds; and the man who holds no true opinion concerning God, but lives in all outrage and blasphemy, despises divine things, breaks the laws, commits outrage against boys and women alike, razes cities unjustly, burns houses with their inhabitants, and devastates a country, and at the same time destroys inhabitants of cities and peoples, and even an entire nation—how in a mortal body could he endure a penalty adequate to these crimes, since death prevents the deserved punishment, and the mortal nature does not suffice for any single one of his deeds? It is proved, therefore, that neither in the present life is there a judgment according to men's deserts, nor after death.

CHAP. XX.—*Man must be possessed both of a body and soul hereafter, that the judgment passed upon him may be just.*

For either death is the entire extinction of life, the soul being dissolved and corrupted along with the body, or the soul remains by itself, incapable of dissolution, of dispersion, of corruption, whilst the body is corrupted and dissolved, retaining no longer any remembrance of past actions, nor sense of what it experienced in connection with the soul. If the life of men is to be utterly extinguished, it is manifest there will be no care for men who are not living, no judgment respecting those who have lived in virtue or in vice; but there will rush in again upon us whatever belongs to a lawless life, and the swarm of absurdities which follow from it, and that which is the summit of this lawlessness—atheism. But if the body were to be corrupted, and each of the dissolved particles to pass to its kindred element, yet the soul to remain by itself as immortal, neither on this supposition would any judgment on the soul take place, since there would be an absence of equity: for it is unlawful to suspect that any judgment can proceed out of God and from God which is wanting in equity. Yet equity *is* wanting to the judgment, if the being is not preserved in existence who practised righteousness or lawlessness: for that which practised each of the things in life on which the judgment is passed was man, not soul by itself. To sum up all in a word, this view will in no case consist with equity.

CHAP. XXI.—*Continuation of the argument.*

For if good deeds are rewarded, the body will clearly be wronged, inasmuch as it has shared with the soul in the toils connected with well-doing, but does not share in the reward of the good deeds, and because, though the soul is often excused for certain faults on the ground of the body's neediness and want, the body itself is deprived of all share in the good deeds done, the toils on behalf of which it helped to bear during life. Nor, again, if faults are judged, is the soul dealt fairly with, supposing it alone to pay the penalty for the faults it committed through being solicited by the body and drawn away by it to its own appetites and motions, at one time being seized upon and carried off, at another attracted in some very violent manner, and sometimes concurring with it by way of kindness and attention to its preservation. How can it possibly be other than unjust for the soul to be judged by itself in respect of things towards which in its own nature it feels no appetite, no motion, no impulse, such as licentiousness, violence, covetousness, injustice, and the unjust acts arising out of these? For if the majority of such evils come from men's not having the mastery of the passions which solicit them, and they are solicited by the neediness and want of the body, and the care and attention required by it (for these are the motives for every acquisition of property, and especially for the using of it, and moreover for marriage and all the actions of life, in which things, and in connection with which, is seen what is faulty and what is not so), how can it be just for the soul alone to be judged in respect of those things which the body is the first to be sensible of, and in which it draws the soul away to sympathy and participation in actions with a view to things which it wants; and that the appetites and pleasures, and moreover the fears and sorrows, in which whatever exceeds the proper bounds is amenable to judgment, should be set in motion by the body, and yet that the sins arising from these, and the punishments for the sins committed, should fall upon the soul alone, which neither needs anything of this sort, nor desires nor fears or suffers of itself any such thing as man is wont to suffer? But even if we hold that these affections do not pertain to the body alone, but to man, in saying which we should speak correctly, because the life of man is one, though composed of the two, yet surely we shall not assert that these things belong to the soul, if we only look simply at its peculiar nature. For if it is absolutely without need of food, it can never desire those things which it does not in the least require for its subsistence; nor can it feel any impulse towards any of those things which it is not at all fitted to use; nor, again, can it be grieved at the want of money or other property, since these are not suited to it. And if, too, it is superior to corruption, it fears nothing whatever as destructive of itself: it has no dread of famine, or disease, or mutilation, or blemish, or fire, or sword, since it cannot suffer from any of these any hurt or pain, because neither bodies nor bodily powers touch it at all. But if it is absurd to attach the passions to the soul as belonging specially to it, it is in the highest degree unjust and unworthy of the judgment of God to lay upon the soul alone the sins which spring from them, and the consequent punishments.

CHAP. XXII.—*Continuation of the argument.*

In addition to what has been said, is it not absurd that, while we cannot even have the notion of virtue and vice as existing separately in the soul (for we recognise the virtues as man's virtues, even as in like manner vice, their opposite, as not belonging to the soul in separation from the body, and existing by itself), yet that the reward or punishment for these should be assigned to the soul alone? How can any one have even the notion of courage or fortitude as existing in the soul alone, when it has no fear of death, or wounds, or maiming, or loss, or maltreatment, or of the pain connected with these, or the suffering resulting from them? And what shall we say of self-control and temperance, when there is no desire drawing it to food or sexual intercourse, or other pleasures and enjoyments, nor any other thing soliciting it from within or exciting it from without? And what of practical wisdom, when things are not proposed to it which may or may not be done, nor things to be chosen or avoided, or rather when there is in it no motion at all or natural impulse towards the doing of anything? And how in any sense can equity be an attribute of souls, either in reference to one another or to anything else, whether of the same or of a different kind, when they are not able from any source, or by any means, or in any way, to bestow that which is equal according to merit or according to analogy, with the exception of the honour rendered to God, and, moreover, have no impulse or motion towards the use of their own things, or abstinence from those of others, since the use of those things which are according to nature, or the abstinence from them, is considered in reference to those who are so constituted as to use them, whereas the soul neither wants anything, nor is so constituted as to use any things or any single thing, and therefore what is called the independent action of the parts cannot be found in the soul so constituted?

Chap. XXIII.—*Continuation of the argument.*

But the most irrational thing of all is this: to impose properly sanctioned laws on men, and then to assign to their souls alone the recompense of their lawful or unlawful deeds. For if he who receives the laws would also justly receive the recompense of the transgression of the laws, and if it was man that received the laws, and not the soul by itself, man must also bear the recompense for the sins committed, and not the soul by itself, since God has not enjoined on souls to abstain from things which have no relation to them, such as adultery, murder, theft, rapine, dishonour to parents, and every desire in general that tends to the injury and loss of our neighbours. For neither the command, "Honour thy father and thy mother," is adapted to souls alone, since such names are not applicable to them, for souls do not produce souls, so as to appropriate the appellation of father or mother, but men produce men; nor could the command, "Thou shalt not commit adultery," ever be properly addressed to souls, or even thought of in such a connection, since the difference of male and female does not exist in them, nor any aptitude for sexual intercourse, nor appetite for it; and where there is no appetite, there can be no intercourse; and where there is no intercourse at all, there can be no legitimate intercourse, namely marriage; and where there is no lawful intercourse, neither can there be unlawful desire of, or intercourse with, another man's wife, namely adultery. Nor, again, is the prohibition of theft, or of the desire of having more, applicable to souls, for they do not need those things, through the need of which, by reason of natural indigence or want, men are accustomed to steal or to rob, such as gold, or silver, or an animal, or something else adapted for food, or shelter, or use; for to an immortal nature everything which is desired by the needy as useful is useless. But let the fuller discussion of these matters be left to those who wish to investigate each point more exactly, or to contend more earnestly with opponents. But, since what has just been said, and that which concurs with this to guarantee the resurrection, suffices for us, it would not be seasonable to dwell any longer upon them; for we have not made it our aim to omit nothing that might be said, but to point out in a summary manner to those who have assembled what ought to be thought concerning the resurrection, and to adapt to the capacity of those present the arguments bearing on this question.

CHAP. XXIV.—*Argument for the resurrection from the chief end of man.*

The points proposed for consideration having been to some extent investigated, it remains to examine the argument from the end or final cause, which indeed has already emerged in what has been said, and only requires just so much attention and further discussion as may enable us to avoid the appearance of leaving unmentioned any of the matters briefly referred to by us, and thus indirectly damaging the subject or the division of topics made at the outset. For the sake of those present, therefore, and of others who may pay attention to this subject, it may be well just to signify that each of those things which are constituted by nature, and of those which are made by art, must have an end peculiar to itself, as indeed is taught us by the common sense of all men, and testified by the things that pass before our eyes. For do we not see that husbandmen have one end, and physicians another; and again, the things which spring out of the earth another, and the animals nourished upon it, and produced according to a certain natural series, another? If this is evident, and natural and artificial powers, and the actions arising from these, must by all means be accompanied by an end in accordance with nature, it is absolutely necessary that the end of men, since it is that of a peculiar nature, should be separated from community with the rest; for it is not lawful to suppose the same end for beings destitute of rational judgment, and of those whose actions are regulated by the innate law and reason, and who live an intelligent life and observe justice. Freedom from pain, therefore, cannot be the proper end for the latter, for this they would have in common with beings utterly devoid of sensibility: nor can it consist in the enjoyment of things which nourish or delight the body, or in an abundance of pleasures; else a life like that of the brutes must hold the first place, while that regulated by virtue is without a final cause. For such an end as this, I suppose, belongs to beasts and cattle, not to men possessed of an immortal soul and rational judgment.

CHAP. XXV.—*Argument continued and concluded.*

Nor again is it the happiness of soul separated from body: for we are not inquiring about the life or final cause of either of the parts of which man consists, but of the being who is composed of both; for such is every man who has a share in this present existence, and there must be some appropriate end proposed for this life. But if it is the end of both parts together, and this can be discovered neither while they are still living in the present state of existence through the numerous causes already mentioned, nor yet when the soul is in a state of separation, because the man cannot be said to exist when the body is dissolved, and indeed entirely scattered abroad, even though the soul continue by itself—it is absolutely necessary that the end of man's being should appear in some reconstitution of the two together, and of the same living being. And as this follows of necessity, there must by all means be a resurrection of the bodies which are dead, or even entirely dissolved, and the same men must be formed anew, since the law of nature ordains the end not absolutely, nor as the end of any men whatsoever, but of the same men who passed through the previous life; but it is impossible for the same men to be reconstituted unless the same bodies are restored to the same souls. But that the same soul should obtain the same body is impossible in any other way, and possible only by the resurrection; for if this takes place, an end befitting the nature of men follows also. And we shall make no mistake in saying, that the final cause of an intelligent life and rational judgment, is to be occupied uninterruptedly with those objects to which the natural reason is chiefly and primarily adapted, and to delight unceasingly in the contemplation of *Him who is*, and of His decrees, notwithstanding that the majority of men, because they are affected too passionately and too violently by things below, pass through life without attaining this object. For the large number of those who fail of the end that belongs to them does not make void the common lot, since the examination relates to individuals, and the reward or punishment of lives ill or well spent is proportioned to the merit of each.

INDEX OF SUBJECTS.

INDEX OF TEXTS.

END OF VOL. II.

MURRAY AND GIBB, PRINTERS, EDINBURGH.

WORKS BY THE LATE WILLIAM CUNNINGHAM, D.D.,

PRINCIPAL AND PROFESSOR OF CHURCH HISTORY, NEW COLLEGE, EDINBURGH.

COMPLETE IN FOUR VOLUMES 8VO, PRICE £2, 2s.

In Two Volumes, demy 8vo, price 21s., Second Edition,

HISTORICAL THEOLOGY:

A REVIEW OF THE PRINCIPAL DOCTRINAL DISCUSSIONS IN THE CHRISTIAN CHURCH SINCE THE APOSTOLIC AGE.

Chapter 1. The Church; 2. The Council of Jerusalem; 3. The Apostles' Creed; 4. The Apostolical Fathers; 5. Heresies of the Apostolical Age; 6. The Fathers of the Second and Third Centuries; 7. The Church of the Second and Third Centuries; 8. The Constitution of the Church; 9. The Doctrine of the Trinity; 10. The Person of Christ; 11. The Pelagian Controversy; 12. Worship of Saints and Images; 13. The Civil and Ecclesiastical Authorities; 14. The Scholastic Theology; 15. The Canon Law; 16. Witnesses for the Truth during Middle Ages; 17. The Church at the Reformation; 18. The Council of Trent; 19. The Doctrine of the Fall; 20. Doctrine of the Will; 21. Justification; 22. The Sacramental Principle; 23. The Socinian Controversy; 24. Doctrine of the Atonement; 25. The Arminian Controversy; 26. Church Government; 27. The Erastian Controversy.

In demy 8vo (624 pages), price 10s. 6d., Second Edition,

THE REFORMERS AND THE THEOLOGY OF THE REFORMATION.

Chapter 1. Leaders of the Reformation; 2. Luther; 3. The Reformers and the Doctrine of Assurance; 4. Melancthon and the Theology of the Church of England; 5. Zwingle and the Doctrine of the Sacraments; 6. John Calvin; 7. Calvin and Beza; 8. Calvinism and Arminianism; 9. Calvinism and the Doctrine of Philosophical Necessity; 10. Calvinism and its Practical Application; 11. The Reformers, and the Lessons from their History.

'This volume is a most magnificent vindication of the Reformation, in both its men and its doctrines, suited to the present time and to the present state of the controversy.' —*Witness.*

In One Volume, demy 8vo, price 10s. 6d.,

DISCUSSIONS ON CHURCH PRINCIPLES:

POPISH, ERASTIAN, AND PRESBYTERIAN.

Chapter 1. The Errors of Romanism; 2. Romanist Theory of Development; 3. The Temporal Sovereignty of the Pope; 4. The Temporal Supremacy of the Pope; 5. The Liberties of the Gallican Church; 6. Royal Supremacy in Church of England; 7. Relation between Church and State; 8. The Westminster Confession on Relation between Church and State; 9. Church Power; 10. Principles of the Free Church; 11. The Rights of the Christian People; 12. The Principle of Non-Intrusion; 13. Patronage and Popular Election.

In Two Volumes, demy 8vo, price 21s.,

INTRODUCTION TO THE PENTATEUCH:

AN INQUIRY, CRITICAL AND DOCTRINAL, INTO THE GENUINENESS, AUTHORITY, AND DESIGN OF THE MOSAIC WRITINGS.

BY REV. D. MACDONALD.

'The object of this work is very opportune at the present time. It contains a full review of the evidences, external and internal, for the genuineness, authenticity, and divine character of the Pentateuch. While it gives full space and weight to the purely critical and historical portions of the inquiry, its special attention is devoted to the certainly more profound and more conclusive considerations derived from the connection between the Pentateuch and the great scheme of revelation of which it forms the basis; and this portion of the work is that upon which the author lays most stress. We entirely agree with him in his view of its importance. The work is singularly complete also in its view of the literature of the subject, as well as in the outline of its plan.'—*Guardian.*

Made in the USA
Lexington, KY
28 September 2010